A Handbook of Family Law Terms

BRYAN A. GARNER
Editor in Chief

CYNDE L. HORNE
Assistant Editor

WEST
GROUP

St. Paul, Minnesota
2001

COPYRIGHT® 2001

By

WEST GROUP

ISBN 0–314–24906–0

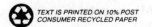 *TEXT IS PRINTED ON 10% POST CONSUMER RECYCLED PAPER*

Preface

Of all legal fields, family law—known also as *domestic-relations law* or simply as *domestic relations*—is the one that affects most people's lives most directly. It is also probably the field that traditional legal lexicography has most neglected over the years. The terminology is varied and vast, and it often differs from state to state.

So this book, the fourth in the line of glossaries known as the Black's Law Dictionary Series, is perhaps the most ambitious one in the series. Far from being a mere culling of family-law terms from the seventh edition of *Black's Law Dictionary*, this work reflects a painstaking review of recent family-law literature.

Although many points of family law are traceable back more than two millennia to Roman law, many others are quite recent. Family law is a fast-changing field. This is perhaps most dramatically illustrated in the fact that it is now possible—thanks to modern technology and developing legal theories of parenthood—for a child to have as many as 16 parents:

- biological mother;
- biological father;
- gestational mother;
- intentional mother;
- intentional father;

- foster mother;
- foster father;
- adoptive mother;
- adoptive father;
- de facto mother;
- de facto father;
- stepmother;
- stepfather;
- psychological mother;
- psychological father;
- legal father (the husband of whoever is found to be the mother).

How could a single child have all these parents? It would be an improbable saga reminiscent of a Charles Dickens or Victor Hugo novel, but it's hardly impossible given today's technology and legal doctrines. An infertile couple decides to have a child (Leslie), so the doctors take sperm from a man (the biological father) and an egg from a woman (the biological mother), and they implant the fertilized egg into a woman (the gestational mother); the infertile couple are the intentional parents who raise Leslie. These parents die, and Leslie is put into the care of two foster parents until she is taken into the home of her adoptive parents. These adoptive parents divorce and both begin living with significant others who support Leslie emotionally and financially; these unmarried significant others become the de facto mother and the de facto father. The adoptive parents leave their significant others and separately remarry the persons who become Leslie's two stepparents. Both of Leslie's adoptive parents begin suffering from a debilitating mental disease, and a woman who is a family friend develops close bonds with Leslie and becomes her psychological mother; the same happens with a male family friend, who becomes her psychological father. Leslie's biological mother then sues for custody, and the court decides in her favor over the stepparents and the psychological parents; the biological mother's husband (married even when she donated the egg several years before) is declared by the court to be legal father.

As all this suggests, traditional notions of what constitutes a family have yielded to newer theories—even to the extent that "family law" now resolves disputes involving unmarried cohabitants and those who participate in novel means of reproduction. As one commentator eloquently says, it's cutting-edge and it's controversial:

> "Family law is now central to many of the most difficult, and emotional, of social issues: Should same-sex couples be able to marry? Should couples who live together without marriage be entitled to benefits that have traditionally been available only to 'family members'? Should a law degree be considered marital property to be 'divided' at divorce? Who is the mother of a child born to one woman with genetic material from another? Should a lesbian 'co-parent' be able to adopt her partner's child? Absent an adoption, should she have an entitlement to visitation when her relationship with the child's mother ends?" [1]

---

1. Harry D. Krause et al., *Family Law: Cases, Comments, and Questions* 8–9 (4th ed. 1998).

From a moral point of view, some people lament the modern trends as indicators of contemporary decadence. Others cheer them as harbingers of more expansive and liberating ways of dealing with clanship in modern society. Still others would view the question in a neutral way: the modern view of family relationships has simply had to evolve in a society in which a majority of the children born today are not reared in a traditional household of two parents of the opposite sex who are married to each other indefinitely. Modern life isn't so tidy—and maybe life never was.

Our vocabulary reflects the realities of a changing world. Sadly, many of the terms in these pages deal with abuse (e.g., *secondary abuse*), neglect (e.g., *developmental neglect*), delinquency (e.g., *blended sentence*), miscellaneous other crimes (e.g., *impairing the morals of a minor*), and broken promises (e.g., *deadbeat dad*). Meanwhile, old categories such as *bastard* and *illegitimate child* don't work very well in a society in which one-third of children are born outside marriage.[2]

The terminology with which we describe family law is a fascinating mixture of the old and the new. Aunts and uncles are pretty much what they used to be, but now we have all kinds of newish words and phrases, from *advance directive* to *family leave* to *parental-consent statute* to *wrongful adoption*.

---

2. Tamar Lewin, *Is Social Stability Subverted If You Answer 'I Don't'?*, N.Y. Times, 4 Nov. 2000, at A21 (contrasting the current figure of 1 in 3 children born out of wedlock to the 1960 figure of 1 in 20).

When you add in legislative neologisms, not to mention names of various federal and uniform statutes, there's enough to keep lexicographers quite busy for nearly a year.

That's what it took to prepare this book, and I had some extraordinary help in preparing it. Cynde L. Horne, a talented lawyer with years of experience in family practice, researched and drafted hundreds of entries and edited the entire manuscript. David W. Schultz researched and drafted dozens of entries. Tiger Jackson painstakingly checked all cross-references and proofread the entire manuscript; she also contributed many draft entries. Once again, as with my other books in recent years, Karen L. Magnuson proofread the manuscript three times and, as always, improved it at each stage.

This book was complicated enough that I decided to engage several specialists to read the manuscript: two academics, a judge, and a practitioner. Professor Lucy McGough of Louisiana State University read and commented extensively on the manuscript in two batches. So did Judge Janice M. Rosa of the New York Family Court in Buffalo. Their erudition has improved every page.

After incorporating Professor McGough's and Judge Rosa's suggestions, I asked Professor Joseph W. McKnight of Southern Methodist University and Dawn Fowler, a Dallas practitioner, to read through the manuscript. They both had many valuable suggestions even at that late stage, and I was fortunate that they were willing to devote the time necessary for a close review on short notice.

For all this excellent help from so many quarters, I am grateful. My hope is that the book will prove helpful not only to family-law judges and practitioners everywhere, but also to anyone who needs a better understanding of this important legal field.

BRYAN A. GARNER

Dallas, Texas
November 2000

A Handbook of Family Law Terms

A

AAML. *abbr.* AMERICAN ACADEMY OF MATRIMONIAL LAWYERS.

abandonment, *n.* The act of leaving a spouse or child willfully and without an intent to return. • Child abandonment is grounds for termination of parental rights. Spousal abandonment is grounds for divorce. — **abandon,** *vb.* Cf. DESERTION.

> *abandonment of minor children.* See NONSUPPORT.

> *constructive abandonment.* See *constructive desertion* under DESERTION.

> *malicious abandonment.* See *voluntary abandonment.*

> *voluntary abandonment.* **1.** As a ground for divorce, a final departure without the consent of the other spouse, without sufficient reason, and without the intention to return. **2.** In the law of adoption, a natural parent's willful act or course of conduct that implies a conscious disregard of or indifference to a child, as if no parental obligation existed. — Also termed *malicious abandonment.*

abatement (ə-**bayt**-mənt), *n*. The reduction of a legacy, general or specific, as a result of the estate's being insufficient to pay all debts and legacies <the abatement of legacies resulted from the estate's insolvency>.

abduction (ab-**dək**-shən), *n*. **1.** The act of leading someone away by force or fraudulent persuasion. ● Some jurisdictions have added various elements to this basic definition, such as that the abductor must have the intent to marry or defile the person, that the abductee must be a child, or that the abductor must intend to subject the abductee to concubinage or prostitution. **2.** *Archaic.* At common law, the crime of taking away a female person without her consent by use of persuasion, fraud, or violence, for the purpose of marriage, prostitution, or illicit sex. **3.** Loosely, KIDNAPPING. — **abduct,** *vb*. — **abductor,** *n*. — **abductee,** *n*. See ENTICEMENT OF A CHILD.

abode, *n*. A home; a fixed place of residence. See DOMICILE.

abominable and detestable crime against nature. See SODOMY.

abortifacient (ə-bor-tə-**fay**-shənt), *n*. A drug, article, or other thing designed or intended to produce an abortion. — **abortifacient,** *adj*.

abortion, *n*. **1.** An artificially induced termination of a pregnancy for the purpose of destroying an embryo or fetus. ● In *Roe v. Wade*, the Supreme Court first recognized a woman's right to choose to end her pregnancy as a privacy right stemming from the Due Process Clause of the 14th Amendment. 410 U.S. 113, 93 S.Ct. 705 (1973). Sixteen years later, in *Webster v. Reproductive Health Services*, the Court permitted states to limit this right by allowing them to enact legislation that (1) prohibits public facilities or employees from performing abortions, (2) prohibits the use of public funds for family planning that includes information on abortion, or (3) severely limits the right to an abortion after a fetus becomes viable — that is, could live independently of its mother. 492 U.S. 490, 109 S.Ct. 3040 (1989). In 1992, the Court held that (1) before viability, a woman has a fundamental right to choose to terminate her pregnancy, (2) a law that imposes an undue burden on the woman's right to choose before viability is unconstitutional, and (3) after viability, the state, in promoting its interest in potential human life, may regulate or prohibit abortion unless it is necessary to preserve the life or health of the mother. *Planned Parenthood of Southeastern Pa. v. Casey*, 505 U.S. 833, 112 S.Ct. 2791 (1992). In 2000, the Court again considered abortion rights and reaffirmed *Casey* in holding the Nebraska law at issue unconstitutional because (1) it failed to provide an exception to preserve the health of the mother, and (2) it unduly burdened a woman's right to choose a late-term abortion, thereby unduly burdening her right to choose abortion itself. *Stenberg v. Carhart*, 120 S.Ct. 2597 (2000). **2.**

The spontaneous expulsion of an embryo or fetus before viability; MISCARRIAGE. — **abort,** *vb.* — **abortionist,** *n.*

> *induced abortion.* An abortion purposely and artificially caused either by the mother herself or by a third party. See ABORTIFACIENT.

> *late-term abortion.* An abortion performed during the latter stages of pregnancy, usu. after the middle of the second trimester.

> *partial-birth abortion.* An abortion in which a viable unborn fetus is partially delivered before being destroyed.

> *spontaneous abortion.* See MISCARRIAGE.

> *therapeutic abortion.* An abortion carried out to preserve the life or health of the mother.

abrogation of adoption. An action brought by an adoptive parent to terminate the parent–child relationship by annulment of the decree of adoption. • An adoption may be nullified if it resulted from fraud, misrepresentation, or undue influence, or if nullification is in the child's best interests. — Also termed *annulment of adoption.* Cf. WRONGFUL ADOPTION.

absent parent. See *noncustodial parent* under PARENT.

absolute delivery. See DELIVERY.

absolute divorce. See *divorce a vinculo matrimonii* under DIVORCE.

absolute gift. See *inter vivos gift* under GIFT.

absolute legacy. See LEGACY.

A-B trust. See *bypass trust* under TRUST.

abuse (ə-**byoos**), *n.* **1.** A departure from legal or reasonable use; misuse. **2.** Physical or mental maltreatment, often resulting in mental, emotional, sexual, or physical injury. — Also termed *cruel and abusive treatment*. Cf. NEGLECT; CRUELTY.

> *abuse of the elderly.* Abuse of a senior citizen by a caregiver. • Examples include deprivation of food or medication, beatings, oral assaults, and isolation. — Also termed *elder abuse*.

> *carnal abuse.* See *sexual abuse* (1).

> *child abuse.* **1.** Intentional or neglectful physical or emotional harm inflicted on a child, including sexual molestation; esp., a parent's or caregiver's act or failure to act that results in a child's exploitation, serious physical or emotional injury, sexual abuse, or death. **2.** An act or failure to act that presents an imminent risk of serious harm to a child. • Child abuse can be either intentional or negligent. The first case of child abuse actually prosecuted occurred in New York City in 1874. An eight-year-old girl named Mary Ellen was

found to have been severely abused. Her abusers were prosecuted under the law for prevention of cruelty to animals, since no law protecting children then existed. Child abuse was first recognized as a medical concern in 1962, when Dr. C. Henry Kempe introduced the medical concept of battered-child syndrome. — Also termed *cruelty to a child*; *cruelty to children*; *child maltreatment*. See *abused child* under CHILD; *battered child* under CHILD; BATTERED-CHILD SYNDROME. Cf. *secondary abuse*.

domestic abuse. See *domestic violence* under VIOLENCE.

elder abuse. See *abuse of the elderly*.

emotional abuse. Physical or mental abuse that causes or could cause serious emotional injury.

secondary abuse. Child abuse suffered by children who, although they are not physically abused, witness domestic violence within their families.

sexual abuse. **1.** An illegal sex act, esp. one performed against a minor by an adult. — Also termed *carnal abuse*. **2.** RAPE (2).

spousal abuse. Physical, sexual, or psychological abuse inflicted by one spouse on the other spouse. See BATTERED-WOMAN SYNDROME.

abuse (ə-**byooz**), *vb.* **1.** To damage (a thing). **2.** To depart from legal or reasonable use in dealing with (a person or thing); to misuse. **3.** To injure (a person) physically or mentally. **4.** In the context of child welfare, to hurt or injure (a child) by maltreatment. ● In most states, a finding of abuse is generally limited to maltreatment that causes or threatens to cause lasting harm to the child.

abused child. See CHILD.

abuse of the elderly. See ABUSE.

abusive (ə-**byoo**-siv), *adj.* **1.** Characterized by wrongful or improper use <abusive discovery tactics>. **2.** (Of a person) that treats another badly <abusive parent>. — **abusively,** *adv.*

a/c. *abbr.* ACCOUNT.

accelerated remainder. See REMAINDER.

access. See VISITATION.

access order. See VISITATION ORDER.

accident and health insurance. See HEALTH INSURANCE.

account, *n.* A detailed statement of the debits and credits between parties to a contract or to a fiduciary relationship; a reckoning of monetary dealings <the trustee balanced the account at the end of each month>. ● In wills and estates, an account is a brief financial statement of the manner in which an executor or administrator has performed the official duties of collecting the estate's assets and paying those who are entitled. An account charges the executor or administrator with the value of the estate as shown by the inventory, plus any increase, and credits the executor with expenses and costs, duly authorized disbursements, and the executor's commission. — Abbr. acct.; a/c. — Also termed *accounting*.

account in trust. An account established by an individual to hold the account's assets in trust for someone else.

annual account. See *intermediate account.*

community account. An account consisting of community funds or commingled funds. See COMMUNITY PROPERTY.

convenience account. An apparent joint account, but without right of survivorship, established by a creator to enable another person to withdraw funds at the creator's direction or for the creator's benefit. • Unlike a true joint account, only one person, the creator, has an ownership interest in the deposited funds. Convenience accounts are often established by those who need a financial manager's help and want to make it easy for the manager to pay bills. Although the manager's name is on the account, he or she does not contribute any personal funds to the account and can write checks or make withdrawals only at the direction of or on behalf of the creator.

custodial account. An account opened on behalf of someone else, such as one opened by a parent for a minor child. ● Custodial accounts most often arise under the Uniform Transfers to Minors Act (1983). All states have enacted either that act or its earlier version, the Uniform Gifts to Minors Act. Property can be set aside by a donor or transferred to a third party as custodian for the benefit of a minor, usually as an irrevocable gift. This is a much simpler mechanism than a trust. The custodian has powers and fiduciary duties similar to those of a trustee, except that the custodian is not under a court's supervision. The custodian must account for the property and turn it over to the beneficiary when he or she reaches majority. See UNIFORM TRANSFERS TO MINORS ACT.

intermediate account. An account filed by an executor, administrator, or guardian after the initial account and before the final account. ● This account is usually filed annually. — Also termed *annual account*.

joint account. A bank or brokerage account opened by two or more people, by which each party has a present right to withdraw all funds in the account and, upon the death of one party, the survivors become the owners of the account, with no right of the deceased party's heirs or devisees to share in it. ● Typically, the account-holders are designated as "joint tenants with right of survivorship" or "joint-and-survivor account-holders." In some jurisdictions, they must be so designated to establish a right of survivorship. — Abbr. JA. — Also termed *joint-and-survivorship account*.

multiple-party account. An account that has more than one owner with a current or future interest in the account. ● Multiple-party accounts include joint accounts, payable-on-death (P.O.D.) accounts, and trust accounts. Unif. Probate Code § 6–201(5).

accountant–client privilege. See PRIVILEGE.

accounting, *n.* **1.** See ACCOUNT. **2.** A rendition of an account, either voluntarily or by court order. ● The term frequently refers to the report of all items of property, income, and expenses prepared by a personal representative, trustee, or guardian and given to heirs, beneficiaries, or the probate court.

acct. *abbr.* ACCOUNT.

accumulated income. See INCOME.

accumulated legacy. See LEGACY.

accumulation trust. See TRUST.

accumulative legacy. See LEGACY.

accusatorial system. See ADVERSARY SYSTEM.

accusatory procedure. See ADVERSARY SYSTEM.

acknowledged father. See FATHER.

acknowledgment. 1. A father's public recognition of a child as his own. — Also termed *acknowledgment of paternity*.

> *formal acknowledgment.* **1.** A father's recognition of a child as his own by a formal, written declaration that meets a state's requirements for execution, typically by signing in the presence of two witnesses. **2.** A father's recognition of a child as his own in the child's registry of birth or at the child's baptism. ● In this sense, a formal acknowledgment typically occurs when a man signs the birth certificate or baptismal certificate as the father or announces at the baptismal service that he is the father. The fact that a man is named as the father on a certificate of birth or baptism is not a formal acknowledgment unless the father signs the document.

> *informal acknowledgment.* A father's recognition of a child as his own not by a written declaration but by receiving the child into his family or supporting the child and otherwise treating the child as his own offspring.

2. A formal declaration made in the presence of an authorized officer, such as a notary public, by someone who signs a document and confirms that the signature is authentic. • In most states, the officer certifies that (1) he or she personally knows the document signer or has established the signer's identity through satisfactory evidence, (2) the signer appeared before the officer on the date and in the place (usu. the county) indicated, and (3) the signer acknowledged signing the document freely. Cf. VERIFICATION.

acknowledgment of paternity. See ACKNOWLEDGMENT (1).

acquaintance rape. See RAPE.

acquest (ə-**kwest**), *n*. See ACQUET.

acquet (a-**kay** *or* ə-**kwet**), *n*. [French *acquêt* "acquisition"] (*usu. pl.*) *Civil law*. **1.** Property acquired by purchase, gift, or any means other than inheritance. • The term is most commonly used to denote a marital acquisition that is presumed to be community property. **2.** Property acquired by either spouse during the marriage. — Also termed *acquest*. See COMMUNITY PROPERTY.

act, *n*. **1.** Something done or performed, esp. voluntarily; a deed. — Also termed *action*. **2.** The process of doing or performing; an occurrence that results from the exertion of a person's will on the external world; ACTION (1). — Also termed *positive act*; *act of* *commission.* **3.** The formal product of a legislature or other deliberative body; esp., a statute.

acting executor. See EXECUTOR.

action. 1. The process of doing something; conduct or behavior. **2.** A thing done; ACT (1). **3.** A civil or criminal judicial proceeding.

> *matrimonial action.* An action relating to the state of marriage, such as an action for separation, annulment, or divorce.

active adoption-registry statute. See ADOPTION-REGISTRY STATUTE.

active euthanasia. See EUTHANASIA.

active trust. See TRUST.

act of commission. See ACT (2).

actual delivery. See DELIVERY.

actual service. See *personal service* under SERVICE.

ADA. *abbr.* AMERICANS WITH DISABILITIES ACT.

additional legacy. See LEGACY.

additional tax. See *stopgap tax* under TAX.

ADEA. *abbr.* AGE DISCRIMINATION IN EMPLOYMENT ACT.

ademption (ə-**demp**-shən), *n. Wills & estates.* The destruction or extinction of a testamentary gift by reason of a bequeathed asset's ceasing to be part of the estate at the time of the testator's death; a beneficiary's forfeiture of a legacy or bequest that is no longer operative. ● There are two theories of ademption. Under the *identity theory of ademption*, a devise of a specific piece of property will fail if that property is not a part of the testator's estate upon his or her death. Under the *intent theory of ademption*, by contrast, when a specific devise is no longer in the testator's estate at the time of his or her death, the devisee will receive a gift of equal value if it can be proved that the testator did not intend the gift to be adeemed. The intent theory has been codified in § 2–606 of the 1990 Uniform Probate Code. — Also termed *extinguishment of legacy*. — **adeem** (ə-**deem**), *vb.* Cf. ABATEMENT; ADVANCEMENT; LAPSE (2).

> **ademption by extinction.** An ademption that occurs because the unique property that is the subject of a specific bequest has been sold, given away, or destroyed, or is not otherwise in existence at the time of the testator's death.

> **ademption by satisfaction.** An ademption that occurs because the testator, while alive, has already given property to the beneficiary in lieu of the testamentary gift.

adjoining owner. See OWNER.

adjudication (ə-joo-di-**kay**-shən), *n.* **1.** The legal process of resolving a dispute; the process of judicially deciding a case. **2.** JUDGMENT.

adjudication hearing. See HEARING.

adjudicative-claims arbitration. See ARBITRATION.

adjudicatory hearing. See *adjudication hearing* under HEARING.

adjusted gross estate. See ESTATE.

administration, *n.* The management and settlement of the estate of an intestate decedent, or of a testator who has no executor, by a person legally appointed and supervised by the court. — **administer,** *vb.* — **administrative,** *adj.*

administration cum testamento annexo (kəm tes-tə-**men**-toh ə-**nek**-soh). [Latin "with the will annexed"] An administration granted when (1) a testator's will does not name any executor or when the executor named is incompetent to act, is deceased, or refuses to act, and (2) no successor executor has been named or is qualified to serve. — Abbr. c.t.a. — Also termed *administration with the will annexed.*

administration de bonis non (dee **boh**-nis non). [Latin "of the goods not administered"] An administration granted for the purpose of settling the remainder of an intestate estate that was not administered by the former administrator. — Abbr. d.b.n.

administration de bonis non cum testamento annexo (de **boh**-nis non kəm tes-tə-**men**-toh ə-**nek**-soh). An administration granted to settle the remainder of a testate estate not settled by a previous administrator or executor. ● This type of administration arises when there is a valid will, as opposed to an *administration de bonis non*, which is granted when there is no will. — Abbr. d.b.n.c.t.a.

administration durante absentia (d[y]uu-**ran**-tee ab-**sen**-shee-ə). An administration granted during the absence of either the executor or the person who has precedence as administrator.

administration durante minore aetate (d[y]uu-**ran**-tee mi-**nor**-ee ee-**tay**-tee). An administration granted during the minority of either a child executor or the person who has precedence as administrator.

administration pendente lite (pen-**den**-tee lı-tee). An administration granted during the pendency of a suit concerning a will's validity. — Also termed *pendente lite administration*; *special administration*. See PENDENTE LITE.

administration with the will annexed. See *administration cum testamento annexo*.

ancillary administration (**an**-sə-ler-ee). An administration that is auxiliary to the administration at the place of the decedent's domicile, such as one in another state. ● The purpose of this process is to collect assets, to transfer and record changed title to real property located there, and to pay any debts in that locality. — Also termed *foreign administration.*

caeterorum administration (set-ə-**ror**-əm). [Latin "of the rest"] An administration granted when limited powers previously granted to an administrator are inadequate to settle the estate's residue.

domiciliary administration (dom-ə-**sil**-ee-er-ee). The handling of an estate in the state where the decedent was domiciled at death.

foreign administration. See *ancillary administration.*

general administration. An administration with authority to deal with an entire estate. Cf. *special administration.*

limited administration. An administration for a temporary period or for a special purpose.

pendente lite administration. See *administration pendente lite.*

public administration. In some jurisdictions, an administration by an officer appointed to administer for an intestate who has left no person entitled to apply for letters (or whose possible representatives refuse to serve).

special administration. **1.** An administration with authority to deal with only some of a decedent's property, as opposed to administering the whole estate. **2.** See *administration pendente lite*. Cf. *general administration*.

temporary administration. An administration in which the court appoints a fiduciary to administer the affairs of a decedent's estate for a short time before an administrator or executor can be appointed and qualified.

administration cum testamento annexo. See ADMINISTRATION.

administration de bonis non. See ADMINISTRATION.

administration de bonis non cum testamento annexo. See ADMINISTRATION.

administration durante absentia. See ADMINISTRATION.

administration durante minore aetate. See ADMINISTRATION.

administration expense. A necessary expenditure made by an administrator in managing and distributing an estate. ● These expenses are tax-deductible even if not actually incurred by the time the return is filed.

administration letters. See LETTERS OF ADMINISTRATION.

administration pendente lite. See ADMINISTRATION.

administration with the will annexed. See *administration cum testamento annexo* under ADMINISTRATION.

administrative officer. An official, other than a judge, who is appointed to preside over child-support matters. See CHILD-SUPPORT-ENFORCEMENT AGENCY. Cf. MASTER (2); JUDGE.

administrator (ad-**min**-ə-stray-tər). A person appointed by the court to manage the assets and liabilities of an intestate decedent. ● This term once referred to males only (as opposed to *administratrix*), but legal writers now generally use *administrator* to refer to someone of either sex. Cf. EXECUTOR (2).

> *administrator ad litem* (ad lɪ-tem *or* -təm). A special administrator appointed by the court to represent the estate's interest in an action usu. either because there is no administrator of the estate or because the current administrator has an interest in the action adverse to that of the estate.

administrator ad prosequendum (ad prahs-ə-**kwen**-dəm). An administrator appointed to prosecute or defend a certain action or actions involving the estate.

administrator cum testamento annexo (kəm tes-tə-**men**-toh ə-**nek**-soh). An administrator appointed by the court to carry out the provisions of a will when the testator has named no executor, or the executors named refuse, are incompetent to act, or have died before performing their duties. — Also termed *administrator c.t.a.*; *administrator with the will annexed.*

administrator de bonis non (dee **boh**-nis non). An administrator appointed by the court to administer the decedent's goods that were not administered by an earlier administrator or executor. ● If there is no will, the administrator bears the name *administrator de bonis non* (abbr. *administrator d.b.n.*), but if there is a will, the full name is *administrator de bonis non cum testamento annexo* (abbr. *administrator d.b.n.c.t.a.*).

administrator pendente lite. See *special administrator* (2).

administrator with the will annexed. See *administrator cum testamento annexo.*

ancillary administrator (**an**-sə-ler-ee). A court-appointed administrator who oversees the distribution of the part of a decedent's estate located in a jurisdiction other than where the decedent was domiciled (the place of the main administration).

foreign administrator. An administrator appointed in another jurisdiction.

general administrator. A person appointed to administer an intestate decedent's entire estate.

public administrator. A state-appointed officer who administers intestate estates that are not administered by the decedent's relatives. ● This officer's right to administer is usually subordinate to the rights of creditors, but in a few jurisdictions the creditors' rights are subordinate.

special administrator. **1.** A person appointed to administer only a specific part of an intestate decedent's estate. **2.** A person appointed to serve as administrator of an estate solely because of an emergency or an unusual situation, such as a will contest. — Also termed (in sense 2) *administrator pendente lite.*

administrator ad litem. See ADMINISTRATOR.

administrator ad prosequendum. See ADMINISTRATOR.

administrator c.t.a. See *administrator cum testamento annexo* under ADMINISTRATOR.

administrator cum testamento annexo. See ADMINISTRATOR.

administrator d.b.n. See *administrator de bonis non* under ADMINISTRATOR.

administrator d.b.n.c.t.a. See *administrator de bonis non* under ADMINISTRATOR.

administrator de bonis non. See ADMINISTRATOR.

administrator de bonis non cum testamento annexo. See *administrator de bonis non* under ADMINISTRATOR.

administrator pendente lite. See *special administrator* (2) under ADMINISTRATOR.

administrator with the will annexed. See *administrator cum testamento annexo* under ADMINISTRATOR.

administratrix (ad-min-ə-**stray**-triks *or* ad-**min**-ə-strə-triks). *Archaic.* A female administrator. Pl. **administratrixes, administratrices.** See ADMINISTRATOR.

adoptability, *n.* **1.** A child's availability to be adopted, esp. by reason of all legal impediments having been removed. **2.** The likelihood of a child's being adopted; a prospective adoptee's desirability from the prospective parents' point of view. — **adoptable,** *adj.*

adopted child. See CHILD; ADOPTEE.

adoptee. A person who has become the legal child of one or two nonbiological parents. — Also termed *adopted child*.

adoption, *n*. The creation of a parent–child relationship by judicial order between two parties who usu. are unrelated. ● This is accomplished only after a determination that the child is an orphan or has been abandoned, or that the parents' parental rights have been terminated by court order. Adoption creates a parent–child relationship between the adopted child and the adoptive parents with all the rights, privileges, and responsibilities that attach to that relationship, though there may be agreed exceptions. There is a distinction between adoption and legitimation, and between adoption and fostering. Adoption usually refers to an act between persons unrelated by blood; legitimation refers to an act between persons related by blood. Universally, a decree of adoption confers legitimate status on the adopted child. — **adopt,** *vb*. — **adoptive,** *adj*. See *adopted child* under CHILD. Cf. LEGITIMATION (2).

adoption by estoppel. **1.** An equitable adoption of a child by a person's promises and acts that preclude the person and his or her estate from denying adopted status to the child. **2.** An adoption decree formerly conferred by a court of equity or, today, by a court exercising equitable powers, treating as done that which ought to have been done. ● In such a case, no final decree of adoption has previously been obtained even though the principals have acted as if an adoption has been achieved. A petitioner must show an agreement of adoption, relinquishment of parental authority by the child's biological parents, assumption of parental responsibility by the foster parents, and a de facto relationship of parent and child over a substantial period. Such a claim typically occurs when an adoptive parent has died intestate, and the child tries to be named an heir. — Also termed *equitable adoption*; *virtual adoption*. See ESTOPPEL (1). **3.** See *de facto adoption*.

adult adoption. The adoption of one adult by another. ● Many jurisdictions do not allow adult adoptions. Those that do often impose restrictions, as by requiring consent of the person to be adopted, but may not look too closely at the purpose for which adoption is sought.

agency adoption. An adoption in which parental rights are terminated and legal custody is relinquished to an agency that finds and approves the adoptive parents. ● An agency adoption can be either public or private. In all states, adoption agencies must be licensed, and in most they are nonprofit entities. Parents who voluntarily place a child for adoption most commonly use a private agency. Cf. *private adoption*.

black-market adoption. **1.** An illegal adoption in which an intermediary (a broker) receives payment for his or her services. **2.** Baby-selling.

closed adoption. An adoption in which the biological parent relinquishes his or her parental rights and surrenders the child to an unknown person or persons; an adoption in which there is no disclosure of the identity of the birth parents, adopting parent or parents, or child. ● Adoptions by stepparents, blood relatives, and foster parents are exceptions to the no-disclosure requirement. — Also termed *confidential adoption.* Cf. *open adoption*; *cooperative adoption*.

cooperative adoption. A process in which the birth parents and adoptive parents negotiate to reach a voluntary agreement about the degree and type of continuing contact after adoption, including direct visitation or more limited arrangements such as communication by telephone or mail, the exchange of either identifying or nonidentifying information, and other forms of contact. Cf. *open adoption*; *closed adoption*.

de facto adoption. An adoption that falls short of the statutory requirements in a particular state. ● The adoption agreement may ripen to a de jure adoption when the statutory formalities have been met or if a court finds that the requirements for adoption by estoppel have been met. — Also termed *adoption by estoppel*.

direct-placement adoption. See *private adoption*.

equitable adoption. See *adoption by estoppel*.

gray-market adoption. See *private adoption.*

independent adoption. See *private adoption.*

intercountry adoption. See *international adoption.*

international adoption. An adoption in which parents domiciled in one nation travel to a foreign country to adopt a child there, usu. in accordance with the laws of the child's nation. • International adoptions first became popular after World War II and escalated after the Korean Conflict because of the efforts of humanitarian programs working to find homes for children left orphaned by the wars. More recently prospective parents have turned to international adoption as the number of healthy babies domestically available for adoption has steadily declined. — Also termed *transnational adoption*; *intercountry adoption.* See MULTIETHNIC PLACEMENT ACT OF 1994.

interracial adoption. See *transracial adoption.*

interstate adoption. An adoption in which the prospective parents live in one state and the child lives in another state. See INTERSTATE COMPACT ON THE PLACEMENT OF CHILDREN.

joint adoption. An adoption in which the prospective parents apply as a couple and are approved or rejected as a couple, as opposed to filing separate and individual applications to adopt a child. • Although the term most often applies to adoption by a married couple, it also applies to an adoption petition by two unmarried partners who are adopting a child.

open adoption. An adoption in which the biological mother (sometimes with the biological father) chooses the adoptive parents and in which the child often continues to have a post-adoption relationship with his or her biological family. ● Typically the birth parents meet the adoptive parents and participate in the separation and placement process. The birth parents relinquish all legal, moral, and nurturing rights over the child, but usually retain the right to continuing contact and to knowledge of the child's welfare and location. Cf. *closed adoption*; *cooperative adoption*.

private adoption. An adoption that occurs independently between the biological mother (and sometimes the biological father) and the adoptive parents without the involvement of an agency. ● A private adoption is usually arranged by an intermediary such as a lawyer, doctor, or counselor. Legal custody — though sometimes not physical custody — remains with the biological parent or parents until the termination and adoption are complete. — Also termed *private-placement adoption*; *direct-placement adoption*; *direct adoption*; *gray-market adoption*; *identified adoption*; *independent adoption.* Cf. *agency adoption*.

private-placement adoption. See *private adoption*.

27

second-parent adoption. An adoption by an unmarried cohabiting partner of a child's legal parent, not involving the termination of a legal parent's rights; esp., an adoption in which a lesbian, gay man, or unmarried heterosexual person adopts his or her partner's biological or adoptive child. See Restatement (Third) of Property: Wills and Other Donative Transfers § 2.5 (Tentative Draft No. 2, 1998). • Although not all jurisdictions recognize second-parent adoption, the practice is becoming more widely accepted. See *In re Adoption of B.L.V.B.*, 628 A.2d 1271 (Vt. 1993); *In re Adoption of Tammy*, 619 N.E.2d 315 (Mass. 1993); *In re Adoption of Evan*, 583 N.Y.S.2d 997 (Sur. Ct. 1992). — Also termed *de facto stepparent adoption*; *pseudo-stepparent adoption*. Cf. *stepparent adoption*.

stepparent adoption. The adoption of a child by a stepfather or stepmother. • Stepparent adoptions are the most common adoptions in the United States. Cf. *second-parent adoption*.

transnational adoption. See *international adoption*.

transracial adoption. An adoption in which at least one adoptive parent is of a race different from that of the adopted child. • Under federal law, child-placement agencies may not use race as a factor in approving adoptions. 42 USCA § 5115a. — Also termed *interracial adoption*. See MULTIETHNIC PLACEMENT ACT OF 1994.

virtual adoption. See *adoption by estoppel.*

wrongful adoption. See WRONGFUL ADOPTION.

adoption agency. A licensed establishment where a biological parent can voluntarily surrender a child for adoption. See *agency adoption* under ADOPTION.

Adoption and Safe Families Act. A 1997 federal law that requires states to provide safe and permanent homes for abused and neglected children within shorter periods than those required by earlier state and federal laws. ● The primary focus is on the safety and well-being of the child, in contrast to previously paramount rights of the parents. The ASFA signaled a dramatic shift in the philosophy of child-protection proceedings that had controlled since 1980 under the Adoption Assistance and Child Welfare Act. — Abbr. ASFA. See ADOPTION ASSISTANCE AND CHILD WELFARE ACT; FOSTER-CARE DRIFT.

Adoption Assistance and Child Welfare Act. A 1980 federal statute whose purpose was to force states to use reasonable efforts (1) to avoid removing children from their homes, (2) to reunite families when children had been removed because of abuse or neglect, and (3) when reunification failed, to terminate parental rights and place the children in permanent homes. 42 USCA § 620 et seq.; § 670 et seq. ● The Act provided funds for foster-care placement, Child Protective Services, family preservation and reunification, and foster-care reform to states complying with the Act. Its aim was to prevent the unnecessary removal of children from homes and to hasten the return of children in foster care to their families. It has now been essentially overruled in philosophy by the 1997 enactment of the Adoption and Safe Families Act. See ADOPTION AND SAFE FAMILIES ACT.

adoption-assistance plan. An employer-sponsored program that provides financial assistance to employees for adoption-related expenses.

adoption by estoppel. See ADOPTION.

adoption by reference. See INCORPORATION BY REFERENCE.

adoption-registry statute. A law that provides for the release of adoption information if the biological parent, the adoptive parent, and the adoptee (after he or she reaches a certain statutorily prescribed age) all officially record their desire for its release. — Also termed *voluntary-registry law*.

    active adoption-registry statute. A registry statute that authorizes a state authority to seek out parties' desires to obtain or release adoption information when one party expresses a desire for that information.

    passive adoption-registry statute. A registry statute allowing parties to register their desires for release of adoption information after an adopted child reaches a specified age.

adoptive parent. See PARENT.

ADR. *abbr*. ALTERNATIVE DISPUTE RESOLUTION.

adult (ə-**dəlt** *or* ad-əlt), *n*. A person who has attained the legal age of majority, generally 18. — Also termed *major*. — **adult** (ə-**dəlt**), *adj*.

adult adoption. See ADOPTION.

adulterine (ə-**dəl**-tə-rin), *adj*. **1.** Illegal; unlicensed. **2.** Born of adultery. **3.** Of or involving adultery.

adulterine, *n*. *Archaic*. An illegitimate child.

adulterine bastard. See BASTARD.

adultery (ə-**dəl**-tə-ree), *n*. Voluntary sexual intercourse between a married person and someone other than the person's spouse. ● In many jurisdictions, adultery is a crime, but it is rarely prosecuted. In states that still permit fault divorce, proof of adultery is a ground on which a divorce may be granted. A court may also use proof of adultery as a reason to reduce the offending spouse's marital-property award in a property division. Judges traditionally viewed adultery as a reason for denying the offending spouse primary custody of a child in a child-custody dispute. But today, only the deleterious effect of immoral behavior on the child is typically considered relevant. — Formerly also

31

termed *spouse-breach*; *avowtry*. — **adulterous,** *adj*. — **adulterer, adulteress,** *n*. Cf. FORNICATION; INFIDELITY.

double adultery. Adultery between persons who are both married to other persons.

incestuous adultery. Adultery between relatives; adultery committed by persons who are closely related.

open and notorious adultery. *Archaic*. Adultery in which the parties reside together publicly, as if married, and the community is generally aware of the living arrangement and the fact that the couple is not married.

single adultery. Adultery in which only one party is married to another person.

Adult Protective Services. A governmental agency with responsibility for investigating allegations of elder abuse and neglect and for responding appropriately. ● Every state has such an agency. — Abbr. APS.

advance directive. 1. A durable power of attorney that takes effect upon one's incompetency and designates a surrogate decision-maker for healthcare matters. ● The Uniform Health-Care Decision Act (1993) states that the power of attorney for healthcare must be in writing and signed by the principal. Unless otherwise stated, the authority is effective only upon a determination that the principal lacks capacity, and it ceases to be effective once the principal regains his capacity. The agent must make decisions in accordance with the principal's relevant instructions, if there are any, or in the principal's best interests. — Also termed *power of attorney for healthcare*; *healthcare proxy*. See POWER OF ATTORNEY; UNIFORM HEALTH-CARE DECISION ACT. **2.** A legal document explaining one's wishes about medical treatment if one becomes incompetent or unable to communicate. — Often shortened to *directive*. — Also termed *medical directive*; *physician's directive*; *written directive*. See NATURAL-DEATH ACT; PROXY DIRECTIVE. Cf. LIVING WILL.

advancement, *n.* A payment or gift to an heir (esp. a child) during one's lifetime as an advance share of one's estate, with the intention of reducing or extinguishing the heir's claim to the estate under intestacy laws. ● In some jurisdictions, the donor's intent is irrelevant if all the statutory elements of an advancement are present. A few jurisdictions define the relationship between the donor and donee to include inter vivos transfers between ancestors and descendants. — **advance,** *vb.* Cf. ADEMPTION.

adversary procedure. See ADVERSARY SYSTEM.

adversary system. A procedural system, such as the Anglo–American legal system, involving active and unhindered parties contesting with each other to put forth a case before an independent decision-maker. — Also termed *adversary procedure*; (in criminal cases) *accusatorial system*, *accusatory procedure*.

AFDC. *abbr.* AID TO FAMILIES WITH DEPENDENT CHILDREN.

affiant (ə-**fī**-ənt), *n.* One who makes an affidavit. — Also termed *deponent*.

affidavit (af-ə-**day**-vit). A voluntary declaration of facts written down and sworn to by the declarant before an officer authorized to administer oaths, such as a notary public. ● A great deal of evidence is submitted by affidavit, especially in pretrial matters such as summary-judgment motions. Cf. DECLARATION.

> ***affidavit of nonprosecution.*** An affidavit in which a crime victim requests that the perpetrator not be prosecuted. ● In many cases, if the victim files an affidavit of nonprosecution, the prosecutor will withdraw or not file criminal charges against the perpetrator on grounds that there is no victim. Sometimes, though, the prosecutor will go forward with the prosecution even if the victim files an affidavit of nonprosecution.

> ***self-proving affidavit.*** An affidavit attached to a will and signed by the testator and witnesses certifying that the statutory requirements of due execution of the will have been complied with. ● The affidavit, which recites the facts of the will's proper execution, permits the will to be probated

without the necessity of having the witnesses appear and prove due execution by their testimony.

affine (ə-**fīn**), *n*. A relative by marriage.

affinity (ə-**fin**-ə-tee). **1.** A close agreement. **2.** The relation that one spouse has to the blood relatives of the other spouse; relationship by marriage. **3.** Any familial relation resulting from a marriage. Cf. CONSANGUINITY. See *relative by affinity* under RELATIVE.

> ***collateral affinity.*** The relationship of a spouse's relatives to the other spouse's relatives. ● An example is a wife's brother and her husband's sister.

> ***direct affinity.*** The relationship of a spouse to the other spouse's blood relatives. ● An example is a wife and her husband's brother.

> ***quasi-affinity.*** *Civil law*. The affinity existing between two persons, one of whom has been engaged to a relative of the other.

> ***secondary affinity.*** The relationship of a spouse to the other spouse's marital relatives. ● An example is a wife and her husband's sister-in-law.

affirmative injunction. See *mandatory injunction* under INJUNCTION.

afterborn child. See CHILD.

afterborn heir. See HEIR.

age, *n.* A period of time; esp., a period of individual existence or the duration of a person's life. ● In American usage, age is stated in full years completed (so that someone *15 years of age* might actually be 15 years and several months old). State statutes define various types of ages, as shown in the subentries.

age of capacity. The age, usu. defined by statute as 18 years, at which a person is legally capable of agreeing to a contract, maintaining a lawsuit, or the like. ● A person may be authorized to make certain critical personal decisions at an earlier age than the general age of capacity, such as the decision whether to bear a child, to donate blood, to obtain treatment for sexually transmitted diseases, to marry, or to write a will. The age of capacity to write a will is typically not 18, but 14. — Also termed *age of majority; legal age; lawful age.* See CAPACITY.

age of consent. The age, usu. defined by statute as 16 years, at which a person is legally capable of agreeing to marriage (without parental consent) or to sexual intercourse. ● If a person over the age of consent has sexual intercourse with a person under the age of consent, the older person may be prosecuted for statutory rape regardless of whether the younger person consented to the act. See *statutory rape* under RAPE.

age of majority. 1. The age, usu. defined by statute as 18 years, at which a person attains full legal rights, esp. civil and political rights such as the right to vote. ● The age of majority must be the same for men and women. In almost all states today, the age of majority is 18, but the age at which a person may legally purchase and consume alcohol is 21. — Also termed *lawful age*; *legal age*. **2.** See *age of capacity*.

age of reason. The age at which a person becomes able to distinguish right from wrong and is thus legally capable of committing a crime or tort. ● The age of reason varies from jurisdiction to jurisdiction, but 7 years is traditionally the age below which a child is conclusively presumed not to have committed a crime or tort, while 14 years is usually the age below which a rebuttable presumption applies. A child of 14 or older has traditionally been considered legally competent to commit a crime and therefore held accountable. With the creation of juvenile courts and their investiture of delinquency jurisdiction over children from birth to age 18, these traditional distinctions have nearly vanished. They surface from time to time in murder cases when a juvenile court considers whether to certify or transfer a very young child for trial in criminal court or when a prosecutor seeks to bypass the juvenile court by filing criminal charges against a young child.

lawful age. **1.** See *age of capacity*. **2.** See *age of majority* (1).

age discrimination. See DISCRIMINATION (2).

Age Discrimination in Employment Act. A federal law prohibiting job discrimination based on a person's age, esp. unfair and discriminatory employment decisions that negatively affect someone who is 40 years old or older. 29 USCA §§ 621–634. ● Passed in 1967, the Act applies to businesses with more than 20 employees and to all governmental entities. — Abbr. ADEA.

agency adoption. See ADOPTION.

agent. One who is authorized to act for or in place of another; a representative.

> *private agent.* An agent acting for an individual in that person's private affairs.

> *universal agent.* An agent authorized to perform all acts that the principal could personally perform.

age of capacity. See AGE.

age of consent. See AGE.

age of majority. See AGE.

age of reason. See AGE.

aggravated kidnapping. See KIDNAPPING.

aggregate income. See INCOME.

aging-out, *n.* A foster child's or minor ward's reaching the age at which any legal right to care expires. ● Aging-out usually occurs when the child reaches the age of majority and becomes ineligible for foster care. Some states allow an extension of eligibility up to age 21 if the child is still in school or cannot live independently, or if it is otherwise in the child's best interests to remain in foster care and the child consents. See INDEPENDENT-LIVING PROGRAM.

agnate (**ag**-nayt), *adj.* Related or akin through male descent or on the father's side.

agnate, *n.* A blood relative whose connection is through the male line. Cf. COGNATE.

agnatic (ag-**nat**-ik), *adj.* (Of a relationship) restricted to affiliations through the male line. — Also termed *agnatical* (ag-**nat**-i-kəl).

agreed decree. See DECREE.

agreed judgment. See JUDGMENT.

agreement. A mutual understanding between two or more persons about their relative rights and duties regarding past or future performances; a manifestation of mutual assent by two or more persons.

agreement incident to divorce. See DIVORCE AGREEMENT.

antenuptial agreement. See PRENUPTIAL AGREEMENT.

cohabitation agreement. See COHABITATION AGREEMENT.

divorce agreement. See DIVORCE AGREEMENT.

living-together agreement. See COHABITATION AGREEMENT.

marital agreement. See MARITAL AGREEMENT.

marital settlement agreement. See DIVORCE AGREEMENT.

negotiated agreement. See NEGOTIATED AGREEMENT.

postnuptial agreement. See POSTNUPTIAL AGREEMENT.

prenuptial agreement. See PRENUPTIAL AGREEMENT.

property settlement agreement. See PROPERTY SETTLEMENT (2).

reconciliation agreement. See RECONCILIATION AGREEMENT.

separation agreement. See SEPARATION AGREEMENT.

surrogate-parenting agreement. See SURRO-GATE-PARENTING AGREEMENT.

trust agreement. See *declaration of trust* (2) under DECLARATION.

agreement incident to divorce. See DIVORCE AGREEMENT.

agreement to marry. See MARRIAGE PROMISE.

agunah (ah-**goo**-nə), *n.* A Jewish woman whose husband will not agree to a divorce.

AID. *abbr.* See *artificial insemination by donor* under ARTIFICIAL INSEMINATION.

Aid to Families with Dependent Children. *Obsolete.* A federally funded, state-administered welfare program that provided financial assistance to needy families with dependent children. ● Aid to Families with Dependent Children has been replaced by Temporary Assistance to Needy Families. — Abbr. AFDC. See TEMPORARY ASSISTANCE TO NEEDY FAMILIES.

AIH. *abbr.* See *artificial insemination by husband* under ARTIFICIAL INSEMINATION.

alien, *vb.* See ALIENATE.

alienable (**ay**-lee-ə-nə-bəl *or* **ayl**-yə-), *adj.* Capable of being transferred to the ownership of another;

transferable <an alienable property interest>. — **alienability,** *n.*

alienate (**ay**-lee-ə-nayt *or* **ayl**-yə-), *vb.* To transfer or convey (property or a property right) to another. — Also termed *alien.*

alienation (ay-lee-ə-**nay**-shən *or* ayl-yə-**nay**-shən), *n.* **1.** Withdrawal from former attachment; estrangement <alienation of affections>. **2.** Conveyance or transfer of property to another <alienation of one's estate>. — **alienative** (**ay**-lee-ə-nay-tiv *or* **ayl**-yə-), *adj.*

alienation of affections. A tort claim for willful or malicious interference with a marriage by a third party without justification or excuse. ● Where the cause of action still exists, the elements are (1) some wrongful conduct by the defendant with the plaintiff's spouse, (2) the loss of affection or loss of consortium of the plaintiff's spouse, and (3) a causal relationship between the defendant's conduct and the loss of consortium. Heartbalm statutes in 26 states and the District of Columbia have now abolished in whole or in part suits for alienation of affections. But the doctrine thrives elsewhere. For example, a North Carolina court has upheld a $1 million award to an ex-wife who filed an alienation-of-affections action against her ex-husband's new wife. *Hutelmyer v. Cox,* 514 S.E.2d 554 (N.C. Ct. App. 1999). See CONSORTIUM; HEARTBALM STATUTE.

alimony (al-ə-moh-nee). A court-ordered allowance that one spouse pays to the other spouse for maintenance and support while they are separated, while they are involved in a matrimonial lawsuit, or after they are divorced. ● Alimony is distinct from a property settlement. Alimony payments are taxable income to the receiving spouse and are deductible by the payor spouse; payments in settlement of property rights are not. The Supreme Court has held unconstitutional a statute that imposed alimony obligations on the husband only. *Orr v. Orr*, 440 U.S. 268, 99 S.Ct. 1102 (1979). — Also termed *spousal support*; *maintenance*. Cf. CHILD SUPPORT; DIVORCE AGREEMENT.

>   *alimony in gross.* Alimony in the form of a single and definite sum not subject to modification. — Also termed *lump-sum alimony*.

>   *alimony pendente lite* (pen-**den**-tee **li**-tee). [Latin *pendente lite* "pending litigation"] See *temporary alimony*.

>   *final alimony.* See *permanent alimony*.

>   *lump-sum alimony.* See *alimony in gross*.

>   *periodic alimony.* See *permanent alimony*.

>   *permanent alimony.* Alimony payable in usu. weekly or monthly installments either indefinitely or until a time specified by court order. ● This kind of alimony may usually be modified for changed circumstances of either party. It termi-

nates upon the death of either spouse and usually upon the remarriage of the obligee. — Also termed *final alimony*; *periodic alimony*.

provisional alimony. See *temporary alimony*.

rehabilitative alimony. Alimony found necessary to assist a divorced person in acquiring the education or training required to find employment outside the home or to reenter the labor force. ● It usually has time limitations, such as a maximum of one or two years. — Also termed *short-term alimony*; *transitional alimony*.

reimbursement alimony. Alimony designed to repay a spouse who during the marriage made financial contributions that directly enhanced the future earning capacity of the other spouse. ● An example is alimony for a wife who worked full-time supporting herself and her husband with separate-property earnings while he earned a medical degree.

temporary alimony. Interim alimony ordered by the court pending an action for divorce or separation in which one party has made a claim for permanent alimony. — Also termed *provisional alimony*; *alimony pendente lite*; *allowance pendente lite*.

transitional alimony. See *rehabilitative alimony*.

alimony in gross. See ALIMONY.

alimony pendente lite. See ALIMONY.

alimony trust. See TRUST.

allegation of faculties. *Archaic.* A statement detailing a husband's or wife's property, made by a spouse who seeks alimony. See FACULTIES.

allowance. 1. A share or portion, esp. of money that is assigned or granted.

 allowance pendente lite. See *temporary alimony* under ALIMONY.

 family allowance. A portion of a decedent's estate set aside by statute for a surviving spouse, children, or parents, regardless of any testamentary disposition or competing claims. ● Every state has a statute authorizing the probate court to award an amount for the temporary maintenance and support of the surviving spouse (and often for dependent children). The allowance may be limited for a fixed period (18 months under the Uniform Probate Code) or may continue until all contests are resolved and a decree of distribution is entered. This support, together with probate homesteads and personal-property allowances, is in addition to whatever interests pass by the will or by intestate succession. See *probate homestead* under HOMESTEAD. Cf. *spousal allowance.*

 gratuitous allowance. A pension voluntarily granted by a public entity. ● The gratuitous (rather than contractual) nature of this type of allowance gives the pensioner no vested rights in the allowance.

spousal allowance. A portion of a decedent's estate set aside by statute for a surviving spouse, regardless of any testamentary disposition or competing claims. ● This allowance is superior to the claims of general creditors. In some states, it is even preferred to the expenses of administration, funeral, and last illness of the spouse. — Also termed *widow's allowance*; *widower's allowance*. See *probate homestead* under HOMESTEAD. Cf. *family allowance*.

widower's allowance. See *spousal allowance*.

widow's allowance. See *spousal allowance*.

2. The sum awarded by a court to a fiduciary as payment for services. **3.** A deduction.

allowance pendente lite. See *temporary alimony* under ALIMONY.

allurement. *Torts.* An attractive object that tempts a trespassing child to meddle when the child ought to abstain. Cf. ATTRACTIVE-NUISANCE DOCTRINE.

alternate legacy. See LEGACY.

alternative devise. See DEVISE.

alternative dispute resolution. A procedure for settling a dispute by means other than litigation, such as arbitration or mediation. — Abbr. ADR. — Also termed *dispute resolution*. See ARBITRATION; MEDIATION.

alternative remainder. See REMAINDER.

Amber alert. A system by which the police can rapidly broadcast to the general public a report of a missing or endangered child by means of radio and television announcements. ● The alert is named for Amber Hagerman of Texas, a nine-year-old who was abducted and murdered in 1996 by an unknown person. The system has been adopted by many communities in the U.S. and Canada. — Also termed *Amber Plan*.

ambulatory, *adj.* Capable of being altered or revised <a will is ambulatory because it is revocable until the testator's death>.

a mensa et thoro (ay **men**-sə et **thor**-oh). [Latin "from board and hearth"] (Of a divorce decree) effecting a separation of the parties rather than a dissolution of the marriage <a separation *a mensa et thoro* was the usual way for a couple to separate under English law up until 1857>. ● Not all states provide for such a proceeding. See *divorce a mensa et thoro* under DIVORCE; SEPARATION; A VINCULO MATRIMONII.

American Academy of Matrimonial Lawyers. A professional organization of attorneys who are invited to become members after showing a proficiency and specialization in the field of matrimonial law. — Abbr. AAML.

Americans with Disabilities Act. A federal statute that prohibits discrimination — in employment, public services, and public accommodations — against any person with a disability ("a physical or mental impairment that substantially limits one or more of the major life activities"). 42 USCA §§ 12101–12213. • Under the ADA, major life activities include any activity that an average person in the general population can perform with little or no difficulty, such as seeing, hearing, sleeping, eating, walking, traveling, and working. The statute applies to both private and governmental entities, but not to a private employer having fewer than 15 employees. 42 USCA § 12111(5)(A). — Abbr. ADA. See DISABILITY.

amicus curiae (ə-**mee**-kəs **kyoor**-ee-ı *or* ə-**mı**-kəs **kyoor**-ee-ee *also* **am**-i-kəs). [Latin "friend of the court"] A person who is not a party to a lawsuit but who petitions the court or is requested by the court to file a brief in the action because that person has a strong interest in the subject matter. — Often shortened to *amicus*. — Also termed *friend of the court*. Pl. **amici curiae** (ə-**mee**-kee *or* ə-**mı**-sı *or* ə-**mı**-kı).

48

Amish exception. An exemption of the Amish from compulsory-school-attendance laws under the Free Exercise Clause of the First Amendment. ● In *Wisconsin v. Yoder*, 406 U.S. 205, 92 S.Ct. 1526 (1972), the Supreme Court held that Amish children could not be compelled to attend high school even though they were within the age range of the state's compulsory-attendance law. The Court has very narrowly construed the Amish exception and has refused to extend it to non-Amish children. See COMPULSORY-ATTENDANCE LAW; FREE EXERCISE CLAUSE.

anatomical gift. See GIFT.

ancestor. See ASCENDANT.

ancestral debt. See DEBT.

ancestral estate. See ESTATE.

ancestry. A line of descent; lineage.

ancillary administration. See ADMINISTRATION.

ancillary administrator. See ADMINISTRATOR.

and his heirs. See HEIR.

animus deserendi (**an**-ə-məs des-ə-**ren**-dɪ). [Latin] The intention to desert (usu. a spouse, child, etc.).

annual account. See *intermediate account* under ACCOUNT.

annual gift-tax exclusion. See *annual exclusion* under EXCLUSION.

annuity trust. See TRUST.

annulment (ə-nəl-mənt), *n*. **1.** The act of nullifying or making void. **2.** A judicial or ecclesiastical declaration that a marriage is void. ● An annulment establishes that the marital status never existed. So annulment and dissolution of marriage (or divorce) are fundamentally different: an annulment renders a marriage void from the beginning, while dissolution of marriage terminates the marriage as of the date of the judgment of dissolution. Although a marriage terminated by annulment is considered never to have occurred, in most states today a child born during the marriage is not considered illegitimate after the annulment. — **annul** (ə-nəl), *vb*. Cf. DIVORCE.

annulment of adoption. See ABROGATION OF ADOPTION.

answer, *n*. A defendant's first pleading that addresses the merits of the case, usu. by denying the plaintiff's allegations. ● An answer usually sets forth the defendant's defenses and counterclaims.

answer, *vb*. **1.** To respond to a pleading or a discovery request <the company failed to answer

the interrogatories within 30 days>. **2.** To assume the liability of another <a guarantor answers for another person's debt>. **3.** To pay (a debt or other liability) <she promised to answer damages out of her own estate>.

antecessor (an-tə-**ses**-ər *or* **an**-tə-ses-ər), *n.* [Latin] *Hist.* An ancestor.

ante mortem. [Latin] Before death.

antenuptial (an-ti-**nəp**-shəl), *adj.* See PRENUPTIAL.

antenuptial agreement. See PRENUPTIAL AGREEMENT.

antenuptial contract. See PRENUPTIAL AGREEMENT.

antenuptial gift. See *prenuptial gift* under GIFT.

antenuptial will. See *prenuptial will* under WILL.

anticontest clause. See NO-CONTEST CLAUSE.

anti-evolution statute. *Hist.* A law that forbids the teaching of the theory of evolution in schools. ● Such statutes were held unconstitutional as violative of the Establishment Clause in *Epperson v. Arkansas*, 393 U.S. 97, 89 S.Ct. 266 (1968). — Also termed *evolution statute.* Cf. CREATION SCIENCE.

anti-heartbalm statute. See HEARTBALM STATUTE.

antilapse statute. A statute that substitutes certain heirs of some types of testamentary beneficiaries when the beneficiary has predeceased the testator and permits them to take the gift, which would otherwise fail and thus pass to the residuary beneficiary (if any) or to the intestate heirs. • Under the common law and the laws of all states, a testamentary beneficiary must survive a testator or else the gift is said to lapse. Although most states have enacted antilapse statutes, their terms vary from state to state. — Also termed *lapse statute*; *nonlapse statute*.

antimarital-facts privilege. See *marital privilege* (2) under PRIVILEGE.

apparent heir. See *heir apparent* under HEIR.

appeal, *n.* A proceeding undertaken to have a decision reconsidered by bringing it to a higher authority; esp., the submission of a lower court's or agency's decision to a higher court for review and possible reversal <the case is on appeal>.

appeal, *vb.* To seek review (from a lower court's decision) by a higher court <petitioner appeals the conviction>. — **appealability,** *n.*

appeals court. See *appellate court* under COURT.

appearance, *n.* A coming into court as a party or interested person, or as a lawyer on behalf of a party or interested person. — **appear,** *vb.*

appearance de bene esse. See *special appearance*.

general appearance. A general-purpose appearance that waives a party's ability later to dispute the court's authority to enter a binding judgment against him or her.

limited appearance. See *special appearance*.

special appearance. **1.** A defendant's pleading that either claims that the court lacks personal jurisdiction over the defendant or objects to improper service of process. **2.** A defendant's showing up in court for the sole purpose of contesting the court's assertion of personal jurisdiction over the defendant. — Also termed *limited appearance*; *appearance de bene esse*.

appearance de bene esse. See *special appearance* under APPEARANCE.

appellant (ə-**pel**-ənt). A party who appeals a lower court's decision, usu. seeking reversal of that decision. Cf. APPELLEE.

appellate (ə-**pel**-it), *adj.* Of or relating to an appeal or to appeals generally.

appellate court. See COURT.

appellee (ap-ə-**lee**). A party against whom an appeal is taken and whose role is to respond to that appeal, usu. seeking affirmance of the lower court's decision. Cf. APPELLANT.

appendant power. See POWER.

applicable exclusion amount. See *unified estate-and-gift tax credit* under TAX CREDIT.

applicant. One who requests something; a petitioner, such as a person who applies for letters of administration.

appointive asset. See ASSET.

apportionment, *n.* **1.** Division into proportionate shares. **2.** The act of allocating or attributing moneys or expenses in a given way, as when a taxpayer allocates part of profits to a particular tax year or part of the use of a personal asset to a business. **3.** The division (by statute or by the testator's instruction) of an estate-tax liability among persons interested in an estate. — **apportion,** *vb.*

APS. *abbr.* ADULT PROTECTIVE SERVICES.

arbitration, *n.* A method of dispute resolution involving one or more neutral third parties who are usu. agreed to by the disputing parties and whose decision is binding. — Also termed (redundantly) *binding arbitration.* — **arbitrate,** *vb.* — **arbitral,** *adj.* Cf. MEDIATION.

   adjudicative-claims arbitration. Arbitration designed to resolve matters usu. handled by courts (such as tort claims), in contrast to arbitration of labor issues, international trade, and other fields traditionally associated with arbitration.

compulsory arbitration. Arbitration required by law or forced by law on the parties.

final-offer arbitration. Arbitration in which each party must submit a "final offer" to the arbitrator, who may choose only one. ● This device gives each party an incentive to make a reasonable offer or risk the arbitrator's accepting the other party's offer. The purpose of this type of arbitration is to counteract arbitrators' tendency to make compromise decisions halfway between the two parties' demands.

judicial arbitration. Court-referred arbitration that is final unless a party objects to the award.

voluntary arbitration. Arbitration by the agreement of the parties.

arbitration act. A federal or state statute providing for the submission of disputes to arbitration.

arbitration clause. A contractual provision mandating arbitration — and thereby avoiding litigation — of disputes about the contracting parties' rights, duties, and liabilities.

arbitrator, *n.* A neutral person who resolves disputes between parties, esp. by means of formal arbitration. — **arbitratorship,** *n.* Cf. MEDIATOR.

array, *n.* **1.** A panel of potential jurors <the array of mostly wealthy professionals seemed to favor the corporate defendant>. **2.** The jurors actually impaneled <the array hearing the case consisted of seven women and five men>. **3.** A list or roster of impaneled jurors <the plaintiff obtained a copy of the array to help prepare for voir dire>. **4.** Order; arrangement <the array of jurors from oldest to youngest>.

array, *vb.* **1.** To impanel a jury for trial. **2.** To call out the names of jurors, one by one, as they are impaneled.

arrear, *n.* (*usu. pl.*) **1.** The state of being behind in the payment of a debt or the discharge of an obligation <the father, who had been ordered to pay child support, was in arrears>. — Also termed *arrearage.* **2.** An unpaid or overdue debt <the creditor reached an agreement with the debtor on settling the arrears>.

ART. *abbr.* ASSISTED REPRODUCTIVE TECHNOLOGY.

art, *n. Archaic.* In a seduction case, the skillful and systematic coaxing of another to engage in sexual activity.

artificial insemination. A process for achieving conception, whereby semen is inserted into a woman's vagina by some means other than intercourse. • If the woman is married when the artificial insemination and the birth occur, and her husband has consented to the insemination, and the insemination is performed by a licensed physician, the husband is considered the father of the child. If the woman is unmarried at the time of the insemination, several factors, varying from jurisdiction to jurisdiction, determine whether the donor is considered the father of the child. Cf. IN VITRO FERTILIZATION; GAMETE INTRAFALLOPIAN TRANSFER; ZYGOTE INTRAFALLOPIAN TRANSFER.

artificial insemination by donor. Artificial insemination in which the semen donor is someone other than the recipient's husband. — Abbr. AID. — Also termed *heterologous artificial insemination*; *exogamous insemination*.

artificial insemination by husband. Artificial insemination in which the semen donor is the recipient's husband. — Abbr. AIH. — Also termed *homologous insemination*; *endogenous insemination*.

endogenous insemination. See *homologous artificial insemination*.

exogamous insemination. See *artificial insemination by donor*.

heterologous artificial insemination. See *artificial insemination by donor*.

homologous artificial insemination. See *artificial insemination by husband*.

ascendant (ə-**sen**-dənt), *n.* One who precedes in lineage, such as a parent or grandparent. — Also termed *ancestor.* — **ascendant,** *adj.* Cf. DESCENDANT.

collateral ascendant. Loosely, an aunt, uncle, or other relative who is not strictly an ancestor. — Also termed *collateral ancestor.*

lineal ascendant. A blood relative in the direct line of ascent; ancestor. • Parents, grandparents, and great-grandparents are lineal ascendants.

ASFA. *abbr.* ADOPTION AND SAFE FAMILIES ACT.

assault, *n.* **1.** *Criminal & tort law.* The threat or use of force on another that causes that person to have a reasonable apprehension of imminent harmful or offensive contact; the act of putting another person in reasonable fear or apprehension of an immediate battery by means of an act amounting to an attempt or threat to commit a battery. **2.** *Criminal law.* An attempt to commit battery, requiring the specific intent to cause physical injury. — Also termed (in senses 1 and 2) *simple assault.* **3.** Loosely, a battery. **4.** Popularly, any attack. — **assault,** *vb.* — **assaultive,** *adj.* Cf. BATTERY.

assault to rape. See *assault with intent to commit rape.*

assault with intent to commit rape. An assault carried out with the additional criminal purpose of intending to rape the victim. — Also termed *assault to rape*.

atrocious assault. An assault that causes severe wounding or maiming.

indecent assault. See *sexual assault* (2).

sexual assault. 1. Sexual intercourse with another person without that person's consent. • Several state statutes have abolished the crime of rape and replaced it with the offense of sexual assault. **2.** Offensive sexual contact with another person, exclusive of rape. — Also termed (in sense 2) *indecent assault*. Cf. RAPE.

assault to rape. See *assault with intent to commit rape* under ASSAULT.

assault with intent to commit rape. See ASSAULT.

assented-to motion. See *agreed motion* under MOTION.

asset. 1. An item that is owned and has value. **2.** (*pl.*) The entries on a balance sheet showing the items of property owned, including cash, inventory, equipment, real estate, accounts receivable, and goodwill. **3.** (*pl.*) All the property of a person (esp. a bankrupt or deceased person) available for paying debts or for distribution.

appointive asset. An asset distributed under a power of appointment.

assets by descent. The portion of an estate that passes to an heir and is sufficient to charge the heir with the decedent's specialty debts. — Also termed *assets per descent.*

assets in hand. The portion of an estate held by an executor or administrator for the payment of debts chargeable to the executor or administrator.

assets per descent. See *assets by descent.*

legal asset. A decedent's asset that by law is subject to the claims of creditors or legacies. — Also termed *probate asset.*

new asset. In the administration of a decedent's estate, property that the administrator or executor receives after the time has expired to file claims against the estate.

nonprobate asset. Property that passes to a named beneficiary upon the owner's death according to the terms of some contract or arrangement other than a will. • Such an asset is not a part of the probate estate and is not ordinarily subject to the probate court's jurisdiction (and fees), though it is part of the taxable estate. Examples include life-insurance contracts, joint property arrangements with right of survivorship, pay-on-death bank accounts, and inter vivos trusts. — Also termed *nonprobate property*. Cf. WILL SUBSTITUTE.

premarital asset. Property that a spouse owned before marrying. ● In most jurisdictions, this is part of the spouse's separate property. See SEPARATE PROPERTY. Cf. COMMUNITY PROPERTY.

probate asset. See *legal asset*.

asset-protection trust. See *self-settled trust* under TRUST.

assets by descent. See ASSET.

assets in hand. See ASSET.

assets per descent. See *assets by descent* under ASSET.

assignment. 1. The transfer of rights or property; the rights or property so transferred. **2.** A welfare recipient's surrender of his or her rights to child support (both current and past due) in favor of the state as a result of his or her receiving governmental financial assistance.

assignment of dower (**dow**-ər). The act of setting apart a widow's share of her deceased husband's real property. See DOWER.

assignment-of-income doctrine. The common-law principle that the person who has earned income is the person taxed on it, regardless of who receives the proceeds. ● Under this doctrine, future income assigned to another is taxable to the assignor. For example, in *Lucas v. Earl*, 281 U.S. 111, 50 S.Ct. 241 (1930), the Court held that a husband who was the sole wage-earner could not assign to his wife half his income and then pay the federal income tax on only the unassigned part.

assignment of property. See EQUITABLE DISTRIBUTION.

assisted conception. The fertilization of a woman's egg with a man's sperm by some means other than sexual intercourse. See ARTIFICIAL INSEMINATION; IN VITRO FERTILIZATION; GAMETE INTRAFALLOPIAN TRANSFER; ZYGOTE INTRAFALLOPIAN TRANSFER.

assisted reproductive technology. Any medical means of aiding human reproduction, esp. through laboratory procedures. — Abbr. ART. — Also termed *assisted reproduction*; *assisted-reproductive therapy*.

assisted self-determination. See *assisted suicide* under SUICIDE (1).

assisted suicide. See SUICIDE (1).

associate judge. See JUDGE.

association. An unincorporated business organization that is not a legal entity separate from the persons who compose it. ● If an association has sufficient corporate attributes, such as centralized management, continuity of existence, and limited liability, it may be classified and taxed as a corporation. — Also termed *unincorporated association*; *voluntary association*.

beneficial association. See *benevolent association*.

benefit association. See *benevolent association*.

benevolent association. An unincorporated, nonprofit organization that has a philanthropic or charitable purpose. — Also termed *beneficial association*; *benefit association*; *benevolent society*; *fraternal society*; *friendly society*.

homeowners' association. 1. An association of people who own homes in a given area and have united to improve or maintain the area's quality. 2. An association formed by a land developer or homebuilder to manage and maintain property in which the developer and the builder own an undivided common interest. ● Homeowners' associations — which are regulated by statute in many states — are commonly formed by restrictive covenant or a declaration of restrictions. — Also spelled *homeowners association*.

asylum. 1. A sanctuary or shelter. 2. An institution for the protection and relief of the unfortunate, esp. the mentally ill. — Also termed (in sense 2) *insane asylum*.

atrocious assault. See ASSAULT.

attachment of wages. The withholding of a certain percentage of an obligor's earnings for satisfaction of judgments for child support and alimony. ● Under the federal garnishment statute, up to 50% of a wage-earner's disposable income can be seized if the wage-earner has another family of dependents and up to 60% if there is only one family. If the obligor is more than three months in arrears, an additional 5% can be seized until the arrearage is paid. 15 USCA § 1673(b)(2). — Also termed *wage-withholding*; *automatic wage-withholding*; *wage assignment*. Cf. INCOME-WITHHOLDING ORDER.

attempted marriage. See MARRIAGE.

attempted suicide. See SUICIDE (1).

attendance officer. See TRUANCY OFFICER.

attestation clause. A provision at the end of an instrument (esp. a will) that is signed by the instrument's witnesses and that recites the formalities required by the jurisdiction in which the instrument might take effect (such as where the will might be probated). ● The attestation strengthens the presumption that all the statutory requirements for executing the will have been satisfied. Cf. TESTIMONIUM CLAUSE.

attested copy. See *certified copy* under COPY.

attested will. See WILL.

attesting witness. See WITNESS.

attorney. 1. Strictly, one who is designated to transact business for another; a legal agent. — Also termed *attorney-in-fact*; *private attorney*. **2.** A person who practices law; lawyer. — Also termed (in sense 2) *attorney-at-law*; *public attorney*. — Abbr. att'y. Pl. **attorneys.**

attorney, power of. See POWER OF ATTORNEY.

attorney ad litem (ad lɪ-tem *or* -təm). A court-appointed lawyer who represents a child during the course of a legal action, such as a divorce, termination, or child-abuse case. ● The attorney owes to the child the duties of loyalty, confidentiality, and competent representation. A child's right to legal representation in a juvenile proceeding was mandated in *In re Gault*, 387 U.S. 1, 87 S.Ct. 1428 (1967). The appointment of an attorney ad litem is a limited one — only for a specific lawsuit. — Also termed *child's attorney*; *attorney for the child*. Cf. *guardian ad litem* under GUARDIAN.

attorney-at-law. See ATTORNEY (2).

attorney–client privilege. See PRIVILEGE.

attorney for the child. See ATTORNEY AD LITEM.

attorney-in-fact. See ATTORNEY (1).

attractive-nuisance doctrine. *Torts.* The rule that a person who owns property on which there is a dangerous thing or condition that will foreseeably lure children to trespass has a duty to protect those children from the danger <the attractive-nuisance doctrine imposed a duty on the school to protect the children from the shallow, polluted pond on school property>. — Also termed *turntable doctrine*; *torpedo doctrine*. Cf. ALLUREMENT.

augmented estate. See ESTATE.

authenticate, *vb.* **1.** To prove the genuineness of (a thing). **2.** To render authoritative or authentic, as by attestation or other legal formality. See UCC § 9–102(a)(5).

authentication, *n.* **1.** Broadly, the act of proving that something (as a document) is true or genuine, esp. so that it may be admitted as evidence; the condition of being so proved <authentication of the handwriting>. **2.** Specif., the assent to or adoption of a writing as one's own.

self-authentication. Authentication without extrinsic evidence of truth or genuineness. ● In federal courts, certain writings, such as notarized documents and certified copies of public records, may be admitted into evidence by self-authentication. Fed. R. Evid. 902.

authority. 1. The right or permission to act legally on another's behalf; the power delegated by a principal to an agent. **2.** Governmental power or jurisdiction. **3.** A legal writing taken as definitive or decisive. **4.** A source, such as a statute, case, or treatise, cited in support of a legal argument.

automatic transfer statute. See TRANSFER STATUTE.

automatic wage-withholding. See ATTACHMENT OF WAGES.

automobile-guest statute. See GUEST STATUTE.

a vinculo matrimonii (ay **ving**-kyə-loh ma-trə-**moh**-nee-I). [Latin] From the bond of matrimony. See *divorce a vinculo matrimonii* under DIVORCE.

avowtry. See ADULTERY.

B

baby act, pleading the. *Slang*. The act of asserting a person's infancy as a defense to a contract claim.

baby-bartering. See BABY-SELLING.

baby-brokering. See BABY-SELLING.

Baby Doe. A generic pseudonym for a very young child involved in litigation, esp. in the context of being provided with medical care. ● Today a gender designation is often added: *Baby Girl Doe* or *Baby Boy Doe*. The generic term is used to shield the child's identity.

baby-selling. The exchange of money or something of value for a child. ● All states have prohibitions against baby-selling. It is not considered baby-selling for prospective adoptive parents to pay money to a birth mother for pregnancy-related expenses. — Also termed *baby-brokering*; *baby-bartering*.

baby-snatching. See *child-kidnapping* under KID-NAPPING.

bad faith, *n*. Dishonesty of belief or purpose. — Also termed *mala fides* (**mal**-ə **fī**-deez).

bank-account trust. See *Totten trust* under TRUST.

banns of matrimony. Public notice of an intended marriage. ● The notice was given to ensure that objections to the marriage would be voiced before the wedding. Banns are still common in some American churches. — Also spelled *bans of matrimony*. — Also termed *banns of marriage*.

bare ownership. See *trust ownership* under OWNERSHIP.

bare possibility. See *naked possibility* under POSSIBILITY.

bare trustee. See TRUSTEE.

bastard. 1. See *illegitimate child* under CHILD. **2.** A child born to a married woman whose husband could not be or is otherwise proved not to be the father. ● Because the word is most commonly used as a slur, its use in family-law contexts is much in decline.

    adulterine bastard. A child born to a married woman whose husband is not the father of the child. ● The rebuttable presumption is generally that a child born of the marriage is the husband's child. A child born to a woman by means of artificial insemination may be termed an *adulterine bastard*, but most jurisdictions prohibit a husband who has consented to the artificial insemination from denying paternity and responsibility for the child. Cf. ARTIFICIAL INSEMINATION.

bastardy. See ILLEGITIMACY.

bastardy proceeding. See PATERNITY SUIT.

bastardy statute. *Archaic.* A criminal statute that punishes an unwed father for failing to support his child. ● These statutes have been found unconstitutional because they unfairly discriminate against fathers and do not punish unwed mothers. They are therefore unenforceable.

battered child. See CHILD.

battered-child syndrome. A constellation of medical and psychological conditions of a child who has suffered continuing injuries that could not be accidental and are therefore presumed to have been inflicted by someone close to the child, usu. a caregiver. ● Diagnosis typically results from a radiological finding of distinct bone trauma and persistent tissue damage caused to a young child by intentional injury, such as twisting or hitting with violence. The phrase was first used by Dr. Henry Kempe and his colleagues in a 1962 article entitled "The Battered Child Syndrome," which appeared in the *Journal of the American Medical Association.* As a result of research on battered-child syndrome, the Children's Bureau of the United States Department of Health, Education, and Welfare drafted a model statute requiring physicians to report serious cases of suspected child abuse. See CHILD-ABUSE AND -NEGLECT REPORTING STATUTE.

battered-person syndrome. See BATTERED-WOMAN SYNDROME.

battered-spouse syndrome. See BATTERED-WOMAN SYNDROME.

battered-wife syndrome. See BATTERED-WOMAN SYNDROME.

battered woman. A woman who is the victim of domestic violence; a woman who has suffered physical, emotional, or sexual abuse at the hands of a spouse or lover. See *domestic violence* under VIOLENCE.

battered-woman syndrome. A constellation of medical and psychological conditions of a woman who has suffered physical, sexual, or emotional abuse at the hands of a spouse or lover. ● Battered-woman syndrome was first described in the early 1970s by Dr. Lenore Walker. It consists of a three-stage cycle of violence: (1) the tension-building phase, which may include verbal and mild physical abuse; (2) the acute battering incident, which includes stronger verbal abuse, increased physical violence, and perhaps rape or other sexual abuse; and (3) the loving-contrition phase, which includes the abuser's apologies, attentiveness, kindness, and gift-giving. This syndrome is sometimes proposed as a defense to justify a woman's killing of a man. — Sometimes (more specif.) termed *battered-wife syndrome*; (more broadly) *battered-spouse syndrome*.

battery, *n.* **1.** *Criminal law.* The application of force to another, resulting in harmful or offensive contact. ● It is a misdemeanor under most modern statutes. — Also termed *criminal battery.* **2.** *Torts.* An intentional and offensive touching of another without lawful justification. — Also termed *tortious battery.* — **batter,** *vb.* Cf. ASSAULT.

> **sexual battery.** The forced penetration of or contact with another's sexual organs or the sexual organs of the perpetrator. Cf. RAPE.

bench warrant. A writ issued directly by a judge to a law-enforcement officer, esp. for the arrest of a person who has been held in contempt, has been indicted, has disobeyed a subpoena, or has failed to appear for a hearing or trial. ● A bench warrant is often issued for the arrest of a child-support obligor who is found in contempt for not having paid the support obligation.

beneficial association. See *benevolent association* under ASSOCIATION.

beneficial owner. See OWNER.

beneficial ownership. See OWNERSHIP.

beneficial power. See POWER.

beneficiary (ben-ə-**fish**-ee-er-ee *or* ben-ə-**fish**-ə-ree), *n.* A person who is designated to benefit from an appointment, disposition, or assignment (as in a will, insurance policy, etc.); one designated to receive something as a result of a legal arrangement or instrument. — **beneficiary,** *adj*.

contingent beneficiary. **1.** A person designated in a life-insurance policy to receive the proceeds if the primary beneficiary is unable to do so. — Also termed *secondary beneficiary.* **2.** A person designated by the testator to receive a gift if the primary beneficiary is unable or unwilling to take the gift. — Also termed *contingency beneficiary.*

direct beneficiary. See *intended beneficiary.*

favored beneficiary. A beneficiary who receives disproportionate amounts of willed property as compared with others having equal claims to the property, raising the specter of the beneficiary's undue influence over the testator. See UNDUE INFLUENCE.

incidental beneficiary. A third-party beneficiary who is not intended to benefit from a contract and thus does not acquire rights under the contract. Cf. *intended beneficiary.*

income beneficiary. A person entitled to income from property; esp., a person entitled to receive trust income.

intended beneficiary. A third-party beneficiary who is intended to benefit from a contract and thus acquires rights under the contract as well as the ability to enforce the contract once those rights have vested. — Also termed *direct benefi-ciary*. Cf. *incidental beneficiary*.

life beneficiary. One who receives payments or other benefits from a trust for life.

primary beneficiary. The person designated in a life-insurance policy to receive the proceeds when the insured dies.

secondary beneficiary. See *contingent beneficia-ry* (1).

unborn beneficiary. A person who, though not yet born, is named in a general way as sharing in an estate or gift. • An example might be a grand-child not yet born when a grandparent specifies, in a will, that Blackacre is to go to "my grandchil-dren."

beneficiary heir. See HEIR.

benefit association. See *benevolent association* under ASSOCIATION.

benefit of clergy. Religious approval as solem-nized by church ritual <the couple had several children without benefit of clergy>. • This common use of the phrase is premised on a misunderstand-ing of its original meaning. At common law, *benefit of clergy* referred to the right of a cleric not to be tried for a felony in the King's Court.

benefit of inventory. *Civil law.* The principle that an heir's liability for estate debts is limited to the value of what is inherited, if the heir so elects and files an inventory of the estate's assets.

benevolent association. See ASSOCIATION.

benevolent society. See *benevolent association* under ASSOCIATION.

bequeath (bə-**kwee***th*), *vb.* To give property (usu. personal property) by will.

bequeathal. See BEQUEST.

bequest (bə-**kwest**), *n.* **1.** The act of giving property (usu. personal property) by will. **2.** Property (usu. personal property other than money) disposed of in a will. — Also termed *bequeathal* (bə-**kwee**-*th*əl). Cf. DEVISE; LEGACY.

  charitable bequest. A bequest given to a philanthropic organization. See CHARITABLE ORGANIZATION.

  conditional bequest. A bequest whose effectiveness or continuation depends on the occurrence or nonoccurrence of a particular event. ● An example might be a testator's gift of "the income from the farm to my daughter, Betty, until she remarries." If a condition prohibits certain legal conduct, such as using tobacco or growing a beard, it is sometimes termed a *reformation condition* or *character-improvement condition.*

demonstrative bequest. A bequest that, by its terms, must be paid out of a specific source, such as a stock fund.

executory bequest. A bequest of a future, deferred, or contingent interest in personalty.

general bequest. **1.** A bequest of a general benefit, rather than a particular asset, such as a gift of money or a gift of all the testator's stocks. **2.** A bequest payable out of the general assets of the estate.

monetary bequest. See *pecuniary bequest*.

money bequest. See *pecuniary bequest*.

pecuniary bequest. A testamentary gift of money; a legacy. — Also termed *monetary bequest*; *money bequest*.

remainder bequest. See *residuary bequest*.

residuary bequest. A bequest of the remainder of the testator's estate, after the payment of the debts, legacies, and specific bequests. — Also termed *remainder bequest*.

specific bequest. A bequest of a specific or unique item of property, such as any real estate or a particular piece of furniture.

bestiality (bes-chee-**al**-ə-tee). Sexual activity between a human and an animal. ● Some authorities restrict the term to copulation between a human and an animal of the opposite sex. See SODOMY.

best interests of the child. A standard by which a court determines what arrangements would be to a child's greatest benefit, often used in deciding child-custody and visitation matters and in deciding whether to approve an adoption or a guardianship. • A court uses many factors to determine what is in the best interests of the child, including the emotional tie between the child and the parent or guardian, the ability of a parent or guardian to give the child love and guidance, the ability of a parent or guardian to provide necessaries, the established living arrangement existing between a parent or guardian and the child, the child's preference if the child is of an age at which the jurisdiction considers that preference in making a custody award, and a parent's ability to foster a healthy relationship between the child and the other parent. — Abbr. BIC. — Also termed *best interest of the child*. Cf. PARENTAL-PREFERENCE DOCTRINE.

best-interests-of-the-child doctrine. The principle that courts should make custody decisions based on whatever best advances the child's welfare, regardless of a claimant's particular status or relationship with the child. • One important factor entering into these decisions is the general belief that normally it is in the child's best interests to be in the custody of parents, as opposed to grandparents or others less closely related than parents. The doctrine is quite old, having been stated, for example, in the early 19th-century case of *Commonwealth v. Briggs*, 33 Mass. 203 (1834). — Sometimes shortened to *best-interests doctrine*; *best-interest doctrine*. See PARENTAL-PREFERENCE DOCTRINE.

bet din. A rabbinical tribunal empowered by Jewish law to decide and enforce matters of Jewish law and custom; esp., a tribunal consisting of three rabbis who decide questions of Jewish law.

betrothal. See ENGAGEMENT (2).

BIC. *abbr.* BEST INTERESTS OF THE CHILD.

bifurcated divorce. See *divisible divorce* under DIVORCE.

bigamous (**big**-ə-məs), *adj.* **1.** (Of a person) guilty of bigamy. **2.** (Of a marriage) involving bigamy.

bigamy, *n.* **1.** The act of marrying one person while legally married to another. ● Bigamy is distinct from adultery. It is a criminal offense if it is committed knowingly. In 1878, the U.S. Supreme Court held that the government was not constitutionally prohibited from banning Mormon polygamy. *Reynolds v. United States*, 98 U.S. (8 Otto) 145 (1878). **2.** *Eccles. law.* The act of marrying a widow or widower, a divorced person, or a person who is unchaste or of questionable morals. ● Somewhat surprisingly, sense 2 is valid even under modern ecclesiastical

law. — **bigamist,** *n.* Cf. POLYGAMY; MONOGAMY; ADUL-
TERY.

binding arbitration. See ARBITRATION.

biological, *adj.* **1.** Of or relating to biology or life.
2. Genetically related.

biological child. See *natural child* under CHILD.

biological father. See FATHER.

biological mother. See MOTHER.

biological parent. See PARENT.

birth certificate. A formal document that records
a person's birthdate, birthplace, and parentage. ● In
all 50 states, an adopted child receives a second
birth certificate reflecting his or her adoptive parents. In such a case, the original birth certificate is
usually sealed and can be opened only by court
order. Some states allow limited access, depending
on the year when an adoptee was born and (sometimes) on whether the birth parents consent. The
trend today is to open records if (1) both the child
and the biological parent consent — for example,
through an adoption registry, or (2) the child requests and, upon notification, the biological parent
does not veto the request. Oregon enacted the first
statute to permit access to birth records upon the
unilateral demand of the adopted child, once the

child reaches the age of majority. See ADOPTION-REGISTRY STATUTE.

birth control. 1. Any means of preventing conception and pregnancy, usu. by mechanical or chemical means, but also by abstaining from intercourse. **2.** More narrowly, contraception.

birth father. See *biological father* under FATHER.

birth injury. Harm that occurs to a fetus during the birth process, esp. during labor and delivery. Cf. PRENATAL INJURY.

birth mother. See MOTHER.

birth parent. See PARENT.

birth records. Statistical data kept by a governmental entity concerning people's birthdates, birthplaces, and parentage.

black-market adoption. See ADOPTION.

blank consent. A general authorization from a natural parent who voluntarily relinquishes a child for private adoption and allows adoption proceedings without further consent. ● Jurisdictions are divided over whether a blank consent is valid if the prospective adoptive parents are not identified and approved by the natural parents. — Also termed *blanket consent*; *general consent*.

blended family. See FAMILY.

blended fund. See FUND (1).

blended sentence. In a juvenile-delinquency disposition, a sanction that combines delinquency sanctions and criminal punishment.

blended trust. See TRUST.

blind trust. See TRUST.

blood. A relationship between persons arising by descent from a common ancestor. See RELATIVE.

entire blood. See *full blood*.

full blood. The relationship existing between persons having the same two parents; unmixed ancestry. — Also termed *whole blood*; *entire blood*.

half blood. The relationship existing between persons having the same father or mother, but not both parents in common. — Sometimes written *half-blood*. See *relative of the half blood* under RELATIVE.

inheritable blood. *Hist.* A relationship between an ancestor and an heir that the law recognizes for purposes of passing good title to property.

mixed blood. The relationship between persons whose ancestors are of different races or nationalities.

whole blood. See *full blood.*

blood border. *Slang.* The dividing line between adjoining states that have different minimum drinking ages. ● The term derives from the fact that juveniles from the state with the higher minimum age drive to the state with a lower minimum age, purchase and consume alcohol, and drive home intoxicated.

blood-grouping test. A test used in paternity and illegitimacy cases to determine whether a particular man could be the father of a child, examples being the genetic-marker test and the human-leukocyte antibody test. ● The test does not establish paternity; rather, it eliminates men who could not be the father. See PATERNITY TEST; GENETIC-MARKER TEST; HUMAN-LEUKOCYTE ANTIBODY TEST.

blood relative. See RELATIVE.

blood test. The medical analysis of blood, esp. to establish paternity or (as required in some states) to test for sexually transmitted diseases in marriage-license applicants. See SEROLOGICAL TEST.

bodily heir. See *heir of the body* under HEIR.

body execution. See CAPIAS.

bogus will. See WILL.

bona fides. See GOOD FAITH.

bond. A written promise to pay money or do some act if certain circumstances occur or a certain time elapses; a promise that is defeasible upon a condition subsequent.

> ***executor's bond.*** A bond given to ensure the executor's faithful administration of the estate.

> ***fiduciary bond.*** A type of surety bond required of a trustee, administrator, executor, guardian, conservator, or other fiduciary to ensure the proper performance of duties.

> ***probate bond.*** A bond, such as that filed by an executor, required by law to be given during a probate proceeding to ensure faithful performance by the person under bond.

bond trust. See TRUST.

boot camp. A military-like facility esp. for juvenile offenders. ● Boot camps are specialized programs for offenders who are generally nonviolent males from 17 to 25 years old. While proponents applaud the success of these programs, others find their long-term success limited at best.

born-alive test. 1. Under the common law, a showing that an infant was completely expelled from the mother's womb and possessed a separate and independent existence from the mother. **2.** A showing that an infant, at the time of birth, was capable of living a separate and independent existence (regardless of how long the infant actually lived).

brain death. See DEATH.

breach of promise. The violation of one's word or undertaking, esp. a promise to marry. See HEART-BALM STATUTE.

breakdown of the marriage. See IRRETRIEVABLE BREAKDOWN OF THE MARRIAGE.

brother. A male having one parent or both parents in common with another person.

> **brother-german.** A full brother; a male child of both of one's own parents. See GERMAN.

> **consanguine brother** (kahn-**sang**-gwin *or* kən-**san**-gwin). *Civil law.* A brother having the same father as another, but a different mother.

> **half brother.** A male sibling with whom one shares the same father or the same mother, but not both; a brother by one parent only.

> **stepbrother.** The son of one's stepparent.

> **uterine brother** (**yoo**-tər-in). *Civil law.* A brother having the same mother as another, but a different father.

brother-in-law. The brother of one's spouse, the husband of one's sister, or the husband of one's spouse's sister. Pl. **brothers-in-law.**

Buckley Amendment. See FAMILY EDUCATIONAL RIGHTS AND PRIVACY ACT.

buggery. See SODOMY.

bum-marriage doctrine. The principle that the marital-witness privilege may not be asserted by a partner in a marriage that is in fact moribund, though legally valid. See *marital privilege* (2) under PRIVILEGE.

business compulsion. See *economic duress* under DURESS.

business homestead. See HOMESTEAD.

bypass trust. See TRUST.

C

caeterorum administration. See ADMINISTRATION.

canonical impediment. See IMPEDIMENT.

capacity. 1. A legal qualification, such as legal age, that determines one's ability to sue or be sued, to enter into a binding contract, and the like <she had full capacity to bind the corporation with her signature>. • Unless necessary to show the court's jurisdiction, a plaintiff's pleadings need not assert the legal capacity of any party. A party wishing to raise the issue of capacity must do so by specific negative pleading. Fed. R. Civ. P. 9(a). — Also termed (specif.) *capacity to sue*. See STANDING. **2.** The mental ability to understand the nature and effect of one's acts <his acute pain reduced his capacity to understand the hospital's admission form>. — Also termed *mental capacity*. See *age of capacity* under AGE.

> **diminished capacity.** An impaired mental condition — short of insanity — that is caused by intoxication, trauma, or disease and that prevents a person from having the mental state necessary to be held responsible for a crime. • In some jurisdictions, a defendant's diminished capacity can be used to determine the degree of the offense or the severity of the punishment. — Also termed *diminished responsibility*. Cf. INSANITY.

> **disposing capacity.** See *testamentary capacity*.

testamentary capacity. The mental ability that a person must have to prepare a valid will. ● This capacity is often described as the ability to recognize the natural objects of one's bounty, the nature and extent of one's estate, and the fact that one is making a plan to dispose of the estate after death. Traditionally, the phrase "of legal age and sound mind" refers to the testator's capacity. — Also termed *disposing capacity*. See *age of capacity* under AGE.

capacity to sue. See CAPACITY (1).

capias (**kay**-pee-əs *or* **kap**-ee-əs). [Latin "that you take"] Any of various types of writs that require an officer to take a named defendant into custody. ● A capias is often issued when a respondent fails to appear or when an obligor has failed to pay child support. — Also termed *writ of capias*; *body execution*.

CAPTA. *abbr.* CHILD ABUSE PREVENTION AND TREATMENT ACT.

care, *n.* The provision of physical or psychological comfort to another, esp. an ailing spouse, child, or parent.

caregiver. A person, usu. not a parent, who has and exercises custodial responsibility for a child or for an elderly or disabled person. — Also termed *caretaker*; *custodian*. See RESIDENTIAL RESPONSIBILITY.

caretaker. See CAREGIVER.

caretaking functions. A parent's or caregiver's task that either involves interaction with a child or directs others' interaction with a child. ● Some caretaking functions include feeding and bathing a child, guiding the child in language and motor-skills development, caring for a sick child, disciplining the child, being involved in the child's educational development, and giving the child moral instruction and guidance. *Principles of the Law of Family Dissolution: Analysis and Recommendations* § 2.03 (ALI, Tentative Draft No. 3, pt. I, 1998). Cf. PARENTING FUNCTIONS.

carnal abuse. See *sexual abuse* (1) under ABUSE.

CASA. *abbr.* COURT APPOINTED SPECIAL ADVOCATES.

CASA volunteer. A specially screened and trained child-welfare volunteer appointed by the court to conduct an independent investigation of both the state agency and the family and to submit a report with findings and recommendations. ● In some jurisdictions such volunteers are provided for statutorily. They sometimes act as guardians ad litem. The CASA volunteer usually (1) provides independent assessment of the child's needs, (2) acts as an advocate for the child, and (3) monitors agency decision-making and court proceedings.

case plan. A written procedure for the care and management of a child who has been removed from his or her home and placed in foster care or in an institution. ● The case plan includes (1) a description of the place where the child has been placed, (2) a plan for providing the child with safe and proper care, and (3) a plan for services that will be provided to the child's parents. Each state must have a case-review system formulated to ensure that the child is placed in the least restrictive and most appropriate place and that the plan is in the best interests of the child; the plan must be reviewed every six months. See ADOPTION AND SAFE FAMILIES ACT.

causa mortis (**kaw**-zə **mor**-tis), *adj.* Done or made in contemplation of one's own death. See *gift causa mortis* under GIFT.

cause list. See DOCKET (2).

caveator. See CONTESTANT.

ceremonial marriage. See MARRIAGE (2).

certified copy. See COPY.

certified juvenile. See JUVENILE.

cestui que trust (**set**-ee [*or* **ses**-twee] kee [*or* kə] trəst). [Law French] *Archaic.* One who possesses equitable rights in property, usu. receiving the rents, issues, and profits from it; BENEFICIARY. — Also termed *fide-commissary*; *fidei-commissarius*.

Pl. **cestuis que trust** or (erroneously) **cestuis que trustent.**

cestui que use (**set**-ee [or **ses**-twee] kee [or kə] **yoos**). *Archaic.* The person for whose use and benefit property is being held by another, who holds the legal title to the property. Pl. **cestuis que use** or (erroneously) **cestuis que usent.**

cestui que vie (**set**-ee [or **ses**-twee] kee [or kə] **vee**). The person whose life measures the duration of a trust, gift, estate, or insurance contract. Cf. MEASURING LIFE.

chancery guardian. See GUARDIAN.

change in circumstances. A modification in the physical, emotional, or financial condition of one or both parents, used to show the need to modify a custody or support order; esp., an involuntary occurrence that, if it had been known at the time of the divorce decree, would have resulted in the court's issuing a different decree, as when an involuntary job loss creates a need to modify the decree to provide for reduced child-support payments. — Also termed *change of circumstances; changed circumstances; material change in circumstances; substantial change in circumstances; change of condition.* See MODIFICATION ORDER.

change of condition. See CHANGE IN CIRCUMSTANCES.

changing fund. See FUND (1).

characterization. The process of classifying property accumulated by spouses as either separate or marital property (or community property).

character-reformation condition. See *conditional bequest* under BEQUEST.

charitable bequest. See BEQUEST.

charitable deduction. A gift to a charitable enterprise that has qualified for tax-exempt status in accordance with IRC (26 USCA) § 501(c)(3) and is entitled to be deducted in full by the donor from the taxable estate or from gross income.

charitable gift. An inter vivos or testamentary donation to a nonprofit organization for the relief of poverty, the advancement of education, the advancement of religion, the promotion of health, governmental, or municipal purposes, and other purposes the accomplishment of which is beneficial to the community. Restatement (Second) of Trusts § 368 (1959).

charitable lead trust. See TRUST.

charitable organization. *Tax.* A tax-exempt organization that (1) is created and operated exclusively for religious, scientific, literary, educational, athletic, public-safety, or community-service purposes, (2) does not distribute earnings for the benefit of private individuals, and (3) does not interfere in any way with political campaigns and decision-making processes. IRC (26 USCA) § 501(c)(3). — Also termed *charity*; *501(c)(3) organization*.

charitable remainder. See REMAINDER.

charitable-remainder annuity trust. See TRUST.

charitable-remainder trust. See TRUST.

charitable-remainder-trust retirement fund. See *charitable-remainder annuity trust* under TRUST.

charitable trust. See TRUST.

charitable use. See *charitable trust* under TRUST.

charity. See CHARITABLE ORGANIZATION.

chief judge. See JUDGE.

child. 1. A person under the age of majority. **2.** *Hist.* At common law, a person who has not reached the age of 14. **3.** A boy or girl; a young person. **4.** A son or daughter. **5.** A baby or fetus. See JUVENILE; MINOR.

> *abused child.* A child who has been subjected to physical or mental neglect or harm. See *child abuse* under ABUSE.

adopted child. A child who has become the son or daughter of a parent or parents by virtue of legal or equitable adoption; ADOPTEE. See ADOPTION.

afterborn child. A child born after execution of a will or after the time in which a class gift closes. — Also spelled *after-born child*. See *after-born heir* under HEIR.

battered child. A child upon whom physical or sexual abuse has been inflicted, usu. by a relative, caregiver, or close family friend. See *child abuse* under ABUSE; *domestic violence* under VIOLENCE; BATTERED-CHILD SYNDROME.

biological child. See *natural child*.

child in need of supervision. A child who has committed an offense that only children can commit, such as being ungovernable and disobedient to parents, running away from home, violating a curfew, being habitually truant from school, violating age restrictions on the purchase or possession of liquor or tobacco, or the like. — Also termed *person in need of supervision*; *minor in need of supervision*. — Abbr. CHINS.

child out of wedlock. See *illegitimate child*.

child with disabilities. Under the Individuals with Disabilities Education Act, a child who needs special-education or related services because of (1) mental retardation, (2) a hearing, language, or visual impairment, (3) a serious emotional distur-

bance, or (4) another health impairment or specific learning disability. See INDIVIDUALS WITH DISABILI-
TIES EDUCATION ACT.

delinquent child. A child who has committed an
offense that would be a crime if committed by an
adult. ● A delinquent child may not be subject to
the jurisdiction of the juvenile court if the child is
under a statutory age. Cf. *child in need of supervision.* See JUVENILE DELINQUENT.

dependent child. A needy child who has been
deprived of parental support or care because of
the parent's or other responsible person's death,
absence from the home, physical or mental incapacity, or (in some cases) unemployment. 42
USCA § 606(a).

deprived child. A child who (1) lacks proper
parental care or control, subsistence, education,
or other care and control for his or her physical,
mental, or emotional well-being, (2) has been
placed for care or adoption in violation of the law,
(3) has been abandoned, or (4) is without a parent, guardian, or legal custodian. Unif. Juvenile
Delinquency Act, 18 USCA §§ 5031 et seq. Cf.
neglected child.

disobedient child. See *incorrigible child.*

foster child. A child whose care and upbringing
are entrusted to an adult other than the child's
natural or adoptive parents, usu. by an agency. ●
A foster child may receive informal, voluntary

care by someone (often a grandparent, other relative, or neighbor) who enters into an agreement with the parent or who simply substitutes for the parent as necessary to ensure the child's protection. More formally, the child may be part of the federal–state foster-care program that identifies, trains, and pays caregivers who will provide family care for children who lack parents or cannot remain safely with their biological parents. — Also termed (archaically) *fosterling*. See *foster parent* under PARENT.

genetic child. See *natural child*.

handicapped child. A child who is mentally retarded, deaf or hearing-impaired, speech-impaired, blind or visually disabled, seriously emotionally disturbed, or orthopedically impaired, or who because of specific learning disabilities requires special education.

illegitimate child. A child who was not conceived or born in lawful wedlock, nor later legitimated. ● At common law, such a child was considered the child of nobody (*nullius filius*) and had no name except what was gained by reputation. Being no one's child, an illegitimate child could not inherit, even from the mother, but all states now allow maternal inheritance. In cases such as *Levy v. Louisiana*, 391 U.S. 68, 88 S.Ct. 1509 (1968), and *Glona v. American Guar. & Liab. Ins. Co.*, 391 U.S. 73, 88 S.Ct. 1515 (1968), the Supreme Court held that limitations on a child's right to inherit from his or her mother were unconstitutional. As a result, states changed their laws to permit full maternal inheritance. Full paternal inheritance is permitted if the child can prove paternity in accordance with state law (the proof varies from state to state). This burden of proof, uniquely imposed on an illegitimate child, is constitutionally permissible. *Lalli v. Lalli*, 439 U.S. 259, 99 S.Ct. 518 (1978). — Also termed *bastard*; *child out of wedlock*; *nonmarital child*; (archaically) *natural child*. Cf. BASTARD.

incorrigible child. A child who refuses to obey his or her parents or guardians. — Also termed *disobedient child*.

intended child. The child that is intended to result from a surrogacy contract. See *surrogate parent* under PARENT; *surrogate mother* under MOTHER; *intentional parent* under PARENT; *legal father* under FATHER; SURROGACY CONTRACT.

legitimate child. 1. At common law, a child conceived or born in lawful wedlock. 2. Modernly, a child conceived or born in lawful wedlock, or legitimated either by the parents' later marriage or by a declaration or judgment of legitimation.

natural child. 1. A child by birth, as distinguished from an adopted child. — Also termed *biological child*; *genetic child*. 2. A child that is genetically related to the mother and father as opposed to a child conceived by donor insemination or by egg donation. 3. *Archaic.* An illegitimate child acknowledged by the father. **4.** *Archa-ic*. An illegitimate child.

neglected child. 1. A child whose parents or legal custodians are unfit to care for him or her because of cruelty, immorality, or incapacity. **2.** A child whose parents or legal custodians refuse to provide the necessary care and medical services for the child. Cf. *deprived child*.

nonmarital child. See *illegitimate child*.

posthumous child. A child born after a parent's death. ● Ordinarily, the phrase *posthumous child* suggests one born after the father's death. But in at least one case, a legally dead pregnant woman was kept on life-support machines until the child could be safely delivered; so it is possible for a mother's posthumous child to be born.

quasi-posthumous child. *Civil law*. A child who becomes a direct heir of a grandfather or other male ascendant because of the death of the child's father.

special-needs child. 1. A child with medical problems or with a physical or emotional handicap. **2.** A child that is likely to be unadoptable because of medical problems or physical or emotional handicaps, or by reason of age or ethnic background. See ADOPTION ASSISTANCE AND CHILD WELFARE ACT.

stepchild. The child of one's spouse by a previous marriage. ● A stepchild is generally not entitled to the same legal rights as a natural or adopted child. For example, a stepchild has no right to a share of an intestate stepparent's property.

unborn child. A child not yet born, esp. at the happening of some event.

child abuse. See ABUSE.

child-abuse and -neglect reporting statute. A state law requiring certain persons, among them healthcare providers, teachers, and child-care workers, to report suspected child abuse. • By 1967, every state had adopted some form of reporting statute. In the Child Abuse Prevention and Treatment Act (42 USCA §§ 5101–5157), Congress provided federal funding for all states that implement federal standards in their reporting statutes and defined child maltreatment broadly. See CHILD ABUSE PREVENTION AND TREATMENT ACT.

Child Abuse Prevention and Treatment Act. A federal statute that provides limited funding to states for preventing, identifying, and treating child abuse and neglect. • Enacted in 1974, the Act was amended in 1996 to reinforce an emphasis on child safety. The Act established the National Center on Child Abuse and Neglect in the Department of Health and Human Services. Its function is to study child abuse, conduct research into its causes, and make grants to agencies for the study, prevention, and treatment of child abuse. 42 USCA

§§ 5101–5157. — Abbr. CAPTA. See CHILD-ABUSE AND -NEGLECT REPORTING STATUTE.

child-access prevention statute. See SAFE-STORAGE STATUTE.

child- and dependent-care tax credit. See TAX CREDIT.

child-benefit theory. See STUDENT-BENEFIT THEORY.

child-care fund. State-government funds set aside to reimburse counties for part of the payments for children's foster care and expenses.

child-care rules. State administrative rules for the care of foster children. ● In most states, departments concerned with social services establish and enforce the rules governing the welfare of foster children. A few states have created agencies expressly dedicated to services for children.

child custody. See CUSTODY.

child destruction. 1. See FETICIDE. **2.** See INFANTICIDE (1).

child endangerment. The placing of a child in a place or position that exposes him or her to danger to life or health. — Also termed *endangering the welfare of a child.*

physical child endangerment. Reckless behavior toward a child that has caused or could cause serious physical injury. — Sometimes shortened to *physical endangerment.*

child in need of supervision. See CHILD.

child-kidnapping. See KIDNAPPING.

child labor. The employment of workers under the age of majority. ● This term typically focuses on abusive practices such as exploitative factory work; slavery, sale, and trafficking in children; forced or compulsory labor such as debt bondage and serfdom; and the use of children in prostitution, pornography, drug-trafficking, or anything else that might jeopardize their health, safety, or morals. Some writers restrict the term to activities forbidden by the International Labor Organization's minimum-age conventions. See ILO Minimum Age Convention ch. 138 (1973). See FAIR LABOR STANDARDS ACT. Cf. CHILD WORK.

oppressive child labor. Under the Fair Labor Standards Act, the employment of workers under the age of 16 in any occupation, or the employment of those 16 to 18 years old in particularly hazardous occupations. 29 USCA § 203(*l*); 29 CFR § 570.1(d). The Secretary of Labor may assess civil penalties of up to $10,000 per violation. 29 USCA § 216(e). — Also termed *harmful child labor.*

child-labor law. A state or federal statute that protects children by prescribing the necessary working conditions for children in a workplace. See FAIR LABOR STANDARDS ACT.

child maltreatment. See *child abuse* under ABUSE.

childnapping. See *child-kidnapping* under KIDNAPPING.

child neglect. See NEGLECT.

child out of wedlock. See *illegitimate child* under CHILD.

child pornography. See PORNOGRAPHY.

Child Protective Services. A governmental agency with responsibility for investigating allegations of child abuse and neglect, providing family services to the parent or guardian of a child who has been abused or neglected, and administering the foster-care program. — Abbr. CPS. — Also termed (in some states) *Department of Social Services*.

child-rearing. The practices and customs followed in the upbringing of children, whether in a particular family or in society generally. — Sometimes written *childrearing*.

children's court. See *juvenile court* under COURT.

child's attorney. See ATTORNEY AD LITEM.

child-sexual-abuse accommodation syndrome.
The supposed medical and psychological condition
of a child who has suffered repeated instances of
sexual abuse, usu. from a relative or family friend. ●
This so-called "syndrome" has been repudiated by
the scientific community. It cannot be validated and
thus cannot discriminate between abuse and non-
abuse cases. — Abbr. CSAAS. — Also termed *child-*
sexual-abuse syndrome.

child's part. An inheritance that, by statute in
some states, a widow may claim in lieu of dower or
what she would receive under her husband's will. ●
The amount is calculated by counting the widow as
a child of the decedent, sharing equally any entitlement with any other child.

child-stealing. See *child-kidnapping* under KIDNAP-
PING.

child support. 1. A parent's legal obligation to
contribute to the economic maintenance and education of a child until the age of majority, the
child's emancipation before reaching majority, or
the child's completion of secondary education. ● The
obligation is enforceable both civilly and criminally.
2. In a custody or divorce action, the money legally
owed by one parent to the other for the expenses
incurred for children of the marriage. ● The right to
child support is the child's right and cannot be

waived, and any divorce-decree provision waiving child support is void. Cf. ALIMONY.

decretal child support. Child support provided for in a divorce decree or modification order.

child-support-enforcement agency. A governmental agency that helps custodial parents collect child support. ● Under Title IV(D) of the Social Security Act, states are required to establish child-support-enforcement agencies to collect support for obligee parents. Although the agencies are governed by a set of federal standards, each state has its own central registry. The CSE agency may operate through the state's Department of Human Services, its Department of Justice, its tax agency, or its Attorney General's office. The agency can help locate a missing parent and establish paternity. The agency works to establish support orders and to enforce those orders. — Abbr. CSE agency. — Also termed *IV-D agency*. See OFFICE OF CHILD-SUPPORT ENFORCEMENT.

child-support guidelines. Statutory provisions that govern the amount of child support that an obligor parent must pay. ● Child-support guidelines have been developed in every state in response to the creation of the Temporary Assistance to Needy Families program. 42 USCA §§ 601–603a.

Child Support Recovery Act of 1994. A statute that made it a federal offense for a person to willfully fail to pay past-due child support for a child who lived in another state. ● This Act has been replaced by the Deadbeat Parents Punishment Act. 42 USCA § 228. See DEADBEAT PARENTS PUNISH-MENT ACT.

child with disabilities. See CHILD.

child work. A minor's salutary employment, esp. within the family. ● This term is sometimes used in contrast to *child labor*, the idea being that child work within the family unit can be a positive experience. Some scholars and courts note that child work can facilitate vocational skills and social adaptation, and is often viewed as an expression of family solidarity. Cf. CHILD LABOR.

CHINS. *abbr.* See *child in need of supervision* under CHILD.

choice. See FREEDOM OF CHOICE.

Christian name. See GIVEN NAME.

circumstance, *n.* (*often pl.*) An accompanying or accessory fact, event, or condition, such as a piece of evidence that indicates the probability of an event. — **circumstantial,** *adj.*

citizen, *n.* A person who, by either birth or naturalization, is a member of a political community, owing allegiance to the community and being entitled to enjoy all its civil rights and protections; a member of the civil state, entitled to all its privileges. Cf. RESIDENT; DOMICILIARY.

federal citizen. A citizen of the United States.

natural-born citizen. A person born within the jurisdiction of a national government.

naturalized citizen. A foreign-born person who attains citizenship by law.

city judge. See *municipal judge* under JUDGE.

civil cognation. See COGNATION (2).

civil commitment. See COMMITMENT.

civil-commitment statute. A law that provides for the confinement of a person who is mentally ill, incompetent, drug-addicted, or the like, often a sexually violent predator. ● Unlike criminal incarceration, civil commitment is for an indefinite period.

civil contempt. See CONTEMPT.

civil death. See DEATH.

civil impediment. See IMPEDIMENT.

civil-liability act. See DRAM-SHOP ACT.

civil liberty. (*usu. pl.*) Freedom from undue governmental interference or restraint. ● This term usually refers to freedom of speech or religion. — Also termed *civil right*.

civil marriage. See MARRIAGE (2).

civil right. (*usu. pl.*) **1.** The individual rights of personal liberty guaranteed by the Bill of Rights and by the 13th, 14th, 15th, and 19th Amendments, as well as by legislation such as the Voting Rights Act. ● Civil rights include especially the right to vote, the right of due process, and the right of equal protection under the law. **2.** CIVIL LIBERTY.

civil-rights act. One of several federal statutes enacted after the Civil War (1861–1865) and, much later, during and after the civil-rights movement of the 1950s and 1960s, intended to implement and give further force to the basic rights guaranteed by the Constitution, and esp. prohibiting discrimination in employment and education on the basis of race, sex, religion, color, or age.

civil union. A marriage-like relationship, often between members of the same sex, recognized by civil authorities within a jurisdiction. ● Vermont was the first state to recognize civil unions. In December 1999, the Vermont Supreme Court ruled that denying gay couples the benefits of marriage amounted to unconstitutional discrimination. *Baker v. State*, 744 A.2d 864 (Vt. 1999). Several months later the legislature passed a civil-unions law, which took effect on July 1, 2000. Cf. DOMESTIC PARTNERSHIP; *same-sex marriage* under MARRIAGE (1).

Claflin **trust.** See *indestructible trust* under TRUST.

Claflin-**trust principle.** The doctrine that a trust cannot be terminated by the beneficiaries if the termination would defeat one of the settlor's material purposes in establishing the trust, even if all the beneficiaries seek its termination. ● The *Claflin* rule, which derives from *Claflin v. Claflin*, 20 N.E. 454 (Mass. 1889), is often cited as the purest illustration of "deadhand control," in which the wishes of the now dead settlor prevail over the wishes and needs of living beneficiaries. If the settlor is alive and consents to the modification or termination of the trust, the trust may usually be terminated, unless it is irrevocable. Trusts in the *Claflin* category are spendthrift trusts, support trusts, trusts in which the trustee has discretion to make distributions, and trusts in which the beneficiary is entitled to income until a certain age and the principal at that age.

clandestine marriage. See MARRIAGE (1).

class, *n.* **1.** A group of people, things, qualities, or activities that have common characteristics or attributes <a class of common-stock shares> <the upper-middle class>. **2.** A group of people, uncertain in number <a class of beneficiaries>.

testamentary class (tes-tə-**men**-tə-ree *or* -tree). A group of beneficiaries who are uncertain in number but whose number will be ascertainable in the future, when each will take an equal or other proportionate share of the gift.

class gift. See GIFT.

clause of accrual. A provision, usu. found in a gift by will or in a deed between tenants in common, that grants a predeceasing beneficiary's shares to the surviving beneficiary. — Also termed *clause of accruer*.

clean-hands doctrine. The principle that a party cannot seek equitable relief or assert an equitable defense if that party has violated an equitable principle, such as good faith. • Such a party is described as having "unclean hands." Section 8 of the Uniform Child Custody Jurisdiction Act contains an unclean-hands provision that forbids a court from exercising jurisdiction in a child-custody suit in certain situations, as when one party has wrongfully removed a child from another state, has improperly retained custody of a child after visitation, or has wrongfully removed a child from the person with custody. — Also termed *unclean-hands doctrine*.

clergyman–penitent privilege. See *priest–penitent privilege* under PRIVILEGE.

client's privilege. See *attorney–client privilege* under PRIVILEGE.

closed adoption. See ADOPTION.

co-administrator. *Wills & estates.* A person appointed to jointly administer an estate with one or more other administrators.

COBRA (**koh**-brə). *abbr.* CONSOLIDATED OMNIBUS BUDGET RECONCILIATION ACT OF 1985.

code state. *Hist.* A state that, at a given time, had already procedurally merged law and equity, so that equity was no longer administered as a separate system. ● This term was current primarily in the early to mid-20th century. Cf. NONCODE STATE.

codicil (**kod**-ə-səl *or* -sil). A supplement or addition to a will, not necessarily disposing of the entire estate but modifying, explaining, or otherwise qualifying the will in some way. ● When admitted to probate, the codicil becomes a part of the will.

coercion (koh-ər-zhən *or* -shən), *n.* **1.** Compulsion by physical force or threat of physical force. ● An act such as signing a will is not legally valid if done under coercion. Also, since a valid marriage requires voluntary consent, coercion or duress is grounds for invalidating a marriage. **2.** *Hist.* A husband's actual or supposed control or influence over his wife's actions. ● Under the common-law doctrine of coer-

cion, a wife who committed a crime in her husband's presence was presumed to have been coerced
by him and thus had a complete defense. Courts
have abolished this doctrine. — **coercive,** *adj.* —
coercer, *n.*

coexecutor. See *joint executor* under EXECUTOR.

cognate, *adj.* See COGNATIC.

cognate, *n.* One who is kin to another. ● In Roman
law, the term implies that the kinship derives from
a lawful marriage. In Scots and later civil law, the
term implies kinship from the mother's side. Cf. AG-
NATE.

cognatic (kog-**nat**-ik), *adj.* (Of a relationship) existing between cognates. — Also termed *cognate.*

cognation (kog-**nay**-shən), *n.* **1.** Relationship by
blood rather than by marriage; relationship arising
through common descent from the same man and
woman, whether the descent is traced through
males or females. **2.** *Civil law.* A relationship existing between two people by blood, by family, or by
both.

civil cognation. A relationship arising by law,
such as that created by adoption.

mixed cognation. A relationship that combines
the ties of blood and family, such as that existing

110

between brothers who are born of the same marriage.

natural cognation. A blood relationship, usu. arising from an illicit connection.

3. Relationship between persons or things of the same or similar nature; likeness.

cohabitation (koh-hab-ə-**tay**-shən), *n.* The fact or state of living together, esp. as partners in life, usu. with the suggestion of sexual relations. — **cohabit** (koh-**hab**-it), *vb.* — **cohabitative** (koh-**hab**-ə-tay-tiv), *adj.* — **cohabitant** (koh-**hab**-ə-tənt), *n.* — **cohabitor** (koh-**hab**-ə-tər), *n.*

illicit cohabitation. **1.** The condition of a man and a woman who, though not married, live together in circumstances that make the arrangement illegal. **2.** The offense committed by an unmarried man and woman who live together as husband and wife and engage in sexual intercourse. ● This offense, where it still exists, is seldom prosecuted. — Also termed *lascivious cohabitation*; *lewd and lascivious cohabitation.* Cf. FORNICATION.

lascivious cohabitation. See *illicit cohabitation.*

matrimonial cohabitation. The living together of husband and wife.

notorious cohabitation. The act of a man and a woman who, though not married, live together openly under circumstances that make the arrangement illegal.

cohabitation agreement. A contract outlining the property and financial arrangements between persons who live together. — Also termed *living-together agreement*. Cf. PRENUPTIAL AGREEMENT.

cohabiting unmarried person of the opposite sex. See CUPOS.

coheir (koh-**air**). One of two or more persons to whom an inheritance descends. See HEIR.

COLA. *abbr.* COST-OF-LIVING ADJUSTMENT.

collate (kə-**layt**), *vb. Civil law.* To return (inherited property) to an estate for division <the grandchildren collated the property they had received>.

collateral (kə-**lat**-ər-əl), *adj.* Not direct in line, but on a parallel or diverging line of descent; of or relating to persons who are related by blood but are neither ancestors nor descendants <an uncle is in a collateral, not a direct, line>. — **collaterality** (kə-lat-ər-**al**-ə-tee), *n.* Cf. LINEAL.

collateral (kə-**lat**-ər-əl), *n.* A person collaterally related to a decedent.

collateral affinity. See AFFINITY.

collateral ancestor. See *collateral ascendant* under ASCENDANT.

collateral ascendant. See ASCENDANT.

collateral consanguinity. See CONSANGUINITY.

collateral descendant. See DESCENDANT.

collateral descent. See DESCENT.

collateral heir. See HEIR.

collateral-inheritance tax. See TAX.

collateral line. See LINE.

collateral relative. See RELATIVE.

collatio bonorum (kə-**lay**-shee-oh bə-**nor**-əm). [Latin "collation of goods"] *Civil law.* The bringing into hotchpot of goods or money advanced by a parent to a child, so that the parent's personal estate will be equally distributed among the parent's children. See HOTCHPOT.

collation (kə-**lay**-shən), *n.* The taking into account of the value of advancements made by an intestate to his or her children so that the estate may be divided in accordance with the intestacy statute. — **collate** (kə-**layt**), *vb.* — **collator** (kə-**lay**-tər), *n.* Cf. HOTCHPOT.

collector of decedent's estate. A person temporarily appointed by a probate court to collect assets and payments due to a decedent's estate, and to settle other financial matters requiring immediate attention. • A collector is often appointed to look after an estate when there is a will contest or a dispute about who should be appointed administrator. The collector's duties end when an executor or administrator is appointed.

collusion (kə-**loo**-zhən), *n.* **1.** An agreement to defraud another or to do or obtain something forbidden by law. **2.** As a defense to divorce, an agreement between a husband and wife to commit or to appear to commit an act that is grounds for divorce. • For example, before the advent of no-fault divorce, a husband and wife might agree to make it appear that one of them had committed adultery. Cf. CONNIVANCE (2); CONDONATION (2); RECRIMINATION. — **collude,** *vb.* — **collusive,** *adj.* — **colluder,** *n.*

colorable, *adj.* **1.** (Of a claim or action) appearing to be true, valid, or right <the pleading did not state a colorable claim>. **2.** Intended to deceive; counterfeit <the court found the conveyance of exempt property to be a colorable transfer, and so set it aside>.

colorable transfer. See TRANSFER.

comingle, *vb.* See COMMINGLE.

comity (**kom**-ə-tee). Courtesy among political entities (as nations, states, or courts of different jurisdictions), involving esp. mutual recognition of legislative, executive, and judicial acts.

commercialized obscenity. See OBSCENITY.

commingle, *vb.* **1.** To put together (as funds or property) into one mass, as by mixing together a spouse's separate property with marital or community property, or mixing together the separate property of both spouses. **2.** (Of a fiduciary) to mix personal funds with those of a beneficiary or client. ● Commingling is usually considered a breach of the fiduciary relationship. Under the Model Rules of Professional Conduct, a lawyer is prohibited from commingling personal funds with those of a client. — Also spelled *comingle*. Cf. TRACING.

commit, *vb.* To send (a person) to a mental health facility, esp. by court order.

commitment, *n.* **1.** The act of confining a person in a mental hospital or other institution. **2.** The order directing an officer to take a person to a mental institution.

    civil commitment. A commitment of a person who is ill, incompetent, drug-addicted, or the like, as contrasted with a criminal sentence.

    voluntary commitment. A commitment of a person who is ill, incompetent, drug-addicted, or the like, upon the request or with the consent of the person being committed.

common ancestor. A person to whom the ancestry of two or more persons is traced.

common disaster. An event that causes two or more persons with related property interests (such as an insured and the beneficiary) to die at very nearly the same time, with no way of determining who died first. See UNIFORM SIMULTANEOUS DEATH ACT; COMMORIENTES.

common-law contempt. See *criminal contempt* under CONTEMPT.

common-law husband. See HUSBAND.

common-law marriage. See MARRIAGE (1).

common-law-property state. See COMMON-LAW STATE.

common-law state. 1. See NONCODE STATE. **2.** Any state that has not adopted a community-property regime. ● The chief difference today between a community-property state and a common-law state is that in a common-law state, a spouse's interest in property held by the other spouse does not vest until (1) a divorce action has been filed, or (2) the death of the other spouse. Cf. COMMUNITY-PROPERTY STATE.

common-law wife. See WIFE.

common tenancy. See *tenancy in common* under TENANCY.

common trust fund. See TRUST FUND.

commorientes (kə-mor-ee-**en**-teez). [fr. Latin *commorior* "to die together"] **1.** (*pl.*) Persons who die at the same time, such as spouses who die in an accident. **2.** *Civil law.* The rule of succession regarding such persons. See *simultaneous death* under DEATH; UNIFORM SIMULTANEOUS DEATH ACT.

commune (**kom**-yoon), *n.* A community of people who share property and responsibilities.

community account. See ACCOUNT.

community debt. See DEBT.

community estate. In a community-property state, the total of the assets and debts making up a married couple's property owned in common.

community-notification law. See MEGAN'S LAW.

community property. Property owned in common by husband and wife as a result of its having been acquired during the marriage by means other than an inheritance or a gift to one spouse, each spouse generally holding a one-half interest in the property. ● Only nine states have community-property systems: Arizona, California, Idaho, Louisiana, Nevada, New Mexico, Texas, Washington, and Wisconsin. See *marital property* under PROPERTY; TITLE DIVISION. Cf. SEPARATE PROPERTY.

quasi-community property. Personal property that, having been acquired in a non-community-property state, would have been community property if acquired in a community-property state. ● If a community-property state is the forum for a divorce or administration of a decedent's estate, state law may allow the court to treat quasi-community property as if it were community property when it determines the spouses' interests.

community-property state. A state in which spouses hold property that is acquired during marriage (other than property acquired by inheritance or individual gift) as community property. See COMMUNITY PROPERTY. Cf. COMMON-LAW STATE.

community trust. An agency organized to administer funds placed in trust for public-health, educational, and other charitable purposes in perpetuity.

comparative-rectitude doctrine. Before the advent of no-fault divorce, the rule providing that when both spouses show grounds for divorce, the party less at fault is granted the requested relief.

compelling-state-interest test. *Constitutional law.* A method for determining the constitutional validity of a law, whereby the government's interest in the law is balanced against the individual's constitutional right to be free of the law, and only if the government's interest is strong enough will the law be upheld. • The compelling-state-interest test is used most commonly in equal-protection analysis when the disputed law requires strict scrutiny. See STRICT SCRUTINY.

compensatory payment. A postmarital spousal payment made by the richer ex-spouse to the poorer one and treated as an entitlement rather than as a discretionary award. • Compensatory payments are set by statute and are based on a formula using the length of the marriage, differences in postdivorce income, role as primary caregiver, and other factors. The purpose is to compensate somewhat for disparate income levels after a failed marriage. Cf. ALIMONY.

competency proceeding. A proceeding to assess a person's mental capacity. • A competency hearing may be held either in a criminal context to determine a defendant's competency to stand trial or as a civil proceeding to assess whether a person should be committed to a mental-health facility.

complaint. The initial pleading that starts a civil action and states the basis for the court's jurisdiction, the basis for the plaintiff's claim, and the demand for relief. • In some states, this pleading is called a *petition*.

amended complaint. A complaint that modifies and replaces the original complaint by adding relevant matters that occurred before or at the time the action began. • In some circumstances, a party must obtain the court's permission to amend its complaint.

complaint for modification. See *motion to modify* under MOTION.

supplemental complaint. An additional complaint that either corrects a defect in the original complaint or adds relevant matters that occurred after the action began. • Generally, a party must obtain the court's permission to file a supplemental complaint.

well-pleaded complaint. An original or initial pleading that sufficiently sets forth a claim for relief — by including the grounds for the court's jurisdiction, the basis for the relief claimed, and a demand for judgment — so that a defendant may draft an answer that is responsive to the issues presented. • A well-pleaded complaint must raise a controlling issue of federal law for a federal court to have federal-question jurisdiction over the lawsuit.

completed gift. See GIFT.

complete interdiction. See *full interdiction* under INTERDICTION.

complete voluntary trust. See *executed trust* under TRUST.

compulsory arbitration. See ARBITRATION.

compulsory-attendance law. A statute requiring minors of a specified age to attend school. ● Compulsory-attendance laws do not apply to married persons. — Also termed *compulsory-school-attendance law*. See AMISH EXCEPTION.

computer matching. The comparing of computer records in two separate systems to determine whether the same record exists in both systems. ● The government, for example, uses computer matching to find persons who are both employed and receiving welfare payments and to find instances in which both divorced parents are claiming the same child on their income-tax returns. See COMPUTER MATCHING AND PRIVACY PROTECTION ACT OF 1988.

Computer Matching and Privacy Protection Act of 1988. An act that allows governmental agencies, with certain limitations, to compare computerized records to establish or verify eligibility for benefits or to recoup payments on benefits. 5 USCA § 552a. See COMPUTER MATCHING.

comstockery (**kom**-stok-ər-ee). (*often cap.*) Censorship or attempted censorship of art or literature that is supposedly immoral or obscene.

Comstock law (**kom**-stok). An 1873 federal statute that tightened rules against mailing "obscene, lewd, or lascivious" books or pictures, as well as "any article or thing designed for the prevention of conception or procuring of abortions." ● Because of the intolerance that led to this statute, the law gave rise to an English word roughly equivalent to *prudery* — namely, *comstockery*.

conciliation, *n.* A relatively unstructured method of dispute resolution in which a third party facilitates communication between parties in an attempt to help them settle their differences. ● Some jurisdictions, such as California, have Family Conciliation Courts to help resolve problems within the family. — Also termed *facilitation.* — **conciliate,** *vb.* — **conciliatory,** *adj.* — **conciliator,** *n.* Cf. MEDIATION; ARBITRATION.

conclusion of fact. A factual deduction drawn from observed or proven facts; an evidentiary inference. Cf. FINDING OF FACT.

conclusion of law. An inference on a question of law, made as a result of a factual showing, no further evidence being required; a legal inference. Cf. FINDING OF FACT.

concubinage (kon-**kyoo**-bə-nij), *n.* **1.** The relationship of a man and woman who cohabit without the benefit of marriage. **2.** The state of being a concubine.

concubine (**kong**-kyə-bɪn). *Archaic.* A woman who cohabits with a man to whom she is not married. ● A concubine is often considered a wife without title. A concubine's status arises from the permanent cohabitation of a man and a woman as husband and wife although without the benefit of marriage. Cf. *common-law wife* under WIFE; COURTESAN.

concurrent jurisdiction. See JURISDICTION.

conditional bequest. See BEQUEST.

conditional delivery. See DELIVERY.

conditional devise. See DEVISE.

conditional legacy. See LEGACY.

conditional will. See WILL.

condonation (kon-də-**nay**-shən), *n.* **1.** A victim's express or (esp.) implied forgiveness of an offense, esp. by treating the offender as if there had been no offense. ● Condonation is not usually a valid defense to a crime. **2.** One spouse's express or implied forgiveness of a marital offense by resuming marital life and sexual intimacy. ● Before the advent of no-fault divorce, one spouse might impliedly forgive the other spouse's infidelity by continuing to live with him or her. If condonation is proved, the forgiving spouse is barred from proof of that offense as a ground for divorce. Cf. COLLUSION (2); CONNIVANCE (2); RECRIMINATION; RECONCILIATION.

confidential adoption. See *closed adoption* under ADOPTION.

confidential communication. A communication made within a certain protected relationship and legally protected from forced disclosure. • Among confidential communications are those between husband and wife, attorney and client, and priest and penitent. Cf. PRIVILEGE.

confidentiality statute. A law that seals adoption records and prevents an adopted child from learning the identity of his or her biological parent and prevents the biological parent from learning the identity of the adoptive parents. — Also termed *sealed-record statute.*

confidential marriage. See MARRIAGE (1).

confidential relationship. See FIDUCIARY RELATIONSHIP.

conflict of laws. 1. A difference between the laws of different states or countries in a case in which a transaction or occurrence central to the case has a connection to two or more jurisdictions. — Often shortened to *conflict.*

   conflict of personal laws. **1.** A difference of laws between a jurisdiction's general laws and the laws of a racial or religious group, such as a conflict between federal law and American Indian tribal law. **2.** A difference between personal laws.

2. The body of jurisprudence that undertakes to reconcile such differences or to decide what law is to govern in these situations; the principles of choice of law. — Often shortened (in sense 2) to *conflicts*.

conformed copy. See COPY.

conjoint will. See *joint will* under WILL.

conjugal (**kon**-jə-gəl), *adj.* Of or relating to the married state, often with an implied emphasis on sexual relations between spouses <the prisoner was allowed a private bed for conjugal visits>.

conjugal rights. The rights and privileges arising from the marriage relationship, including the mutual rights of companionship, support, and sexual relations. ● Loss of conjugal rights amounts to loss of consortium. See CONSORTIUM.

connivance (kə-**nı**-vənts), *n.* **1.** The act of promoting, encouraging, or setting up another's wrongdoing. **2.** As a defense to divorce, one spouse's corrupt consent, express or implied, to have the other commit adultery or some other act of sexual misconduct. ● Consent is an essential element of connivance. The complaining spouse must have consented to the act complained of. — **connive,** *vb.* Cf. COLLUSION (2); CONDONATION (2); RECRIMINATION.

consanguine brother. See BROTHER.

consanguinity (kon-sang-**gwin**-ə-tee), *n.* The relationship of persons of the same blood or origin. — **consanguineous,** *adj.* See *prohibited degree* under DEGREE. Cf. AFFINITY.

> *collateral consanguinity.* The relationship between persons who have the same ancestor but do not descend or ascend from one another (for example, uncle and nephew, cousins, etc.).

> *lineal consanguinity.* The relationship between persons who are directly descended or ascended from one another (for example, mother and daughter, great-grandfather and grandson, etc.).

conscious-presence test. A method for judging whether a testator is in the presence of a witness to a will, whereby if the testator can sense the presence of the witness — even if the witness cannot be seen — the witness is present. Restatement (Third) of Property: Wills and Other Donative Transfers § 3.1 (Tentative Draft No. 2, 1998). — Also termed *conscious presence.* See PRESENCE-OF-THE-TESTATOR RULE.

consensual marriage. See *common-law marriage* under MARRIAGE.

consent, *n.* Agreement, approval, or permission as to some act or purpose, esp. given voluntarily by a competent person. — **consent,** *vb.* — **consensual,** *adj.*

blank consent. See BLANK CONSENT.

informed consent. **1.** A person's agreement to allow something to happen, made with full knowledge of the risks involved and the alternatives. **2.** A patient's knowing choice about a medical treatment or procedure, made after a physician or other healthcare provider discloses whatever information a reasonably prudent provider in the medical community would provide to a patient regarding the risks involved in the proposed treatment or procedure. — Also termed *knowing consent.*

knowing consent. See *informed consent.*

voluntary consent. Consent that is given freely and that has not been coerced.

consent calendar. A schedule of informal hearings involving a child, usu. arranged when it appears that the child's best interests will be served if the case is heard informally. ● The child and all interested parties must first consent before the case goes on the consent calendar.

consent judgment. See *agreed judgment* under JUDGMENT.

conservator (kən-**sər**-və-tər *or* **kon**-sər-vay-tər), *n*. A guardian, protector, or preserver. ● *Conservator* is the modern equivalent of the common-law *guardian*. Judicial appointment and supervision are still required, but a conservator has far more flexible authority than a guardian, including the same investment powers that a trustee enjoys. The Uniform Probate Code uses the term *conservator*, and Article 5 is representative of modern conservatorship laws. — **conservatorship,** *n*.

managing conservator. **1.** A person appointed by a court to manage the estate or affairs of someone who is legally incapable of doing so; GUARDIAN (1). **2.** In the child-custody laws of some states, the parent who has primary custody of a child, with the right to establish the child's primary domicile. See CUSTODY.

possessory conservator. See *noncustodial parent* under PARENT.

Consolidated Omnibus Budget Reconciliation Act of 1985. A federal statute requiring employers that offer group health coverage to their employees to continue to do so for a prescribed period (usu. 18 to 36 months) after employment has terminated so that the former employee can continue to benefit from group-health rates until becoming a member of another health-insurance plan. ● The statute temporarily continues group coverage for a person no longer entitled to receive it, such as a terminated employee or an overage dependent. One of the "qualifying events" justifying the continuation of group-health-insurance benefits is divorce or legal separation. So COBRA often provides critical transitional coverage until a divorced spouse and children can arrange for new health insurance. The period of transitional coverage is up to 36 months, and an applicant spouse of the employee must make written application to the employer within 60 days of the separation or divorce. — Abbr. COBRA.

consortium (kən-**sor**-shee-əm). The benefits that one person, esp. a spouse, is entitled to receive from another, including companionship, cooperation, affection, aid, and (between spouses) sexual relations <a claim for loss of consortium>. See LOSS OF CONSORTIUM; CONJUGAL RIGHTS.

> *filial consortium* (**fil**-ee-əl). A child's society, affection, and companionship given to a parent.

> *parental consortium.* A parent's society, affection, and companionship given to a child.

> *spousal consortium.* A spouse's society, affection, and companionship given to the other spouse.

constitutional homestead. See HOMESTEAD.

constructive abandonment. See DESERTION.

constructive delivery. See DELIVERY.

constructive desertion. See DESERTION.

constructive emancipation. See EMANCIPATION.

constructive parent. See *equitable parent* under PARENT.

constructive trust. See TRUST.

consular marriage. See MARRIAGE (1).

consumer. A person who buys goods or services for personal, family, or household use, with no intention of resale; a natural person who uses products for personal rather than business purposes. 40 CFR § 721(b)(1).

Consumer Credit Protection Act. A federal statute that safeguards consumers in the use of credit by (1) requiring full disclosure of the terms of loan agreements, including finance charges, (2) restricting the garnishment of wages, and (3) regulating the use of credit cards. 15 USCA §§ 1601–1693. ● Many states have also adopted consumer-credit-protection acts. — Also termed *Truth in Lending Act*.

Consumer Product Safety Commission. A federal agency that promulgates and oversees safety regulations for consumer products.

consumer-protection law. A state or federal statute designed to protect consumers against unfair trade and credit practices involving consumer goods, as well as to protect consumers against faulty and dangerous goods.

consummate (kən-**səm**-it *or* **kahn**-sə-mit), *adj.* Completed; fully accomplished. ● *Consummate* was often used at common law to describe the status of a contract or an estate, such as the transformation of a husband's interest in his wife's inheritance from that of a tenant by the curtesy *initiate* to a tenant by curtesy *consummate* upon the wife's death (assuming that a child had been born during the marriage). See *curtesy consummate* under CURTE-SY.

consummate (**kon**-sə-mayt), *vb.* To bring to completion; esp., to make (a marriage) complete by sexual intercourse.

consummate dower. See DOWER.

consummation of marriage. The first postmarital act of sexual intercourse between a husband and wife. ● Under canon law, a refusal to consummate the marriage may be grounds for an annulment or for divorce. But this is not so at common law or under modern state law.

contemplation of death. The thought of dying, not necessarily from imminent danger, but as the compelling reason to transfer property to another. See *gift causa mortis* under GIFT.

contemporary community standards. The gauge by which a fact-finder decides whether material is obscene, judging by its patent offensiveness and its pruriency in the locale at a given time. See OBSCENITY (1).

contempt, *n.* Conduct that defies the authority or dignity of a court or legislature. • Because such conduct interferes with the administration of justice, it is punishable, usually by fine or imprisonment. — Also termed *contempt of court.* — **contemptuous,** *adj.*

 civil contempt. The failure to obey a court order that was issued for another party's benefit. • A civil-contempt proceeding is coercive or remedial in nature. The usual sanction is to confine the contemner until he or she complies with the court order. In post-divorce proceedings, the purpose of a civil-contempt proceeding is to compel the defendant to comply with the divorce decree, often to comply with a child-support or visitation order. The act (or failure to act) complained of must be within the defendant's power to perform, and the contempt order must state how the contempt may be purged. Imprisonment for civil contempt is indefinite and for a term that lasts until the defendant complies with the decree.

 common-law contempt. See *criminal contempt.*

 criminal contempt. An act that obstructs justice or attacks the integrity of the court. • A criminal-contempt proceeding is punitive in nature. The purpose of criminal-contempt proceedings is to punish repeated or aggravated failure to comply with a court order. All the protections of criminal law and procedure apply, and the commitment must be for a definite period. — Also termed *common-law contempt*.

contempt of court. See CONTEMPT.

contestability clause (kən-tes-tə-**bil**-ə-tee). *Insurance*. A policy provision setting forth when and under what conditions the insurer may contest a claim or void the policy based on a representation or omission made when the policy was issued. ● Contestability clauses usually lapse after two years. — Also termed *contestable clause*. Cf. INCON-TESTABILITY CLAUSE.

contestant. One who contests the validity of a will. — Also termed *objectant*; *caveator*.

contested divorce. See DIVORCE.

contested hearing. See HEARING.

contingency beneficiary. See *contingent beneficiary* (2) under BENEFICIARY.

contingent legacy. See LEGACY.

contingent ownership. See OWNERSHIP.

contingent remainder. See REMAINDER.

contingent trust. See TRUST.

contingent will. See WILL.

continuance, *n.* The adjournment or postponement of a trial or other proceeding to a future date <motion for continuance>. — **continue,** *vb.*

continued-custody hearing. See *shelter hearing* under HEARING.

continuing jurisdiction. See JURISDICTION.

continuing-jurisdiction doctrine. The rule that once a court has acquired jurisdiction over a child-custody or support case, that court continues to have jurisdiction to modify orders, even if the child or a parent moves to another state.

contract of insurance. See INSURANCE POLICY.

contributing to the delinquency of a minor. The offense of an adult's engaging in conduct involving a minor — or in the presence of a minor — likely to result in delinquent conduct. ● Examples include encouraging a minor to shoplift, to lie under oath, or to commit vandalism. — Often shortened to *contributing to delinquency.* See JUVENILE DELINQUENCY. Cf. IMPAIRING THE MORALS OF A MINOR; CORRUPTING.

contributory pension plan. See PENSION PLAN.

control-your-kid law. See PARENTAL-RESPONSIBILITY STATUTE.

contumacy (**kon**-t[y]uu-mə-see), *n.* Contempt of court; the refusal of a person to follow a court's order or direction. — **contumacious,** *adj.* See CONTEMPT.

conversion divorce. See DIVORCE.

convertible divorce. See *conversion divorce* under DIVORCE.

cooling-off period. An automatic delay between a person's taking some legal action and the consequence of that action, such as between the filing of divorce papers and the divorce hearing.

cooperative adoption. See ADOPTION.

coordinate jurisdiction. See *concurrent jurisdiction* under JURISDICTION.

coparcenary (koh-**pahr**-sə-ner-ee), *n.* An estate that arises when two or more persons jointly inherit from one ancestor, the title and right of possession being shared equally by all. ● Coparcenary was a form of coownership created by common-law rules of descent upon intestacy when two or more persons together constituted the decedent's heirs. Typically, this situation arose when the decedent was survived by no sons but by two or more daughters, so that the daughters took as coparceners. — Also termed *parcenary*; *tenancy in coparcenary*. — **coparcenary,** *adj*.

copy, *n*. An imitation or reproduction of an original.

> *attested copy.* See *certified copy*.

> *certified copy.* A duplicate of an original (usu. official) document, certified as an exact reproduction usu. by the officer responsible for issuing or keeping the original. — Also termed *attested copy*; *exemplified copy*; *verified copy*.

> *conformed copy.* An exact copy of a document bearing written explanations of things that were not or could not be copied, such as a note on the document indicating that it was signed by a person whose signature appears on the original.

> *exemplified copy.* See *certified copy*.

> *verified copy.* See *certified copy*.

corespondent. In a divorce suit based on adultery, the person with whom the spouse is accused of having committed adultery.

corporal punishment. See PUNISHMENT.

corporate trustee. See TRUSTEE.

corporeal hereditament. See HEREDITAMENT.

corporeal ownership. See OWNERSHIP.

corpus (**kor**-pəs), *n.* [Latin "body"] **1.** The property for which a trustee is responsible; the trust principal. — Also termed *res*; *trust estate*; *trust fund*; *trust property*; *trust res*. **2.** PRINCIPAL (3). Pl. **corpora** (**kor**-pə-rə), **corpuses** (**kor**-pə-səz).

corrupting, *n.* See CORRUPTION OF A MINOR.

corruption of a minor. 1. The crime of engaging in sexual activity with a minor; specif., the offense of having sexual intercourse or engaging in sexual activity with a person who is not the actor's spouse and who (1) is under the legal age of consent, the actor being considerably older than the victim (usu. four or more years), or (2) is less than 21 years old (or other age established by the particular jurisdiction), the actor being the person's guardian or otherwise responsible for the victim's welfare. Model Penal Code § 213.3. ● In some jurisdictions, the definition has been broadened to include aiding or encouraging a minor to commit a criminal offense. Cf. IMPAIRING THE MORALS OF A MINOR. **2.** A parent's or caregiver's act of stimulating or encouraging a child to engage in destructive antisocial behavior. — Also termed *corrupting*. Cf. CONTRIBUTING TO THE DELINQUENCY OF A MINOR.

cost, *n.* The amount paid or charged for something; price or expenditure. Cf. EXPENSE.

cost-of-living adjustment. An automatic increase or decrease in the amount of money, usu. support or maintenance, to be paid by one party to another, the adjustment being tied to the cost-of-living-adjustment figures maintained and updated by the federal government. — Abbr. COLA.

cotenancy. See TENANCY.

cotrustee. One of two or more persons in whom the administration of a trust is vested. ● The cotrustees form a collective trustee and exercise their powers jointly. — Also termed *joint trustee*. See TRUSTEE.

counter will. See *mutual will* under WILL.

county agent. See JUVENILE OFFICER.

county court. See *probate court* under COURT.

county judge. See JUDGE.

court, *n*. **1.** A governmental body consisting of one or more judges who sit to adjudicate disputes and administer justice <a question of law for the court to decide>. **2.** The judge or judges who sit on such a governmental body <the court asked the parties to approach the bench>. **3.** A legislative assembly <in Massachusetts, the General Court is the legislature>. **4.** The locale for a legal proceeding <an out-of-court statement>. **5.** The building where the judge or judges convene to adjudicate disputes and administer justice <the lawyers agreed to meet at the court at 8:00 a.m.>. — Also termed (in sense 5) *courthouse*.

appeals court. See *appellate court*.

appellate court. A court with jurisdiction to review decisions of lower courts or administrative agencies. — Also termed *appeals court*; *appeal court*; *court of appeals*; *court of appeal*; *court of review*.

children's court. See *juvenile court* (1).

county court. See *probate court*.

court of appeals. See *appellate court*.

court of domestic relations. See *family court*.

court of first instance. See *trial court*.

court of instance. See *trial court*.

court of ordinary. See *probate court*.

court of review. See *appellate court*.

dependency court. A court having jurisdiction over matters involving abused and neglected children, foster care, the termination of parental rights, and (sometimes) adoption.

domestic court. 1. A court having jurisdiction at the place of a party's residence or domicile. **2.** See *family court*.

domestic-relations court. See *family court.*

drug court. A court that hears cases against nonviolent adults and juveniles, who are often first-time offenders and who are usu. charged with possession of a controlled substance or with committing a minor drug-related crime. ● Drug courts focus on treatment rather than on incarceration.

family court. A court having jurisdiction over matters involving divorce, child custody and support, paternity, domestic violence, and other family-law issues. — Also termed *domestic-relations court; court of domestic relations; domestic court.*

instance court. See *trial court.*

juvenile court. **1.** A court having jurisdiction over cases involving children under a specified age, usu. 18. ● Illinois enacted the first statewide juvenile-court act in 1899. Today every state has a specialized juvenile or family court with exclusive original delinquency jurisdiction. — Also termed *children's court.* **2.** A court having special jurisdiction over orphaned, delinquent, dependent, and neglected children. ● This type of juvenile court is created by statute and derives its power from the specific wording of the statute, usually having exclusive original jurisdiction over matters involving abuse and neglect, adoption, status offenses, and delinquency. Generally, juvenile courts are special courts of a paternal nature that have jurisdiction over the care, custody, and control of children (as defined by the statute). The jurisdiction of the juvenile court is exercised as between the state (for the child) and the parents of the child and is not concerned with a custody controversy that does not affect the morale, health, or welfare of the child. A juvenile court is not a criminal court. The primary concern of a juvenile court is the child's immediate welfare. See UNIFORM JUVENILE COURT ACT.

orphan's court. See *probate court*.

probate court. A court with the power to declare wills valid or invalid, to oversee the administration of estates, and in some states to appoint guardians and approve the adoption of minors. — Also termed *surrogate's court*; *surrogate court*; *court of ordinary*; *county court*; *orphan's court* (abbr. o.c.). See PROBATE.

surrogate's court. See *probate court*.

teen court. A group of teenagers who (1) hear cases involving juveniles, usu. first-time offenders, who have acknowledged their guilt or responsibility, and (2) impose sanctions within a fixed range, usu. involving counseling, community service, or restitution. • Some local jurisdictions in more than half the states have provided for this type of tribunal. The juvenile offender consents to the assessment of punishment by this jury of peers. The American Bar Association encourages the formation of these kinds of courts. — Also termed *youth court*.

trial court. A court of original jurisdiction where the evidence is first received and considered. — Also termed *court of first instance*; *instance court.*

unified family court. In some jurisdictions, a court that hears all family matters, including matters of divorce, juvenile delinquency, adoption, abuse and neglect, and criminal abuse. • A unified family court also hears matters typically heard in family court (in jurisdictions that have statutory family courts) or in courts of general jurisdiction, such as divorce, paternity, and emancipation proceedings. Proponents of unified family courts cite the benefits of having all family-related matters heard by one court — for instance, the benefit of having a child testify only once rather than forcing the child to testify in one court in a divorce proceeding, in a different court in criminal proceedings against an abuser, and in yet another in a civil proceeding initiated by Child Protective Services.

youth court. See *teen court.*

Court Appointed Special Advocates. A federally funded program in which trained laypersons act on behalf of children in abuse and neglect cases. • The CASA program began in 1977 in Seattle, Washington. In 1989, the American Bar Association endorsed using a combination of CASA volunteers and attorneys in abuse and neglect cases. CASA volunteers are sanctioned by the ABA as permissible guardians ad litem. — Abbr. CASA.

court calendar. See DOCKET (2).

courtesan. 1. A court mistress. **2.** A loose woman. **3.** A prostitute. — Also spelled *courtezan*. Cf. CONCUBINE.

courthouse. See COURT (5).

court of appeals. See *appellate court* under COURT.

court of domestic relations. See *family court* under COURT.

court of first instance. See *trial court* under COURT.

court of instance. See *trial court* under COURT.

court of ordinary. See *probate court* under COURT.

court of review. See *appellate court* under COURT.

court order. See ORDER.

cousin. 1. A child of one's aunt or uncle. — Also termed *first cousin*; *full cousin*; *cousin-german*. **2.** A relative descended from one's ancestor (such as a grandparent) by two or more steps in a diverging line. **3.** Any distant relative by blood or marriage; a kinsman or kinswoman.

cousin-german. A first cousin; a child of a full sibling of one's mother or father. See COUSIN (1); GERMAN.

cousin-in-law. **1.** A husband or wife of one's cousin. **2.** A cousin of one's husband or one's wife.

cousin once removed. **1.** A child of one's cousin. **2.** A cousin of one's parent.

cousin twice removed. **1.** A grandchild of one's cousin. **2.** A cousin of one's grandparent.

first cousin. See COUSIN (1).

second cousin. A person related to another by descending from the same great-grandfather or great-grandmother.

third cousin. A person related to another by descending from the same great-great-grandfather or great-great-grandmother.

covenant marriage. See MARRIAGE (1).

coverture (**kəv**-ər-chər *also* -tyoor), *n. Archaic.* The condition of being a married woman <under former law, a woman under coverture was allowed to sue only through the personality of her husband>. — **covert** (**kəv**-ərt), *adj.* See *feme covert* under FEME.

CPS. *abbr.* CHILD PROTECTIVE SERVICES.

CRAT. *abbr.* Charitable-remainder annuity trust. See TRUST.

creation science. The teaching of the biblical version of the creation of the universe. ● The United States Supreme Court has held unconstitutional a Louisiana law that forbade the teaching of the theory of evolution unless biblical creation was also taught. The Court found the law violative of the Establishment Clause of the First Amendment because it lacked a "clear secular purpose." *Edwards v. Aguillard*, 482 U.S. 578, 107 S.Ct. 2573 (1987). Cf. ANTI-EVOLUTION STATUTE.

creator. See SETTLOR.

credit. See TAX CREDIT.

credit-shelter trust. See *bypass trust* under TRUST.

crim. con. *abbr.* CRIMINAL CONVERSATION.

crime against nature. See SODOMY.

criminal battery. See BATTERY (1).

criminal contempt. See CONTEMPT.

criminal conversation. *Archaic.* A tort action for adultery, brought by a husband against a third party who engaged in sexual intercourse with his wife. ● Criminal conversation has been abolished in most jurisdictions. — Abbr. crim. con. See HEART-BALM STATUTE.

criminal-court judge. See JUDGE.

criminal desertion. See DESERTION.

criminal neglect of family. See NONSUPPORT.

criminal nonsupport. See NONSUPPORT.

cross-marriage. See MARRIAGE (1).

cross-remainder. See REMAINDER.

cruel and abusive treatment. See ABUSE (2).

cruel and inhumane treatment. See *extreme cruelty* under CRUELTY.

cruelty. The intentional and malicious infliction of mental or physical suffering on a living creature, esp. a human; abusive treatment; outrage. Cf. ABUSE; INHUMAN TREATMENT; INDIGNITY.

    cruelty to a child. See *child abuse* under ABUSE.

    extreme cruelty. As a ground for divorce, one spouse's physical violence toward the other spouse, or conduct that destroys or severely impairs the other spouse's mental health. — Also termed *cruel and inhumane treatment.* Cf. ABUSE (2).

legal cruelty. Cruelty that will justify granting a divorce to the injured party; specif., one's spouse's conduct that endangers the life, person, or health of the other spouse, or creates a reasonable apprehension of bodily or mental harm.

mental cruelty. As a ground for divorce, one spouse's course of conduct (not involving actual violence) that creates such anguish that it endangers the life, physical health, or mental health of the other spouse. See EMOTIONAL DISTRESS.

physical cruelty. As a ground for divorce, actual personal violence committed by one spouse against the other.

cruelty to children. See *child abuse* under ABUSE.

Crummey power. The right of a beneficiary of a Crummey trust to withdraw gifts made to the trust up to a maximum amount (often the lesser of the annual exclusion or the value of the gift made to the trust) for a certain period after the gift is made. ● The precise characteristics of a Crummey power are established by the settlor of a Crummey trust. Typically, the power is exercisable for 30 days after the gift is made and permits withdrawals up to $5,000 or 5% of the value of the trust. A beneficiary may allow the power to lapse without making any demand for distribution. See *Crummey trust* under TRUST; *annual exclusion* under EXCLUSION.

Crummey trust. See TRUST.

CSAAS. *abbr.* CHILD-SEXUAL-ABUSE-ACCOMMODATION SYN-DROME.

CSE agency. *abbr.* CHILD-SUPPORT-ENFORCEMENT AGEN-CY.

c.t.a. See *administration cum testamento annexo* under ADMINISTRATION.

cultural defense. A defense to prosecution for a criminal act — often child abuse, child neglect, or child endangerment — that, according to the defendant, results from his or her cultural background. • This defense is sometimes raised by those accused of female genital mutilation. See FEMALE GENITAL MUTILATION.

cum testamento annexo (kəm tes-tə-**men**-toh ə-**nek**-soh). See *administration cum testamento annexo* under ADMINISTRATION.

cumulative legacy. See *accumulative legacy* under LEGACY.

cumulatively harmful behavior. See HARMFUL BEHAVIOR.

CUPOS. *abbr.* A cohabiting unmarried person of the opposite sex. • Although this term is intended to be synonymous with "POSSLQ" (a person of the opposite sex sharing living quarters), it is more literally precise because it excludes married persons. See POSSLQ.

curator (**kyuur**-ə-tər *or* **kyuur**-ay-tər *or* kyuu-**ray**-tər), *n.* **1.** A temporary guardian or conservator appointed by a court to care for the property or person of a minor or incapacitated person.

> *interim curator. Archaic.* A person appointed by a justice of the peace to hold a felon's property until a royal administrator could be assigned the task.

2. In the civil law, a guardian who manages the estate of a minor, an absent person, or an incapacitated person.

> *curator ad hoc* (**kyuur**-ə-tər ad **hok**). A court-appointed curator who manages a single matter or transaction. See *special guardian* under GUARD-IAN.

curatorship. The office of a curator or guardian.

curfew. A regulation that forbids people (or certain classes of them, such as minors) from being outdoors between certain hours.

curtesy (**kər**-tə-see). At common law, a husband's right, upon his wife's death, to a life estate in the land that his wife owned during their marriage, assuming that a child was born alive to the couple. ● This right has been largely abolished. Traditionally, the full phrase was *estate by the curtesy of England*. Cf. DOWER.

    curtesy consummate (kər-tə-see kən-**səm**-it *or* **kahn**-sə-mit). The interest the husband has in his wife's estate after her death.

    curtesy initiate (kər-tə-see i-**nish**-ee-it). The interest the husband has in his wife's estate after the birth of issue capable of inheriting, and before the death of the wife.

custodial account. See ACCOUNT.

custodial interference. 1. The abduction of a child or the inducement of a minor child to leave the parent legally entitled to custody or not to return to the parent entitled to legal custody. **2.** Any hindrance to a parent's rightful access to a child. ● The Restatement (Second) of Torts § 700 (1977) provides for an action in tort by the parent entitled to custody against one who, with knowledge that the parent does not consent, either takes the child or compels or induces the child to leave or not to return to the parent legally entitled to custody. — Also termed *custody interference*.

custodial parent. See PARENT.

custodial responsibility. Physical child custody and supervision, usu. including overnight responsibility for the child. ● This term encompasses visitation and sole, joint, and shared custody. Both parents share responsibility for the child regardless of the amount of time they spend with the child. *Principles of the Law of Family Dissolution: Analysis and Recommendations* § 2.03 (ALI, Tentative Draft No. 3, pt. I, 1998). See CUSTODY.

custodial trust. See TRUST.

custodian, *n.* A person or institution that has charge or custody (of a child, property, papers, or other valuables); GUARDIAN. • In reference to a child, a custodian has either legal or physical custody. — **custodianship,** *n.* See CAREGIVER.

custody, *n.* The care, control, and maintenance of a child awarded by a court to a responsible adult. • Custody involves legal custody (decision-making authority) and physical custody (caregiving authority), and an award of custody usually grants both rights. In a divorce or separation proceeding between the parents, the court usually awards custody to one of them, unless both are found to be unfit, in which case the court may award custody to a third party, typically a relative. In a case involving parental dereliction, such as abuse or neglect, the court may award custody to the state for placing the child in foster care if no responsible relative or family friend is willing and able to care for the child. — Also termed *child custody*; *legal custody*; *managing conservatorship*; *parental functions*. See *managing conservator* (2) under CONSERVATOR; PARENTING PLAN.

> **divided custody.** An arrangement by which each parent has exclusive physical custody and full

control of and responsibility for the child part of the time, with visitation rights in the other parent. ● For example, a mother might have custody during the school year, and the father might have custody during the summer vacation.

joint custody. An arrangement by which both parents share the responsibility for and authority over the child at all times, although one parent may exercise primary physical custody. ● In most jurisdictions, there is a rebuttable presumption that joint custody is in the child's best interests. Joint-custody arrangements are favored unless there is so much animosity between the parents that the child or children will be adversely affected by a joint-custody arrangement. An award of joint custody does not necessarily mean an equal sharing of time; it does, however, mean that the parents will consult and share equally in the child's upbringing and in decision-making about upbringing. In a joint-custody arrangement, the rights, privileges, and responsibilities are shared, though not necessarily the physical custody. In a joint-custody arrangement, physical custody is usually given to one parent. In fact, awards of joint physical custody, in the absence of extraordinary circumstances, are usually found not to be in the best interests of the child. — Also termed *shared custody*; *joint managing conservatorship*.

legal custody. **1.** CUSTODY. **2.** DECISION-MAKING RESPONSIBILITY.

physical custody. **1.** The right to have the child live with the person awarded custody by the court. — Also termed *residential custody*. **2.** Possession of a child during visitation.

residential custody. See *physical custody* (1).

shared custody. See *joint custody*.

sole custody. An arrangement by which one parent has full control and sole decision-making responsibility — to the exclusion of the other parent — on matters such as health, education, religion, and living arrangements.

split custody. An arrangement in which one parent has custody of one or more children, while the other parent has custody of the remaining children. ● Split custody is fairly uncommon, since most jurisdictions favor keeping siblings together.

custody determination. A court order determining custody and visitation rights. ● The order typically does not include any instructions on child support or other monetary obligations.

custody evaluation. See HOME-STUDY REPORT.

custody hearing. See HEARING.

custody interference. See CUSTODIAL INTERFERENCE.

custody proceeding. An action to determine who is entitled to legal or physical custody of a child. ● Legal custody gives one the right to make significant decisions regarding the child, and physical custody gives one the right to physical care and control of the child. See CUSTODY; *custody hearing* under HEARING.

cy pres (see **pray** *or* SI). [Law French "as near as"] The equitable doctrine under which a court reforms a written instrument with a gift to charity as closely to the donor's intention as possible, so that the gift does not fail. ● Courts use *cy pres* especially in construing charitable gifts when the donor's original charitable purpose cannot be fulfilled. Cf. DOCTRINE OF APPROXIMATION.

D

D. *abbr.* DEFENDANT.

date rape. See RAPE.

daughter. A parent's female child; a female child in a parent–child relationship.

daughter-in-law. The wife of one's son.

d.b.n. See *administration de bonis non* under ADMINISTRATION.

d.b.n.c.t.a. See *administration de bonis non cum testamento annexo* under ADMINISTRATION.

deadbeat. *Slang.* A person who does not pay debts or financial obligations (such as for child support), usu. with the suggestion that the person is also adept or experienced at evading creditors.

deadbeat dad. *Slang.* A father who has not paid or who is behind in making child-support payments.

deadbeat mom. *Slang.* **1.** A mother who has not paid or who is behind in making child-support payments. ● This term is used far less frequently than either *deadbeat dad* or *deadbeat parent*, probably because nearly ten times as many men as women fail to support (or are ordered to support) their children financially after divorce. **2.** An able-bodied mother whose income is derived from welfare payments, not from gainful employment.

Deadbeat Parents Punishment Act. A 1998 federal statute that makes it a felony, punishable by up to two years in prison, for failure to pay child support if the obligor has crossed state lines in an attempt to avoid paying the support. ● The Act provides felony penalties if (1) a person travels across state lines intending to evade a child-support obligation that is over $5,000 or that has remained unpaid longer than one year, or (2) a person willfully fails to pay support for a child living in a different state if that obligation is greater than $10,000 or if it remains unpaid for more than two years. The Act supersedes the Child Support Recovery Act of 1994. The greatest change in the new statute is the provision regarding the obligor's crossing of state lines in an effort to evade the support obligation. 42 USCA § 228. — Abbr. DPPA. See CHILD SUPPORT RECOVERY ACT OF 1994.

deadborn. See STILLBORN.

deadhand control. The convergence of various legal doctrines that allow a decedent's control of wealth to influence the conduct of a living beneficiary; esp., the use of executory interests that vest at some indefinite and remote time in the future to restrict alienability and to ensure that property remains in the hands of a particular family or organization. ● Examples include the lawful use of conditional gifts, contingent future interests, and the *Claflin*-trust principle. The rule against perpetuities restricts certain types of deadhand control, which is sometimes referred to either as the power of the *mortua manus* (dead hand) or as trying to retain property *in mortua manu*. See RULE AGAINST PERPETUITIES.

dead man's part. *Archaic.* By custom in certain places, the portion of a dead man's estate given to the administrator. ● That portion ranged from one-third (if the deceased had a wife and children) to the entire estate amount (if the deceased had no wife or children). — Also termed *death's part*; (in Scots law) *dead's part*.

dead man's statute. A law prohibiting the admission of a decedent's statement as evidence in certain circumstances, as when an opposing party or witness seeks to use the statement to support a claim against the decedent's estate. — Also termed *dead person's statute*.

dead's part. See DEAD MAN'S PART.

death. The ending of life; the cessation of all vital functions and signs. — Also termed *decease*; *demise*.

brain death. The bodily condition of showing no response to external stimuli, no spontaneous movements, no breathing, no reflexes, and a flat reading (usu. for a full day) on a machine that measures the brain's electrical activity. — Also termed *legal death*.

civil death. **1.** *Archaic*. At common law, the loss of rights — such as the rights to vote, make contracts, inherit, and sue — by a person who has been outlawed or convicted of a serious crime, or who is considered to have left the temporal world for the spiritual by entering a monastery. **2.** In some states, the loss of rights — such as the rights to vote and hold public office — by a person serving a life sentence. — Also termed *legal death*. Cf. *civil disability* under DISABILITY (2).

immediate death. **1.** See *instantaneous death*. **2.** A death occurring within a short time after an injury or seizure, but not instantaneously.

instantaneous death. Death occurring in an instant or within an extremely short time after an injury or seizure. ● It is a factor in determining an award of damages for the victim's pain and suffering. — Sometimes also termed *immediate death*.

legal death. **1.** See *brain death*. **2.** See *civil death*.

natural death. **1.** Bodily death, as opposed to civil death. **2.** Death from causes other than accident or violence; death from natural causes. — Also termed *mors naturalis*. See NATURAL-DEATH ACT.

presumptive death. Death inferred from proof of the person's long, unexplained absence, usu. after seven years. See ENOCH ARDEN LAW.

simultaneous death. The death of two or more persons in the same mishap, under circumstances that make it impossible to determine who died first. See UNIFORM SIMULTANEOUS DEATH ACT; COMMON DISASTER; COMMORIENTES.

death, contemplation of. See CONTEMPLATION OF DEATH.

death action. See WRONGFUL-DEATH ACTION.

deathbed declaration. See *dying declaration* under DECLARATION.

death benefits. A sum or sums paid to a beneficiary from a life-insurance policy on the death of an insured.

death case. See WRONGFUL-DEATH ACTION.

death certificate. An official document issued by a public registry verifying that a person has died, with information such as the date and time of death, the cause of death, and the signature of the attending or examining physician.

death's part. See DEAD MAN'S PART.

death statute. A law that protects the interests of a decedent's family and other dependents, who may recover in damages what they would reasonably have received from the decedent if the death had not occurred. Cf. SURVIVAL STATUTE.

death tax. See *estate tax* under TAX.

debt. Liability on a claim; a specific sum of money due by agreement or otherwise <the debt amounted to $2,500>.

    ancestral debt. An ancestor's debt that an heir can be compelled to pay.

    community debt. A debt that is chargeable to the community of husband and wife. See COMMUNITY PROPERTY.

decease. See DEATH.

deceased. See DECEDENT.

decedent (di-**see**-dənt), *n.* A dead person, esp. one who has died recently. • This term is little used outside law. It typically appears in legal proceedings or administrative inquiries. — Also termed *deceased*.

    nonresident decedent. A decedent who was domiciled outside the jurisdiction in question (such as probate jurisdiction) at the time of death.

decedent's estate. See ESTATE.

decision-making responsibility. The authority to make significant decisions on a child's behalf, including decisions about education, religious training, and healthcare. — Also termed (in some states) *legal custody*. *Principles of the Law of Family Dissolution: Analysis and Recommendations* § 2.03 (ALI, Tentative Draft No. 3, pt. I, 1998). See CUSTODY.

declaration, *n.* **1.** A formal statement, proclamation, or announcement, esp. one embodied in an instrument. Cf. AFFIDAVIT.

deathbed declaration. See *dying declaration*.

declaration of homestead. A statement required to be filed with a state or local authority to prove property ownership in order to claim homestead-exemption rights. See HOMESTEAD.

declaration of legitimacy. A formal or legal pronouncement that a child is legitimate.

declaration of trust. 1. The act by which the person who holds legal title to property or an estate acknowledges that the property is being held in trust for another person or for certain specified purposes. **2.** The instrument that creates a trust. — Also termed (in sense 2) *trust instrument*; *trust deed*; *trust agreement*.

dying declaration. A statement by a person who believes that death is imminent, relating to the cause or circumstances of the person's impending death. ● The statement is admissible in evidence as an exception to the hearsay rule. — Also termed *deathbed declaration*.

2. DECLARATORY JUDGMENT. **3.** See DECLARATION OF RIGHTS.

declaration of a desire for a natural death. See LIVING WILL.

declaration of homestead. See DECLARATION.

declaration of legitimacy. See DECLARATION.

declaration of rights. 1. An action in which a litigant requests a court's assistance not because any rights have been violated but because those rights are uncertain. ● Examples include suits for a declaration of legitimacy, for declaration of nullity of marriage, and for the authoritative interpretation of a will. **2.** DECLARATORY JUDGMENT. — Often shortened to *declaration*.

declaration of trust. See DECLARATION.

declaratory decree. See DECLARATORY JUDGMENT.

declaratory judgment. A binding adjudication that establishes the rights and other legal relations of the parties without providing for or ordering enforcement. — Also termed *declaratory decree*; *declaration*; *declaration of rights*.

decree, *n.* **1.** Traditionally, a judicial decision in a court of equity, admiralty, divorce, or probate — similar to a judgment of a court of law <the judge's decree in favor of the will's beneficiary>. **2.** Any court order, but esp. one in a matrimonial case <divorce decree>. See JUDGMENT; ORDER.

    agreed decree. A final judgment, the terms of which are agreed to by the parties.

    custody decree. A decree awarding or modifying child custody. ● The decree may be included in the decree for a related proceeding — such as a divorce — or it may be a separate order.

    decree of distribution. An instrument by which heirs receive the property of a deceased person.

    decree of insolvency. A probate-court decree declaring an estate's insolvency.

    decree of nullity. A decree declaring a marriage to be void *ab initio*. See NULLITY OF MARRIAGE.

    divorce decree. A final judgment in a suit for divorce. ● A divorce decree dissolves the marriage and usually resolves all matters concerning property and children. Generally, matters concerning children can be modified in a post-divorce action if there has been a substantial change in circumstances.

decree of distribution. See DECREE.

decree of insolvency. See DECREE.

decree of nullity. See DECREE.

decretal child support. See CHILD SUPPORT.

deduction, *n.* **1.** An amount subtracted from gross income when calculating adjusted gross income, or from adjusted gross income when calculating taxable income. — Also termed *tax deduction.* Cf. TAX CREDIT.

> **deduction in respect of a decedent.** A deduction that accrues to the point of death but is not recognizable on the decedent's final income-tax return because of the accounting method used, such as an accrued-interest expense of a cash-basis debtor.

> **marital deduction.** A federal tax deduction allowed for lifetime and testamentary transfers from one spouse to another. IRC (26 USCA) §§ 2056, 2523.

2. The portion of a succession to which an heir is entitled before a partition. — **deduct,** *vb.*

deduction in respect of a decedent. See DEDUCTION (1).

deemed transferor. *Tax.* A person who holds an interest in a generation-skipping trust on behalf of a beneficiary, and whose death will trigger the imposition of a generation-skipping transfer tax. • A *deemed transferor* is often a child of the settlor.

For example, a grandfather could establish a trust with income payable for life to his son (who, because he is only one generation away from his father, is also known as a *nonskip person*) with the remainder to his grandson, a beneficiary also known as the *skip person*. When the son dies, the trust will be included in his gross estate for determining the generation-skipping transfer tax. IRC (26 USCA) §§ 2601–2663. See GENERATION-SKIPPING TRANSFER; *generation-skipping transfer tax* under TAX; *generation-skipping trust* under TRUST; SKIP PERSON; NONSKIP PERSON.

de facto adoption. See ADOPTION.

de facto father. See *de facto parent* under PARENT.

de facto marriage. See MARRIAGE (1).

de facto mother. See *de facto parent* under PARENT.

de facto parent. See PARENT.

de facto stepparent adoption. See *second-parent adoption* under ADOPTION.

default (**dee**-fawlt), *n.* The omission or failure to perform a legal or contractual duty; esp., the failure to pay a debt when due. — **default** (di-**fawlt**), *vb.* — **defaulter,** *n.*

default judgment. See JUDGMENT.

default jurisdiction. See JURISDICTION.

defeasible remainder. See REMAINDER.

defective trust. See TRUST.

defendant (di-**fen**-dənt). A person sued in a civil proceeding or accused in a criminal proceeding. — Abbr. D. Cf. PLAINTIFF.

Defense of Marriage Act. A federal statute that (1) provides that no state can be required to recognize or give effect to same-sex marriages, (2) defines the term "marriage" for purposes of federal law as the union of a man and a woman as husband and wife, and (3) defines "spouse" for purposes of federal law as being only a person of the opposite sex. 28 USCA § 1738C. • The Defense of Marriage Act was enacted in response to the fear that if one state sanctioned same-sex marriages, other states might then have to give full faith and credit to those marriages. — Abbr. DOMA.

defined benefit plan. See EMPLOYEE BENEFIT PLAN.

defined-contribution plan. See EMPLOYEE BENEFIT PLAN.

defined pension plan. See PENSION PLAN.

definitive judgment. See *final judgment* under JUDGMENT.

defunct marriage. See MARRIAGE (1).

degree. In the line of descent, a measure of removal determining the proximity of a blood or marital relationship <the council member did not participate in the vote because he was related to one of the bidders within the first degree of consanguinity>. • In the civil law, and in the degree-of-relationship system used by many American jurisdictions, an intestate estate passes to the closest of kin, counting degrees of kinship. To calculate the degree of relationship of the decedent to the claimant, one counts the steps (one for each generation) up from the decedent to the nearest common ancestor of the decedent and the claimant, and on down to the claimant from the common ancestor. The total number of steps is the degree of relationship. For example, a decedent's cousin stands in the fourth degree of relationship. Degrees of relationship are used not only to determine who is the closest heir but also to establish the incest prohibition in marriage requirements. — Also termed *degree of kin*; *degree of relationship*. See AFFINITY (2); CONSANGUINITY.

equal degree. A relationship between two or more relatives who are the same number of steps away from a common ancestor.

prohibited degree. A degree of relationship so close (as between brother and sister) that marriage between the persons is forbidden by law. • Generally, with slight variations from jurisdiction to jurisdiction, the law forbids marriages between all persons lineally related and within the third civil-law degree of relationship. That is, aunt–nephew and uncle–niece relations are prohibited. Prohibited degrees are also known as *Levitical degrees*, since the incest prohibition is pronounced in the Bible in Leviticus 18:6–18. — Also termed *forbidden degree*.

degree of kin. See DEGREE.

degree of relationship. See DEGREE.

delinquency, *n.* **1.** A failure or omission; a violation of a law or duty. See JUVENILE DELINQUENCY. **2.** A debt that is overdue in payment.

delinquency jurisdiction. See JURISDICTION.

delinquent, *adj.* **1.** (Of a person) failing to perform an obligation. **2.** (Of a person) guilty of serious antisocial or criminal conduct. **3.** (Of an obligation) past due or unperformed.

delinquent, *n.* **1.** A person who fails to perform an obligation. **2.** A person guilty of serious antisocial or criminal conduct. **3.** JUVENILE DELINQUENT.

delinquent child. See CHILD.

delinquent minor. See JUVENILE DELINQUENT.

delivery, *n.* **1.** The formal act of transferring or conveying something, such as a deed; the giving or yielding possession or control of something to another. **2.** The thing so transferred or conveyed. — **deliver,** *vb.* Cf. LIVERY.

absolute delivery. A delivery that is complete upon the actual transfer of the instrument from the grantor's possession. ● Such a delivery does not usually depend on recordation.

actual delivery. The act of giving real and immediate possession to the buyer or the buyer's agent.

conditional delivery. A delivery that passes possession only upon the happening of a specified event.

constructive delivery. An act that amounts to a transfer of title by operation of law when actual transfer is impractical or impossible. ● For example, the delivery of a deposit-box key by someone who is ill and immobile amounts to a constructive delivery of the box's contents even though the box may be miles away.

symbolic delivery. The constructive delivery of the subject matter of a sale by the actual delivery of an article that represents the item, that renders access to it possible, or that provides evidence of the purchaser's title to it, such as the key to a warehouse or a bill of lading for goods on shipboard.

unconditional delivery. A delivery that immediately passes both possession and title and that takes effect immediately.

demise. See DEATH.

demonstrative bequest. See BEQUEST.

demonstrative devise. See DEVISE.

demonstrative legacy. See LEGACY.

Department of Social Services. See CHILD PROTECTIVE SERVICES. — Abbr. DSS.

dependency court. See COURT.

dependency exemption. A tax exemption granted to an individual taxpayer for each dependent whose gross income is less than the exemption amount and for each child who is younger than 19 or, if a student, younger than 24.

dependency hearing. See *shelter hearing* under HEARING.

dependent, *n.* **1.** One who relies on another for support; one not able to exist or sustain oneself without the power or aid of someone else.

lawful dependent. **1.** One who receives an allowance or benefits from the public, such as social security. **2.** One who qualifies to receive a benefit from private funds as determined within the terms of the laws governing the distribution.

legal dependent. A person who is dependent according to the law; a person who derives principal support from another and usu. may invoke laws to enforce that support.

2. *Tax.* A relative, such as a child or parent, for whom a taxpayer may claim a personal exemption if the taxpayer provides more than half of the person's support during the taxable year. — **dependent,** *adj.*

dependent child. See CHILD.

dependent relative revocation. A common-law doctrine that operates to undo an otherwise sufficient revocation of a will when there is evidence that the testator's revocation was conditional rather than absolute. • Typically, the doctrine applies when a testator has physically revoked the will and believes that a new will is valid, although this belief is mistaken. The doctrine undoes only the revocation; it does not always accomplish the testator's intent or validate an otherwise invalid will. — Also termed *dependent-relative-revocation doctrine*; *ineffective revocation*; *doctrine of ineffective revocation*.

deponent. See AFFIANT.

deprived child. See CHILD.

171

derogatory clause. A clause that a testator secretly inserts in a will, containing a provision that any later will not having that precise clause is invalid. ● A derogatory clause seeks to protect against a later will extorted by undue influence, duress, or violence.

descend, *vb.* To pass (a decedent's property) by intestate succession.

descendant (di-**sen**-dənt), *n.* One who follows in lineage, in direct (not collateral) descent from a person. ● Examples are children and grandchildren. — **descendant,** *adj.* Cf. ASCENDANT.

    collateral descendant. Loosely, a blood relative who is not strictly a descendant, like a niece or nephew.

    lineal descendant. A blood relative in the direct line of descent. ● Children, grandchildren, and great-grandchildren are lineal descendants.

descendible, *adj.* (Of property) capable of passing by descent or being inherited.

descent, *n.* **1.** The acquisition of real property by law, as by inheritance; the passing of intestate real property to heirs. See SUCCESSION (2). Cf. DISTRIBUTION (1); PURCHASE. **2.** The fact or process of originating from a common ancestor. — **descend,** *vb.*

    collateral descent. Descent in a collateral or oblique line, from brother to brother or cousin to cousin. ● With collateral descent, the donor and donee are related through a common ancestor.

direct-line descent. See *lineal descent.*

immediate descent. **1.** A descent directly to an heir, as from a grandmother to granddaughter, brought about by the earlier death of the mother. **2.** A direct descent without an intervening link in consanguinity, as from mother to daughter.

lineal descent. Descent in a direct or straight line, as from father or grandfather to son or grandson. — Also termed *direct-line descent.*

maternal-line descent. Descent between two persons, traced through the mother of the younger.

mediate descent. **1.** A descent not occurring immediately, as when a granddaughter receives land from her grandmother, which first passed to the mother. **2.** A direct descent occurring through a link in consanguinity, as when a granddaughter receives land from her grandfather directly.

paternal-line descent. Descent between two persons, traced through the father of the younger.

descent and distribution. 1. INTESTATE SUCCESSION. **2.** Broadly, the rules by which a decedent's property is passed, whether by intestate succession or by will.

desertion. The willful and unjustified abandonment of a person's duties or obligations, esp. to a spouse or family. ● The five elements of spousal desertion are usually described as (1) a cessation of cohabitation, (2) the lapse of a statutory period, (3) AN INTENTION TO ABANDON, (4) a lack of consent from the abandoned spouse, and (5) a lack of spousal misconduct that might justify the abandonment. Cf. ABANDONMENT.

> **constructive desertion.** One spouse's misconduct that forces the other spouse to leave the marital abode. ● The actions of the offending spouse must be serious enough that the spouse who is forced from the home finds the continuation of the marriage to be unendurable or dangerous to his or her safety and well-being, and finds it necessary to seek safety outside the marital domicile. — Also termed *constructive abandonment.*

> **criminal desertion.** One spouse's willful failure without just cause to provide for the care, protection, or support of the other spouse who is in ill health or needy circumstances.

> **obstinate desertion.** Desertion by a spouse who persistently refuses to return to the marital home, so that the other spouse has grounds for divorce. ● Before the advent of no-fault divorce, this term was commonly used in divorce statutes. The term was often part of the longer phrase *willful, continued, and obstinate desertion.*

willful, continued, and obstinate desertion.
See *obstinate desertion*.

destructible trust. See TRUST.

detention, pretrial. See PRETRIAL DETENTION.

detention hearing. See HEARING.

determinative judgment. See *final judgment* under JUDGMENT.

deuterogamy (d[y]oo-tər-**og**-ə-mee), *n.* [fr. Greek *deuterogamia* "second marriage"] A second marriage after the death of or divorce from the first spouse, or after an annulment of a first marriage. — Also termed *digama*; *digamy*.

developmental disability. See DISABILITY (1).

developmental neglect. See NEGLECT.

devise (di-**viz**), *n.* **1.** The act of giving property by will. ● Although this term traditionally referred to gifts of real property — and in British usage the term is still confined to real property — in American usage the term has been considerably broadened. In both the Restatement of Property and the Uniform Probate Code, a disposition of any property by will is a devise. In the United States today, it is pedantry to insist that the noun *devise* be restricted to real property. **2.** The provision in a will containing such a gift. **3.** Property disposed of in a will. **4.** A will disposing of property. Cf. TESTAMENT (1). — **devise,** *vb.* Cf. BEQUEST; LEGACY.

alternative devise. A devise that, under the terms of the will, is designed to displace another devise if one or more specified events occur.

conditional devise. A devise that depends on the occurrence of some uncertain event.

demonstrative devise. A devise, usu. of a specific amount of money or quantity of property, that is primarily payable from a designated source, but that may be payable from the estate's general assets if the designated property is insufficient. Restatement (Third) of Property: Wills and Other Donative Transfers § 5.1 (Tentative Draft No. 2, 1998). Cf. *pecuniary devise.*

executory devise. An interest in land, created by will, that takes effect in the future and depends on a future contingency; a limitation, by will, of a future estate or interest in land when the limitation cannot, consistently with legal rules, take effect as a remainder. • An executory devise, which is a type of conditional limitation, differs from a remainder in three ways: (1) it needs no particular estate to support it, (2) with it a fee simple or lesser estate can be limited after a fee simple, and (3) with it a remainder can be limited in a chattel interest after a particular estate for life is created in that interest.

general devise. **1.** A devise, usu. of a specific amount of money or quantity of property, that is payable from the estate's general assets. Restatement (Third) of Property: Wills and Other Donative Transfers § 5.1 (Tentative Draft No. 2, 1998). **2.** A devise that passes the testator's lands without specifically enumerating or describing them.

lapsed devise. A devise that fails because the devisor outlives the named recipient.

pecuniary devise. A demonstrative devise consisting of money. Cf. *demonstrative devise*.

primary devise. A devise to the first person named as taker. ● For example, a devise of "Blackacre to A, but if A does not survive me then to B" names A as the recipient of the primary devise and B as the recipient of the secondary or alternative devise.

residuary devise. A devise of the remainder of the testator's property left after other specific devises are taken.

secondary devise. See *alternative devise*.

specific devise. A devise that passes a particular piece of property.

younger-generation devise. An alternative devise to a descendant of the recipient of a primary devise. Unif. Probate Code § 206-3. ● A devise of "Blackacre to A but if A does not survive me then

to A's child B" creates a younger-generation devise in A's descendant, B. See *alternative devise*.

devisee (dev-ə-**zee** *or* di-vī-**zee**). A recipient of
property by will. Cf. LEGATEE.

> *first devisee.* The first devisee designated to
> receive an estate under a will.

> *next devisee.* The devisee who receives the re-
> mainder of an estate in tail, as distinguished from
> the first devisee. See FEE TAIL.

> *residuary devisee.* The person named in a will
> who takes the testator's property that remains
> after the other devises.

devisor. One who disposes of property (usu. real
property) in a will.

digamy. See DEUTEROGAMY.

dilatory fiduciary. See FIDUCIARY.

diminished capacity. See CAPACITY.

diminished responsibility. See *diminished capacity* under CAPACITY.

direct adoption. See *private adoption* under ADOP-
TION.

direct affinity. See AFFINITY.

direct beneficiary. See *intended beneficiary* under BENEFICIARY.

directive. See ADVANCE DIRECTIVE.

directive to physicians. See LIVING WILL.

direct line. See LINE.

direct-line descent. See *lineal descent* under DESCENT.

directory trust. See TRUST.

direct payment. A child-support payment made directly to the obligee parent rather than through the court.

direct placement. See PRIVATE PLACEMENT.

direct-placement adoption. See *private adoption* under ADOPTION.

direct skip. *Tax.* A generation-skipping transfer of assets, either directly or through a trust. ● A direct skip may be subject to a generation-skipping transfer tax — either a gift tax or an estate tax. IRC (26 USCA) §§ 2601–2602. See GENERATION-SKIPPING TRANSFER; *generation-skipping transfer tax* under TAX; SKIP PERSON.

direct trust. See *express trust* under TRUST.

diriment impediment. See IMPEDIMENT.

disability. 1. The inability to perform some function; an objectively measurable condition of impairment, physical or mental <his disability entitled him to workers'-compensation benefits>. — Also termed *incapacity*.

> *developmental disability.* An impairment of general intellectual functioning or adaptive behavior.

> *partial disability.* A worker's inability to perform all the duties that he or she could do before an accident or illness, even though the worker can still engage in some gainful activity on the job.

> *permanent disability.* A disability that will indefinitely prevent a worker from performing some or all of the duties that he or she could do before an accident or illness.

> *physical disability.* An incapacity caused by a physical defect or infirmity, or by bodily imperfection or mental weakness.

> *temporary disability.* A disability that exists until an injured worker is as far restored as the nature of the injury will permit.

> *temporary total disability.* Total disability that is not permanent.

total disability. A worker's inability to perform employment-related duties because of a physical or mental impairment.

2. Incapacity in the eyes of the law <most of a minor's disabilities are removed when he or she turns 18>. — Also termed *incapacity*.

civil disability. The condition of a person who has had a legal right or privilege revoked as a result of a criminal conviction, as when a person's driver's license is revoked after a DWI conviction. Cf. *civil death* (2) under DEATH.

disability retirement plan. See EMPLOYEE BENEFIT PLAN.

disclaimer, *n.* **1.** A renunciation of one's legal right or claim. **2.** A repudiation of another's legal right or claim. **3.** A writing that contains such a renunciation or repudiation. **4.** RENUNCIATION (2). — **disclaim,** *vb.*

discretionary-transfer statute. See TRANSFER STATUTE.

discretionary trust. See TRUST.

discrimination, *n.* **1.** The effect of a law or established practice that confers privileges on a certain class or that denies privileges to a certain class because of race, age, sex, nationality, religion, or handicap. • Federal law, including Title VII of the

Civil Rights Act, prohibits employment discrimination based on any one of those characteristics. Other federal statutes, supplemented by court decisions, prohibit discrimination in voting rights, housing, credit extension, public education, and access to public facilities. State laws provide further protections against discrimination. **2.** Differential treatment; esp., a failure to treat all persons equally when no reasonable distinction can be found between those favored and those not favored.

age discrimination. Discrimination based on age. ● Federal law prohibits age discrimination in employment against people who are age 40 or older.

gender discrimination. See *sex discrimination.*

invidious discrimination (in-**vid**-ee-əs). Discrimination that is offensive or objectionable, esp. because it involves prejudice or stereotyping.

racial discrimination. Discrimination based on race.

reverse discrimination. Preferential treatment of minorities, usu. through affirmative-action programs, in a way that adversely affects members of a majority group.

sex discrimination. Discrimination based on gender, esp. against women. ● The Supreme Court has established an intermediate-scrutiny standard of review for gender-based classifications, which must serve an important governmental interest and be substantially related to the achievement of that objective. *Craig v. Boren*, 429 U.S. 190, 97 S.Ct. 451 (1976). — Also termed *gender discrimination*.

viewpoint discrimination. Discrimination based on the content of a communication. • If restrictions on the content of speech are reasonable and not calculated to suppress a particular set of views or ideas, a governmental body may limit speech in a nonpublic forum to expressions that serve a specific purpose. For example, an agency holding a workshop to inform state employees of laws related to the agency's functions may reasonably prohibit the expression of opinions regarding the motives of the legislators. But if speech favorable to the legislators' intent is allowed and opponents are denied the opportunity to respond, the restriction would constitute viewpoint discrimination.

3. The effect of state laws that favor local interests over out-of-state interests. • Such a discriminatory state law may still be upheld if it is narrowly tailored to achieve an important state interest. — **discriminate,** *vb.* — **discriminatory,** *adj.*

disherison (dis-**her**-ə-zən). See DISINHERITANCE.

disheritor (dis-**her**-ə-tər *or* -tor). *Archaic.* A person who deprives someone of an inheritance.

disinherison. See DISINHERITANCE.

disinheritance, *n.* **1.** The act by which an owner of an estate deprives a would-be heir of the expectancy to inherit the estate. • A testator may expressly exclude or limit the right of a person or a class to inherit property that the person or class would have inherited through intestate succession. **2.** The state of being disinherited. — Also termed *disherison*; *disinherison*. — **disinherit,** *vb.* See *forced heir* under HEIR.

Disneyland parent. See PARENT.

disobedient child. See *incorrigible child* under CHILD.

disposable portion. The portion of property that can be willed to anyone the testator chooses.

disposing capacity. See *testamentary capacity* under CAPACITY.

disposition (dis-pə-**zish**-ən), *n.* The act of transferring something to another's care or possession, esp. by deed or will; the relinquishing of property <a testamentary disposition of all the assets>.

dispositional hearing. 1. See *disposition hearing* under HEARING. **2.** See *permanency hearing* under HEARING.

disposition hearing. See HEARING.

dispute resolution. See ALTERNATIVE DISPUTE RESO-LUTION.

dissipation, *n.* The use of an asset for an illegal or inequitable purpose, such as a spouse's use of com-munity property for personal benefit when a divorce is imminent. — **dissipate,** *vb.*

dissociative amnesia. See REPRESSED-MEMORY SYN-DROME.

dissolution of marriage. 1. DIVORCE. **2.** *Archaic.* A divorce-like remedy available when both spouses have signed a separation agreement that deals with (1) the issue of alimony (providing either some or none), and (2) if there are children, the issues of support, custody, and visitation. ● Under a dissolu-tion of marriage in this sense, the court is bound by the separation agreement and cannot later modify alimony payments. Courts in jurisdictions where the term has been used in this specific sense tradi-tionally distinguish it from *divorce*, which was for-merly available only on certain grounds and which allowed the court to modify alimony payments.

distributee (di-strib-yoo-**tee**), *n.* **1.** A beneficiary entitled to payment. **2.** An heir, esp. one who ob-tains personal property from the estate of an intes-tate decedent.

legal distributee. A person whom the law would entitle to take property under a will.

distribution, *n*. **1.** At common law, the passing of personal property to an intestate decedent's heirs. Cf. DESCENT (1). **2.** The act or process of apportioning or giving out. — **distribute,** *vb*.

> ***probate distribution.*** The judicially supervised apportionment and division — usu. after the payment of debts and charges — of assets of an estate among those legally entitled to share.

> ***trust distribution.*** The cash or other property paid or credited to a trust beneficiary.

distributive clause. A will or trust provision governing the distribution of income and gifts.

distributive deviation. A trustee's authorized or unauthorized departure from the express distributional terms of a trust. ● A trustee must apply to the court for authority to deviate from the terms of a trust. In American law, courts rarely authorize deviation unless all the beneficiaries consent and there is no material purpose of the settlor yet to be served. Some state statutes provide that deviation is permitted if the court finds that deviation would effectuate the settlor's intention, though the modification is not expressly authorized by the trust's provisions. The Pulitzer trust illustrates the possibility that extraordinary circumstances not anticipated by the settlor may justify deviation, even despite an express prohibition within the trust.

Joseph Pulitzer set up a testamentary trust with shares of *World* newspaper stock; his will directed that the sale of these shares was not authorized under any circumstances. Nonetheless, the court later approved the stock sale when given evidence that because of hemorrhaging losses, the trust's continuation was jeopardized. *In re Pulitzer's Estate*, 249 N.Y.S. 87 (Sur. Ct. 1931).

distributive share. The share that an heir or beneficiary receives from the legal distribution of an estate.

district judge. See JUDGE.

diversion program. A community-based program or set of services designed to prevent the need for court intervention in matters of child neglect, minor juvenile delinquency, truancy, or incorrigibility. ● Sustained by government funding, the program provides services quickly and in a nonadversarial manner so that there is no need for a formal court trial.

divided custody. See CUSTODY.

divisible divorce. See DIVORCE.

division of property. See PROPERTY SETTLEMENT (1).

divorce. The legal dissolution of a marriage by a court. — Also termed *marital dissolution*; *dissolution of marriage*. — **divorce,** *vb.* Cf. ANNULMENT.

absolute divorce. See *divorce a vinculo matrimonii.*

bifurcated divorce. See *divisible divorce.*

contested divorce. 1. A divorce that one spouse opposes in court. 2. A divorce in which the spouses litigate. ● In this sense, although both spouses may want the divorce, they disagree on the terms of the divorce decree. Cf. *uncontested divorce.*

conversion divorce. A divorce granted after (1) a legal separation has been granted or the parties have signed a separation agreement, and (2) the parties have lived separately for a statutorily prescribed period. — Also termed *convertible divorce.*

divisible divorce. A divorce whereby the marriage itself is dissolved but the issues incident to the divorce, such as alimony, child custody, and visitation, are reserved until a later proceeding. ● This type of divorce can be granted when the court has subject-matter jurisdiction but lacks personal jurisdiction over the defendant-spouse. The doctrine of divisible divorce was recognized by the Supreme Court in *Estin v. Estin*, 334 U.S. 541, 68 S.Ct. 1213 (1948), and *Vanderbilt v. Vanderbilt*, 354 U.S. 416, 77 S.Ct. 1360 (1957). — Also termed *bifurcated divorce.*

divorce a mensa et thoro (ay **men**-sə et **thor**-oh). [Latin "(divorce) from board and hearth"] *Hist.* A partial or qualified divorce by which the parties were separated and forbidden to live together, but remained technically married. ● This type of divorce, abolished in England in 1857, was the forerunner of modern judicial separation. — Also termed *separation a mensa et thoro*; *separation from bed and board*; *limited divorce*; *legal separation*; *judicial separation*.

divorce a vinculo matrimonii (ay **ving**-kyə-loh ma-trə-**moh**-nee-ı). [Latin "(divorce) from the chains of marriage"] A total divorce of husband and wife, dissolving the marriage tie and releasing the parties wholly from their matrimonial obligations. ● At common law, this type of divorce bastardized any children from the marriage and was granted on grounds that existed before the marriage. In England, the Matrimonial Causes Act of 1857 introduced statutory divorce *a vinculo matrimonii*. — Usu. shortened to *divorce*. — Also termed *absolute divorce*. Cf. *limited divorce*.

Dominican divorce. See *Mexican divorce*.

ex parte divorce (eks **pahr**-tee). A divorce proceeding in which only one spouse participates or appears in court.

fault divorce. A divorce granted to one spouse on the basis of some proven wrongful act (grounds for divorce) by the other spouse. ● Although all states now have some form of no-fault divorce, some jurisdictions still consider a spouse's fault in precipitating the divorce, especially when dividing marital property or when awarding alimony. Traditionally, the common grounds for a fault divorce were adultery, abandonment, imprisonment, and physical or mental cruelty; the defenses to alleged fault in a petition for divorce were condonation, connivance, collusion, recrimination, and insanity. Section 303(e) of the Uniform Marriage and Divorce Act has abolished the defenses to divorce. Cf. *no-fault divorce.*

foreign divorce. A divorce obtained outside the state or country in which one spouse resides.

hotel divorce. *Slang.* A form of collusive divorce — occurring before widespread passage of no-fault divorce laws — in which the spouses agree to fake an adultery scene to create "fault." Cf. *no-fault divorce.*

legislative divorce. *Hist.* The legal termination of a particular marriage, enacted by the legislature rather than by a court. ● In the 18th century, Colonial American legislatures granted these special statutes. In 1816, the House of Burgesses of Virginia granted a divorce to Rachel Robards Jackson, the wife of then President Andrew Jackson, from a former spouse. Mrs. Jackson's untimely death was attributed to her reaction to the scandal that she had married Jackson before the divorce was procured. Now only state courts have authority to grant decrees of divorce. — Also termed *parliamentary divorce.*

limited divorce. **1.** A divorce that ends the legal relationship of marriage by court order but does not address financial support, property distribution, or care and custody of children. • In the days before no-fault divorce, a spouse might seek a quick divorce in a state with a short residency requirement (such as Nevada). Then courts in the home state would give full faith and credit only to the dissolution of the marital res, while maintaining sole jurisdiction over property-division, support, and custody issues. **2.** Loosely, a legal separation. **3.** See *divorce a mensa et thoro.* Cf. *divorce a vinculo matrimonii.*

mail-order divorce. *Slang.* A divorce obtained by parties who are not physically present or domiciled in the jurisdiction purporting to grant the divorce. • Such a divorce is not recognized in the United States because of the absence of the usual bases for jurisdiction.

Mexican divorce. A divorce obtained in Mexico by mail order or by the appearance of one spouse who does not have a Mexican domicile. • Neither type is recognized in the United States. — Also termed *Dominican divorce* (if granted in the Dominican Republic).

migratory divorce. A divorce obtained in a jurisdiction other than the marital domicile; esp., a divorce obtained by a spouse who moves to, or temporarily resides in, another state or country to get the divorce.

no-fault divorce. A divorce in which the parties are not required to prove fault or grounds beyond a showing of the irretrievable breakdown of the marriage or irreconcilable differences. ● The system of no-fault divorce has been adopted throughout the United States. By 1974, 45 states had adopted no-fault divorce; by 1985, every state but New York had adopted some form of it. In New York — one of the last bastions of fault grounds for divorce — the closest equivalent is a conversion divorce one year after legal separation or a legal-separation agreement. Cf. *fault divorce*; *hotel divorce*.

parliamentary divorce. See *legislative divorce*.

pro–con divorce. *Slang.* An uncontested divorce granted after only the plaintiff appears at the proceeding (since the defendant contests nothing).

quickie divorce. *Slang.* A fast divorce granted with minimal paperwork. — Also termed *quick divorce*.

rabbinical divorce. A divorce granted under the authority of a rabbi. ● This type of divorce affects the relationship of the parties under the tenets of Judaism. It affects particularly a Jewish woman's ability to remarry in accordance with Judaic law. In the United States, it is not generally a divorce recognized in civil courts. — Also termed *get*.

uncontested divorce. A divorce that is unopposed by the spouse who did not initiate it. Cf. *contested divorce*.

divorce agreement. A contractual agreement that sets out divorcing spouses' rights and responsibilities regarding property, alimony, custody, visitation, and child support. ● The divorce agreement usually becomes incorporated by court order as a part of the divorce decree and thus is enforceable by contempt, among other remedies. — Also termed *agreement incident to divorce*; *marital settlement agreement*; *separation agreement*. Cf. PROPERTY SETTLEMENT.

divorce *a mensa et thoro.* See DIVORCE.

divorce *a vinculo matrimonii.* See DIVORCE.

divorce decree. See DECREE.

divorce proctor. A person (such as a guardian) who is appointed to protect the interest of the state or children in a divorce action. — Sometimes shortened to *proctor*.

DNA identification. A method of comparing a person's deoxyribonucleic acid (DNA) — a patterned chemical structure of genetic information — with the DNA in a biological specimen (such as blood, tissue, or hair) to determine whether the person is the source of the specimen. — Also termed *DNA fingerprinting*; *genetic fingerprinting*. Cf. HU-MAN-LEUKOCYTE ANTIGEN TEST.

docket, *n.* **1.** A formal record in which a judge or court clerk briefly notes all the proceedings and filings in a court case <review the docket to determine the filing date>. — Also termed *judicial record*. **2.** A schedule of pending cases <the case is third on Monday's trial docket>. — Also termed *court calendar*; *cause list*; *trial calendar*.

docket, *vb.* **1.** To make a brief entry in the docket of the proceedings and filings in a court case <to docket the filing date>. **2.** To schedule (a case) for trial or some other event <the case was docketed for a May trial>.

docket number. A number that the court clerk assigns to a case on the court's docket.

doctor–patient privilege. See PRIVILEGE.

doctrine of approximation. A doctrine that authorizes a court to vary the details of a trust's administration to preserve the trust and to carry out the donor's intentions. — Also termed *equitable doctrine of approximation*. Cf. CY PRES.

doctrine of ineffective revocation. See DEPENDENT RELATIVE REVOCATION.

doctrine of legal unities. See LEGAL-UNITIES DOCTRINE.

doctrine of marital privacy. See MARITAL-PRIVACY DOCTRINE.

doctrine of necessaries. 1. The rule holding a parent or spouse liable to anyone who sells goods or provides medical services to that person's child or spouse if the goods or services are required for sustenance, support, or healthcare. **2.** *Archaic.* The common-law rule holding a husband or father liable to anyone who sells goods to his wife or child if the goods are required for sustenance or support. See NECESSARIES.

doctrine of separate spheres. See SEPARATE-SPHERES DOCTRINE.

doctrine of spousal unity. See SPOUSAL-UNITY DOCTRINE.

doctrine of substituted judgment. See SUBSTITUTED-JUDGMENT DOCTRINE.

doctrine of worthier title. See WORTHIER-TITLE DOCTRINE.

DOMA. *abbr.* DEFENSE OF MARRIAGE ACT.

domestic abuse. See ABUSE.

domestic authority. 1. The legal power to use nondeadly force when reasonably necessary to protect a person for whom one is responsible. **2.** A defense allowing a person responsible for another (such as a parent responsible for a child) to use nondeadly force when reasonably necessary to protect the person being cared for.

domestic court. See COURT.

domestic dispute. A disturbance, usu. at a residence and usu. within a family, involving violence and often resulting in a call to a law-enforcement agency. — Also termed *domestic disturbance*; *family disturbance*. See *domestic violence* under VIOLENCE.

domestic disturbance. See DOMESTIC DISPUTE.

domestic guardian. See GUARDIAN.

domestic partnership. 1. A nonmarital relationship between two persons of the same or opposite sex who share a residence and live as a couple for a significant period of time. *Principles of the Law of Family Dissolution: Analysis and Recommendations* § 6.01 (ALI, Tentative Draft No. 4, 2000). **2.** A relationship that an employer or governmental entity recognizes as equivalent to marriage for the purpose of extending employee-partner benefits otherwise reserved for the spouses of employees. — **domestic partner,** *n*. Cf. CIVIL UNION; *same-sex marriage* under MARRIAGE (1).

domestic-partnership law. A legislative enactment, often a municipal ordinance, that grants unmarried adults living in economically or emotionally based relationships, regardless of their sexual preference, some of the rights of a civil marriage without attempting to change the traditional definition of marriage.

domestic-partnership period. The period beginning when domestic partners begin sharing a primary residence, unless both partners show that they did not begin sharing a life as a couple until a later time, and ending when the partners stop sharing a primary residence. *Principles of the Law of Family Dissolution: Analysis and Recommendations* § 6.04 (ALI, Tentative Draft No. 4, 2000). See DO-MESTIC PARTNERSHIP.

domestic-partnership property. See PROPERTY.

domestic relations. See FAMILY LAW.

domestic-relations court. See *family court* under COURT.

domestic-relations exception. The exclusion of suits regarding the granting of divorce, alimony, and child custody from federal diversity jurisdiction. • The domestic-relations exemption to federal diversity jurisdiction originated as dictum in *Barber v. Barber*, 62 U.S. (21 How.) 582 (1858). Federal courts do not have jurisdiction to grant divorces, award alimony, or determine child custody. In general, matters of domestic relations are left to the states. But the federal courts may hear other diversity matters involving family members, such as tort claims or suits seeking to enforce alimony orders. *Ankenbrandt v. Richards*, 504 U.S. 689, 112 S.Ct. 2206 (1992).

domestic-relations law. See FAMILY LAW.

domestic tort. See *marital tort* under TORT.

domestic violence. See VIOLENCE.

domicile (**dom**-ə-sɪl), *n.* **1.** The place at which a person is physically present and that the person regards as home; a person's true, fixed, principal, and permanent home, to which that person intends to return and remain even though currently residing elsewhere. — Also termed *permanent abode*. **2.** The residence of a person or corporation for legal purposes. — Also termed (in sense 2) *legal residence*. Cf. RESIDENCE.

> **domicile of choice. 1.** A domicile established by physical presence within a state or territory, coupled with the intention to make it home. **2.** The domicile that a person chooses after reaching majority or being emancipated.

> **domicile of origin.** The domicile of a person at birth, derived from the custodial parent or imposed by law. — Also termed *natural domicile*. See *necessary domicile*.

> **domicile of succession.** The domicile that determines the succession of a person's estate.

domicile of trustee. The domicile where a trustee is appointed.

matrimonial domicile. A domicile that a husband and wife, as a married couple, have established as their home. — Also termed *marital domicile*; *matrimonial home.*

natural domicile. See *domicile of origin.*

necessary domicile. A domicile legally fixed and independent of choice, as in the domicile of origin. See *domicile of origin.*

domicile of choice. See DOMICILE.

domicile of origin. See DOMICILE.

domicile of succession. See DOMICILE.

domicile of trustee. See DOMICILE.

domiciliary (dom-ə-**sil**-ee-er-ee), *adj.* Of or relating to domicile <domiciliary jurisdiction>.

domiciliary (dom-ə-**sil**-ee-er-ee), *n.* A person who resides in a particular place with the intention of making it a principal place of abode; one who is domiciled in a particular jurisdiction. Cf. RESIDENT; CITIZEN.

domiciliary administration. See ADMINISTRATION.

domiciliary parent. See PARENT.

Dominican divorce. See *Mexican divorce* under DI-VORCE.

donatio causa mortis. See *gift causa mortis* under GIFT.

donatio mortis causa, *n.* See *gift causa mortis* under GIFT. Pl. **donationes mortis causa.**

donative intent. See INTENT.

donative trust. See TRUST.

donee (doh-**nee**). One to whom a gift is made.

donee of power. The recipient of a power of appointment.

donor. 1. One who gives something without receiving consideration for the transfer. **2.** SETTLOR.

dos rationabilis. See *dower by the common law* under DOWER.

dotal property. See PROPERTY.

double adultery. See ADULTERY.

double will. See *mutual will* under WILL.

dower (**dow**-ər). At common law, the right of a wife, upon her husband's death, to a life estate in one-third of the land that he owned in fee. ● With few exceptions, the wife could not be deprived of dower by any transfer made by her husband during his lifetime. Although most states have abolished dower, many states retaining the concept have expanded the wife's share to a life estate in all the land that her husband owned in fee. — Also termed *dowment*. Cf. CURTESY.

>*consummate dower* (kən-**səm**-it *or* **kahn**-sə-mit). A wife's interest in her deceased husband's estate until that interest is legally assigned to her.

>*dower by the common law*. The regular dower, consisting of a life interest in one-third of the lands that the husband held in fee. — Also termed *dos rationabilis*.

>*inchoate dower* (in-**koh**-it). A wife's interest in her husband's estate while both are living.

dower by the common law. See DOWER.

doweress. See DOWRESS.

dowment. See DOWER.

dowress (**dow**-ris). *Archaic*. **1.** A woman legally entitled to dower. **2.** A tenant in dower. — Also spelled *doweress*.

dowry (**dow**-ree). *Archaic*. The money, goods, or property that a woman brings to her husband in marriage. — Also termed *marriage portion*; *marita-gium* (mar-ə-**tay**-jee-əm); *maritage* (**ma**-ri-tij).

DPPA. *abbr.* DEADBEAT PARENTS PUNISHMENT ACT.

drug court. See COURT.

dry trust. See *passive trust* under TRUST.

DSS. *abbr.* DEPARTMENT OF SOCIAL SERVICES.

dual inheritance. See INHERITANCE.

dual-residential parent. See PARENT.

due course of law. See DUE PROCESS.

due process. The conduct of legal proceedings according to established rules and principles for the protection and enforcement of private rights, including notice and the right to a fair hearing before a tribunal with the power to decide the case. — Also termed *due process of law*; *due course of law*. See FUNDAMENTAL-FAIRNESS DOCTRINE.

> **procedural due process.** The minimal requirements of notice and a hearing guaranteed by the Due Process Clauses of the 5th and 14th Amendments, esp. if the deprivation of a significant life, liberty, or property interest may occur. ● The Supreme Court has ruled that the fundamental guarantees of due process apply to children as well as to adults and that they apply in situations

in which a juvenile may be deprived of liberty even though the juvenile proceedings may be labeled civil rather than criminal. *In re Gault*, 387 U.S. 1, 87 S.Ct. 1428 (1967). In that case, the Court held that an accused child was entitled to notice of the charges, the privilege against self-incrimination, the right to confront witnesses, and the right to summon witnesses on his or her own behalf. Justice Abe Fortas wrote the majority opinion in *Gault*, and Chief Justice Earl Warren predicted that it would come to be called the "Magna Carta for juveniles."

substantive due process. The doctrine that the Due Process Clauses of the 5th and 14th Amendments require legislation to be fair and reasonable in content and to further a legitimate governmental objective.

Due Process Clause. The constitutional provision that prohibits the government from unfairly or arbitrarily depriving a person of life, liberty, or property. • There are two Due Process Clauses in the U.S. Constitution, one in the 5th Amendment applying to the federal government, and one in the 14th Amendment applying to the states (although the 5th Amendment's Due Process Clause also applies to the states under the incorporation doctrine). Cf. EQUAL PROTECTION CLAUSE.

due process of law. See DUE PROCESS.

due-process rights. The rights (as to life, liberty, and property) so fundamentally important as to require compliance with due-process standards of fairness and justice. See DUE PROCESS; DUE PROCESS CLAUSE; FUNDAMENTAL-FAIRNESS DOCTRINE.

duplicate will. See WILL.

durable power of attorney. See POWER OF ATTORNEY.

duress (d[y]uu-**res**). **1.** Strictly, the physical confinement of a person or the detention of a contracting party's property. ● In the field of torts, duress is considered a species of fraud in which compulsion takes the place of deceit in causing injury. **2.** Broadly, the threat of confinement or detention, or other threat of harm, used to compel a person to do something against his or her will or judgment. ● A marriage that is induced by duress is generally voidable. **3.** The use or threatened use of unlawful force — usu. that a reasonable person cannot resist — to compel someone to commit an unlawful act. ● Duress is a recognized defense to a crime, contractual breach, or tort. See Model Penal Code § 2.09. See COERCION.

duress of imprisonment. The wrongful confining of a person to force the person to do something.

duress of the person. Compulsion of a person by imprisonment, by threat, or by a show of force that cannot be resisted.

duress per minas (pər **mɪ**-nəs). [Law Latin] Duress by threat of loss of life, loss of limb, mayhem, or other harm to a person.

economic duress. An unlawful coercion to perform by threatening financial injury at a time when one cannot exercise free will. — Also termed *business compulsion.*

moral duress. An unlawful coercion to perform by unduly influencing or taking advantage of the weak financial position of another. ● Moral duress focuses on the inequities of a situation while economic duress focuses on the lack of will or capacity of the person being influenced.

duressor (d[y]ə-**res**-ər). A person who coerces another person to do something against his or her will or judgment.

duty. 1. A legal obligation that is owed or due to another and that needs to be satisfied; an obligation for which somebody else has a corresponding right. **2.** Any action, performance, task, or observance owed by a person in an official or fiduciary capacity.

fiduciary duty (fi-**d**[**y**]**oo**-shee-er-ee). A duty of utmost good faith, trust, confidence, and candor owed by a fiduciary (such as a lawyer or corporate officer) to the beneficiary (such as a lawyer's client or a shareholder); a duty to act with the highest degree of honesty and loyalty toward another person and in the best interests of the other person (such as the duty that one partner owes to another). See FIDUCIARY; FIDUCIARY RELATIONSHIP.

3. A tax imposed on a commodity or transaction, esp. on imports. ● A duty in this sense is imposed on things, not persons.

legacy duty. See *legacy tax* under TAX.

probate duty. A duty assessed by the government either on every will admitted to probate or on the gross value of the decedent's personal property.

dying declaration. See DECLARATION.

dying without issue. See FAILURE OF ISSUE.

dynasty trust. See TRUST.

E

earning capacity. A person's ability or power to earn money, given the person's talent, skills, training, and experience. ● Earning capacity is one element considered when measuring the damages recoverable in a personal-injury lawsuit. And in family law, earning capacity is considered when awarding child support and spousal maintenance (or alimony) and in dividing property between spouses upon divorce. — Also termed *earning power*. See LOST EARNING CAPACITY.

earnings. Revenue gained from labor or services, from the investment of capital, or from assets. See INCOME.

educational neglect. See NEGLECT.

educational trust. See TRUST.

EEOC. *abbr.* EQUAL EMPLOYMENT OPPORTUNITY COMMISSION.

egg donation. A type of assisted-reproductive therapy in which eggs are removed from one woman and transplanted into the uterus of another woman who carries and delivers the child. ● In egg donation, the egg is usually fertilized in vitro. See IN VITRO FERTILIZATION; ASSISTED-REPRODUCTIVE TECHNOLOGY.

elder abuse. See *abuse of the elderly* under ABUSE.

elder law. The field of law dealing with the elderly, including such issues as estate planning, retirement benefits, social security, age discrimination, and healthcare.

election, *n.* **1.** The exercise of a choice; esp., the act of choosing from several possible rights or remedies in a way that precludes the use of other rights or remedies <the taxpayers' election to file jointly instead of separately>. **2.** The doctrine by which a person is compelled to choose between accepting a benefit under a legal instrument and retaining some property right to which the person is already entitled; an obligation imposed on a party to choose between alternative rights or claims, so that the party is entitled to enjoy only one. — Also termed *equitable election*. See RIGHT OF ELECTION.

election dower. A name sometimes given to a law specifying a widow's statutory share of her deceased husband's estate if she chooses to reject her share under a will. See RIGHT OF ELECTION.

elective share. The percentage of a deceased spouse's estate, set by statute, that a surviving spouse (or sometimes a child) may choose to receive instead of taking under a will or in the event of being unjustifiably disinherited. — Also termed *forced share*; *statutory share*; *statutory forced share*. See RIGHT OF ELECTION.

Electronic Communications Privacy Act. A federal statute that limits the circumstances under which the federal and state government may gain access to oral, wire, and electronic communications. 18 USCA § 2510.

elope, *vb.* **1.** *Archaic.* To run away; escape. **2.** *Archaic.* To abandon one's husband and run away with a lover. **3.** To run away secretly for the purpose of getting married, often without parental consent. — **elopement,** *n.*

emancipate, *vb.* **1.** To set free from legal, social, or political restraint; esp., to free from slavery or bondage. **2.** To release (a child) from the control, support, and responsibility of a parent or guardian. — **emancipative, emancipatory,** *adj.* — **emancipator,** *n.*

emancipated minor. See MINOR.

emancipation. 1. The act by which one who was under another's power and control is freed. **2.** A surrender and renunciation of the correlative rights and duties concerning the care, custody, and earnings of a child; the act by which a parent (historically a father) frees a child and gives the child the right to his or her own earnings. • This act also frees the parent from all legal obligations of support. Emancipation may take place by agreement between the parent and child, by operation of law (as when the parent abandons or fails to support the child), or when the child gets legally married or enters the armed forces. A "partial emancipation"

209

frees a child for only a part of the period of minority, or from only a part of the parent's rights, or for only some purposes.

> ***constructive emancipation.*** Emancipation by implication of law, as opposed to a voluntary act of the parent. • Constructive emancipation may occur in several ways, as by (1) conduct of the parents that is inconsistent with the performance of parental duties, (2) marriage of the child, or (3) the child's service in the armed forces.

emancipation act. See MARRIED WOMEN'S PROPERTY ACTS.

embryo (**em**-bree-oh). A developing but unborn or unhatched animal; esp., an unborn human from conception until the development of organs (i.e., until about the eighth week of pregnancy). Cf. FETUS; ZYGOTE.

emergency jurisdiction. See JURISDICTION.

emotional abuse. See ABUSE.

emotional distress. A highly unpleasant mental reaction (such as anguish, grief, fright, humiliation, or fury) that results from another person's conduct; emotional pain and suffering. • Emotional distress, when severe enough, can form a basis for the recovery of tort damages. — Also termed *emotional harm*; *mental anguish*; *mental distress*; *mental suffering*. Cf. MENTAL CRUELTY.

emotional harm. See EMOTIONAL DISTRESS.

employee benefit plan. A written stock-purchase, savings, option, bonus, stock-appreciation, profit-sharing, thrift, incentive, pension, or similar plan solely for employees, officers, and advisers of a company. ● The term includes an employee-welfare benefit plan, an employee-pension benefit plan, or a combination of those two. But the term excludes any plan, fund, or program (other than an apprenticeship or training program) in which no employees are plan participants. — Often shortened to *plan*. Cf. PENSION PLAN.

defined-benefit plan. Under ERISA, a plan established and maintained by an employer primarily to provide systematically for the payment of definitely determinable benefits to employees over a period of years, usu. for life, after retirement. ● Retirement benefits under a defined-benefit plan are measured by and based on various factors such as years of service rendered and compensation earned. The amount of benefits and the employer's contributions do not depend on the employer's profits. The employer has the entire investment risk and must cover any funding shortfall. Any plan that is not a defined-contribution plan is a defined-benefit plan. 29 USCA § 1002(35). Cf. *defined-contribution plan.*

defined-contribution plan. Under ERISA, an employee retirement plan in which each employee has a separate account — funded by the employee's contributions and the employer's contributions (usu. in a preset amount), the employee being entitled to receive the benefit generated by the individual account. 29 USCA § 1002(34). — Also termed *defined-contribution pension plan; individual account plan.* Cf. *defined-benefit plan.*

disability retirement plan. 1. A plan that is invoked when a covered person is disabled from working to normal retirement age. **2.** A plan that provides increased benefits if a person retires because of a disability.

employee-stock-ownership plan. A profit-sharing plan designed primarily to give an employee retirement benefits and a stake in the company, but also used to allow employees to purchase their employer company if it is closing. IRC (26 USCA) § 4975(e)(7)(A). — Abbr. ESOP.

excess benefit plan. An employee benefit plan maintained by an employer solely for the purpose of providing benefits for certain employees in excess of the statutory limitations on contributions and benefits.

401(k) plan. A retirement and savings plan that allows an employee to invest pretax contributions from a certain portion of gross wages. • Many employers match the employee's contributions. The contributions and their earnings are accumulated tax-free until they are withdrawn. The contributions are invested, usually in investments that the employees choose from a list of options.

The employer's contributions and the growth on those contributions are usually not fully vested in the employee unless the employee has achieved a certain duration of service with the employer. IRC (26 USCA) § 401(k).

403(b) plan. A tax-deferred retirement plan for employees of public educational systems and certain tax-exempt organizations, funded primarily with employee contributions (through deferred compensation) and the employer's matching contributions. ● The contributions accumulate earnings on a tax-deferred basis, so that neither the contributions nor the earnings are taxed until they are distributed to the employee. IRC (26 USCA) § 403(b). — Also termed *tax-sheltered annuity*; *tax-deferred annuity*.

governmental plan. An employee benefit plan established and maintained by the government for its employees at any level, including plans established or maintained in accordance with collective-bargaining agreements between governmental entities and labor unions if those plans are funded by, and cover only employees of, governmental entities. — Also termed *governmental employee benefit plan*; *government plan*.

individual account plan. See *defined-contribution plan*.

Keogh plan. See KEOGH PLAN.

money-purchase plan. An employee benefit plan that provides a benefit based on the total amount of employer contributions in a participant's account. ● A money-purchase plan can be a qualified plan if the contributions are fixed and not geared to profits.

nonqualified deferred-compensation plan. A compensation arrangement (such as providing stock options), frequently offered to executives, that defers the recognition of taxable income to a later date. ● It is termed "nonqualified" because it is not covered under ERISA regulations and does not receive various tax-avoidance advantages.

retirement plan. An employee benefit plan — such as a pension plan or Keogh plan — provided by an employer (or a self-employed person) for an employee's retirement.

simplified employee pension plan. An individual retirement account or annuity established for an employee and funded by employee contributions and by discretionary contributions from the employer. ● A simplified employee pension plan operates much like a 401(k) plan, in that the employee contributions can be made by deferred compensation and the employer can contribute. But the plan is attractive to small employers because it is much easier to administer than a 401(k) plan and gives the employer complete discretion on whether to make an annual contribution. IRC (26 USCA) § 408(k). — Abbr. SEP.

split-funded plan. A retirement plan combining elements of both life-insurance and investment plans.

target benefit plan. A money-purchase plan that sets a "targeted" benefit to be met by actuarially determined contributions.

Employee Retirement Income Security Act. A federal statute that regulates private pension plans and employee benefit plans and that established the Pension Benefit Guaranty Corporation. 29 USCA §§ 1001 et seq. — Abbr. ERISA.

employee-stock-ownership plan. See EMPLOYEE BENEFIT PLAN.

enabling power. See POWER OF APPOINTMENT.

endangering the welfare of a child. See CHILD ENDANGERMENT.

endogenous insemination. See *artificial insemination by husband* under ARTIFICIAL INSEMINATION.

enforcement, *n.* The act or process of compelling compliance with a law, mandate, command, decree, or agreement.

engagement, *n.* **1.** A contract or agreement involving mutual promises. **2.** An agreement to marry; the period after which a couple has agreed to marry but before they do so. — Also termed (in sense 2) *betrothal.*

Enoch Arden law (**ee**-nək **ahrd**-ən). A statute that grants a divorce or an exemption from liability so that a person can remarry when his or her spouse has been absent without explanation for a specified number of years (usu. five or seven). • This type of law is named after a Tennyson poem, in which the eponymous hero, having been shipwrecked for years on a desert island, returns home to find that his wife has remarried. He selflessly conceals his identity from her so that she can remain with her new husband. — Also spelled *Enoc Arden law.* See *presumptive death* under DEATH; ABANDONMENT.

entail. See FEE TAIL.

entailed estate. See FEE TAIL.

enticement of a child. *Criminal law.* The act or offense of inviting, persuading, or attempting to persuade a child to enter a vehicle, building, room, or secluded place with the intent of committing an unlawful sexual act against the child. — Often shortened to *enticement.*

enticement of a parent. *Rare.* The tortious interference with a child's rights and interests in maintaining the parent–child relationship, usu. caused by a third person who induces a parent to abandon the child. • Actions based on enticement, where they are recognized, are rarely successful because many states do not recognize a child's legal right to a parent's consortium or affection.

entire blood. See *full blood* under BLOOD.

en ventre sa mere (*on* **von**-trə sa **mair**). [Law French "in utero"] (Of a fetus) in the mother's womb <child *en ventre sa mere*>. • This phrase refers to an unborn child, usually in the context of a discussion of that child's rights. If the child is *en ventre sa mere* at the time of a decedent's death and is subsequently born alive, the child is treated as having been in existence at the time of the decedent's death for purposes of inheritance. — Also spelled *in ventre sa mere*.

Equal Access Act of 1984. A federal law that prohibits school districts receiving federal funds and allowing extracurricular activities to be held in its facilities from denying secondary-school students the right to meet for religious and other purposes in public-school facilities. 20 USCA § 4071. • The constitutionality of the Act was upheld in *Board of Education of Westside Community Schools v. Mergens*, 496 U.S. 226, 110 S.Ct. 2356 (1990).

Equal Credit Opportunity Act. A federal statute that prohibits creditors from discriminating against credit applicants on the basis of race, color, religion, national origin, age, sex, or marital status with respect to any aspect of a credit transaction. 15 USCA §§ 1691 et seq. — Abbr. ECOA.

equal degree. See DEGREE.

Equal Employment Opportunity Commission. A federal agency created under the Civil Rights Act of 1964 to end discriminatory employment practices and to promote nondiscriminatory employment programs. ● The EEOC investigates alleged discriminatory employment practices and encourages mediation and other nonlitigious means of resolving employment disputes. A claimant must file a charge of discrimination with the EEOC before pursuing a claim under Title VII of the Civil Rights Act and certain other employment-related statutes. — Abbr. EEOC.

equal-management rule. The doctrine that each spouse alone may manage community property unless the law provides otherwise. Cf. HEAD-AND-MASTER RULE.

Equal Pay Act. A federal law mandating that all who perform substantially the same work must be paid equally. 29 USCA § 206.

equal protection. The 14th Amendment guarantee that the government must treat a person or class of persons the same as it treats other persons or classes in like circumstances. ● In today's constitutional jurisprudence, equal protection means that legislation that discriminates must have a rational basis for doing so. And if the legislation affects a fundamental right (such as the right to vote) or involves a suspect classification (such as race), it is unconstitutional unless it can withstand strict scrutiny. — Also termed *equal protection of the laws*; *equal protection under the law*. See RATIONAL-BASIS TEST; STRICT SCRUTINY.

Equal Protection Clause. The 14th Amendment provision requiring the states to give similarly situated persons or classes similar treatment under the law. Cf. DUE PROCESS CLAUSE.

equal protection of the laws. See EQUAL PROTECTION.

equal protection under the law. See EQUAL PROTECTION.

equitable adoption. See *adoption by estoppel* under ADOPTION.

equitable distribution. The division of marital property by a court in a divorce proceeding, under statutory guidelines that provide for a fair, but not necessarily equal, allocation of the property between the spouses. ● With equitable distribution, when a marriage ends in divorce, property acquired during the marriage is divided equitably between the spouses regardless of who holds title to the property. The courts consider many factors in awarding property, including a spouse's monetary contributions, nonmonetary assistance to a spouse's career or earning potential, the efforts of each spouse during the marriage, and the length of the marriage. The court may take into account the relative earning capacity of the spouses and the fault of either spouse. Equitable distribution is applied in 47 states (i.e., all the states except California, Louisiana, and New Mexico, which are "equal division" community-property states). — Also termed *equitable division*; *assignment of property*. Cf. TITLE DIVISION; COMMUNITY PROPERTY.

equitable division. See EQUITABLE DISTRIBUTION.

equitable doctrine of approximation. See DOCTRINE OF APPROXIMATION.

equitable election. See ELECTION.

equitable life tenant. See LIFE TENANT.

equitable owner. See *beneficial owner* under OWNER.

equitable ownership. See *beneficial ownership* under OWNERSHIP.

equitable parent. See PARENT.

equitable-parent doctrine. The principle that a spouse who is not the biological parent of a child born or conceived during the marriage may, in a divorce action, be considered the child's natural father or mother if (1) the other spouse and the child both acknowledge a parent–child relationship, esp. when that other spouse has cooperated in the development of this relationship before the divorce action, (2) the nonbiologically related spouse wants parental rights, and (3) he or she is willing to take on the responsibility of paying support. • The doctrine sometimes applies to nonspousal partners as well. Very few jurisdictions apply the doctrine. See Carolee Kvoriak Lezuch, *Michigan's Doctrine of Equitable Parenthood*, 45 Wayne L. Rev. 1529 (1999). — Also termed *equitable-parenthood doctrine*.

equity to a settlement. A wife's equitable right, arising when her husband sues in equity for the reduction of her equitable estate to his own possession, to have all or part of that estate settled upon herself and her children. — Also termed *wife's equity*; *wife's settlement*.

erectile dysfunction. See IMPOTENCE.

ERISA (ee- *or* ə-**ris**-ə). *abbr*. EMPLOYEE RETIREMENT INCOME SECURITY ACT.

escalator clause. A provision in a divorce decree or divorce agreement providing for the automatic increase of alimony payments upon the occurrence of any of various triggering events, such as cost-of-living increases or an increase in the obligor's salary. • Escalation clauses for child support are often unenforceable.

escheat (es-**cheet**), *n.* **1.** Reversion of property (esp. real property) to the state upon the death of an owner who has neither a will nor any legal heirs. **2.** Property that has so reverted. — **escheat,** *vb.* See *heirless estate* under ESTATE.

ESOP. *abbr.* See *employee-stock-ownership plan* under EMPLOYEE BENEFIT PLAN.

espousals (ǝ-**spow**-zǝlz), *n.* A mutual promise between a man and a woman to marry one another.

Establishment Clause. The First Amendment provision that prohibits the government from creating or favoring a particular religion. U.S. Const. amend. I. Cf. FREE EXERCISE CLAUSE.

estate. 1. The amount, degree, nature, and quality of a person's interest in land or other property. **2.** All that a person or entity owns, including both real and personal property. **3.** The property that one leaves after death; the collective assets and liabilities of a dead person.

> ***adjusted gross estate. 1.** The total value of a decedent's property after subtracting administration expenses, funeral expenses, creditors' claims,*

and casualty losses. ● The value of the adjusted gross estate is used in computing the federal estate tax. Cf. *net probate estate* under PROBATE ES-TATE. **2.** See *gross estate* (1).

ancestral estate. An estate that is acquired by descent or by operation of law with no other consideration than that of blood.

augmented estate. A refinement of the elective share to which a surviving spouse is entitled, whereby the "fair share" is identified by using a sliding scale that increases with each year of marriage. ● Under this concept, a surviving spouse has accrued full marital-property rights after 15 years of marriage. This percentage of spousal entitlement is applied to a reconceptuali-zation of the decedent's estate to take into ac-count more than just the assets remaining in the probate estate at death. Also added into the calcu-lation are the value of certain inter vivos trans-fers that the decedent made to others in a way that depleted the probate estate; the value of similar transfers made to others by the spouse as well as the value of the marital property owned by the spouse at the decedent's death; and the value of inter vivos transfers of property made by the decedent to the spouse. The Uniform Probate Code adopted the augmented-estate concept in an attempt to equalize the treatment of surviving spouses in non-community-property states vis-à-vis community-property states. Unif. Probate Code § 2–202. See FORCED SHARE.

decedent's estate. The real and personal property that a person possesses at the time of death and that passes to the heirs or testamentary beneficiaries.

estate by curtesy. An estate owned by a wife, to which the husband is entitled upon her death. See CURTESY.

estate by entirety. A common-law estate in which each spouse is seised of the whole of the property. ● An estate by entirety is based on the legal fiction that a husband and wife are a single unit. The estate consists of five unities: time, title, interest, possession, and marriage. The last of these unities distinguishes the estate by entirety from the joint tenancy. A joint tenancy can exist with any number of persons, while an estate by entirety can be held only by a husband and wife and is not available to any other persons. And it can be acquired only during the marriage. This estate has a right of survivorship, but upon the death of one spouse, the surviving spouse retains the entire interest rather than acquiring the decedent's interest. Most jurisdictions have abolished this estate. — Also termed *estate by the entirety*; *estate by entireties*; *estate by the entireties*; *tenancy by the entirety*; *tenancy by the entireties*. Cf. *joint tenancy* under TENANCY; *tenancy in common* under TENANCY.

estate by the curtesy of England. See CURTESY.

estate for life. See *life estate*.

estate in common. See *tenancy in common* under TENANCY.

estate of inheritance. An estate that may descend to heirs.

gross estate. **1.** The total value of a decedent's property without any deductions. **2.** Loosely, adjusted gross estate.

heirless estate. The property of a person who dies intestate and without heirs. See ESCHEAT.

joint estate. Any of the following five types of estates: (1) a joint tenancy, (2) a tenancy in common, (3) an estate in coparcenary (a common-law estate in which coheirs hold as tenants in common), (4) a tenancy by the entirety, or (5) an estate in partnership.

legal life estate. See *life estate.*

life estate. An estate held only for the duration of a specified person's life, usu. the possessor's. • Most life estates — created, for example, by a grant "to Jane for life" — are beneficial interests under trusts, the corpus often being personal property, not real property. — Also termed *estate for life*; *legal life estate*; *life tenancy*. See LIFE TENANT.

life estate pur autre vie (pər **oh**-trə **vee**). A life estate for which the measuring life — the life whose duration determines the duration of the estate — is someone other than the possessor's. — Also spelled *life estate per autre vie.*

minor's estate. A minor's property that must be administered by a court-appointed fiduciary.

net estate. See *net probate estate* under PROBATE ESTATE.

net probate estate. See PROBATE ESTATE.

nonancestral estate. An estate from any source other than the owner's ancestors.

probate estate. See PROBATE ESTATE.

residuary estate. The part of a decedent's estate remaining after payment of all debts, expenses, statutory claims, taxes, and testamentary gifts (special, general, and demonstrative) have been made. — Also termed *residual estate*; *residue*; *residuary*; *residuum.*

separate estate. The individual property of one of two persons who stand in a marital or business relationship. See SEPARATE PROPERTY.

settled estate. An estate created or limited under a settlement; an estate in which the powers of alienation, devising, and transmission according to the ordinary rules of descent are restrained by the settlement's terms.

taxable estate. A decedent's gross estate reduced by allowable deductions (such as administration costs and ESOP deductions). IRC (26 USCA) § 2051. ● The taxable estate is the amount that is subject to the federal unified transfer tax at death.

vested estate. An estate with a present right of enjoyment or a present fixed right of future enjoyment.

estate by curtesy. See ESTATE.

estate by entirety. See ESTATE.

estate by the curtesy of England. See CURTESY.

estate by entirety. See ESTATE.

estate for life. See *life estate* under ESTATE.

estate freeze. An estate-planning maneuver whereby an owner of a closely held business exchanges common stock for dividend-paying preferred stock and gives the common stock to his or her children, thus guaranteeing a pension and avoiding estate tax.

estate in common. See *tenancy in common* under TENANCY.

estate in expectancy. See FUTURE INTEREST.

estate in fee simple. See FEE SIMPLE.

estate in tail. See FEE TAIL.

estate of inheritance. See ESTATE.

estate planning. 1. The preparation for the distribution and management of a person's estate at death through the use of wills, trusts, insurance policies, and other arrangements, esp. to reduce administration costs and estate-tax liability. **2.** A branch of law that involves the arrangement of a person's estate, taking into account the laws of wills, taxes, insurance, property, and trusts.

estate tail. See FEE TAIL.

estate tax. See TAX.

estate trust. See TRUST.

estoppel (e-**stop**-əl), *n*. **1.** A bar that prevents one from asserting a claim or right that contradicts what one has said or done before or what has been legally established as true. **2.** A bar that prevents the relitigation of issues. **3.** An affirmative defense alleging good-faith reliance on a misleading representation and an injury or detrimental change in position resulting from that reliance. — **estop,** *vb*.

estrange, *vb*. **1.** To separate, to keep away (a person or thing), or to keep away from (a person or thing). **2.** To destroy or divert affection, trust, and loyalty. — **estrangement,** *n*.

et uxor (et ə**k**-sor). [Latin] *Archaic*. And wife. ●
This phrase was formerly common in case names
and legal documents (especially abstracts of title)
involving a husband and wife jointly. It usually
appears in its abbreviated form, *et ux*. <conveyed
the land to Donald Baird et ux.>. See UXOR.

et vir (et **veer**). [Latin] *Archaic*. And husband. See
VIR.

euthanasia (yoo-thə-**nay**-zhə), *n*. The act or practice of killing or bringing about the death of a
person who suffers from an incurable disease or
condition, esp. a painful one, for reasons of mercy. ●
Euthanasia is sometimes regarded by the law as
second-degree murder, manslaughter, or criminally
negligent homicide. — Also termed *mercy killing*. —
euthanasic (yoo-thə-**nay**-zik), *adj*. See LIVING WILL;
ADVANCE DIRECTIVE. Cf. *assisted suicide* under SUICIDE.

active euthanasia. Euthanasia performed by a
facilitator (such as a healthcare practitioner) who
not only provides the means of death but also
carries out the final death-causing act.

involuntary euthanasia. Euthanasia of a competent, nonconsenting person.

nonvoluntary euthanasia. Euthanasia of an
incompetent, and therefore nonconsenting, person.

passive euthanasia. The act of allowing a terminally ill person to die by either withholding or

withdrawing life-sustaining support such as a respirator or feeding tube.

voluntary euthanasia. Euthanasia performed with the terminally ill person's consent.

evolution statute. See ANTI-EVOLUTION STATUTE.

exceptio plurium concubentium **defense.** See MULTIPLE ACCESS.

excess benefit plan. See EMPLOYEE BENEFIT PLAN.

excision. See FEMALE GENITAL MUTILATION.

exclusion, *n. Tax.* An item of income excluded from gross income. — Also termed *income exclusion.*

annual exclusion. The amount (currently as much as $10,000) allowed as nontaxable gift income during the calendar year. ● The purpose of the annual exclusion is both to serve as an estate-planning mechanism (so that gifts made during the donor's lifetime remain nontestamentary and nontaxable) and to eliminate the administrative inconvenience of taxing relatively small gifts. For an individual, the first $10,000 in gifts can be excluded; for married persons, the exclusion is $20,000 per donee for joint gifts, regardless of which spouse supplied the donated property. IRC (26 USCA) § 2503. — Also termed *annual gift-tax exclusion.*

exculpatory clause. A contractual provision relieving a party from any liability resulting from a negligent or wrongful act. • A will or a trust may contain an exculpatory clause purporting to immunize a fiduciary from a breach of duty; the clause may reduce the degree of care and prudence required of the fiduciary. But courts generally find that if an exculpatory clause in a will or trust seeks to confer absolute immunity, it is void as being against public policy.

ex delicto trust. See TRUST.

executed remainder. See *vested remainder* under REMAINDER.

executed trust. See TRUST.

executor, *n.* **1.** (**ek**-sə-kyoo-tər) One who performs or carries out some act. **2.** (eg-**zek**-yə-tər) A person named by a testator to carry out the provisions in the testator's will. — **executorial,** *adj.* — **executorship,** *n.* Cf. ADMINISTRATOR.

   acting executor. One who assumes the role of executor — usu. temporarily — but is not the legally appointed executor or the executor-in-fact. — Also termed *temporary executor.*

   coexecutor. See *joint executor.*

   executor a lege constitutus (ay [*or* ah] **lee**-jee kon-sti-**t[y]oo**-təs). [Law Latin] *Eccles. law.* One authorized by law to be an executor; the ordinary of the diocese.

executor a testatore constitutus (ay [*or* ah] tes-tə-**tor**-ee kon-sti-**t**[**y**]**oo**-təs). [Law Latin] *Eccles. law.* An executor appointed by a testator. — Also termed *executor testamentarius*.

executor de son tort (də sawn [*or* son] **tor**[**t**]). [Law French "executor of his own wrong"] A person who, without legal authority, takes on the responsibility to act as an executor or administrator of a decedent's property, usu. to the detriment of the estate's beneficiaries or creditors.

executor testamentarius. See *executor a testatore constitutus.*

executor to the tenor. *Eccles. law.* A person who is not named executor in the will but who performs duties similar to those of an executor.

general executor. An executor who has the power to administer a decedent's entire estate until its final settlement.

independent executor. An executor who, unlike an ordinary executor, can administer the estate with very little supervision by the probate court. • Only a few states — mostly in the West and Southwest — allow testators to designate independent executors. But lawyers routinely write wills that relieve a trusted executor from obtaining appraisals, from providing inventories and surety bonds, and from obtaining court approval "to the maximum extent permitted by law." The Uniform Probate Code endorses independent administration, and it is the usual process unless a party demands court-supervised administration. — Also termed *nonintervention executor*.

joint executor. One of two or more persons named in a will as executor of an estate. — Also termed *coexecutor*.

limited executor. An executor whose appointment is restricted in some way, such as time, place, or subject matter.

nonintervention executor. See *independent executor*.

special executor. An executor whose power is limited to a portion of the decedent's estate.

substituted executor. An executor appointed to act in the place of an executor who cannot or will not perform the required duties.

temporary executor. See *acting executor*.

executor a lege constitutus. See EXECUTOR.

executor a testore constitutus. See EXECUTOR.

executor de son tort. See EXECUTOR.

executor fund. See FUND (1).

executor's bond. See BOND.

executor testamentarius. See *executor a testatore constitutus* under EXECUTOR.

executor to the tenor. See EXECUTOR.

executory bequest. See BEQUEST.

executory devise. See DEVISE.

executory interest. A future interest, held by a third person, that either cuts off another's interest or begins after the natural termination of a preceding estate. Cf. REMAINDER.

executory remainder. See *contingent remainder* under REMAINDER.

executory trust. See TRUST.

executress. See EXECUTRIX.

executrix (eg-**zek**-yə-triks), *n. Archaic.* A female executor. — Abbr. exrx. — Also termed *executress.* Pl. **executrixes** (eg-**zek**-yə-trik-səz), **executrices** (eg-zek-yə-**trɪ**-seez). See EXECUTOR.

exemplified copy. See *certified copy* under COPY.

exempt property. 1. A debtor's holdings and possessions that, by law, a creditor cannot attach to satisfy a debt. • All the property that creditors may lawfully reach is known as *nonexempt property*. Many states provide a homestead exemption that excludes a person's house and household items, up to a certain amount, from the liens of most creditors. The purpose of the exemption is to prevent debtors from becoming destitute. See HOMESTEAD. Cf. NONEXEMPT PROPERTY. **2.** Personal property that a surviving spouse is automatically entitled to receive from the decedent's estate.

Exercise Clause. See FREE EXERCISE CLAUSE.

ex officio service (eks ə-**fish**-ee-oh). A service that the law imposes on an official by virtue of the office held, such as a local sheriff's duty to perform marriage ceremonies.

exogamous insemination. See *artificial insemination by donor* under ARTIFICIAL INSEMINATION.

exoneration. 1. The removal of a burden, charge, responsibility, or duty. **2.** The right to be reimbursed by reason of having paid money that another person should have paid. **3.** The equitable right of a surety — confirmed by statute in many states — to proceed to compel the principal debtor to satisfy the obligation when, even though the surety would have a right of reimbursement, it would be inequitable for the surety to be compelled to perform if the principal debtor can satisfy the obligation. • When a testator leaves a gift of property encumbered by a

mortgage or lien, the doctrine of exoneration operates to satisfy the encumbrance from the general
assets of the estate. Many states have abandoned
the common-law rule in favor of exoneration.

exordium clause (ek-**sor**-dee-əm). The introducto-
ry phrase of a will identifying the testator and
declaring that the document is the testator's will.

ex parte, *adj.* Done or made at the instance and for
the benefit of one party only, and without notice to,
or argument by, any person adversely interested; of
or relating to court action taken by one party without notice to the other, usu. for temporary or emergency relief <an ex parte hearing> <an ex parte
injunction>. — Sometimes spelled *exparte*. — **ex
parte,** *adv.*

ex parte divorce. See DIVORCE.

ex parte injunction. See INJUNCTION.

expectancy, *n.* The possibility that an heir apparent, an heir presumptive, or a presumptive next of
kin will acquire property by devolution on intestacy,
or the possibility that a presumptive beneficiary will
acquire property by will.

expectant heir. See HEIR.

expense, *n.* An expenditure of money, time, labor,
or resources to accomplish a result; esp., a business

expenditure chargeable against revenue for a specific period. — **expense,** *vb.* Cf. COST.

funeral expense. (*usu. pl.*) An expense necessarily and reasonably incurred in procuring the burial, cremation, or other disposition of a corpse, including the funeral or other ceremonial rite, a casket and vault, a monument or tombstone, a burial plot and its care, and a visitation (or wake).

general administrative expense. (*usu. pl.*) An expense incurred in running a business, as distinguished from an expense incurred in manufacturing or selling; overhead.

expenses of administration. Expenses incurred by a decedent's representatives in administering the estate.

exploitation. See SEXUAL EXPLOITATION.

express active trust. See TRUST.

express private passive trust. See TRUST.

express trust. See TRUST.

extended family. See FAMILY.

extinguishment of legacy. See ADEMPTION.

extradotal property. See PROPERTY.

extreme cruelty. See CRUELTY.

F

FACE. *abbr.* FREEDOM OF ACCESS TO CLINIC ENTRANCES ACT.

facilitated negotiation. See MEDIATION.

facilitation. See CONCILIATION.

fact-finder. One or more persons — such as jurors in a trial or administrative-law judges in a hearing — who hear testimony and review evidence to rule on a factual issue. — Also termed *finder of fact*. See FINDING OF FACT.

factum of a will. The formal ceremony of making a will; a will's execution by the testator and attestation by the witnesses.

faculties. *Archaic.* The extent of a husband's estate; esp., the ability to pay alimony. See ALLEGATION OF FACULTIES.

failed legacy. See *lapsed legacy* under LEGACY.

failure. 1. Deficiency; lack; want. **2.** An omission of an expected action, occurrence, or performance. See LAPSE (2).

> *failure of trust.* The invalidity of a trust because the instrument creating it has a defect or because of its illegality or other legal impediment.

failure of issue. The fact of dying without descendants, esp. if they would have inherited the decedent's estate. — Also termed *dying without issue*. See ISSUE.

> *indefinite failure of issue.* A failure of issue whenever it happens, without any certain period within which it must happen.

failure of trust. See FAILURE.

failure to protect. The refusal or inability of a parent or guardian to prevent abuse of a child under his or her care.

failure-to-supervise statute. See PARENTAL-LIABILITY STATUTE.

failure to thrive. 1. A medical and psychological condition in which a child's height, weight, and motor development fall significantly below average growth rates. ● Failure to thrive is sometimes asserted as a ground for alleging abuse or neglect by a parent or caregiver. **2.** A condition, occurring during the first three years of a child's life, in which the child suffers marked retardation or ceases to grow. — Abbr. FTT.

Fair Credit Billing Act. A federal law that facilitates the correction of billing errors by credit-card companies and makes those companies more responsible for the quality of goods purchased by cardholders. 15 USCA §§ 1666–1666j.

fair-credit-reporting act. A federal or state law that regulates the keeping of credit reports and ensures the right of consumers to get and correct their credit reports. ● The federal Fair Credit Reporting Act was enacted in 1970. 15 USCA §§ 1681–1681u.

Fair Labor Standards Act. A federal law, enacted in 1938, that regulates minimum wages, overtime pay, and the employment of minors. 29 USCA §§ 201–219. — Abbr. FLSA.

faith-healing exemption. In a child-abuse or child-neglect statute, a provision that a parent who provides a child with faith healing (in place of standard medical treatment) will not, for that reason alone, be charged with abuse or neglect. ● Nearly all states have enacted some form of faith-healing exemption. But the statutes differ greatly. For example, they differ on whether the exemption is available as a defense to manslaughter or murder charges brought against a parent whose child dies as a result of the parent's having refused to consent to medical treatment. — Also termed *religious-exemption statute*; *spiritual-treatment exemption*. Cf. *medical neglect* under NEGLECT.

false-memory syndrome. The supposed recovery of memories of traumatic or stressful episodes that did not actually occur, often in session with a mental-health therapist. ● This term is most frequently applied to claims by adult children that repressed memories of prolonged and repeated child sexual abuse, usually by parents, have surfaced, even though there is no independent evidence to substantiate the claims. Cf. REPRESSED-MEMORY SYNDROME.

False Memory Syndrome Foundation. An organization of parents who claim that their adult children have falsely accused them of childhood sexual abuse. • The organization was formed for the purpose of aiding persons who claim to have been wrongly accused as a result of the recovery of repressed memories. — Abbr. FMSF. Cf. VICTIMS OF CHILD ABUSE LAWS.

family, *n.* **1.** A group of persons connected by blood, by affinity, or by law, esp. within two or three generations. **2.** A group consisting of parents and their children. **3.** A group of persons who live together and have a shared commitment to a domestic relationship. — **familial,** *adj.* See RELATIVE.

blended family. The combined families of persons with children from earlier marriages or relationships.

extended family. **1.** The immediate family together with the collateral relatives who make up a clan; GENS. **2.** The immediate family together with collateral relatives and close family friends.

immediate family. **1.** A person's parents, spouse, children, and siblings. **2.** A person's parents, spouse, children, and siblings, as well as those of the person's spouse. ● Stepchildren and adopted children are usually immediate family members. For some purposes, such as taxes, a person's immediate family may also include the spouses of children and siblings.

intact family. A family in which both parents live together with their children.

family allowance. See ALLOWANCE (1).

Family and Medical Leave Act. A 1993 federal statute providing that employees may take unpaid, job-protected leave for certain family reasons, as when a family member is sick or when a child is born. 29 USCA §§ 2601 et seq. ● The statute applies to businesses with 50 or more employees. An employee may take up to 12 weeks of unpaid leave per year under the FMLA. — Abbr. FMLA. Cf. FAMI-LY LEAVE.

family arrangement. An informal agreement among family members, usu. to distribute property in a manner other than what the law provides for. — Also termed *family settlement.*

family-automobile doctrine. See FAMILY-PURPOSE RULE.

family-autonomy doctrine. See PARENTAL-AUTONO-MY DOCTRINE.

family-car doctrine. See FAMILY-PURPOSE RULE.

family court. See COURT.

family-court judge. See JUDGE.

family disturbance. See DOMESTIC DISPUTE.

Family Educational Rights and Privacy Act. An act that prescribes minimum standards for the maintenance and dissemination of student records by educational institutions. 20 USCA § 1232g. — Abbr. FERPA. — Also termed *Buckley Amendment*.

family-expense statute. 1. A state law that permits a charge against the property of a spouse for family debts such as rent, food, clothing, and tuition. **2.** A section of the federal tax code providing that a person may not deduct expenses incurred for family, living, or personal purposes. IRC (26 USCA) § 262. See NECESSARIES.

family home. A house that was purchased during marriage and that the family has resided in, esp. before a divorce. ● In some jurisdictions, the court may award the family home to the custodial parent until (1) the youngest child reaches the age of 18 or is otherwise emancipated, (2) the custodial parent moves, or (3) the custodial parent remarries. In making such an award, the court reasons that it is in the best interests of the child to remain in the family home. — Also termed *marital home*; *marital residence*.

family-income insurance. An agreement to pay benefits for a stated period following the death of the insured. ● At the end of the payment period, the face value is paid to the designated beneficiary.

family law. 1. The body of law dealing with marriage, divorce, adoption, child custody and support, child abuse and neglect, paternity, juvenile delinquency, and other domestic-relations issues. — Also termed *domestic relations*; *domestic-relations law*. **2.** (More broadly) the bodies of law dealing with wills and estates, property, constitutional rights, contracts, employment, and finance as they relate to families.

family leave. An unpaid leave of absence from work taken to have or care for a baby or to care for a sick family member. See FAMILY AND MEDICAL LEAVE ACT.

family partnership. A business partnership in which the partners are related. IRC (26 USCA) § 704(e). See FAMILY-PARTNERSHIP RULES.

family-partnership rules. Laws or regulations designed to prevent the shifting of income among partners, esp. family members, who may not be dealing at arm's length.

family-pot trust. See TRUST.

family-purpose rule. The principle that a vehicle's owner is liable for injuries or damage caused by a family member's negligent driving. ● Many states have abolished this rule. — Also termed *family-purpose doctrine*; *family-automobile doctrine*; *family-car doctrine*. Cf. GUEST STATUTE.

family reunification. See REUNIFICATION.

family settlement. See FAMILY ARRANGEMENT.

family shelter. See *women's shelter* under SHELTER.

family support. A combined award of child support and alimony that does not apportion the amount of each.

Family Support Act of 1988. A federal statute requiring states to develop and implement child-support guidelines. 42 USCA § 667. See CHILD-SUPPORT GUIDELINES.

family trust. See TRUST.

family violence. See *domestic violence* under VIOLENCE.

FAS. *abbr.* FETAL ALCOHOL SYNDROME.

father. A male parent. See PARENT.

acknowledged father. The admitted biological father of a child born to unmarried parents. See ACKNOWLEDGMENT (1).

adoptive father. See *adoptive parent* under PAR-
ENT.

biological father. The man whose sperm im-
pregnated the child's biological mother. — Also
termed *natural father*; *birth father*; *genetic father*.

birth father. See *biological father*.

de facto father. See *de facto parent* under PAR-
ENT.

filiated father. The proven biological father of a
child born to unmarried parents. See FILIATION.

foster father. See *foster parent* under PARENT.

genetic father. See *biological father*.

godfather. See GODPARENT.

intentional father. See *intentional parent* under
PARENT.

legal father. The man recognized by law as the
male parent of a child. ● A man is the legal father
of a child if he was married to the child's natural
mother when the child was born, if he has recognized or acknowledged the child, or if he has been
declared the child's natural father in a paternity
action. If a man consents to the artificial insemination of his wife, he is the legal father of the
child that is born as a result of the artificial
insemination even though he may not be the
genetic father of the child.

natural father. See *biological father*.

presumed father. The man presumed to be the father of a child for any of several reasons: (1) because he was married to the child's natural mother when the child was conceived or born (even though the marriage may have been invalid), (2) because the man married the mother after the child's birth and agreed either to have his name on the birth certificate or to support the child, or (3) because the man welcomed the child into his home and held out the child as his own. • This term represents a complicated category, and state laws vary in their requirements. See PRE-SUMPTION OF PATERNITY.

psychological father. See *psychological parent* under PARENT.

putative father (**pyoo**-tə-tiv). The alleged biological father of a child born out of wedlock.

stepfather. The husband of one's mother by a later marriage.

fault divorce. See DIVORCE.

favored beneficiary. See BENEFICIARY.

favor legitimationis (**fay**-vər lə-jit-ə-may-shee-**oh**-nis). [Latin "(in) favor of legitimacy"] The principle that a court should attempt to uphold a child's legitimacy.

favor matrimonii (**fay**-vər ma-trə-**moh**-nee-ı). [Latin "(in) favor of marriage"] The principle that a court should attempt to uphold the validity of a marriage.

favor paternitatis (**fay**-vər pə-tər-nə-**tay**-tis). [Latin "(in) favor of paternity"] The principle that a court should interpret facts so as to uphold the paternity of a child.

favor testamenti (**fay**-vər tes-tə-**men**-tı). [Latin "(in) favor of the testament"] The principle that a court should attempt to uphold a will's validity.

federal citizen. See CITIZEN.

Federal Food Stamp Act. A federally funded program that provides needy families with a means of obtaining a nutritionally adequate diet. ● The Secretary of Agriculture administers the Act.

federal-juvenile-delinquency jurisdiction. See JURISDICTION.

Federal Kidnapping Act. A federal law punishing kidnapping for ransom or reward when the victim is transported interstate or internationally. ● The law presumes that a victim has been transported in violation of the law if the victim is not released within 24 hours. The Federal Kidnapping Act, by express provision, does not apply to the kidnapping of a minor by either parent. 18 USCA § 1201. —

Also termed *Lindbergh Act.* Cf. PARENTAL KIDNAPPING PREVENTION ACT.

Federal Parent Locator Service. A federal program created for the purpose of enforcing child-support obligations. • In an effort to increase the collection of child support, Congress authorized the use of all information contained in the various federal databases to help locate absent, delinquent child-support obligors. Although initially information could be released only if the family was receiving public assistance, any judgment obligee can now apply to receive the last known address of a delinquent child-support obligor. 42 USCA § 653.

fee. See FEE SIMPLE.

fee simple. An interest in land that, being the broadest property interest allowed by law, endures until the current holder dies without heirs; esp., a fee simple absolute. — Often shortened to *fee.* — Also termed *estate in fee simple; fee-simple title.*

fee-simple title. See FEE SIMPLE.

fee tail. An estate that is inheritable only by specified descendants of the original grantee, and that endures until its current holder dies without issue (e.g., "to Albert and the heirs of his body"). • Most jurisdictions — except Delaware, Maine, Massachusetts, and Rhode Island — have abolished the fee tail. — Also termed *entailed estate*; *estate tail*; *estate in tail*; *tenancy in tail*; *entail*.

felony de se. See SUICIDE.

felony injury to a child. The act of causing or allowing a child to suffer in circumstances likely to produce great bodily harm or death, or inflicting unjustifiable pain or mental suffering in those circumstances.

female genital mutilation. 1. Female circumcision. **2.** The act of cutting, or cutting off, one or more female sexual organs. ● Female genital mutilation is practiced primarily among certain tribes in Africa, but it also occurs among some immigrant populations in the United States and in other Western nations. There are three commonly identified types: *sunna*, in which the hood of the clitoris is cut off; *excision*, in which the entire clitoris is cut off; and *infibulation*, in which the clitoris, the labia minora, and much of the labia majora are cut off. In the United States, Congress has outlawed female genital mutilation, specifically prohibiting the use of a cultural defense for persons accused of performing the act. 18 USCA § 16. — Abbr. FGM. See CULTURAL DEFENSE.

feme (fem), *n.* [Law French] *Archaic.* **1.** A woman. **2.** A wife. — Also spelled *femme*.

feme covert (fem **kəv**-ərt). [Law French "covered woman"] *Archaic.* A married woman. ● The notion, as Blackstone put it, was that the husband was the one "under whose wing, protection, and cover, she performs every thing." 1 William Blackstone, *Commentaries on the Law of England* 430 (1766). See COVERTURE.

feme sole (fem **sohl**). [Law French] *Archaic.* **1.** An unmarried woman. **2.** A married woman handling the affairs of her separate estate. — Also termed (in sense 2) *feme sole trader*.

FERPA. *abbr.* FAMILY EDUCATIONAL RIGHTS AND PRIVACY ACT.

fertile-octogenarian rule. The legal fiction, assumed under the rule against perpetuities, that a woman can become pregnant as long as she is alive. ● The case that gave rise to this fiction was *Jee v. Audley*, 1 Cox 324, 29 Eng. Rep. 1186 (ch. 1787). See W. Barton Leach, *Perpetuities: New Hampshire Defertilizes Octogenarians*, 77 Harv. L. Rev. 729 (1963). — Also termed *presumption-of-fertility rule*.

fetal alcohol syndrome. A variety of birth defects caused by the mother's alcohol consumption during pregnancy. ● The birth defects include facial abnormalities, mental retardation, and growth deficiencies. — Abbr. FAS.

feticide (**fee**-tə-sɪd). **1.** The act or an instance of killing a fetus, usu. by assaulting and battering the mother. **2.** An intentionally induced miscarriage. —

Also spelled *foeticide*. — Also termed *child destruction*. — **feticidal,** *adj*. Cf. INFANTICIDE (1).

fetus. A developing but unborn mammal, esp. in the latter stages of development. — Also spelled *foetus*. Cf. EMBRYO; ZYGOTE.

fide-commissary (fī-dee **kom**-ə-ser-ee). See CESTUI QUE TRUST.

fide-committee. A beneficiary; CESTUI QUE TRUST. — Also termed *fidei-commissarius*.

fidei-commissarius. See CESTUI QUE TRUST.

fiduciary (fi-**d[y]oo**-shee-er-ee), *n*. **1.** One who owes to another the duties of good faith, trust, confidence, and candor <the corporate officer is a fiduciary to the shareholders>. **2.** One who must exercise a high standard of care in managing another's money or property <the beneficiary sued the fiduciary for investing in speculative securities>. — **fiduciary,** *adj*.

    dilatory fiduciary (**dil**-ə-tor-ee). A trustee or other fiduciary who causes undue delays in administering an estate.

    successor fiduciary. A fiduciary who is appointed to succeed or replace a prior one.

    temporary fiduciary. An interim fiduciary appointed by the court until a regular fiduciary can be appointed.

fiduciary bond. See BOND.

fiduciary duty. See DUTY (2).

fiduciary relationship. A relationship in which one person is under a duty to act for the benefit of another on matters within the scope of the relationship. • Fiduciary relationships — such as trustee–beneficiary, guardian–ward, principal–agent, and attorney–client — require the highest duty of care. Fiduciary relationships usually arise in one of four situations: (1) when one person places trust in the faithful integrity of another, who as a result gains superiority or influence over the first, (2) when one person assumes control and responsibility over another, (3) when one person has a duty to act for or give advice to another on matters falling within the scope of the relationship, or (4) when there is a specific relationship that has traditionally been recognized as involving fiduciary duties, as with a lawyer and a client or a stockbroker and a customer. — Also termed *fiduciary relation*; *confidential relationship*. Cf. SPECIAL RELATIONSHIP.

file, *vb.* **1.** To deliver a legal document to the court clerk or record custodian for placement into the official record <the lawyer asked for an extension to file the amended petition>. **2.** To commence a lawsuit <Terry filed for divorce on Monday>.

filial consortium. See CONSORTIUM.

filiated father. See FATHER.

filiation (fil-ee-**ay**-shən). **1.** The fact or condition of being a son or daughter; relationship of a child to a parent. **2.** Judicial determination of paternity. — **filiate,** *vb.* See PATERNITY; *filiated father* under FATHER.

filius nullius (**fil**-ee-əs nə-**lı**-əs). [Latin "son of nobody"] *Hist.* An illegitimate child. — Also termed *filius populi.*

filius populi. See FILIUS NULLIUS.

final alimony. See *permanent alimony* under ALIMONY.

final appealable judgment. See *final judgment* under JUDGMENT.

final appealable order. See *final judgment* under JUDGMENT.

final decision. See *final judgment* under JUDGMENT.

final decree. See *final judgment* under JUDGMENT.

final injunction. See *permanent injunction* under INJUNCTION.

final judgment. See JUDGMENT.

final-offer arbitration. See ARBITRATION.

final settlement. See SETTLEMENT.

financial statement. See INCOME-AND-EXPENSE DEC-LARATION.

finder of fact. See FACT-FINDER.

finding. See FINDING OF FACT.

finding of fact. A determination by a judge, jury, or administrative agency of a fact supported by the evidence in the record, usu. presented at the trial or hearing <he agreed with the jury's finding of fact that the driver did not stop before proceeding into the intersection>. — Often shortened to *finding*. See FACT-FINDER. Cf. CONCLUSION OF FACT; CONCLUSION OF LAW.

First Amendment. The constitutional amendment, ratified with the Bill of Rights in 1791, guaranteeing the freedoms of speech, religion, press, assembly, and petition.

first cousin. See COUSIN (1).

first devisee. See DEVISEE.

501(c)(3) organization. See CHARITABLE ORGANIZATION.

fixed-benefit plan. See *defined pension plan* under PENSION PLAN.

fixed trust. See TRUST.

FLSA. *abbr.* FAIR LABOR STANDARDS ACT.

FMLA. *abbr.* FAMILY AND MEDICAL LEAVE ACT.

FMSF. *abbr.* FALSE MEMORY SYNDROME FOUNDATION.

foeticide. See FETICIDE.

foetus. See FETUS.

FOIA. *abbr.* FREEDOM OF INFORMATION ACT.

forbidden degree. See *prohibited degree* under DEGREE.

forced heir. See HEIR.

forced portion. See LEGITIME.

forced share. See ELECTIVE SHARE.

foreign administration. See *ancillary administration* under ADMINISTRATION.

foreign administrator. See ADMINISTRATOR.

foreign divorce. See DIVORCE.

foreign guardian. See GUARDIAN.

foreign-situs trust. See TRUST.

foreign support order. See SUPPORT ORDER.

foreign trust. See *foreign-situs trust* under TRUST.

forfeiture clause. See NO-CONTEST CLAUSE.

formal acknowledgment. See ACKNOWLEDGMENT.

fornication, *n.* **1.** Voluntary sexual intercourse between two unmarried persons. ● Fornication is still a crime in some states, such as Virginia. **2.** *Hist.* Voluntary sexual intercourse with an unmarried woman. ● At common law, the status of the woman determined whether the offense was adultery or fornication — *adultery* was sexual intercourse between a man, single or married, and a married woman; *fornication* was sexual intercourse between a man, single or married, and a single woman. — **fornicate,** *vb.* Cf. ADULTERY.

forum non conveniens (for-əm non kən-**vee**-nee-enz). [Latin "an unsuitable court"] The doctrine that an appropriate forum — even though competent under the law — may divest itself of jurisdiction if, for the convenience of the litigants and the witnesses, it appears that the action should proceed in another forum in which the action might originally have been brought.

foster, *adj.* **1.** (Of a relationship) involving parental care given by someone not related by blood <foster home>. **2.** (Of a person) giving or receiving parental care to or from someone not related by blood <foster parent> <foster child>.

foster, *vb.* To give care to (something or someone); esp., to give parental care to (a child who is not one's natural child).

fosterage, *n.* **1.** The act of caring for another's child. **2.** The entrusting of a child to another. **3.** The condition of being in the care of another. **4.** The act of encouraging or promoting.

foster care. 1. A federally funded child-welfare program providing substitute care for abused and neglected children who have been removed by court order from their parents' care or for children voluntarily placed by their parents in the temporary care of the state because of a family crisis. 42 USCA §§ 670–679a. • The state welfare agency selects, trains, supervises, and pays those who serve as foster parents.

> ***long-term foster care.*** The placing of a child in foster care for extended periods, perhaps even for the child's entire minority, in lieu of family reunification, termination and adoption, or guardianship. • Although most courts do not generally find this arrangement to be in a child's best interests, sometimes it is the only possibility, as when the child, because of age or disability, is

unlikely to be adopted or when, although the parent cannot be permanently reunited with the child, limited contact with the parent would serve the child's best interests. Under the Adoption and Safe Families Act, long-term foster care is the permanent placement of last resort.

2. The area of social services concerned with meeting the needs of children who participate in these types of programs.

foster-care drift. The phenomenon that occurs when children placed in foster care remain in that system, in legal limbo, for too many years of their developmental life before they are reunited with their parents or freed for adoption and placed in permanent homes. • The Adoption and Safe Families Act was passed in 1997 to help rectify this problem. See ADOPTION AND SAFE FAMILIES ACT.

foster-care placement. The (usu. temporary) act of placing a child in a home with a person or persons who provide parental care for the child. Cf. OUT-OF-HOME PLACEMENT.

foster-care review board. A panel of screened and trained volunteers who routinely review cases of children placed in foster care, examine efforts at permanency planning, and report to the court.

foster child. See CHILD.

foster father. See *foster parent* under PARENT.

foster home. A household in which foster care is provided to a child who has been removed from his or her natural parents, usu. for abuse or neglect. ● A foster home is usually an individual home, but it can also be a group home.

fosterling. See *foster child* under CHILD.

foster mother. See *foster parent* under PARENT.

foster parent. See PARENT.

founder. See SETTLOR.

foundling. A deserted or abandoned infant.

foundling hospital. A charitable institution, found esp. in Europe, the purpose of which is to care for abandoned children.

IV-D agency. See CHILD-SUPPORT-ENFORCEMENT AGEN-CY.

401(k) plan. See EMPLOYEE BENEFIT PLAN.

403(b) plan. See EMPLOYEE BENEFIT PLAN.

fraternal society. See *benevolent association* under ASSOCIATION.

fraudulent marriage. See MARRIAGE (1).

Freedom of Access to Clinic Entrances Act. A 1994 federal statute that provides for criminal sanctions, private civil causes of action, and civil action by the U.S. Attorney General against a person who uses force, threat of force, or physical obstruction to injure, intimidate, or interfere with a provider or patient of reproductive services or who damages a reproductive-services facility. — Abbr. FACE.

freedom of assembly. See RIGHT OF ASSEMBLY.

freedom of association. The right to join with others in a common undertaking that would be lawful if pursued individually. ● This right is protected by the First Amendment to the U.S. Constitution. The government may not prohibit outsiders from joining an association, but the insiders do not necessarily have a right to exclude others. Cf. RIGHT OF ASSEMBLY.

freedom of choice. 1. The liberty embodied in the exercise of one's rights. **2.** The parents' opportunity to select a school for their child in a unitary, integrated school system that is devoid of de jure segregation. **3.** The liberty to exercise one's right of privacy, esp. the right to have an abortion. — Also termed *right to choose*; *choice*.

freedom of contract. The doctrine that people have the right to bind themselves legally; a judicial concept that contracts are based on mutual agreement and free choice, and thus should not be ham-

261

pered by external control such as governmental interference. ● This is the principle that people are able to fashion their relations by private agreements, especially as opposed to the assigned roles of the feudal system. — Also termed *liberty of contract*.

freedom of expression. The freedom of speech, press, assembly, or religion as guaranteed by the First Amendment; the prohibition of governmental interference with those freedoms. Cf. FREEDOM OF SPEECH.

Freedom of Information Act. The federal statute that establishes guidelines for public disclosure of documents and materials created and held by federal agencies. 5 USCA § 552. — Abbr. FOIA.

freedom of religion. The right to adhere to any form of religion or none, to practice or abstain from practicing religious beliefs, and to be free from governmental interference with or promotion of religion, as guaranteed by the First Amendment and Article VI, § 3 of the U.S. Constitution.

freedom of speech. The right to express one's thoughts and opinions without governmental restriction, as guaranteed by the First Amendment. — Also termed *liberty of speech*. Cf. FREEDOM OF EXPRESSION.

freedom of the press. The right to print and publish materials without governmental intervention, as guaranteed by the First Amendment. — Also termed *liberty of the press*.

Free Exercise Clause. The constitutional provision (U.S. Const. amend. I) prohibiting the government from interfering in people's religious practices or forms of worship. — Also termed *Exercise Clause*. Cf. ESTABLISHMENT CLAUSE.

friendly-parent law. A statute that requires or allows a judge to consider as a factor in awarding custody the extent to which one parent encourages or thwarts the child's relationship with the other parent.

friendly society. See *benevolent association* under ASSOCIATION.

friend of the court. 1. AMICUS CURIAE. **2.** In some jurisdictions, an official who investigates and advises the court in domestic-relations cases involving minors. ● The friend of the court may also help enforce court orders in those cases.

frottage. Sexual stimulation by rubbing the genitals against another person. ● This may be accomplished without removing clothing. When a child is involved, it is a form of sexual abuse.

FTT. *abbr.* FAILURE TO THRIVE.

full adversary hearing. See *adjudication hearing* under HEARING.

full age. The age of legal majority; legal age.

full blood. See BLOOD.

full cousin. See COUSIN (1).

Full Faith and Credit Clause. U.S. Const. art. IV, § 1, which requires states to give effect to the acts, public records, and judicial decisions of other states.

Full Faith and Credit for Child-Support Orders Act. A 1994 federal statute designed to facilitate interstate child-support collection. ● Under the Act, the state first issuing a child-support order maintains continuing, exclusive jurisdiction to modify the order as long as the child or one or both of the litigants continue to reside there, unless all the contestants agree in writing to change jurisdiction. An order from one state may be registered for enforcement in another state. 28 USCA § 1738B.

full interdiction. See INTERDICTION.

fund, *n.* **1.** A sum of money or other liquid assets established for a specific purpose <a fund reserved for unanticipated expenses>.

> **blended fund.** A fund created by income from more than one source, usu. from the sale of a testator's real and personal property.

changing fund. A fund, esp. a trust fund, that changes its form periodically as it is invested and reinvested.

executor fund. A fund established for an executor to pay an estate's final expenses.

trust fund. See TRUST FUND.

2. (*usu. pl.*) Money or other assets, such as stocks, bonds, or working capital, available to pay debts, expenses, and the like <Sue invested her funds in her sister's business>.

fundamental-fairness doctrine. The rule that applies the principles of due process to a judicial proceeding. ● The term is commonly considered synonymous with *due process*.

fundamental interest. See FUNDAMENTAL RIGHT.

fundamental right. 1. A right derived from natural or fundamental law. 2. *Constitutional law.* A significant component of liberty, encroachments of which are rigorously tested by courts to ascertain the soundness of purported governmental justifications. ● A fundamental right triggers strict scrutiny to determine whether the law violates the Due Process Clause or the Equal Protection Clause of the 14th Amendment. As enunciated by the Supreme Court, fundamental rights include voting, interstate travel, and various aspects of privacy (such as marriage and contraception rights). — Also termed *fundamental interest*. See STRICT SCRUTINY. Cf. SUSPECT CLASSIFICATION.

funding, *n.* The transfer of property to a trust.

funeral expense. See EXPENSE.

future estate. See FUTURE INTEREST.

future interest. A property interest in which the privilege of possession or of other enjoyment is future and not present. ● A future interest can exist in either the grantor (as with a reversion) or the grantee (as with a remainder or executory interest). Today, most future interests are equitable interests in stocks and debt securities, with power of sale in a trustee. — Also termed *future estate*; *estate in expectancy*. Cf. PRESENT INTEREST.

G

GAL. *abbr.* See *guardian ad litem* under GUARDIAN.

gamete intrafallopian transfer. A procedure in which mature eggs are implanted in a woman's fallopian tubes and fertilized with semen. — Abbr. GIFT. — Also termed *gamete intrafallopian-tube transfer.* Cf. ZYGOTE INTRAFALLOPIAN TRANSFER; ARTIFICIAL INSEMINATION; IN VITRO FERTILIZATION.

ganancial (gə-**nan**-shəl), *adj.* Of, relating to, or consisting of community property <a spouse's ganancial rights>. See COMMUNITY PROPERTY.

gang. A group of persons who go about together or act in concert, esp. for antisocial or criminal purposes. • Many gangs (especially those made up of adolescents) have common identifying signs and symbols, such as hand signals and distinctive colors. — Also termed *street gang.*

gay marriage. See *same-sex marriage* under MARRIAGE.

gdn. *abbr.* GUARDIAN.

gender discrimination. See *sex discrimination* under DISCRIMINATION (2).

general administration. See ADMINISTRATION.

general administrative expense. See EXPENSE.

267

general administrator. See ADMINISTRATOR.

general appearance. See APPEARANCE.

general bequest. See BEQUEST.

general devise. See DEVISE.

general executor. See EXECUTOR.

general guardian. See GUARDIAN.

general legacy. See LEGACY.

general legatee. See LEGATEE.

general owner. See OWNER.

general power. See POWER (4).

general power of appointment. See POWER OF AP-
POINTMENT.

general power of attorney. See POWER OF ATTOR-
NEY.

generation. 1. A single degree or stage in the
succession of persons in natural descent. 2. The
average time span between the birth of parents and
the birth of their children.

generation-skipping tax. See TAX.

generation-skipping transfer. A conveyance of assets to a person more than one generation removed from the transferor, that is, a skip person. ● For example, a conveyance either directly or in trust from a grandparent to a grandchild is a generation-skipping transfer subject to a generation-skipping transfer tax. IRC (26 USCA) §§ 2601–2663. See *generation-skipping transfer tax* under TAX; *generation-skipping trust* under TRUST; SKIP PERSON.

generation-skipping transfer tax. See TAX.

generation-skipping trust. See TRUST.

genetic child. See *natural child* under CHILD.

genetic father. See *biological father* under FATHER.

genetic fingerprinting. See DNA IDENTIFICATION.

genetic-marker test. A medical method of testing tissue samples used in paternity and illegitimacy cases to determine whether a particular man could be the father of a child. ● This test represents a medical advance over blood-grouping tests. It analyzes DNA and is much more precise in assessing the probability of paternity. — Abbr. GMT. See PATERNITY TEST. Cf. BLOOD-GROUPING TEST; HUMAN-LEUKOCYTE ANTIBODY TEST.

genetic mother. See *biological mother* under MOTHER.

genetic parent. See *biological parent* under PAR-
ENT.

gens (jenz), *n.* [Latin] *Roman law.* A clan or group
of families who share the same name and (supposedly) a common ancestor; extended family. • Members of a *gens* are freeborn and possess full civic
rights. Pl. *gentes.*

german (jər-mən), *adj.* Having the same parents
or grandparents; closely related.

> **brother-german.** See BROTHER.

> **cousin-german.** See COUSIN.

> **sister-german.** See SISTER.

gestational carrier. See *surrogate mother* (1) under MOTHER.

gestational mother. See *birth mother* under MOTH-
ER.

gestational surrogacy. See SURROGACY.

gestational surrogate. See *surrogate mother* (1)
under MOTHER.

get, *n.* **1.** A rabbinical divorce; a Jewish divorce. **2.**
Under Jewish law, a document signed by a rabbi to
grant a divorce. • Under Jewish law, a Jewish
divorce can be obtained only after the husband has
given the get to the wife, who must voluntarily

accept it. — Also spelled *gett*. Pl. **gittin.** See *rabbinical divorce* under DIVORCE.

GIFT. *abbr.* GAMETE INTRAFALLOPIAN TRANSFER.

gift, *n.* **1.** The act of voluntarily transferring property to another without compensation. **2.** A thing so transferred. — **gift,** *vb.*

absolute gift. See *inter vivos gift.*

anatomical gift. A testamentary donation of a bodily organ or organs, esp. for transplant or for medical research. ● The procedures for making an anatomical gift are set forth in the Uniform Anatomical Gift Act, which has been adopted in every state.

antenuptial gift. See *prenuptial gift.*

class gift. A gift to a group of persons, uncertain in number at the time of the gift but to be ascertained at a future time, who are all to take in definite proportions, the share of each being dependent on the ultimate number in the group.

completed gift. A gift that is no longer in the donor's possession and control. ● Only a completed gift is taxable under the gift tax.

gift causa mortis (**kaw**-zə **mor**-tis). A gift made in contemplation of the donor's imminent death. ● The three essentials are that (1) the gift must be made with a view to the donor's present illness or peril, (2) the donor must actually die from that illness or peril, without ever recovering, and (3) there must be a delivery. Even though *causa mortis* is the more usual word order in mòdern law, the correct Latin phrasing is *mortis causa* — hence *gift mortis causa*. — Also termed *donatio causa mortis*; *donatio mortis causa*; *gift in contemplation of death*; *transfer in contemplation of death*. See CONTEMPLATION OF DEATH.

gift in contemplation of death. See *gift causa mortis*.

gift inter vivos. See *inter vivos gift*.

gift in trust. A gift of legal title to property to someone who will act as trustee for the benefit of a beneficiary.

gift over. A property gift (esp. by will) that takes effect after the expiration of a preceding estate in the property (such as a life estate or fee simple determinable) <to Sarah for life, with gift over to Don in fee>.

gift splitting. See *split gift*.

gratuitous gift. A gift made without consideration, as most gifts are. ● Strictly speaking, the term looks redundant, but it answers to the *donum gratuitum* of Roman law.

inter vivos gift (**in**-tər **vi**-vohs *or* **vee**-vohs). A gift of personal property made during the donor's lifetime and delivered to the donee with the intention of irrevocably surrendering control over the property. — Also termed *gift inter vivos*; *lifetime gift*; *absolute gift*.

lifetime gift. See *inter vivos gift*.

onerous gift (**ohn**-ə-rəs *or* **on**-ə-rəs). A gift made subject to certain conditions imposed on the recipient.

prenuptial gift (pree-**nəp**-shəl). A gift of property from one spouse to another before marriage. ● In community-property states, prenuptial gifts are often made to preserve the property's classification as separate property. — Also termed *antenuptial gift*.

split gift. *Tax.* A gift that is made by one spouse to a third person and that, for gift-tax purposes, both spouses treat as being made one-half by each spouse; a gift in which the spouses combine their annual gift-tax exclusions. ● A split gift, for example, is eligible for two annual exclusions of $10,000 each, or a total of $20,000 for one gift. — Also termed *gift-splitting*; *gift-splitting election*. See *annual exclusion* under EXCLUSION.

substitute gift. A testamentary gift to one person in place of another who is unable to take under the will for some reason. — Also termed *substitutional gift*.

taxable gift. A gift that, after adjusting for the annual exclusion and applicable deductions, is subject to the federal unified transfer tax. IRC (26 USCA) § 2503.

testamentary gift (tes-tə-**men**-tə-ree *or* -tree). A gift made in a will.

vested gift. An absolute gift, being neither conditional nor contingent, though its use or enjoyment might not occur until sometime in the future.

gift in contemplation of death. See *gift causa mortis* under GIFT.

gift inter vivos. See *inter vivos gift* under GIFT.

gift in trust. See GIFT.

gift over. See GIFT.

gift-splitting. See *split gift* under GIFT.

Gifts to Minors Act. See UNIFORM TRANSFERS TO MINORS ACT.

gift tax. See TAX.

gift-tax exclusion. See *annual exclusion* under EXCLUSION.

give, devise, and bequeath, *vb.* To transfer property by will <I give, devise, and bequeath all the rest, residue, and remainder of my estate to my

beloved daughter Sarah>. • This wording has long been criticized as redundant. In modern usage, *give* ordinarily suffices. See BEQUEST.

given name. The name assigned to a person at his or her birth or baptism. — Also termed *Christian name*. Cf. MAIDEN NAME; SURNAME.

GMT. *abbr.* GENETIC-MARKER TEST.

godparent. *Eccles. law.* A person, usu. a close family friend or relative, who accepts a parent's invitation to assume part of the responsibility for the religious education of a newly baptized child. • Often, too, there is an understanding that the god-parent would help support and rear the child if the parents were to die or become incapacitated. The spiritual parent–child relationship creates a canoni-cal impediment to marriage. — Also termed (more specifically) *godmother*; *godfather*; (in *eccles. law*) *sponsor*.

good faith, *n.* A state of mind consisting in (1) honesty in belief or purpose, (2) faithfulness to one's duty or obligation, (3) observance of reason-able commercial standards of fair dealing in a given trade or business, or (4) absence of intent to de-fraud or to seek unconscionable advantage. — Also termed *bona fides*. — **good-faith,** *adj.* Cf. BAD FAITH.

governmental employee benefit plan. See *gov-ernmental plan* under EMPLOYEE BENEFIT PLAN.

governmental plan. See EMPLOYEE BENEFIT PLAN.

governmental trust. See TRUST.

government plan. See *governmental plan* under EMPLOYEE BENEFIT PLAN.

gradual method. An intestate-inheritance scheme that gives priority to relatives who are nearest in degree of consanguinity. ● This method dates back to the English Statute of Distributions (1670). Cf. PARENTELIC METHOD; UNIVERSAL INHERITANCE RULE.

grandparent rights. A grandfather's or grandmother's rights in seeking visitation with a grandchild. ● By statute in most states, in certain circumstances a grandparent may seek court-ordered visitation with a grandchild. Typically these circumstances include the death of the grandparents' child (the child's parent) and the divorce of the child's parents. But the United States Supreme Court has held that the primary, constitutionally protected right of decision-making regarding association with a child lies with the child's parents. As a general rule, if the parent is a fit and proper guardian and objects to visitation, the parent's will prevails. *Troxel v. Granville*, 120 S.Ct. 2054 (2000).

grandparent visitation. See VISITATION.

grantor. See SETTLOR.

grantor-retained annuity trust. See TRUST.

grantor-retained income trust. See TRUST.

grantor-retained unitrust. See TRUST.

grantor trust. See TRUST.

GRAT. *abbr.* GRANTOR-RETAINED ANNUITY TRUST.

gratuitous allowance. See ALLOWANCE (1).

gratuitous gift. See GIFT.

gratuitous trust. See *donative trust* under TRUST.

gray-market adoption. See *private adoption* under ADOPTION.

green-card marriage. See MARRIAGE (1).

Gretna-Green marriage. See MARRIAGE (1).

GRIT. *abbr.* GRANTOR-RETAINED INCOME TRUST.

gross estate. See ESTATE.

gross up, *vb. Slang. Tax.* To add back to a decedent's gross estate the gift taxes paid by the decedent or the decedent's estate on gifts made by the decedent or the decedent's spouse during the three-year period preceding the decedent's death. IRC (26 USCA) § 2035.

group insurance. A form of insurance offered to a member of a group, such as the employees of a business, as long as that person remains a member of the group. • Group insurance is typically health or life (usually term life) insurance issued under a master policy between the insurer and the employer, who usually pays all or part of the premium for the insured person. Other groups, such as unions and associations, often offer group insurance to their members.

GRUT. *abbr.* GRANTOR-RETAINED UNITRUST.

GST supertrust. See *dynasty trust* under TRUST.

guarantor trust. See TRUST.

guardian, *n.* One who has the legal authority and duty to care for another's person or property, esp. because of the other's infancy, incapacity, or disability. • A guardian may be appointed either for all purposes or for a specific purpose. — Abbr. gdn. — Also termed *custodian*. See CONSERVATOR. Cf. WARD.

  chancery guardian (**chan**-sər-ee). A guardian appointed by a court of chancery to manage both the person and the estate of the ward.

  domestic guardian. A guardian appointed in the state in which the ward is domiciled.

foreign guardian. A guardian appointed by a court in a state other than the one in which the ward is domiciled. ● A foreign guardian cares for the ward's property that is located in the state of appointment.

general guardian. A guardian who has general care and control of the ward's person and estate.

guardian ad litem (ad lı-tem *or* -təm). A guardian, usu. a lawyer, appointed by the court to appear in a lawsuit on behalf of an incompetent or minor party. — Abbr. GAL. — Also termed *special guardian*; *law guardian*. Cf. NEXT FRIEND; CHILD'S ATTORNEY; ATTORNEY AD LITEM.

guardian by election. A guardian chosen by a ward who would otherwise be without one.

guardian by estoppel. See *quasi-guardian*.

guardian by statute. See *statutory guardian*.

guardian de son tort (də sawn [*or* son] **tor**[t]). See *quasi-guardian*.

guardian of property. See *guardian of the estate*.

guardian of the estate. A guardian responsible for taking care of the property of someone who is incapable of caring for his or her own property because of infancy, incapacity, or disability. — Also termed *guardian of property*.

guardian of the person. A guardian responsible for taking care of someone who is incapable of caring for himself or herself because of infancy, incapacity, or disability.

law guardian. See *guardian ad litem*.

natural guardian. **1.** In the absence of statute, the father of a legitimate child until the child reaches the age of 21. ● A father of illegitimate children may be appointed as their guardian upon the mother's death. **2.** Most commonly and by statute, either the father or the mother of a minor child — each bearing the title simultaneously. ● If one parent dies, the other is the natural guardian.

partial guardian. A guardian whose rights, duties, and powers are strictly limited to those specified in a court order.

quasi-guardian. A guardian who assumes that role without any authority. ● Such a person may be made to account as guardian. — Also termed *guardian by estoppel*; *guardian de son tort*.

special guardian. **1.** A guardian who has special or limited powers over the ward's person or estate. ● Examples are guardians who have custody of the estate but not of the person, those who have custody of the person but not of the estate, and guardians ad litem. — Also termed (in civil law) *curator ad hoc*. See CURATOR (2). **2.** See *guardian ad litem*.

standby guardian. A parent-designated guardian who is appointed to assume responsibility for a child at a future date if the child's parent becomes incapable of caring for the child but who does not divest the parent of custodial rights. • Several states have enacted statutes providing for a standby guardian in the case of a terminally ill single parent. A standby guardian assumes responsibility for a child during periods of the parent's incapacity and upon the parent's death.

statutory guardian. A guardian appointed by a court having special statutory jurisdiction. — Also termed *guardian by statute*.

successor guardian. An alternate guardian named in a parent's will against the possibility that the first nominee cannot or will not serve as guardian.

testamentary guardian. A guardian nominated by a parent's will for the person and property of a child until the latter reaches the age of majority.

guardian ad litem. See GUARDIAN.

guardian by election. See GUARDIAN.

guardian by estoppel. See *quasi-guardian* under GUARDIAN.

guardian by statute. See *statutory guardian* under GUARDIAN.

guardian de son tort. See *quasi-guardian* under GUARDIAN.

guardian of property. See *guardian of the estate* under GUARDIAN.

guardian of the estate. See GUARDIAN.

guardian of the person. See GUARDIAN.

guardian of the property. See *guardian of the estate* under GUARDIAN.

guardianship. 1. The fiduciary relationship between a guardian and a ward or other incapacitated person, whereby the guardian assumes the power to make decisions about the ward's person or property. • A guardianship is almost always an involuntary procedure imposed by the state on the ward. Cf. CONSERVATORSHIP; INTERDICTION. **2.** The duties and responsibilities of a guardian.

> *guardianship of the estate.* A guardianship in which the guardian can make decisions only about matters regarding the ward's assets and property.

> *guardianship of the person.* A guardianship in which the guardian is authorized to make all significant decisions affecting the ward's well-being, including the ward's physical custody, education, health, activities, personal relationships, and general welfare.

plenary guardianship. A guardianship in which the guardian can make decisions about both the ward's estate and the ward's person.

standby guardianship. A guardianship in which a parent designates a guardian to assume responsibility for a child at a future date, if the child's parent becomes incapable of caring for the child, but without divesting the parent of custodial rights.

guardianship of the estate. See GUARDIANSHIP.

guardianship of the person. See GUARDIANSHIP.

guest statute. A law that bars a nonpaying passenger in a noncommercial vehicle from suing the host-driver for damages resulting from the driver's ordinary negligence. • Though once common, guest statutes remain in force in only a few states. — Also termed *automobile-guest statute.* Cf. FAMILY-PURPOSE RULE.

Gun-Free Schools Act. A federal law designed to eliminate weapons in schools. 20 USCA § 8921. • The Gun-Free Schools Act provides that each state receiving federal funds under the Act must require school districts to expel for one year any student found to have brought a weapon to school. The Act does, however, provide for a case-by-case modification of the expulsion requirement.

H

habitual residence. See RESIDENCE.

Hague Convention on Protection of Children and Cooperation in Respect of Intercountry Adoption. A 1993 international agreement intended to create a uniform process by which ratifying countries will conduct intercountry adoptions. ● The Convention has not been widely adopted. The U.S. has signed but not ratified it.

Hague Convention on the Civil Aspects of International Child Abduction. An international convention (established in 1980) that seeks to counteract international child-snatching by noncustodial parents. ● The Hague Convention is a private legal mechanism available to parents seeking the return of, or access to, their children. Its purpose is to secure the prompt return of children who have been wrongfully taken from one country to another, and to enforce custody and visitation rights in the contracting countries. The procedure is summary in nature and does not contemplate continuing hearings on the merits of a dispute. More than 46 countries are parties to the Convention, including the United States, which became a signatory on July 1, 1988. 42 USCA §§ 11601–11610. — Often shortened to *Hague Convention*.

half blood. See BLOOD.

half brother. See BROTHER.

half nephew. See NEPHEW (1).

half niece. See NIECE.

half orphan. See ORPHAN (2).

half sister. See SISTER.

handfasting. See *handfast marriage* under MAR-RIAGE (1).

handfast marriage. See MARRIAGE (1).

hardship. A condition that makes it onerous or impossible for a child-support obligor to make the required child-support payment.

harmful behavior. Conduct that could injure an-other person, esp. a child.

> *cumulatively harmful behavior.* Seriously harmful parental (or caregiver) behavior that, if continued for a significant period, will over time cause serious harm to a child.

> *immediately harmful behavior.* Seriously harmful parental (or caregiver) behavior that could have caused serious injury to a child but that, because of the intervention of an outside force or a fortuitous event, did not result in any injury.

seriously harmful behavior. Parental (or care-giver) behavior that is capable of causing serious injury to a child in the person's care. ● Some examples of seriously harmful behavior are physical battering, physical neglect, sexual abuse, and abandonment.

harmful child labor. See *oppressive child labor* under CHILD LABOR.

hate crime. A crime motivated by the victim's race, color, ethnicity, religion, or national origin. ● Certain groups have lobbied to expand the definition by statute to include a crime motivated by the victim's disability, gender, or sexual orientation.

hate speech. See SPEECH.

head-and-master rule. *Hist.* The doctrine that the husband alone is authorized to manage community property. ● Some courts have held that the rule is unconstitutional gender-based discrimination. — Also termed *lord-and-master rule.* Cf. EQUAL-MANAGE-MENT RULE.

head of family. A person who supports one or more people related by birth, adoption, or marriage and with whom those persons maintain their permanent domicile. ● The phrase *head of family* appears most commonly in homestead law. For a person to have the status of head of family, there must, of necessity, be at least two people in the family. — Also termed *head of a family*. Cf. HEAD OF HOUSEHOLD.

head of household. 1. The primary income-provider within a family. **2.** For income-tax purposes, an unmarried or separated person (other than a surviving spouse) who provides a home for dependents for more than one-half of the taxable year. • A head of household is taxed at a lower rate than a single person who is not head of a household. Cf. HEAD OF FAMILY; HOUSEHOLDER.

healthcare proxy. See ADVANCE DIRECTIVE (1).

health insurance. Insurance covering medical expenses resulting from sickness or injury. — Also termed *accident and health insurance*; *sickness and accident insurance*.

health-insurance order. An order requiring a parent either to obtain health insurance for a child or to add a child to an existing health-insurance policy. • Health-insurance orders often include dental insurance.

hearing. A judicial session, usu. open to the public, held for the purpose of deciding issues of fact or of law, sometimes with witnesses testifying.

adjudication hearing. **1.** In child-abuse and neglect proceedings, the trial stage at which the court hears the state's allegations and evidence and decides whether the state has the right to intervene on behalf of the child. **2.** In a juvenile-delinquency case, a hearing at which the court hears evidence of the charges and makes a finding of whether the charges are true or not true. — Also termed *adjudicatory hearing*. See *procedural due process* under DUE PROCESS. Cf. *disposition hearing*.

adjudicatory hearing (ə-**joo**-di-kə-tor-ee). See *adjudication hearing*.

contested hearing. A hearing in which at least one of the parties has objections regarding one or more matters before the court.

continued-custody hearing. See *shelter hearing*.

custody hearing. A judicial examination of the facts relating to child custody, typically in a divorce or separation proceeding. ● Child-neglect and dependency matters are also often dealt with in custody hearings. — Also termed *custody proceeding*.

dependency hearing. See *shelter hearing*.

detention hearing. 1. A hearing held by a juvenile court to determine whether a juvenile accused of delinquent conduct should be detained, continued in confinement, or released pending an adjudicatory hearing. Cf. *adjudication hearing*; *disposition hearing*. **2.** See *shelter hearing*.

dispositional hearing. See *disposition hearing*.

disposition hearing. **1.** In child-abuse and neglect proceedings, after an adjudication hearing at
which the state proves its allegations, a hearing
at which the court hears evidence and enters
orders for the child's care, custody, and control. •
Typically, the judge determines a plan for services
aimed at reunifying or rehabilitating the family.
2. In a juvenile-delinquency case, after an adjudication hearing at which the state proves its case
against the juvenile or after a juvenile's pleading
true to the charges against him, a hearing at
which the court determines what sanctions, if
any, will be imposed on the juvenile. • At a
disposition hearing, the court balances the best
interests of the child against the need to sanction
the child for his or her actions. If the juvenile is
adjudicated a delinquent, the probation staff pre-
pares a social history of the youth and his family
and recommends a disposition. After reviewing
the social history and various recommendations,
the court enters a disposition. Among the possible
juvenile sanctions are a warning, probation, restitution, counseling, or placement in a juvenile-
detention facility. Probation is the most common
sanction. — Also termed *dispositional hearing.*
Cf. *adjudication hearing.* **3.** See *permanency hearing.*

full adversary hearing. See *adjudication hearing.*

neglect hearing. A judicial hearing involving
alleged child abuse or some other situation in

which a child has not been properly cared for by a parent or person legally responsible for the child's care. ● At issue is the civil culpability of the parent or responsible party and the possible loss of children into foster care or — in extreme cases — the termination of parental rights.

permanency hearing. Under the Adoption and Safe Families Act, a judicial proceeding to determine the future, permanent status of a child in foster care. ● Under the Act, the term *permanency hearing* replaces the term *disposition hearing*. The permanency hearing must occur within 12 months of a child's being placed in foster care. The purpose of the hearing is to determine the final direction of the case, whether that means going forward with termination proceedings or continuing plans for family reunification. — Also termed *permanency-planning hearing*.

preliminary protective hearing. See *shelter hearing*.

probable-cause hearing. See *shelter hearing*.

review hearing. After a finding of child abuse or neglect, a hearing to assess the progress in the case plan. See CASE PLAN.

shelter hearing. A hearing shortly after the state's removal of a child for suspected abuse or neglect. ● The hearing is generally held within 24 to 72 hours after the removal. The purpose of the hearing is to determine whether the state has adequate cause to maintain the children in protective care. — Also termed *shelter-care hearing*; *continued-custody hearing*; *preliminary protective hearing*; *probable-cause hearing*; *detention hearing*; *dependency hearing*.

termination-of-parental-rights hearing. A trial or court proceeding, usu. initiated by a state agency, that seeks to sever the legal ties between a parent and child, usu. so that the child can be adopted. ● The standard of proof in a termination-of-parental-rights hearing is clear and convincing evidence. *Santosky v. Kramer*, 455 U.S. 745, 102 S.Ct. 1388 (1982). — Often shortened to *termination hearing*.

transfer hearing. In a juvenile-court case, a hearing to determine whether the case should be transferred to adult criminal court where the juvenile will be tried as an adult. ● Every state, as well as the District of Columbia, has a transfer statute. The United States Supreme Court defined the due-process requirements for transfer hearings in *Kent v. United States*, 383 U.S. 541, 86 S.Ct. 1045 (1966). See TRANSFER STATUTE; MANDATORY WAIVER; STATUTORY EXCLUSION.

uncontested hearing. A hearing in which either (1) the parties are in agreement as to all matters before the court, or (2) one of the parties has failed to answer the lawsuit.

hearsay. 1. Traditionally, testimony that is given by a witness who relates not what he or she knows personally, but what others have said, and that is therefore dependent on the credibility of someone other than the witness. ● Such testimony is generally inadmissible under the rules of evidence. **2.** In federal law, a statement (either a verbal assertion or nonverbal assertive conduct), other than one made by the declarant while testifying at the trial or hearing, offered in evidence to prove the truth of the matter asserted. Fed. R. Evid. 801(c). — Also termed *hearsay evidence*; *secondhand evidence*.

> **double hearsay.** A hearsay statement that contains further hearsay statements within it, none of which is admissible unless exceptions to the rule against hearsay can be applied to each level <the double hearsay was the investigation's report stating that Amy admitted to running the red light>. Fed. R. Evid. 805. — Also termed *multiple hearsay*; *hearsay within hearsay*.

hearsay exception. Any of several deviations from the hearsay rule, allowing the admission of otherwise inadmissible statements because the circumstances surrounding the statements provide a basis for considering the statements reliable.

> **tender-years hearsay exception.** A hearsay exception for an out-of-court statement by a child ten years of age or younger, usu. describing an act of physical or sexual abuse, when the child is unavailable to testify and the court determines that the time, content, and circumstances of the statement make it reliable.

hearsay rule. The rule that no assertion offered as testimony can be received unless it is or has been open to test by cross-examination or an opportunity for cross-examination, except as provided otherwise by the rules of evidence, by court rules, or by statute. ● The chief reasons for the rule are that out-of-court statements amounting to hearsay are not made under oath and are not subject to cross-examination. Fed. R. Evid. 802. Rule 803 provides 23 explicit exceptions to the hearsay rule, regardless of whether the out-of-court declarant is available to testify, and Rule 804 provides five more exceptions for situations in which the declarant is unavailable to testify.

hearsay within hearsay. See *double hearsay* under HEARSAY.

heartbalm statute. A state law that abolishes the rights of action for monetary damages as solace for the emotional trauma occasioned by a loss of love and relationship. ● The abolished rights of action include alienation of affections, breach of promise to marry, criminal conversation, and seduction of a person over the legal age of consent. Many states today have enacted heartbalm statutes primarily because of the highly speculative nature of the injury and the potential for abusive prosecution, as well as the difficulties of determining the cause of a loss. The terminology in this field is somewhat confusing, since a *heartbalm statute* abolishes lawsuits that were known as *heartbalm suits*; some scholars therefore call the abolitionary statutes *anti-heartbalm statutes*. But the prevailing term is *heartbalm statute*. — Also written *heart-balm statute*. — Also termed *heartbalm act*; *anti-heartbalm statute*; *anti-heartbalm act*.

heightened scrutiny. See INTERMEDIATE SCRUTINY.

heir (air). **1.** A person who, under the laws of intestacy, is entitled to receive an intestate decedent's property. — Also termed *legal heir*; *heir at law*; *lawful heir*; *heir general*. **2.** Loosely (in common-law jurisdictions), a person who inherits real or personal property, whether by will or by intestate succession. **3.** Popularly, a person who has inherited or is in line to inherit great wealth. **4.** *Civil law*. A person who succeeds to the rights and occupies the place of, or is entitled to succeed to the estate of, a decedent, whether by an act of the decedent or by operation of law. ● The term *heir* under the civil law has a more expanded meaning than under the common law.

> *afterborn heir.* One born after the death of an intestate from whom the heir is entitled to inherit. See *afterborn child* under CHILD.

> *and his heirs.* A term of art formerly required to transfer complete title (a fee simple absolute) to real estate <A conveys Blackacre to B and his heirs>. ● This phrasing originated in the translation of a Law French phrase used in medieval

grants (*a lui et a ses heritiers pour toujours* "to him and his heirs forever"). See FEE SIMPLE.

apparent heir. See *heir apparent*.

beneficiary heir (ben-ə-**fish**-ee-er-ee). In the civil law, an heir who accepts an inheritance but files a benefit of inventory to limit his or her liability for estate debts to the value of the inheritance. — Also termed *heir beneficiary*. See BENEFIT OF INVENTORY. Cf. *unconditional heir*.

bodily heir. See *heir of the body*.

collateral heir. One who is neither a direct descendant nor an ancestor of the decedent, but whose kinship is through a collateral line, such as a brother, sister, uncle, aunt, nephew, niece, or cousin. Cf. *lineal heir*.

expectant heir. An heir who has a reversionary or future interest in property, or a chance of succeeding to it. — Also termed *heir expectant*. See REVERSION; REMAINDER. Cf. *prospective heir*.

forced heir. *Civil law.* Under Louisiana law, a person whom the testator or donor cannot disinherit because the law reserves part of the estate for that person. See LEGITIME.

heir apparent. An heir who is certain to inherit unless he or she dies first or is excluded by a valid will. — Also termed *apparent heir*. Cf. *heir presumptive*.

heir beneficiary. See *beneficiary heir*.

heir by adoption. A person who has been adopted by (and thus has become an heir to) the deceased. ● By statute in most jurisdictions, an adopted child has the same right of succession to intestate property as a biological child unless the deceased clearly expresses a contrary intention. Jurisdictions differ on whether an adopted child may in addition inherit from his or her biological parents or family. The clear majority view, however, is that upon adoption, a complete severance of rights and obligations occurs and the child forfeits inheritance from all biological relatives.

heir by devise. One to whom lands are given by will.

heir conventional. In the civil law, one who takes a succession because of a contract or settlement entitling him or her to it.

heir expectant. See *expectant heir*.

heir of the blood. An heir who succeeds to an estate because of consanguinity with the decedent, in either the ascending or descending line.

heir of the body. *Archaic.* A lineal descendant of the decedent, excluding a surviving spouse, adopted children, and collateral relations. ● The term of art *heirs of the body* was formerly used to create a fee tail <A conveys Blackacre to B and the heirs of his body>. — Also termed *bodily heir*.

heir presumptive. An heir who will inherit if the potential intestate dies immediately, but who may be excluded if another, more closely related heir is born. — Also termed *presumptive heir.* Cf. *heir apparent.*

joint heir. **1.** A coheir. **2.** A person who is or will be an heir to both of two designated persons at the death of the survivor of them, the word *joint* being here applied to the ancestors rather than the heirs.

known heir. An heir who is present to claim an inheritance, the extent of which depends on there being no closer relative.

laughing heir. Slang. An heir distant enough to feel no grief when a relative dies and leaves an inheritance (generally viewed as a windfall) to the heir.

lineal heir. A person who is either an ancestor or a descendant of the decedent, such as a parent or a child. Cf. *collateral heir.*

natural heir. An heir by consanguinity as distinguished from an heir by adoption, or a statutory heir (such as a person's spouse).

presumptive heir. See *heir presumptive.*

pretermitted heir (pree-tər-**mit**-id). A child or spouse who has been omitted from a will, as when a testator makes a will naming his or her two children and then, sometime later, has two more

children who are not mentioned in the will. —
Also termed (more specif.) *pretermitted child*; *pre-termitted spouse*. See PRETERMITTED-HEIR STATUTE.

prospective heir. An heir who may inherit but
may be excluded; an heir apparent or an heir
presumptive. Cf. *expectant heir*.

testamentary heir (tes-tə-**men**-tə-ree *or* -tree).
In the civil law, a person who is appointed heir in
the decedent's will.

unconditional heir. In the civil law, a person
who chooses — expressly or tacitly — to inherit
without any reservation or without making an
inventory. Cf. *beneficiary heir*.

heir apparent. See HEIR.

heir at law. See HEIR.

heir beneficiary. See *beneficiary heir* under HEIR.

heir by adoption. See HEIR.

heir by devise. See HEIR.

heir conventional. See HEIR.

heirdom. The state of being an heir; succession by
inheritance.

heiress. 1. *Archaic.* A female heir. See HEIR. **2.** A
woman or girl who has inherited or is in line to
inherit great wealth.

heir expectant. See *expectant heir* under HEIR.

heir general. See HEIR.

heir-hunter. A person whose business is to track down missing heirs.

heirless estate. See ESTATE.

heirloom. 1. An item of personal property that by local custom, contrary to the usual legal rule, descends to the heir along with the inheritance, instead of passing to the executor or administrator of the last owner. ● Traditional examples are an ancestor's coat of armor, family portraits, title deeds, and keys. Blackstone gave a false etymology that many have copied: "The termination, *loom*, is of Saxon origin; in which language it signifies a limb or member; so that an heirloom is nothing else, but a limb or member of the inheritance." 2 William Blackstone, *Commentaries on the Law of England* 427 (1766). In fact, *loom* derives from Old English *geloma* "utensil," and *loom* meant "implement, tool." **2.** Popularly, a treasured possession of great sentimental value passed down through generations within a family.

heir of the blood. See HEIR.

heir of the body. See HEIR.

heir presumptive. See HEIR.

heirship. 1. The quality or condition of being an heir. **2.** The relation between an ancestor and an heir.

hereditament (her-ə-**dit**-ə-mənt *or* hə-**red**-i-tə-mənt). **1.** Any property that can be inherited; anything that passes by intestacy. **2.** Real property; land.

> *corporeal hereditament* (kor-**por**-ee-əl). A tangible item of property, such as land, a building, or a fixture.

> *incorporeal hereditament* (in-kor-**por**-ee-əl). An intangible right in land, such as an easement. • The various types at common law were advowsons, annuities, commons, dignities, franchises, offices, pensions, rents, tithes, and ways.

hereditary, *adj.* Of or relating to inheritance; that descends from an ancestor to an heir.

hereditary succession. See *intestate succession* under SUCCESSION (2).

heredity. 1. *Archaic.* Intestate succession; the taking of an inheritance by common-law succession. **2.** The hereditary transmission of characteristics from a parent to a child; the biological law by which characteristics of a living being tend to repeat themselves in the being's descendants.

heritable (**her**-i-tə-bəl), *adj.* INHERITABLE.

heritable obligation. See *inheritable obligation* under OBLIGATION.

heterologous artificial insemination. See *artificial insemination by donor* under ARTIFICIAL INSEMINATION.

high-test marriage. See *covenant marriage* under MARRIAGE (1).

HLA test. See HUMAN-LEUKOCYTE ANTIGEN TEST.

holograph (**hol**-ə-graf), *n.* A document (such as a will or deed) that is handwritten by its author. ● The majority rule is that a holographic will need not be entirely handwritten — only the "material provisions" — to take into account the popular use of fill-in-the-blank will forms. This is also the position of the Uniform Probate Code. — Also termed *olograph*. — **holographic,** *adj.* Cf. ONOMASTIC; SYMBOLIC.

holographic will. See WILL.

homeless shelter. See SHELTER.

homeowners' association. See ASSOCIATION.

homeowner's insurance. Insurance that covers both damage to the insured's residence and liability claims made against the insured (esp. those arising from the insured's negligence).

home state. In an interstate child-custody dispute governed by the Uniform Child Custody Jurisdiction and Enforcement Act, the state where a child has lived with a parent or a person acting as a parent for at least six consecutive months immediately before the proceeding. See *home-state jurisdiction* under JURISDICTION.

home-state jurisdiction. See JURISDICTION.

homestead. 1. The house, outbuildings, and adjoining land owned and occupied by a person or family as a residence. ● As long as the homestead does not exceed in area or value the limits fixed by law, in most states it is exempt from forced sale for collection of a debt. — Also termed *homestead estate*. See HOMESTEAD LAW.

   business homestead. The premises on which a family's business is located. ● In some states, business homesteads are exempt from execution or judicial sale for most kinds of debt.

   constitutional homestead. A homestead, along with its exemption from forced sale, conferred on the head of a household by a state constitution.

   probate homestead. A homestead created by a probate court from a decedent's estate for the benefit of the decedent's surviving spouse and minor children. ● Under most statutes providing for the creation of a probate homestead, it is exempt from forced sale for the collection of decedent's debts. The family can remain in the home at least until the youngest child reaches the age of majority. Many states allow the surviving spouse to live in the home for life. In a few states, such as Texas, the right to a probate homestead is constitutional. See *family allowance, spousal allowance* under ALLOWANCE; HOMESTEAD LAW. Cf. *life estate* under ESTATE.

2. A surviving spouse's right of occupying the family home for life. ● In some states, the right is extended to other dependents of a decedent.

homesteader. One who acquires or occupies a homestead.

homestead estate. See HOMESTEAD.

homestead exemption. See HOMESTEAD LAW.

homestead-exemption statute. See HOMESTEAD LAW.

homestead law. A statute exempting a homestead from execution or judicial sale for debt, unless all owners, usu. a husband and wife, have jointly mortgaged the property or otherwise subjected it to creditors' claims. — Also termed *homestead exemption*; *homestead-exemption statute*.

home-study report. A summary of an investigation into a child's home, family environment, and background, usu. prepared by a social worker when a child has been removed from his or her home because of abuse or neglect, but also prepared after a similar investigation of the home of potential adoptive parents. — Often shortened to *home study*. — Also termed *custody evaluation*; *social study*.

homicide by abuse. Homicide in which the perpetrator, under circumstances showing an extreme indifference to human life, causes the death of the perpetrator's dependent — usu. a child or mentally retarded person.

homologous artificial insemination. See ARTIFICIAL INSEMINATION.

homosexual marriage. See *same-sex marriage* under MARRIAGE (1).

honorary trust. See TRUST.

horizontal equality. In per capita distribution of an estate, a system that results in equal distribution among members of the same generation. Restatement (Third) of Property: Wills and Other Donative Transfers § 2.3 (Tentative Draft No. 2, 1998). See PER CAPITA. Cf. VERTICAL EQUALITY.

hotchpot (**hoch**-pot), *n*. **1.** The blending of items of property to secure equality of division, esp. as practiced either in cases of divorce or in cases in which advancements of an intestate's property must be made up to the estate by a contribution or by an accounting. — Also termed *hotchpotch*. **2.** In a community-property state, the property that falls within the community estate. See COLLATIO BONORUM.

hotel divorce. See DIVORCE.

householder. **1.** A person who keeps house with his or her family; the head or master of a family. **2.** A person who has a household. **3.** An occupier of a house. Cf. HEAD OF HOUSEHOLD.

H.R. 10 plan. See KEOGH PLAN.

human-leukocyte antigen test. A medical process of analyzing the blood sample of a man in a paternity or legitimacy case by comparing certain indicators with the child's blood. — Abbr. HLA test. See BLOOD-GROUPING TEST. Cf. GENETIC-MARKER TEST.

husband. A married man; a man who has a lawful wife living. ● Etymologically, the word signified the *house bond*, the man who, according to Saxon ideas and institutions, held around him the family, for which he was legally responsible.

> ***common-law husband.*** The husband in a common-law marriage; a man who contracts an informal marriage with a woman and then holds himself out to the community as being married to her. See *common-law marriage* under MARRIAGE (1).

husband–wife immunity. The immunity of one spouse from a tort action by the other spouse for personal injury. • As of 1992, 38 states and the District of Columbia had abolished interspousal tort immunity either by judicial opinion or by statute. Nine states had abolished the rule only in specific instances such as intentional or vehicular torts. — Also termed *interspousal immunity*; *interspousal tort immunity*; *marital immunity*.

husband–wife privilege. See *marital privilege* under PRIVILEGE.

Hyde Amendment. A federal law that prohibits the use of Medicaid funds for abortions except when necessary to save the mother's life, and that prohibits federally funded family-planning programs from providing abortion counseling. • The bill was sponsored by Representative Henry Hyde of Illinois.

I

ICPC. *abbr*. INTERSTATE COMPACT ON THE PLACEMENT OF CHILDREN.

ICWA. *abbr*. INDIAN CHILD WELFARE ACT.

IDEA. *abbr*. INDIVIDUALS WITH DISABILITIES EDUCATION ACT.

identified adoption. See *private adoption* under ADOPTION.

IFP. *abbr*. IN FORMA PAUPERIS.

ignoring, *n*. A parent's or caregiver's pattern of depriving a child of essential intellectual or emotional stimulation or of otherwise stifling emotional growth and intellectual development, essentially by being unavailable. Cf. ISOLATING; REJECTING.

illegitimacy. **1.** Unlawfulness. **2.** The status of a person who is born outside a lawful marriage and who is not later legitimated by the parents. — Also termed *bastardy*. Cf. LEGITIMACY.

illegitimate, *adj*. (Of a child) born out of lawful wedlock and never having been legitimated <illegitimate son>. • A child conceived while the mother is married but born after she is divorced or widowed is considered legitimate.

illegitimate child. See CHILD.

illicit cohabitation. See COHABITATION.

illusory-transfer doctrine. The rule that the law disregards an inter vivos gift over which the donor retains so much control that there is no good-faith intent to relinquish the transferred property. ● The illusory-transfer doctrine is usually applied to inter vivos trusts in which the settlor retains an excessive control or an interest — for instance, one in which the settlor retains the income for life, the power to revoke, and substantial managerial powers. The leading case on this doctrine is *Newman v. Dore*, 9 N.E.2d 966 (N.Y. 1937). See *colorable transfer* under TRANSFER.

illusory trust. See TRUST.

immediate death. See DEATH.

immediate descent. See DESCENT.

immediate family. See FAMILY.

immediately harmful behavior. See HARMFUL BEHAVIOR.

impairing the morals of a minor. The offense of an adult's engaging in sex-related acts, short of intercourse, with a minor. ● Examples of this conduct are fondling, taking obscene photographs, and showing pornographic materials. Cf. CONTRIBUTING TO

THE DELINQUENCY OF A MINOR; CORRUPTION OF A MINOR; CORRUPTING.

impediment (im-**ped**-ə-mənt). A hindrance or obstruction; esp., one that constitutes a ground for annulling a marriage.

canonical impediment. A ground for annulment recognized by canon law and developed by the ecclesiastical courts of the Roman Catholic Church. • Canonical impediments include affinity, impotence, disparity of worship, and previous religious profession.

civil impediment. A ground for annulment recognized by civil law of contracts, such as minority, unsoundness of mind, fraud, and duress. • The defects of fraud and duress may be waived, and the parties may confirm the marriage.

diriment impediment. A fact that raises an absolute bar to marriage and renders a contracted marriage void. • Diriment impediments include consanguinity within a prohibited degree and prior undissolved marriage.

imperfect trust. See *executory trust* under TRUST.

implied intent. See INTENT.

implied trust. See *constructive trust* under TRUST; *resulting trust* under TRUST.

impotence (**im**-pə-tənts). A man's inability to achieve an erection and therefore to have sexual intercourse. ● Because an impotent husband cannot consummate a marriage, impotence has often been cited as a ground for annulment. — Also termed *impotency*; *physical incapacity*; *erectile dysfunction*.

improper influence. See UNDUE INFLUENCE.

in being. Existing in life <life in being plus 21 years>. ● In property law, this term includes children conceived but not yet born. — Also termed *in esse*. See life in being.

incapacity. 1. Lack of physical or mental capabilities. **2.** Lack of ability to have certain legal consequences attach to one's actions. ● For example, a five-year-old has an incapacity to make a binding contract. **3.** DISABILITY (1). **4.** DISABILITY (2). Cf. INCOMPETENCY.

testimonial incapacity. The lack of capacity to testify.

incest, *n.* **1.** Sexual relations between family members or close relatives, including children related by adoption. ● Incest was not a crime under English common law but was punished as an ecclesiastical offense. Modern statutes make it a felony. **2.** Intermarriage between persons related in any degree of consanguinity or affinity within which marriage is prohibited — for example, through the uncle–niece or aunt–nephew relationship. — **incestuous,** *adj.*

incestuous adultery. See ADULTERY.

inchoate dower. See DOWER.

incidental beneficiary. See BENEFICIARY.

income. The money or other form of payment that one receives, usu. periodically, from employment, business, investments, royalties, gifts, and the like. See EARNINGS.

> *accumulated income.* Income that is retained in an account; esp., income that a trust has generated, but that has not yet been reinvested or distributed by the trustee.

> *aggregate income.* The combined income of a husband and wife who file a joint tax return.

> *income in respect of a decedent.* Income earned by a person, but not collected before death. ● This income is included in the decedent's gross estate for estate-tax purposes. For income-tax purposes, it is taxed to the estate or, if the estate does not collect the income, it is taxed to the eventual recipient. — Abbr. IRD.

> *split income.* An equal division between spouses of earnings reported on a joint tax return, allowing for equal tax treatment in community-property and common-law states.

income-and-expense declaration. In child-support litigation, a document that contains information on a parent's income, assets, expenses, and liabilities. — Also termed *financial statement*.

income beneficiary. See BENEFICIARY.

income exclusion. See EXCLUSION.

income in respect of a decedent. See INCOME.

income-shifting. The practice of transferring income to a taxpayer in a lower tax bracket, such as a child, to reduce tax liability. See *kiddie tax* under TAX.

income-withholding order. A court order providing for the withholding of a person's income by an employer, usu. to enforce a child-support order. — Also termed *wage-withholding order*; *wage-assignment order*; *wage assignment*. Cf. ATTACHMENT OF WAGES.

incompatibility, *n.* Conflict in personality and disposition, usu. leading to the breakup of a marriage. • Every state now recognizes some form of incompatibility as a no-fault ground for divorce. See *no-fault divorce* under DIVORCE. Cf. IRRECONCILABLE DIFFERENCES; IRRETRIEVABLE BREAKDOWN OF THE MARRIAGE.

incompetency, *n.* Lack of legal ability in some respect, esp. to stand trial or to testify <once the defense lawyer established her client's incompetency, the client did not have to stand trial>. — Also termed *incompetence*; *mental incompetence.* — **in-competent,** *adj.* Cf. INCAPACITY.

incomplete transfer. See TRANSFER.

in contemplation of death. See CONTEMPLATION OF DEATH.

incontestability clause. *Insurance.* An insurance-policy provision (esp. found in a life-insurance policy) that prevents the insurer, after a specified period (usu. one or two years), from disputing the policy's validity on the basis of fraud or mistake; a clause that bars all defenses except those reserved (usu. conditions and the payment of premiums). • Most states require that a life-insurance policy contain a clause making the policy incontestable after it has been in effect for a specified period, unless the insured does not pay premiums or violates policy conditions relating to military service. Some states also require similar provisions in accident and sickness policies. — Also termed *noncontestability clause*; *incontestable clause*; *uncontestable clause.* Cf. CONTESTABILITY CLAUSE.

incorporation by reference. A method of making a secondary document part of a primary document by including in the primary document a statement that the secondary document should be treated as if it were contained within the primary one. • A separate writing, existing when a will is signed, may be incorporated by reference into the will if the testator so intends and if the writing is described sufficiently to permit its identification. Unif. Probate Code § 2–510. Not all jurisdictions follow this rule. — Often shortened to *incorporation*. — Also termed *adoption by reference*.

incorporeal hereditament. See HEREDITAMENT.

incorporeal ownership. See OWNERSHIP.

incorrigibility (in-kor-ə-jə-**bil**-ə-tee *or* in-kahr-), *n*. Serious or persistent misbehavior by a child, making reformation by parental control impossible or unlikely. — **incorrigible,** *adj*. Cf. JUVENILE DELINQUENCY.

incorrigible child. See CHILD.

indecency, *n*. The state or condition of being outrageously offensive, esp. in a vulgar or sexual way. ● Unlike obscene material, indecent speech is protected under the First Amendment. — **indecent,** *adj*. Cf. OBSCENITY.

indecent assault. See *sexual assault* (2) under ASSAULT.

indecent liberties. Improper behavior, usu. toward a child, esp. of a sexual nature.

indefeasible remainder. See REMAINDER.

indefeasibly vested remainder. See *indefeasible remainder* under REMAINDER.

indefinite failure of issue. See FAILURE OF ISSUE.

indenture of trust. See TRUST INDENTURE.

indenture trustee. See TRUSTEE.

independent adoption. See *private adoption* under ADOPTION.

independent executor. See EXECUTOR.

independent-living program. A training course designed to enable foster children who are near the age of majority to leave the foster-care system and manage their own affairs as adults. • Independent living programs provide education, training, and financial and employment counseling. They also help many foster youth in locating suitable post-foster-care housing. Permanency planning orders or case plans can — but are not required to — provide for independent living as a goal for a child in long-term foster care and describe how it is to be accomplished. See AGING-OUT; PERMANENCY PLAN.

independent personal representative. See *personal representative* under REPRESENTATIVE.

independent probate. See *informal probate* under PROBATE (1).

independent-significance doctrine. The principle that effect will be given to a testator's disposition that is not done solely to avoid the requirements of a will. • An example is a will provision that gives the contents of the testator's safe-deposit box to his niece. Because the safe-deposit box has utility ("significance") independent of the will, the gift of its contents at the testator's death is valid.

indestructible trust. See TRUST.

Indian child. Under the Indian Child Welfare Act, any unmarried person under the age of 18 who either is a member of an Indian tribe or is both eligible for membership in an Indian tribe and the biological child of a member of an Indian tribe. See INDIAN CHILD WELFARE ACT.

Indian Child Welfare Act. A federal act that governs child-custody proceedings — including foster-care placement, preadoptive placement, adoptive placement, and termination of parental rights — in cases involving a child of American Indian descent. 25 USCA §§ 1911 et seq. • Congress enacted the Act to help protect the best interests of Indian children, to promote the stability and security of Indian tribes and families, and to counteract the disproportionate foster-care placement and adoption of Indian children by non-Indians. The Act provides minimum federal standards for removing Indian children from their families and for placing them in foster or adoptive homes that will provide an environment reflecting the values of the Indian culture. The Act has an important jurisdictional feature: in a custody dispute involving an Indian child who resides in or is domiciled within an Indian reservation, the tribe and its tribal courts have exclusive jurisdiction. And in a custody dispute involving an Indian child who lives off a reservation, upon petition, any state court should usually defer and transfer the case to the tribal court unless a party demonstrates good cause to the contrary. — Abbr. ICWA.

indigent (in-di-jənt), *n.* **1.** A poor person. **2.** A person who is found to be financially unable to pay filing fees and court costs and so is allowed to proceed in *forma pauperis*. ● The Supreme Court has recognized an indigent petitioner's right to have certain fees and costs waived in divorce and termination-of-parental-rights cases. *Boddie v. Connecticut*, 401 U.S. 371, 91 S.Ct. 780 (1971); *M.L.B. v. S.L.J.*, 519 U.S. 102, 117 S.Ct. 555 (1996). — **indigent,** *adj.* See PAUPER; IN FORMA PAUPERIS.

indigent defendant. A person who is too poor to hire a lawyer and who, upon indictment, becomes eligible to receive aid from a court-appointed attorney and a waiver of court costs. ● In some jurisdictions, an indigent defendant in a termination-of-parental-rights case is entitled to court-appointed representation. See IN FORMA PAUPERIS. Cf. PAUPER.

indignity (in-**dig**-ni-tee), *n.* A ground for divorce consisting in one spouse's pattern of behavior calculated to humiliate the other. — Also termed *personal indignity*. Cf. CRUELTY.

individual account plan. See *defined-contribution plan* under EMPLOYEE BENEFIT PLAN.

individualized education program. A specially designed plan of educational instruction for a child with disabilities. ● The individualized education program is a written plan that details the particular child's abilities, the child's educational goals, and the services to be provided. See CHILD WITH DISABILITIES; INDIVIDUALS WITH DISABILITIES EDUCATION ACT.

individual property. See SEPARATE PROPERTY (1).

individual retirement account. A savings or brokerage account to which a person may contribute up to a specified amount of earned income each year ($2,000 under current law). ● The contributions, along with any interest earned in the account, are not taxed until the money is withdrawn after a participant reaches 59½ (or before then, if a 10% penalty is paid). — Abbr. IRA. Cf. KEOGH PLAN.

Roth IRA. An IRA in which contributions are nondeductible when they are made. ● No further taxes are assessed on the contributions (or accrued interest) when the money is withdrawn (if all applicable rules are followed). This term takes its name from Senator William Roth, who sponsored the legislation creating this type of IRA.

Individuals with Disabilities Education Act. A federal statute that governs the public education of children with physical or mental handicaps and attempts to ensure that these children receive a free public education that meets their unique needs. ● The Education of All Handicapped Children Act (enacted in 1975) was renamed the Individuals with Disabilities Education Act in 1990, and this Act was substantially amended in 1997. All states currently participate in this joint federal–state initiative. 20 USCA §§ 1400–1485. — Abbr. IDEA.

induced abortion. See ABORTION.

ineffective revocation. See DEPENDENT RELATIVE REVOCATION.

in esse (in **es**-ee *also* **es**-ay). [Latin "in being"] IN BEING <the court was concerned only with the rights of the children *in esse*>. Cf. IN POSSE.

infancy. 1. MINORITY. **2.** Early childhood.

natural infancy. At common law, the period ending at age seven, during which a child was presumed to be without criminal capacity.

3. The beginning stages of anything.

infant. 1. A newborn baby. **2.** MINOR.

infanticide (in-**fant**-ə-sıd). **1.** The act of killing a newborn child, esp. by the parents or with their consent. ● In archaic usage, the word referred also to the killing of an unborn child. — Also termed *child destruction*; *neonaticide*. Cf. FETICIDE. **2.** The practice of killing newborn children. **3.** One who kills a newborn child. — **infanticidal,** *adj.* Cf. PRO-LICIDE.

infertile, *adj.* Unable to conceive or bear offspring; sterile. — **infertility,** *n.*

infibulation. See FEMALE GENITAL MUTILATION.

infidelity. Unfaithfulness to an obligation; esp., marital unfaithfulness. Cf. ADULTERY.

informal acknowledgment. See ACKNOWLEDGMENT.

informal marriage. See *common-law marriage* under MARRIAGE (1).

informal probate. See PROBATE.

in forma pauperis (in **for**-mə **paw**-pə-ris), *adv.* [Latin "in the manner of a pauper"] In the manner of an indigent who is permitted to disregard filing fees and court costs <when suing, a poor person is generally entitled to proceed *in forma pauperis*>. ● For instance, in many jurisdictions, an indigent divorce petitioner's filing fees and court costs are waived. — Abbr. IFP.

informed consent. See CONSENT.

inherit, *vb.* **1.** To receive (property) from an ancestor under the laws of intestate succession upon the ancestor's death. **2.** To receive (property) as a bequest or devise.

inheritable, *adj.* **1.** (Of property) capable of being inherited. **2.** (Of a person) capable of inheriting. — Also termed *heritable*.

inheritable blood. See BLOOD.

inheritable obligation. See OBLIGATION.

inheritance. 1. Property received from an ancestor under the laws of intestacy. **2.** Property that a person receives by bequest or devise.

   dual inheritance. An adopted child's intestate inheritance through both his adopted family and his natural parent. ● The problem of dual inheritance occurs only if a relative of the birth parent adopts the child. For instance, if a child's mother dies and the maternal grandparents adopt the grandchild, and if a grandparent then dies intestate, the child qualifies for two separate shares — one as a child and the other as a grandchild. In some jurisdictions, by statute, such a child is allowed to inherit only the adopted child's share. Under the Uniform Probate Code, the child takes the larger of the two shares.

   several inheritance. An inheritance that descends to two persons severally, as by moieties.

universal inheritance. A system by which an intestate's estate escheats to the state only if the decedent leaves no surviving relatives, no matter how distant. ● Universal inheritance has been almost universally abandoned in Anglo–American jurisdictions. See Restatement (Third) of Property: Wills and Other Donative Transfers § 2.4 (Tentative Draft No. 2, 1998). See UNIVERSAL-INHERITANCE RULE.

inheritance tax. See TAX.

inheritor. A person who inherits; HEIR.

inheritrix. *Archaic.* A female heir; HEIRESS.

inhuman treatment. Physical or mental cruelty so severe that it endangers life or health. ● Inhuman treatment is usually grounds for divorce. See CRUELTY.

injunction (in-**jəngk**-shən), *n.* A court order commanding or preventing an action. ● To get an injunction, the complainant must show that there is no plain, adequate, and complete remedy at law and that an irreparable injury will result unless the relief is granted. — Also termed *writ of injunction.*

   affirmative injunction. See *mandatory injunction.*

   ex parte injunction. A preliminary injunction issued after the court has heard from only the moving party. — Also termed *temporary restraining order*.

final injunction. See *permanent injunction*.

interlocutory injunction. See *preliminary injunction*.

mandatory injunction. An injunction that orders an affirmative act or mandates a specified course of conduct. — Also termed *affirmative injunction*. Cf. *prohibitory injunction*.

permanent injunction. An injunction granted after a final hearing on the merits. • Despite its name, a permanent injunction does not necessarily last forever. — Also termed *perpetual injunction*; *final injunction*.

perpetual injunction. See *permanent injunction*.

preliminary injunction. A temporary injunction issued before or during trial to prevent an irreparable injury from occurring before the court has a chance to decide the case. • A preliminary injunction will be issued only after the defendant receives notice and an opportunity to be heard. — Also termed *interlocutory injunction*; *temporary injunction*; *provisional injunction*. Cf. EX PARTE INJUNCTION; TEMPORARY RESTRAINING ORDER.

preventive injunction. An injunction designed to prevent a loss or injury in the future. Cf. *reparative injunction*.

prohibitory injunction. An injunction that forbids or restrains an act. ● This is the most common type of injunction. Cf. *mandatory injunction.*

provisional injunction. See *preliminary injunction.*

reparative injunction (ri-**par**-ə-tiv). An injunction requiring the defendant to restore the plaintiff to the position that the plaintiff occupied before the defendant committed a wrong. Cf. *preventive injunction.*

temporary injunction. See *preliminary injunction.*

in-law, *n.* A relative by marriage.

in loco parentis (in **loh**-koh pə-**ren**-tis), *adv. & adj.* [Latin "in the place of a parent"] Of, relating to, or acting as a temporary guardian or caretaker of a child, taking on all or some of the responsibilities of a parent. ● The Supreme Court has recognized that during the school day, a teacher or administrator may act *in loco parentis.* See *Vernonia Sch. Dist. v. Acton,* 515 U.S. 646, 115 S.Ct. 2386 (1995). See PERSON IN LOCO PARENTIS.

in mortua manu (in **mor**-choo-ə **man**-yoo), *adj. & adv.* [Law Latin "in a dead hand"] *Hist.* (Of property) perpetually controlled according to a decedent's directions. ● Land held by a religious society was described this way because the church could hold property perpetually without rendering feudal service. — Also termed *in manu mortua*. See DEADHAND CONTROL.

innocent spouse. A spouse who may be relieved of liability for taxes on income that the other spouse did not include on a joint tax return. ● The innocent spouse must prove that the other spouse omitted the income, that the innocent spouse did not know and had no reason to know of the omission, and that it would be unfair under the circumstances to hold the innocent spouse liable.

inofficious testament. See TESTAMENT.

inofficious will. See *inofficious testament* under TESTAMENT.

in posse (in **pos**-ee). [Latin] Not currently existing, but ready to come into existence under certain conditions in the future; potential <the will contemplated both living children and children *in posse*>. Cf. IN ESSE.

***in propria persona*,** *adv. & adj.* See PRO SE.

insane asylum. See ASYLUM (2).

insane delusion. An irrational, persistent belief in an imaginary state of facts resulting in a lack of capacity to undertake acts of legal consequence, such as making a will. See CAPACITY (2).

insanity, *n.* Any mental disorder severe enough that it prevents a person from having legal capacity and excuses the person from criminal or civil responsibility. ● Insanity is a legal, not a medical, standard. — Also termed *legal insanity*; *lunacy*. Cf. *diminished capacity* under CAPACITY; SANITY.

insinuation of a will. *Civil law.* The first production of a will for probate.

instance court. See *trial court* under COURT.

instantaneous death. See DEATH.

in stirpes. See PER STIRPES.

instruction directive. A document that contains specific directions concerning the declarant's wishes for healthcare decisions. Cf. ADVANCE DIRECTIVE; LIVING WILL; PROXY DIRECTIVE.

insurance policy. 1. A contract of insurance. **2.** A document detailing such a contract. — Often shortened to *policy*. — Also termed *policy of insurance*; *contract of insurance*.

 lapsed policy. 1. An insurance policy on which there has been a default in premium payments. **2.** An insurance policy that, because of statutory provisions, remains in force after a default in premium payments. ● Statutes normally provide a 30- or 31-day grace period after nonpayment of premiums.

insurance trust. See TRUST.

intangible property. See PROPERTY.

integrated property settlement. See PROPERTY SETTLEMENT (2).

integration. 1. The process of making whole or combining into one. **2.** *Wills & estates.* The combining of more than one writing into a single document to form the testator's last will and testament. ● The other writing must be present at the time of execution and intended to be included in the will. The issue of integration is more complicated when it concerns a holographic will, which may be composed of more than one document written at different times.

intended beneficiary. See BENEFICIARY.

intended child. See CHILD.

intended parent. See *intentional parent* under PARENT.

intent. The state of mind accompanying an act, esp. a forbidden act. ● While motive is the inducement to do some act, intent is the mental resolution or determination to do it. When the intent to do an act that violates the law exists, motive becomes immaterial.

donative intent. The intent to surrender dominion and control over the gift that is being made.

implied intent. A person's state of mind that can be inferred from speech or conduct, or from language used in an instrument to which the person is a party.

testamentary intent. A testator's intent that a particular instrument function as his or her last will and testament. • Testamentary intent is required for a will to be valid.

intentional parent. See PARENT.

intercept, *n.* A mechanism by which a portion of an obligor's unemployment benefits, disability income, income-tax refund, or lottery winnings is automatically diverted to a child-support-enforcement agency to satisfy past-due support obligations.

intercountry adoption. See *international adoption* under ADOPTION.

interdict (in-tər-**dikt**), *vb.* **1.** To forbid or restrain. **2.** *Civil law.* To remove a person's right to handle personal affairs because of mental incapacity.

interdiction. 1. The act of forbidding or restraining. **2.** *Civil law.* The act of depriving a person of the right to handle his or her own affairs because of mental incapacity. Cf. GUARDIANSHIP (1); CURATORSHIP; CURATOR (2).

complete interdiction. See *full interdiction.*

full interdiction. The complete removal of one's right to care for oneself and one's affairs or estate because of mental incapacity. — Also termed *complete interdiction.*

partial interdiction. The partial removal of one's right to care for oneself and one's affairs or estate because of mental incapacity.

interested witness. See WITNESS.

interim curator. See CURATOR (1).

interlocutory decree. See *interlocutory judgment* under JUDGMENT.

interlocutory injunction. See *preliminary injunction* under INJUNCTION.

interlocutory judgment. See JUDGMENT.

intermediate account. See ACCOUNT.

intermediate scrutiny. *Constitutional law.* A standard lying between the extremes of rational-basis review and strict scrutiny. ● Under the standard, if a statute contains a quasi-suspect classification (such as gender or legitimacy), the classification must be substantially related to the achievement of an important governmental objective. — Also termed *middle-level scrutiny*; *mid-*

level scrutiny; *heightened scrutiny*. Cf. STRICT SCRUTINY; RATIONAL-BASIS TEST.

International Parental Kidnapping Crime Act of 1993. A federal statute that ratified and implemented the Hague Convention on the Civil Aspects of International Child Abduction. 18 USCA § 1204. See HAGUE CONVENTION ON THE CIVIL ASPECTS OF INTERNATIONAL CHILD ABDUCTION.

international will. See WILL.

interracial adoption. See *transracial adoption* under ADOPTION.

interracial marriage. See MISCEGENATION.

in terrorem **clause.** See NO-CONTEST CLAUSE.

interspousal, *adj.* Between husband and wife.

interspousal immunity. See HUSBAND–WIFE IMMUNITY.

interspousal tort immunity. See HUSBAND–WIFE IMMUNITY.

Interstate Compact on the Placement of Children. An agreement whose purpose is to ensure that when states are involved in the placement or adoption of children across state lines, the states cooperate with each other to facilitate the process and to protect the children. ● This compact is intended to secure states' cooperation in investigating the suitability of proposed adoptive homes in an interstate adoption and also to alleviate conflicts that often occur when the agencies and courts of more than one state are involved. The compact has been enacted in almost identical form in all 50 states as well as in the District of Columbia and the Virgin Islands. — Abbr. ICPC. — Often shortened to *Interstate Compact.*

inter vivos (**in**-tər **vi**-vohs *or* **vee**-vohs), *adj.* [Latin "between the living"] Of or relating to property conveyed not by will or in contemplation of an imminent death, but during the conveyor's lifetime. — *inter vivos, adv.*

inter vivos gift. See GIFT.

inter vivos transfer. See TRANSFER.

inter vivos trust. See TRUST.

intestacy (in-**tes**-tə-see). The state or condition of a person's having died without a valid will. Cf. TESTACY.

intestate (in-**tes**-tayt), *adj.* **1.** Of or relating to a person who has died without a valid will <having revoked her will without making a new one, she was intestate when she died>. **2.** Of or relating to the property owned by a person who died without a valid will <an intestate estate>. **3.** Of or relating to intestacy <a spouse's intestate share>. Cf. TESTATE.

intestate, *n.* One who has died without a valid will. Cf. TESTATOR.

> ***partial intestate.*** One who has died with a valid will that does not dispose of all of his or her net probate estate.

intestate law. The relevant statute governing succession to estates of those who die without a valid will.

intestate succession. See SUCCESSION.

invalid will. See WILL.

invasion of privacy. An unjustified exploitation of one's personality or intrusion into one's personal activity, actionable under tort law and sometimes under constitutional law. • The four types of invasion of privacy in tort are (1) an appropriation of another's name or likeness for one's own benefit, (2) an offensive, intentional interference with a person's seclusion or private affairs, (3) the public disclosure of private information about another in an objectionable manner, and (4) the use of publicity to place another in a false light in the public eye. See RIGHT OF PRIVACY.

inventory. 1. An executor's or administrator's detailed list of the probate-estate assets. See PROBATE

ESTATE; ACCOUNTING. **2.** A divorcing spouse's detailed list of all his or her marital and separate assets and liabilities. — Also termed *inventory and appraisement.*

in ventre sa mere. See EN VENTRE SA MERE.

investment trust. See *investment company* under COMPANY.

invidious discrimination. See DISCRIMINATION (2).

in vitro fertilization. A procedure by which an egg is fertilized outside a woman's body and then inserted into the womb for gestation. — Abbr. IVF. Cf. ARTIFICIAL INSEMINATION; ZYGOTE INTRAFALLOPIAN TRANSFER; GAMETE INTRAFALLOPIAN TRANSFER.

in vivo fertilization. The process in which an egg is fertilized inside a woman's body. Cf. ARTIFICIAL INSEMINATION; ZYGOTE INTRAFALLOPIAN TRANSFER; GAMETE INTRAFALLOPIAN TRANSFER.

involuntary euthanasia. See EUTHANASIA.

involuntary trust. See *constructive trust* under TRUST.

IRA (ı-ahr-**ay** *or* ı-rə). *abbr.* INDIVIDUAL RETIREMENT ACCOUNT.

IRD. *abbr.* See *income in respect of a decedent* under INCOME.

irreconcilable differences. Persistent and unresolvable disagreements between spouses, leading to the breakdown of the marriage. ● These differences may be cited — without specifics — as grounds for a no-fault divorce. At least 33 states have provided that irreconcilable differences are a basis for divorce. Cf. IRRETRIEVABLE BREAKDOWN OF THE MARRIAGE; INCOMPATIBILITY.

irregular succession. See SUCCESSION (2).

irremediable breakdown of the marriage. See IRRETRIEVABLE BREAKDOWN OF THE MARRIAGE.

irretrievable breakdown of the marriage. A ground for divorce that is based on incompatibility between marriage partners and that is used in many states as the sole ground of no-fault divorce. — Also termed *irretrievable breakdown; irremediable breakdown of the marriage; irremediable breakdown.* Cf. IRRECONCILABLE DIFFERENCES; INCOMPATIBILITY.

irrevocable power of attorney. See POWER OF ATTORNEY.

irrevocable trust. See TRUST.

isolating, *n.* A parent's or caregiver's pattern of cutting a child off from normal social experiences, preventing the child from forming friendships, or making the child believe that he or she is alone in the world. Cf. IGNORING; REJECTING.

issue, *n.* Lineal descendants; offspring.

> ***lawful issue.*** Descendants, including descendants more remote than children. ● At common law, the term included only those who were children of legally recognized subsisting marriages. See DESCENDANT; HEIR.

IVF. *abbr.* IN VITRO FERTILIZATION.

J

jactitation of marriage. *Hist.* **1.** False and actionable boasting or claiming that one is married to another. **2.** An action against a person who falsely boasts of being married to the complainant.

joint account. See ACCOUNT.

joint and mutual will. See WILL.

joint and reciprocal will. See *joint and mutual will* under WILL.

joint-and-survivorship account. See *joint account* under ACCOUNT.

joint custody. See CUSTODY.

joint estate. See ESTATE.

joint executor. See EXECUTOR.

joint heir. See HEIR.

joint legal custody. See *joint custody* under CUSTODY.

joint managing conservatorship. See *joint custody* under CUSTODY.

joint ownership. See OWNERSHIP.

joint physical custody. See *joint custody* under CUSTODY.

joint tenancy. See *joint tenancy* under TENANCY.

joint tenant. See *joint tenancy* under TENANCY.

joint trustee. See COTRUSTEE.

jointure (**joyn**-chər). **1.** *Archaic.* A woman's freehold life estate in land, made in consideration of marriage in lieu of dower and to be enjoyed by her only after her husband's death; a settlement under which a wife receives such an estate. ● The four essential elements are that (1) the jointure must take effect immediately upon the husband's death, (2) it must be for the wife's own life, and not for another's life or for a term of years, (3) it must be held by her in her own right and not in trust for her, and (4) it must be in lieu of her entire dower. See DOWER. **2.** An estate in lands given jointly to a husband and wife before they marry.

joint will. See WILL.

judge, *n.* A public official appointed or elected to hear and decide legal matters in court. — Abbr. J. (and, in plural, JJ.).

> **associate judge.** An appellate judge who is neither a chief judge nor a presiding judge. — Also termed *puisne judge*.

chief judge. The judge who presides over the sessions and deliberations of a court, while also overseeing the administration of the court. — Abbr. C.J.

city judge. See *municipal judge*.

county judge. A local judge having criminal or civil jurisdiction, or sometimes both, within a county.

criminal-court judge. A judge who hears criminal matters.

district judge. A judge in a federal or state judicial district. — Abbr. D.J.

family-court judge. A judge who hears matters relating to domestic relations, such as divorce and child-custody matters.

judge of probate. See *probate judge*.

judge pro tempore. See *visiting judge*.

juvenile-court judge. A judge who hears matters involving juveniles, such as suits involving child abuse and neglect, matters involving status offenses, and, sometimes, suits to terminate parental rights.

municipal judge. A local judge having criminal or civil jurisdiction, or sometimes both, within a city. — Also termed *city judge*.

probate judge. A judge having jurisdiction over probate, inheritance, guardianships, and the like. — Also termed *judge of probate*; *surrogate*; *register*.

puisne judge (**pyoo**-nee). See *associate judge.*

temporary judge. See *visiting judge.*

visiting judge. A judge appointed by the presiding judge of an administrative region to sit temporarily on a given court, usu. in the regular judge's absence. — Also termed *temporary judge*; *judge pro tempore.*

judge of probate. See *probate judge* under JUDGE.

judge pro tempore. See *visiting judge* under JUDGE.

judgment. A court's final determination of the rights and obligations of the parties in a case. • The term *judgment* includes a decree and any order from which an appeal lies. Fed. R. Civ. P. 54. — Abbr. J. — Also spelled (esp. in BrE) *judgement.*

agreed judgment. A settlement that becomes a court judgment when the judge sanctions it. — Also termed *consent judgment*; *stipulated judgment.*

consent judgment. See *agreed judgment.*

default judgment. **1.** A judgment entered against a defendant who has failed to plead or otherwise defend against the plaintiff's claim. **2.** A judgment entered as a penalty against a party who does not comply with an order, esp. an order to comply with a discovery request. — Also termed *judgment by default*.

definitive judgment. See *final judgment*.

determinative judgment. See *final judgment*.

final appealable judgment. See *final judgment*.

final judgment. A court's last action that settles the rights of the parties and disposes of all issues in controversy, except for the award of costs (and, sometimes, attorney's fees) and enforcement of the judgment. — Also termed *final appealable judgment*; *final decision*; *final decree*; *definitive judgment*; *determinative judgment*; *final appealable order*.

interlocutory judgment (in-tər-**lok**-[y]ə-tor-ee). An intermediate judgment that determines a preliminary or subordinate point or plea but does not finally decide the case. — Also termed *interlocutory decree*.

judgment by default. See *default judgment*.

judgment homologating the tableau (hə-**mahl**-ə-gay-ting / ta-**bloh** or **tab**-loh). *Civil law.* A judgment approving a plan for distributing the property in a decedent's estate. • The distribution plan is known as the tableau of distribution. La. Code Civ. Proc. art. 3307.

stipulated judgment. See *agreed judgment*.

judgment by default. See *default judgment* under JUDGMENT.

judgment homologating the tableau. See JUDGMENT.

judicial arbitration. See ARBITRATION.

judicial-bypass provision. 1. A statutory provision that allows a court to assume a parental role when the parent or guardian cannot or will not act on behalf of a minor or an incompetent. **2.** A statutory provision that allows a minor to circumvent the necessity of obtaining parental consent by obtaining judicial consent.

judicial order. See ORDER.

judicial record. See DOCKET (1).

judicial separation. 1. See SEPARATION. **2.** See *divorce a mensa et thoro* under DIVORCE.

judicial trustee. See TRUSTEE.

jurisdiction, *n*. A court's power to decide a case or issue a decree <the constitutional grant of federal-question jurisdiction>. — **jurisdictional,** *adj.*

concurrent jurisdiction. Jurisdiction exercised simultaneously by more than one court over the same subject matter and within the same territory, with the litigant having the right to choose the court in which to file the action. — Also termed *coordinate jurisdiction*; *overlapping jurisdiction*.

continuing jurisdiction. A court's power to retain jurisdiction over a matter after entering a judgment, allowing the court to modify its previous rulings or orders. See CONTINUING-JURISDICTION DOCTRINE.

coordinate jurisdiction. See *concurrent jurisdiction*.

default jurisdiction. In a child-custody matter, jurisdiction conferred when it is in the best interests of the child and either (1) there is no other basis for jurisdiction under the Uniform Child Custody Jurisdiction Act or the Parental Kidnapping Prevention Act, or (2) when another state has declined jurisdiction in favor of default jurisdiction. • Jurisdiction is rarely based on default because either home-state jurisdiction or significant-connection/substantial-evidence jurisdiction almost always applies, or else emergency jurisdiction is invoked. Default jurisdiction arises only if none of those three applies, or a state with jurisdiction on any of those bases declines to exercise it and default jurisdiction serves the best interests of the child.

delinquency jurisdiction. The power of the court to hear matters regarding juvenile acts that, if committed by an adult, would be criminal. Cf. *status-offense jurisdiction.*

emergency jurisdiction. A court's ability to take jurisdiction of a child who is physically present in the state when that child has been abandoned or when necessary to protect the child from abuse. ● Section 3(a)(3) of the Uniform Child Custody Jurisdiction Act allows for emergency jurisdiction. It is usually temporary, lasting only as long as is necessary to protect the child.

federal-juvenile-delinquency jurisdiction. A federal court's power to hear a case in which a person under the age of 18 violates federal law. ● In such a case, the federal court derives its jurisdictional power from 18 USCA §§ 5031 et seq. The Act severely limits the scope of federal-juvenile-delinquency jurisdiction because Congress recognizes that juvenile delinquency is essentially a state issue. The acts that typically invoke federal jurisdiction are (1) acts committed on federal lands (military bases, national parks, Indian reservations), and (2) acts that violate federal drug laws or other federal criminal statutes.

home-state jurisdiction. In interstate child-custody disputes governed by the Uniform Child Custody Jurisdiction and Enforcement Act, jurisdiction based on the child's having been a resident of the state for at least six consecutive months immediately before the commencement of the suit. See HOME STATE.

long-arm jurisdiction. Jurisdiction over a non-resident defendant who has had some contact with the jurisdiction in which the petition is filed.

overlapping jurisdiction. See *concurrent jurisdiction*.

probate jurisdiction. Jurisdiction over matters relating to wills, settlement of decedents' estates, and (in some states) guardianship and the adoption of minors.

significant-connection/substantial-evidence jurisdiction. In a child-custody matter, jurisdiction based on (1) the best interests of the child, (2) at least one parent's (or litigant's) significant connection to the state, and (3) the presence in the state of substantial evidence about the child's present or future care, protection, training, and personal relationships. • This type of jurisdiction is conferred by both the Uniform Child Custody Jurisdiction Act and the Parental Kidnapping Prevention Act. Generally, the home state will also be the state with significant connections and substantial evidence. Jurisdiction based on a significant connection or substantial evidence alone is conferred only when the child has no home state. See HOME STATE.

status-offense jurisdiction. The power of the court to hear matters regarding noncriminal conduct committed by a juvenile. See STATUS OFFENSE. Cf. *delinquency jurisdiction*.

jus accrescendi. See RIGHT OF SURVIVORSHIP.

jus soli (jəs **soh**-lı), *n.* [Latin "right of the soil"] The rule that a child's citizenship is determined by place of birth. ● This is the U.S. rule, as affirmed by the 14th Amendment to the Constitution.

juvenile (**joo**-və-nəl *or* -nıl), *n.* A person who has not reached the age (usu. 18) at which one should be treated as an adult by the criminal-justice system; MINOR. — **juvenile,** *adj.* — **juvenility** (joo-və-**nil**-ə-tee), *n.*

   certified juvenile. A juvenile who has been certified to be tried as an adult.

juvenile court. See COURT.

juvenile-court judge. See JUDGE.

juvenile delinquency. Antisocial behavior by a minor; esp., behavior that would be criminally punishable if the actor were an adult, but instead is usu. punished by special laws pertaining only to minors. Cf. INCORRIGIBILITY.

Juvenile Delinquency Prevention Act. A federal statute whose purpose is (1) to help states and local communities provide preventive services to youths who are in danger of becoming delinquent,

(2) to help in training personnel employed in or preparing for employment in occupations that involve the provision of those services, and (3) to give technical assistance in this field. 42 USCA §§ 3801 et seq.

juvenile delinquent. A minor who is guilty of criminal behavior, usu. punishable by special laws not pertaining to adults. — Sometimes shortened to *delinquent*. — Also termed *juvenile offender*; *youthful offender*; *delinquent minor*.

Juvenile Justice and Delinquency Prevention Act. A federal statute whose broad scope is to provide funding, assistance, training, and support to state-operated juvenile-justice programs, initiatives, and court systems. 42 USCA §§ 5601–5785.

juvenile-justice system. The collective institutions through which a youthful offender passes until any charges have been disposed of or the assessed punishment has been concluded. ● The system comprises juvenile courts (judges and lawyers), law enforcement (police), and corrections (probation officers and social workers).

juvenile offender. See JUVENILE DELINQUENT.

juvenile officer. A juvenile-court employee, sometimes a social worker or probation officer, who works with the judge to direct and develop the court's child-welfare work. — Also termed *county agent*.

K

Keogh plan (**kee**-oh). A tax-deferred retirement program developed for the self-employed. ● This plan is also known as an *H.R. 10 plan*, after the House of Representatives bill that established the plan. — Also termed *self-employed retirement plan.* Cf. INDIVIDUAL RETIREMENT ACCOUNT.

ketubah (ke-**too**-vah), *n.* A Jewish marriage contract.

kiddie tax. See TAX.

kidnap, *vb.* To seize and take away (a person) by force or fraud, often with a demand for ransom.

kidnapping. 1. At common law, the crime of forcibly abducting a person from his or her own country and sending the person to another. ● This offense amounted to false imprisonment aggravated by moving the victim to another country. **2.** The crime of seizing and taking away a person by force or fraud. — Also termed *simple kidnapping*; (loosely) *abduction*; (archaically) *manstealing.* See ABDUCTION.

> *aggravated kidnapping.* Kidnapping accompanied by some aggravating factor (such as a demand for ransom or injury of the victim).

> *child-kidnapping.* The kidnapping of a minor, often without the element of force or fraud (as when someone walks off with another's baby). —

Also termed *child-stealing*; *baby-snatching*; *child-napping*.

kidnapping for ransom. The offense of unlawfully seizing a person and then confining the person in a secret place while attempting to extort ransom. ● This grave crime is sometimes made a capital offense. In addition to the abductor, a person who acts as a go-between to collect the ransom is generally considered guilty of the crime.

parental kidnapping. The kidnapping of a child by one parent in violation of the other parent's custody or visitation rights. See PARENTAL KIDNAPPING PREVENTION ACT.

simple kidnapping. Kidnapping not accompanied by an aggravating factor.

kidnapping for ransom. See KIDNAPPING.

kin, *n.* **1.** One's relatives; family. — Also termed *kindred*. **2.** A relative by blood, marriage, or adoption, though usu. by blood only; a kinsman or kinswoman.

kindred. See KIN; KINSHIP.

kinship. Relationship by blood, marriage, or adoption. — Also termed *kindred*.

kinsman. See RELATIVE.

knowing consent. See *informed consent* under CONSENT.

known heir. See HEIR.

L

lapse, *n.* The failure of a testamentary gift, esp. when the beneficiary dies before the testator dies. See ANTILAPSE STATUTE. Cf. ADEMPTION.

lapse, *vb.* **1.** (Of an estate or right) to pass away or revert to someone else because conditions have not been fulfilled or because a person entitled to possession has failed in some duty. See *lapsed policy* under INSURANCE POLICY. **2.** (Of a devise, grant, etc.) to become void.

lapsed devise. See DEVISE.

lapsed legacy. See LEGACY.

lapsed policy. See INSURANCE POLICY.

lapse statute. See ANTILAPSE STATUTE.

lascivious cohabitation. See *illicit cohabitation* under COHABITATION.

last-in-time-marriage presumption. A presumption that the most recently contracted marriage is valid. ● This presumption generally arises in a situation similar to this: A person, believing himself or herself to be divorced, remarries. This person dies, and the new spouse makes a claim for the decedent's pension benefits. Then a former spouse, claiming that there was never a valid divorce, also claims the right to receive the benefits. The last-in-time-marriage presumption operates so that the former spouse bears the burden of proving that there was no valid divorce.

last will. See WILL.

last will and testament. See WILL.

laughing heir. See HEIR.

lawful age. 1. See *age of capacity* under AGE. **2.** See *age of majority* (1) under AGE.

lawful dependent. See DEPENDENT (1).

lawful heir. See HEIR (1).

lawful issue. See ISSUE.

lawful representative. See REPRESENTATIVE.

law guardian. See *guardian ad litem* under GUARD-IAN.

lawyer, *n.* One who is licensed to practice law. — **lawyerly, lawyerlike,** *adj.* — **lawyerdom,** *n.* Cf. ATTORNEY.

lawyer–client privilege. See *attorney–client privilege* under PRIVILEGE.

left-handed marriage. See *morganatic marriage* under MARRIAGE.

legacy (**leg**-ə-see), *n*. A gift by will, esp. of personal property and often of money. Cf. BEQUEST; DEVISE.

> *absolute legacy.* A legacy given without condition and intended to vest immediately. Cf. *vested legacy.*

> *accumulated legacy.* A legacy that has not yet been paid to a legatee.

> *accumulative legacy.* See *additional legacy.*

> *additional legacy.* A second legacy given to a legatee in the same will (or in a codicil to the same will) that gave another legacy. • An additional legacy is supplementary to another and is not considered merely a repeated expression of the same gift. — Also termed *accumulative legacy*; *cumulative legacy.*

> *alternate legacy.* A legacy by which the testator gives the legatee a choice of one of two or more items.

> *conditional legacy.* A legacy that will take effect or be defeated subject to the occurrence or nonoccurrence of an event.

> *contingent legacy.* A legacy that depends on an uncertain event and thus has not vested. • An example is a legacy given to one's granddaughter "if she attains the age of 21."

cumulative legacy. See *additional legacy.*

demonstrative legacy (di-**mon**-strə-tiv). A lega-cy paid from a particular source if that source has enough money. ● If it does not, the amount of the legacy not paid from that source is taken from the estate's general assets.

failed legacy. See *lapsed legacy.*

general legacy. A gift of personal property that the testator intends to come from the general assets of the estate, payable in money or items indistinguishable from each other, such as shares of stock.

lapsed legacy. A legacy to a legatee who dies either before the testator dies or before the legacy is payable. ● It falls into the residual estate unless the jurisdiction has an antilapse statute. — Also termed *failed legacy.* See ANTILAPSE STATUTE.

modal legacy (**moh**-dəl). A legacy accompanied by directions about the manner in which it will be applied to the legatee's benefit <a modal legacy for the purchase of a business>.

pecuniary legacy (pi-**kyoo**-nee-er-ee). A legacy of a sum of money.

residuary legacy (ri-**zij**-oo-er-ee). A legacy of the estate remaining after the satisfaction of all claims and all specific, general, and demonstra-tive legacies.

special legacy. See *specific legacy*.

specific legacy. A legacy of a specific or unique item of property, such as any real estate or a particular piece of furniture. — Also termed *special legacy*.

substitutional legacy. A legacy that replaces a different legacy already given to a legatee.

trust legacy. A legacy of personal property to trustees to be held in trust, with the income usu. paid to a specified beneficiary.

vested legacy. A legacy given in such a way that the legatee has a fixed, indefeasible right to its payment. ● A legacy is said to be vested when the testator's words making the bequest convey a transmissible interest, whether present or future, to the legatee. Thus, a legacy to be paid when the legatee reaches the age of 21 is a vested legacy because it is given unconditionally and absolutely. Although the legacy is vested, the legatee's enjoyment of it is deferred. Cf. *absolute legacy*.

void legacy. A legacy that never had any legal existence. ● The subject matter of such a legacy is treated as a part of the estate and passes under the residuary clause of a will or (in the absence of a residuary clause) under the rules for intestate succession.

legacy duty. See *legacy tax* under TAX.

legacy tax. See TAX.

legal age. 1. See *age of capacity* under AGE. **2.** See *age of majority* (1) under AGE.

legal asset. See ASSET.

legal cruelty. See CRUELTY.

legal custody. 1. CUSTODY. **2.** DECISION-MAKING RE-SPONSIBILITY.

legal death. 1. See *brain death* under DEATH. **2.** See *civil death* under DEATH.

legal dependent. See DEPENDENT.

legal distributee. See DISTRIBUTEE.

legal father. See FATHER.

legal heir. See HEIR (1).

legal insanity. See INSANITY.

legal liability. See LIABILITY.

legal life estate. See *life estate* under ESTATE.

legal life tenant. See LIFE TENANT.

legal owner. See OWNER.

legal parent. See PARENT.

legal–personal representative. See REPRESENTA-TIVE.

legal portion. See LEGITIME.

legal representative. 1. See *personal representative* under REPRESENTATIVE. **2.** See *lawful representative* under REPRESENTATIVE.

legal residence. See DOMICILE (2).

legal separation. 1. SEPARATION. **2.** See *divorce a mensa et thoro* under DIVORCE.

legal succession. See SUCCESSION.

legal-unities doctrine. *Obsolete.* The common-law rule that a wife had no separate existence from her husband. — Also termed *doctrine of legal unities*; *unities doctrine of marriage.* See MARRIED WOMEN'S PROPERTY ACTS; SPOUSAL-UNITY DOCTRINE.

legatary, *n. Archaic.* See LEGATEE.

legate (lə-**gayt**), *vb.* To give or leave as a legacy; to make a testamentary gift of (property); BEQUEATH.

legatee (leg-ə-**tee**). **1.** One who is named in a will to take personal property; one who has received a legacy or bequest. **2.** Loosely, one to whom a devise of real property is given. — Also termed (archaically) *legatary*. Cf. DEVISEE.

general legatee. A person whose bequest is of a specified quantity to be paid out of the estate's personal assets.

residuary legatee (ri-**zij**-oo-er-ee). A person designated to receive the residue of a decedent's estate. See *residuary estate* under ESTATE.

specific legatee. The recipient, under a will, of designated property that is transferred by the owner's death.

universal legatee. A residuary legatee that receives the entire residuary estate.

legator (lə-**gay**-tər *or* leg-ə-**tor**). *Rare.* One who bequeaths a legacy; TESTATOR.

legislative divorce. See DIVORCE.

legitim. See LEGITIME.

legitimacy. 1. Lawfulness. **2.** The status of a person who is born within a lawful marriage or who acquires that status by later action of the parents. Cf. ILLEGITIMACY.

legitimacy presumption. See PRESUMPTION OF PATERNITY.

legitimate (lə-**jit**-ə-mət), *adj.* **1.** Complying with the law; lawful <a legitimate business>. **2.** Born of legally married parents <a legitimate child>. **3.** Genuine; valid <a legitimate complaint>.

legitimate child. See CHILD.

legitimate portion. See LEGITIME.

legitimation, *n.* **1.** The act of making something lawful; authorization. **2.** The act or process of authoritatively declaring a person legitimate, esp. a child whose parentage has been unclear. Cf. ADOPTION. — **legitimate** (lə-**jit**-ə-mayt), *vb.*

legitime (**lej**-ə-tim), *n.* In the civil law, the part of a testator's free movable property that his or her children (and occasionally other heirs) are legally entitled to regardless of the will's terms. See La. Civ. Code art. 1494. ● The legitime cannot be denied the children without legal cause. In Roman law, the amount of the legitime was one-fourth of the claimant's share on intestacy. — Also spelled (esp. in Scotland) *legitim.* — Also termed *legal portion*; *legitimate portion*; *forced portion.* See *forced heir* under HEIR.

***Lemon* test.** A legal standard for judging the state's violation of the Establishment Clause of the First Amendment. ● The *Lemon* test has most often been used in school-related cases. It employs a three-pronged test to determine the state's action:

(1) Does the state's action have a religious purpose? (2) Does the state's action have the primary effect of either promoting or inhibiting religion? (3) Does the state's action create an "excessive entanglement" between church and state? *Lemon v. Kurtzman*, 403 U.S. 602, 91 S.Ct. 2105 (1971). In recent years, the Court has not overturned *Lemon* but has declined to apply it when deciding Establishment Clause cases.

letter of attorney. See POWER OF ATTORNEY (1).

letters. A court order giving official authority to a fiduciary to conduct appointed tasks. ● Examples are letters of administration, letters of conservatorship, letters of guardianship, and letters testamentary. Unif. Probate Code § 1–201(23).

letters of administration. A formal document issued by a probate court to appoint the administrator of an estate. ● Letters of administration originated in the Probate of Testaments Act of 1357 (31 Edw. 3, ch. 4), which provided that in case of intestacy the ordinary (a high-ranking ecclesiastical official within a territory) should depute the decedent's closest friends to administer the estate; a later statute, the Executors Act of 1529 (21 Hen. 8, ch. 4), authorized the ordinary to grant administration to the surviving spouse, to next of kin, or to both of them jointly. — Also termed *administration letters*. See ADMINISTRATION. Cf. LETTERS TESTAMENTARY.

letters of administration c.t.a. Letters of administration appointing an administrator *cum testamento annexo* (with the will annexed) either because the will does not name an executor or because the named executor does not qualify. See *administration cum testamento annexo* under AD-MINISTRATION.

letters of administration d.b.n. Letters of administration appointing an administrator *de bonis non* (concerning goods not yet administered) because the named executor failed to complete the estate's probate. See *administration de bonis non* under ADMINISTRATION.

letters of administration c.t.a. See LETTERS OF ADMINISTRATION.

letters of administration d.b.n. See LETTERS OF ADMINISTRATION.

letters of guardianship. A court order appointing a guardian to care for a minor's or an incapacitated adult's well-being, property, and affairs. • It defines the scope of the guardian's rights and duties, including the extent of control over the ward's education and medical issues. See GUARDIAN.

letters testamentary. A probate-court order approving the appointment of an executor under a will and authorizing the executor to administer the estate. Cf. LETTERS OF ADMINISTRATION.

Levitical degrees. See *prohibited degree* under DE-GREE.

lewd and lascivious cohabitation. See *illicit co-habitation* under COHABITATION.

liability, *n.* **1.** The quality or state of being legally obligated or accountable; legal responsibility to another or to society, enforceable by civil remedy or criminal punishment <liability for injuries caused by negligence>. — Also termed *legal liability*. **2.** (*often pl.*) A financial or pecuniary obligation; debt <tax liability> <assets and liabilities>.

liberty of contract. See FREEDOM OF CONTRACT.

liberty of speech. See FREEDOM OF SPEECH.

liberty of the press. See FREEDOM OF THE PRESS.

life beneficiary. See BENEFICIARY.

life estate. See ESTATE.

life estate pur autre vie. See ESTATE.

life in being. Under the rule against perpetuities, anyone alive when a future interest is created, whether or not the person has an interest in the estate. See IN BEING; RULE AGAINST PERPETUITIES. Cf. MEASURING LIFE.

life insurance. An agreement between an insurance company and the policyholder to pay a specified amount to a designated beneficiary on the insured's death.

ordinary life insurance. See *whole life insurance.*

straight life insurance. See *whole life insurance.*

term life insurance. Life insurance that covers the insured for only a specified period. • It pays a fixed benefit to a named beneficiary upon the insured's death but has no cash value during the insured's life.

whole life insurance. Life insurance that covers an insured for life, during which the insured pays fixed premiums, accumulates savings from an invested portion of the premiums, and receives a guaranteed benefit upon death, to be paid to a named beneficiary. — Also termed *ordinary life insurance*; *straight life insurance.*

life-insurance trust. See TRUST.

life-owner. See LIFE TENANT.

life-rent. See USUFRUCT.

life tenancy. See *life estate* under ESTATE.

life tenant. A person who, until death, is beneficially entitled to property; the holder of a life estate. — Also termed *tenant for life*; *life-owner*. See *life estate* under ESTATE.

> **legal life tenant.** A life tenant who is automatically entitled to possession by virtue of a legal estate.

lifetime gift. See *inter vivos gift* under GIFT.

limited administration. See ADMINISTRATION.

limited appearance. See *special appearance* under APPEARANCE.

limited divorce. See DIVORCE.

limited executor. See EXECUTOR.

limited owner. See OWNER.

limited power of appointment. See POWER OF APPOINTMENT.

limited-purpose marriage. See MARRIAGE.

limited trust. See TRUST.

Lindbergh Act. See FEDERAL KIDNAPPING ACT.

line, *n.* The ancestry of a person; lineage <the Fergusons came from a long line of wheat farmers>.

collateral line. A line of descent connecting persons who are not directly related to each other as ascendants or descendants, but whose relationship consists in common descent from the same ancestor.

direct line. A line of descent traced through only those persons who are related to each other directly as ascendants or descendants.

maternal line. A person's ancestry or relationship with another traced through the mother.

paternal line. A person's ancestry or relationship with another traced through the father.

lineage (lin-ee-əj). Ancestry and progeny; family, ascending or descending.

lineal (lin-ee-əl), *adj*. Derived from or relating to common ancestors, esp. in a direct line; hereditary. Cf. COLLATERAL.

lineal, *n*. A lineal descendant; a direct blood relative.

lineal ascendant. See ASCENDANT.

lineal consanguinity. See CONSANGUINITY.

lineal descendant. See DESCENDANT.

lineal descent. See DESCENT.

lineal heir. See HEIR.

liquidating trust. See TRUST.

lis pendens (lis **pen**-dənz). [Latin "a pending law-suit"] **1.** A pending lawsuit. **2.** The jurisdiction, power, or control acquired by a court over property while a legal action is pending. **3.** A notice, recorded in the chain of title to real property, required or permitted in some jurisdictions to warn all persons that certain property is the subject matter of litigation, and that any interests acquired during the pendency of the suit are subject to its outcome. — Also termed (in sense 3) *notice of lis pendens*; *notice of pendency*. Cf. PENDENTE LITE.

livery (**liv**-ə-ree *or* **liv**-ree). The delivery of the possession of real property. Cf. DELIVERY.

living separate and apart. (Of spouses) residing in different places and having no intention of re-suming marital relations. ● One basis for no-fault divorce in many states exists if the spouses have lived apart for a specified period.

living-together agreement. See COHABITATION AGREEMENT.

living trust. See *inter vivos trust* under TRUST.

living will. An instrument, signed with the formal-ities statutorily required for a will, by which a person directs that his or her life not be artificially prolonged by extraordinary measures when there is no reasonable expectation of recovery from extreme physical or mental disability. ● Most states have living-will legislation. — Also termed *declaration of a desire for a natural death*; *directive to physicians*. See NATURAL-DEATH ACT; UNIFORM HEALTH-CARE DECISION ACT. Cf. ADVANCE DIRECTIVE; INSTRUCTION DIRECTIVE.

lollipop syndrome. A situation in which one or both parents, often in a custody battle, manipulate the child with gifts, fun, good times, and minimal discipline in an attempt to win over the child. See *Disneyland parent* under PARENT. Cf. RESCUE SYNDROME.

long-arm jurisdiction. See JURISDICTION.

long-arm statute. A statute providing for jurisdiction over a nonresident defendant who has had contacts with the territory where the statute is in effect. ● Most state long-arm statutes extend this jurisdiction to its constitutional limits. — Also termed *single-act statute*. See *long-arm jurisdiction* under JURISDICTION.

long-term foster care. See FOSTER CARE (1).

lord-and-master rule. See HEAD-AND-MASTER RULE.

Lord Langdale's Act. See WILLS ACT (2).

Lord Lyndhurst's Act. See LYNDHURST'S ACT.

Lord Mansfield's rule. The principle that neither spouse may testify about whether the husband had access to the wife at the time of a child's conception. ● In effect, this rule — which has been abandoned by most states — made it impossible to bastardize a child born during a marriage.

loss of consortium (kən-**sor**-shee-əm). **1.** A loss of the benefits that one spouse is entitled to receive from the other, including companionship, cooperation, aid, affection, and sexual relations. ● Loss of consortium can be recoverable as damages from a tortfeasor in a personal-injury or wrongful-death action. Originally, only the husband could sue for loss of consortium. But in 1950, nearly a century after the enactment of the married women's property acts, a wife's action for negligent impairment of consortium was first recognized. *Hitaffer v. Argonne Co.*, 183 F.2d 811 (D.C. Cir. 1950). Today 48 states and the District of Columbia recognize both a husband's and a wife's right to sue for loss of consortium (Utah and Virginia do not). **2.** A similar loss of benefits that one is entitled to receive from a parent or child. See CONSORTIUM.

lost earning capacity. A person's diminished earning power resulting from an injury. ● This impairment is recoverable as an element of damages in a tort action.

lost will. See WILL.

lucid interval. 1. A brief period during which an insane person regains sanity sufficient to have the legal capacity to contract and act on his or her own behalf. **2.** A period during which a person has enough mental capacity to understand the concept of marriage and the duties and obligations it imposes. **3.** A period during which an otherwise incompetent person regains sufficient testamentary capacity to execute a valid will. — Also termed *lucid moment*.

lucid moment. See LUCID INTERVAL.

lump-sum alimony. See *alimony in gross* under ALIMONY.

lunacy. See INSANITY.

Lyndhurst's Act. *Hist.* An English statute that rendered marriages within certain degrees of kinship null and void. Marriage Act of 1835, 5 & 6 Will. 4, ch. 54. — Also termed *Lord Lyndhurst's Act.*

M

maiden name. A woman's childhood surname (which may or may not remain her surname for life). Cf. GIVEN NAME; SURNAME.

mail-order divorce. See DIVORCE.

maintenance. Financial support given by one person to another, usu. paid as a result of a legal separation or divorce; esp., ALIMONY. • Maintenance may end after a specified time or upon the death, cohabitation, or remarriage of the receiving party.

    maintenance in gross. A fixed amount of money to be paid upon divorce by one former spouse to the other, in a lump sum or in installments. • Typically, the total amount is unmodifiable regardless of any change in either person's circumstances.

    separate maintenance. Money paid by one married person to another for support if they are no longer living together as husband and wife. • This type of maintenance is often mandated by a court order. An action for separate maintenance is not maintainable after the entry of a divorce decree. — Also termed *separate support*.

maintenance in gross. See MAINTENANCE.

major. See ADULT.

majority. The status of one who has attained the age of majority (usu. 18). See AGE OF MAJORITY. Cf. MINORITY.

mala fides. See BAD FAITH.

malicious abandonment. See *voluntary abandonment* under ABANDONMENT.

managing conservator. See CONSERVATOR.

managing conservatorship. See CUSTODY.

mandatory injunction. See INJUNCTION.

mandatory trust. See TRUST.

mandatory waiver. The mandatory transfer, without judicial discretion, of a case from juvenile court to criminal court once the prosecutor has charged a juvenile with one of certain statutorily enumerated serious crimes. See TRANSFER STATUTE. Cf. STATUTORY EXCLUSION.

mansealing. *Archaic.* See KIDNAPPING.

mariage de convenance. See *marriage of convenience* under MARRIAGE (1).

mariner's will. See *soldier's will* under WILL.

maritage (**ma**-ri-tij), *n.* See DOWRY.

maritagium (ma-ri-**tay**-jee-əm), *n*. See DOWRY.

marital, *adj*. Of or relating to the marriage relationship <marital property>.

marital agreement. An agreement between spouses concerning the division and ownership of marital property during marriage or upon dissolution by death or divorce; esp., a premarital contract or separation agreement that is primarily concerned with dividing marital property in the event of divorce. — Also termed *marriage settlement*; *property settlement*. See PRENUPTIAL AGREEMENT; POSTNUPTIAL AGREEMENT.

marital-communications privilege. See *marital privilege* (1) under PRIVILEGE.

marital deduction. See DEDUCTION (1).

marital-deduction trust. See TRUST.

marital dissolution. See DIVORCE.

marital domicile. See *matrimonial domicile* under DOMICILE.

marital estate. See *marital property* under PROPERTY.

marital home. See FAMILY HOME.

marital immunity. See HUSBAND–WIFE IMMUNITY.

marital life-estate trust. See *bypass trust* under TRUST.

marital misconduct. Any of the various statutory grounds for a fault divorce, such as adultery or cruelty. See *fault divorce* under DIVORCE.

marital portion. In the civil law, the portion of a deceased spouse's estate to which the surviving spouse is entitled.

marital-privacy doctrine. A principle that limits governmental intrusion into private family matters, such as those involving sexual relations between married persons. • The marital-privacy doctrine was first recognized in *Griswold v. Connecticut*, 381 U.S. 479, 85 S.Ct. 1678 (1965). The doctrine formerly deterred state intervention into incidents involving domestic violence. Today, with the trend toward individual privacy rights, the doctrine does not discourage governmental protection from domestic violence. — Also termed *doctrine of marital privacy*.

marital privilege. See PRIVILEGE.

marital property. See PROPERTY.

marital rape. See RAPE.

marital residence. See FAMILY HOME.

marital rights. Rights and incidents (such as property or cohabitation rights) arising from the marriage contract.

marital settlement agreement. See DIVORCE AGREEMENT.

marital status. The condition of being single, married, divorced, or widowed.

marital tort. See TORT.

mariticide. **1.** The murder of one's husband. **2.** A woman who murders her husband. — **mariticidal,** *adj.* Cf. UXORICIDE.

marriage, *n.* **1.** The legal union of a man and woman as husband and wife. ● The essentials of a valid marriage are (1) parties legally capable of contracting to marry, (2) mutual consent or agreement, and (3) an actual contracting in the form prescribed by law. Although the common law regarded marriage as a civil contract, it is now often regarded as the civil status or relationship existing between a man and a woman who agree to and do live together as spouses. Marriage has important consequences in many areas of the law: tort, criminal, evidence, debtor–creditor, property, and contract, for example. — Also termed *matrimony.*

> ***clandestine marriage*** (klan-**des**-tin). **1.** A marriage that rests merely on the agreement of the parties. **2.** A marriage entered into in a secret

way, as one solemnized by an unauthorized person or without all required formalities.

common-law marriage. A marriage that takes legal effect, without license or ceremony, when two people capable of marrying live together as husband and wife, intend to be married, and hold themselves out to others as a married couple. ● The common-law marriage traces its roots to the English ecclesiastical courts, which until 1753 recognized a kind of informal marriage known as *sponsalia per verba de praesenti*, which was entered into without ceremony. Today a common-law marriage, which is the full equivalent of a ceremonial marriage, is authorized in 11 states and in the District of Columbia. If a common-law marriage is established in a state that recognizes such marriages, other states, even those that do not authorize common-law marriage, must give full faith and credit to the marriage. A common-law marriage can be dissolved only by annulment, divorce, or death. — Also termed *consensual marriage*; *informal marriage*. See *common-law husband* under HUSBAND; *common-law wife* under WIFE.

confidential marriage. In some jurisdictions (such as California), a marriage between a man and a woman in which only the two parties and the officiant are present at the ceremony. ● Confidential marriages are neither witnessed nor recorded in public records. They are recorded in nonpublic records. Although rarely performed, they are generally legal. To obtain a confidential marriage, the parties must each be at least 18, must be of the opposite sex, and usually must have lived together for an extended period. In ecclesiastical law, such a marriage is termed an *occult marriage* or, if performed in the strictest secrecy, a *marriage of conscience*.

consensual marriage. Marriage by consent alone, without any formal process. See *common-law marriage*.

consular marriage. A marriage solemnized in a foreign country by a consul or diplomatic official of the United States. ● Consular marriages are recognized in some jurisdictions.

covenant marriage. A special type of marriage in which the parties agree to more stringent requirements for marriage and divorce than are otherwise imposed by state law for ordinary marriages. ● In the late 1990s, several states (beginning with Louisiana) passed laws providing for covenant marriages. The requirements vary, but most of these laws require couples who opt for covenant marriage to undergo premarital counseling. A divorce will be granted only after the couple has undergone marital counseling and has been separated for a specified period (usually at least 18 months). The divorce prerequisites typically can be waived with proof that a spouse has committed adultery, been convicted of a felony, abandoned the family for at least one year, or physically or sexually abused the other spouse or a child. — Also termed (in slang) *high-test marriage*.

cross-marriage. A marriage by a brother and sister to two people who are also brother and sister.

de facto marriage (di **fak**-toh). A marriage that, despite the parties' living as husband and wife, is defective for some reason.

defunct marriage. A marriage in which both parties, by their conduct, indicate their intent to no longer be married.

fraudulent marriage. A marriage based on a misrepresentation regarding some issue of fundamental importance to the innocent party, who relies on the misrepresentation in the decision to marry. • The misrepresentation must concern something of fundamental importance to a marriage, such as religious beliefs, the ability to have sexual relations, or the ability or desire to have children. Cf. *sham marriage*.

green-card marriage. *Slang.* A sham marriage in which a U.S. citizen marries a foreign citizen for the sole purpose of allowing the foreign citizen to become a permanent U.S. resident. • The Marriage Fraud Amendments were enacted to regulate marriages entered into for the purpose of circumventing U.S. immigration laws. 8 USCA §§ 1154 (h), 1255(e). See *sham marriage*.

Gretna-Green marriage. *Slang.* A marriage entered into in a jurisdiction other than where the parties reside to avoid some legal impediment that exists where they live; a runaway marriage. • Gretna Green is a Scottish village close to the English border that served as a convenient place for eloping English couples to wed.

handfast marriage. **1.** *Hist.* A marriage, often lacking only solemnization by clergy, characterized by the couple's joining of hands to conclude a marriage contract. **2.** *Hist.* A betrothal with all the binding effects of a marriage, including conjugal rights and cohabitation, followed by a later formal marriage. **3.** A trial or probationary marriage wherein the couple agrees to cohabit and behave as spouses for a definite period, usu. one year, at the end of which they will mutually decide to separate or go through a permanently binding marriage. • The legal status of such a marriage is unsettled, as many such trial marriages are initiated with a ritual ceremony including an exchange of vows before a presiding officer legally empowered to perform marriages, yet the couple intends to remain free to end the relationship without legal proceedings. Cf. *marriage in jest*; *common-law marriage*. **4.** A binding form of marriage practiced by some modern pagan religions. • Unlike in sense 3, such marriages are entered into with the expectation of permanent duration. — Also termed (in senses 3 and 4) *handfasting*.

high-test marriage. See *covenant marriage.*

homosexual marriage. See *same-sex marriage.*

informal marriage. See *common-law marriage.*

left-handed marriage. See *morganatic marriage.*

limited-purpose marriage. A marriage in which the parties agree to be married only for certain reasons. ● An example is a marriage in which the parties agree to marry so that a child will not be born illegitimate but agree not to live together or to have any duties toward each other. Courts have usually found these marriages to be binding for all purposes. Cf. *sham marriage*; *green card-marriage.*

mariage de convenance. See *marriage of convenience.*

marriage in jest. A voidable marriage in which the parties lack the requisite intent to marry.

marriage of conscience. *Eccles. law.* See *confidential marriage.*

marriage of convenience. **1.** A marriage entered into for social or financial advantages rather than out of mutual love. — Also termed *mariage de convenance.* **2.** Loosely, an ill-considered marriage that, at the time, is convenient to the parties involved.

marriage of the left hand. See *morganatic marriage.*

mixed marriage. See MISCEGENATION.

morganatic marriage (mor-gə-**nat**-ik). *Hist.* A marriage between a man of superior status to a woman of inferior status, with the stipulation that the wife and her children cannot participate in the title or possessions of the husband. ● By extension, the term later referred to the marriage of a woman of superior status to a man of inferior status. — Also termed *left-handed marriage*; *marriage of the left hand*; *salic marriage.*

occult marriage. *Eccles. law.* See *confidential marriage.*

plural marriage. A marriage in which one spouse is already married to someone else; a bigamous or polygamous union; POLYGAMY.

putative marriage (**pyoo**-tə-tiv). A marriage in which either the husband or the wife believes in good faith that the two are married, but for some technical reason they are not formally married (as when the ceremonial official was not authorized to perform a marriage). ● A putative marriage is typically treated as valid to protect the innocent spouse. The concept of a putative marriage was adopted from the Napoleonic Code in those states having a civil-law tradition, such as California, Louisiana, and Texas. This type of marriage is also recognized in the Uniform Marriage and

Divorce Act. The legal rule by which putative marriages exist is sometimes referred to as the *putative-spouse doctrine*.

salic marriage. See *morganatic marriage*.

same-sex marriage. The ceremonial union of two people of the same sex; a marriage-like relationship between two women or two men. ● A same-sex marriage does not endow the couple with the legal status of spouses because, in the United States, persons of the same sex cannot legally marry. Same-sex couples have tried, so far without success, to challenge the laws against same-sex marriage. See *Baehr v. Lewin*, 852 P.2d 44 (Haw. 1993); *Baehr v. Miike*, 994 P.2d 566 (Haw. 1999); *Baker v. State*, 744 A.2d 864 (Vt. 1999). — Also termed *gay marriage*; *homosexual marriage*. Cf. CIVIL UNION; DOMESTIC PARTNERSHIP.

Scotch marriage. A marriage by consensual contract, without the necessity of a formal ceremony, so called because this kind of marriage was recognized as valid under Scots law until 1940.

sham marriage. A purported marriage in which all the formal requirements are met or seemingly met, but in which the parties go through the ceremony with no intent of living together as husband and wife. Cf. *green-card marriage*; *fraudulent marriage*; *limited-purpose marriage*.

voidable marriage. A marriage that is initially invalid but that remains in effect unless terminated by court order. ● For example, a marriage is voidable if either party is underage or otherwise legally incompetent, or if one party used fraud, duress, or force to induce the other party to enter the marriage. The legal imperfection in such a marriage can be inquired into only during the lives of both spouses, in a proceeding to obtain a judgment declaring it void. A voidable marriage can be ratified once the impediment to a legal marriage has been removed.

void marriage. A marriage that is invalid from its inception, that cannot be made valid, and that can be terminated by either party without obtaining a divorce or annulment. ● For example, a marriage is void if the parties are too closely related or if either party is already married. A void marriage does not exist, has never existed, and needs no formal act to be dissolved — although a judicial declaration may be obtained. See NULLITY OF MARRIAGE (1).

2. MARRIAGE CEREMONY. — **marital,** *adj*.

ceremonial marriage. A wedding that follows all the statutory requirements and that has been solemnized before a religious or civil official.

civil marriage. A wedding ceremony conducted by an official, such as a judge, or by some other authorized person — as distinguished from one solemnized by a member of the clergy.

proxy marriage. A wedding in which someone stands in for an absent bride or groom, as when one party is stationed overseas in the military. ● Proxy marriages are prohibited in most states.

marriage article. A premarital stipulation between spouses who intend to incorporate the stipulation in a postnuptial agreement.

marriage bonus. *Tax.* The difference between the reduced income-tax liability owed by a married couple filing a joint income-tax return and the greater amount they would have owed had they been single and filed individually. — Also termed *singles' penalty.* Cf. MARRIAGE PENALTY.

marriage broker. One who arranges a marriage in exchange for consideration. ● A marriage broker may be subject to criminal liability.

marriage-brokerage contract. An agreement under which a person, acting for compensation, procures someone for a marriage. ● Traditionally, these contracts have been void as being against public policy.

marriage ceremony. The religious or civil proceeding that solemnizes a marriage. — Sometimes shortened to *marriage.* — Also termed *wedding.*

marriage certificate. A document that is executed by the religious or civil official presiding at a marriage ceremony and filed with a public authority (usu. the county clerk) as evidence of the marriage.

marriage in jest. See MARRIAGE (1).

marriage license. A document, issued by a public authority, that grants a couple permission to marry.

marriage-notice book. An English registry of marriage applications and licenses.

marriage of conscience. See *confidential marriage* under MARRIAGE.

marriage of convenience. See MARRIAGE (1).

marriage of the left hand. See *morganatic marriage* under MARRIAGE (1).

marriage penalty. *Tax.* The difference between the greater income-tax liability owed by a married couple filing a joint income-tax return and the lesser amount they would owe had they been single and filed individually. Cf. MARRIAGE BONUS.

marriage portion. See DOWRY.

marriage promise. A betrothal; an engagement to be married. — Also termed *agreement to marry*; *promise to marry*.

marriage records. Government or church records containing information on prospective couples (such as a woman's maiden name and address) and on wedding services performed.

marriage settlement. See MARITAL AGREEMENT; PRE-NUPTIAL AGREEMENT.

married woman's separate estate in equity. *Obsolete.* At common law, a trust that a rich family could set up for a daughter so that she would not lose control of her own money and property to her husband. ● The daughter could escape the severe limits of coverture by having her family establish a separate estate in equity, allowing her the benefit of income that was not controlled by her husband even if the husband was named as trustee. See COVERTURE; MARRIED WOMEN'S PROPERTY ACTS.

married women's property acts. (*sometimes cap.*) Statutes enacted to remove a married woman's disabilities; esp., statutes that abolished the common-law prohibitions against a married woman's contracting, suing and being sued, or acquiring, holding, and conveying property in her own right, free from any restrictions by her husband. ● For example, these acts abolished the spousal-unity doctrine. In actual usage, the term almost always appears in the plural form (*acts*, not *act*), except when referring to a particular statute. — Also termed *married women's acts*; *married woman's property acts*; *married woman's acts*; *emancipation*

acts; *married women's emancipation acts*. See MERG-
ER DOCTRINE OF HUSBAND AND WIFE; LEGAL-UNITIES DOC-
TRINE.

master, *n*. **1.** One who has personal authority over
another's services; EMPLOYER <the law of master and
servant>. **2.** A parajudicial officer (such as a refer-
ee, an auditor, an examiner, or an assessor) specially appointed to help a court with its proceedings. •
A master may take testimony, hear and rule on
discovery disputes, enter temporary orders, and
handle other pretrial matters, as well as computing
interest, valuing annuities, investigating encum-
brances on land titles, and the like — usually with a
written report to the court. Fed. R. Civ. P. 53. —
Also termed *special master*.

material change in circumstances. See CHANGE
IN CIRCUMSTANCES.

maternal line. See LINE.

maternal-line descent. See DESCENT.

maternal-preference presumption. The belief
that custody of a child, regardless of age, should
generally be awarded to the mother in a divorce
unless she is found to be unfit. • Most jurisdictions
no longer adhere to the maternal-preference presumption. — Also termed *maternal-preference doctrine*. Cf. PRIMARY-CAREGIVER DOCTRINE; TENDER-YEARS
DOCTRINE.

maternal property. See PROPERTY.

maternity (mə-tər-ni-tee). The state or condition of being a mother, esp. a biological one; motherhood. Cf. FILIATION.

maternity presumption. See PRESUMPTION OF MATERNITY.

matrimonial action. See ACTION.

matrimonial cohabitation. See COHABITATION.

matrimonial domicile. See DOMICILE.

matrimonial home. See *matrimonial domicile* under DOMICILE.

matrimonial res. **1.** The marriage estate. **2.** The state of marriage; the legal relationship between married persons, as opposed to the property and support obligations arising from the marriage.

matrimony, *n*. The act or state of being married; MARRIAGE (1). — **matrimonial,** *adj*.

mature-minor doctrine. A rule holding that an adolescent, though not having reached the age of majority, may make decisions about his or her health and welfare if the adolescent demonstrates an ability to articulate reasoned preferences on those matters. • The mature-minor doctrine was recognized as constitutionally protected in medical decisions (abortion rights) in *Planned Parenthood of Cent. Missouri v. Danforth*, 428 U.S. 52, 96 S.Ct. 2831 (1976). Not all states recognize the common-law mature-minor doctrine. Cf. PARENTAL-CONSENT STATUTE.

measuring life. Under the rule against perpetuities, the last beneficiary to die who was alive at the testator's death and who usu. holds a preceding interest. ● A measuring life is used to determine whether an interest will vest under the rule against perpetuities. See RULE AGAINST PERPETUITIES. Cf. LIFE IN BEING.

mediate descent. See DESCENT.

mediation (mee-dee-**ay**-shən), *n*. A method of non-binding dispute resolution involving a neutral third party who tries to help the disputing parties reach a mutually agreeable solution; CONCILIATION. — Also termed *facilitated negotiation*. — **mediate** (**mee**-dee-ayt), *vb*. — **mediatory** (**mee**-dee-ə-tor-ee), *adj*. Cf. ARBITRATION.

mediator (**mee**-dee-ay-tər), *n*. A neutral person who tries to help disputing parties reach an agreement. Cf. ARBITRATOR.

Medicaid. A cooperative federal–state program that pays for medical expenses for those who cannot afford private medical services. ● The program is authorized under the Social Security Act. — Also termed *Medical Assistance*; (in California) *MediCal*.

Medicaid-qualifying trust. See TRUST.

MediCal. See MEDICAID.

Medical Assistance. See MEDICAID.

medical directive. See ADVANCE DIRECTIVE.

medical neglect. See NEGLECT.

Medicare. A federal program — established under the Social Security Act — that provides health insurance for the elderly and the disabled. Cf. MEDIGAP INSURANCE.

medigap insurance. *Slang.* A private insurance policy for Medicare patients to cover the costs not covered by Medicare. Cf. MEDICARE.

Megan's law (**meg**-ən *or* **may**-gən). A statute that requires sex offenders who are released from prison to register with a local board and that provides for community dissemination of information about the registrants. • Although many of these statutes were enacted in the late 1980s, they took their popular name from Megan Kanka of New Jersey, a seven-year-old who in 1994 was raped and murdered by a twice-convicted sex offender who lived across the street from her house. All states have these laws, but only some require community notification (as by publishing offenders' pictures in local newspapers); in others, people must call a state hotline or submit names of persons they suspect. The federal version of Megan's law may be found at 42 USCA § 14071. — Also termed *registration and community-notification law*; *community-notification law*.

Melson formula. A method of calculating a non-custodial parent's child-support obligation to ensure that (1) neither parent falls below the poverty level in meeting child-support obligations, and (2) a child of a wealthier noncustodial parent shares in that parent's higher standard of living. ● Named for Judge Elwood F. Melson of Delaware Family Court, the formula has been adopted in several states, such as Delaware, Hawaii, Montana, and West Virginia. The formula works as follows. A self-support reserve is first deducted from the parent-obligor's net income. Next, a primary support amount per child is calculated at an established subsistence level, added to actual work-related child-care expenses, and allocated between the parents. After deducting the support obligor's self-support reserve and pro rata share of the child's adjusted primary support amount, a percentage of the obligor's remaining income is allocated to additional child support as a cost-of-living adjustment. Total child support is determined by adding together the noncustodial parent's share of primary support and the standard-of-living allowance.

mensa et thoro (**men**-sə et **thor**-oh). [Latin] Bed and board. See A MENSA ET THORO; *divorce a mensa et thoro* under DIVORCE.

mental anguish. See EMOTIONAL DISTRESS.

mental capacity. See CAPACITY (2).

mental cruelty. See CRUELTY.

mental distress. See EMOTIONAL DISTRESS.

mental incompetence. See INCOMPETENCY.

mental suffering. See EMOTIONAL DISTRESS.

MEPA. *abbr.* MULTIETHNIC-PLACEMENT ACT OF 1994.

mercy killing. See EUTHANASIA.

meretricious (mer-ə-**trish**-əs), *adj.* **1.** Involving prostitution <a meretricious encounter>. **2.** (Of a romantic relationship) involving either unlawful sexual connection or lack of capacity on the part of one party; of or relating to an unlawful sexual nature <a meretricious marriage>.

meretricious relationship. *Archaic.* A stable, marriage-like relationship in which the parties co-habit knowing that a lawful marriage between them does not exist.

merger doctrine of husband and wife. *Obsolete.* The common-law principle that, upon marriage, the husband and wife combined to form one legal entity. — Often shortened to *merger*; *merger doctrine*. See SPOUSAL-UNITY DOCTRINE; LEGAL-UNITIES DOCTRINE.

Mexican divorce. See DIVORCE.

middle-level scrutiny. See INTERMEDIATE SCRUTINY.

mid-level scrutiny. See INTERMEDIATE SCRUTINY.

migratory divorce. See DIVORCE.

military allotment. A child-support deduction from the salary of an obligor parent on active duty in the United States military and paid to the obligee parent. See ATTACHMENT OF WAGES.

military testament. See *soldier's will* under WILL.

Miller **trust.** See TRUST.

minimal scrutiny. See RATIONAL-BASIS TEST.

minimum scrutiny. See RATIONAL-BASIS TEST.

ministerial trust. See *passive trust* under TRUST.

minor, *n.* A person who has not reached full legal age; a child or juvenile. — Also termed *infant.*

emancipated minor. A minor who is self-supporting and independent of parental control, usu. as a result of a court order. See EMANCIPATION.

minor in need of supervision. See *child in need of supervision* under CHILD. — Abbr. MINS.

minority. The state or condition of being under legal age. — Also termed *infancy*; *nonage*. Cf. MAJORITY.

minor's estate. See ESTATE.

minor's trust. See *2503(c) trust* under TRUST.

MINS. *abbr.* Minor in need of supervision. See *child in need of supervision* under CHILD.

miscarriage. Spontaneous and involuntary premature expulsion of a nonviable fetus. — Also termed *spontaneous abortion*.

miscegenation (mi-sej-ə-**nay**-shən). A marriage between persons of different races, formerly considered illegal in some jurisdictions. ● In 1967, the U.S. Supreme Court held that laws banning interracial marriages are unconstitutional. *Loving v. Virginia*, 388 U.S. 1, 87 S.Ct. 1817 (1967). But for years, such laws technically remained on the books in some states. The last remaining state-law ban on interracial marriages was a provision in the Alabama constitution. The Alabama legislature voted to repeal the ban, subject to a vote of the state's citizens, in 1999. — Also termed *mixed marriage*; *interracial marriage*.

mixed blood. See BLOOD.

mixed cognation. See COGNATION (2).

mixed marriage. See MISCEGENATION.

mixed property. See PROPERTY.

mixed trust. See TRUST.

modal legacy. See LEGACY.

Model Marriage and Divorce Act. See UNIFORM MARRIAGE AND DIVORCE ACT.

Model Putative Fathers Act. See UNIFORM PUTATIVE AND UNKNOWN FATHERS ACT.

modification order. A post-divorce order that changes the terms of child support, custody, visitation, or alimony. • A modification order may be agreed to by the parties or may be ordered by the court. The party wishing to modify an existing order must show a material change in circumstances from the time when the order sought to be modified was entered. See CHANGE IN CIRCUMSTANCES.

monetary bequest. See *pecuniary bequest* under BEQUEST.

money bequest. See *pecuniary bequest* under BE-QUEST.

money purchase plan. See EMPLOYEE BENEFIT PLAN.

monogamy (mə-**nog**-ə-mee), *n.* **1.** The custom prevalent in most modern cultures restricting a person to one spouse at a time. **2.** The fact of being married to only one spouse. — **monogamous,** *adj.* — **monogamist,** *n.* Cf. BIGAMY; POLYGAMY.

moral duress. See DURESS.

morganatic marriage. See MARRIAGE (1).

mors naturalis. See *natural death* under DEATH.

mortmain statute. A law that limits gifts and other dispositions of land to corporations (esp. char-itable ones) and that prohibits corporations from holding land in perpetuity. ● In England, laws such as the Provisions of Westminster and Magna Carta essentially required the Crown's authorization be-fore land could vest in a corporation. The object was to prevent lands from being held by religious corpo-rations in perpetuity. Although this type of restric-tion was not generally part of the common law in the United States, it influenced the enactment of certain state laws restricting the amount of proper-ty that a corporation could hold for religious or charitable purposes. — Also termed *mortmain act*; *statute of mortmain*.

mortua manus. See DEADHAND CONTROL.

mother. A woman who has given birth to, provided the egg for, or legally adopted a child. ● The term is sometimes interpreted as including a pregnant woman who has not yet given birth.

adoptive mother. See *adoptive parent* under PARENT.

biological mother. The woman who provides the egg that develops into an embryo. ● With today's genetic-engineering techniques, the biological mother may not be the birth mother, but she is usually the legal mother. — Also termed *genetic mother*; *natural mother*.

birth mother. The woman who carries an embryo during the gestational period and who delivers the child. ● When a child is conceived through artificial insemination, the birth mother may not be the genetic or biological mother. And she may not be the legal mother. — Also termed *gestational mother*. See *surrogate mother*; *natural mother*; *biological mother*.

de facto mother. See *de facto parent* under PARENT.

foster mother. See *foster parent* under PARENT.

genetic mother. See *biological mother*.

gestational mother. See *birth mother*.

godmother. See GODPARENT.

intentional mother. See *intentional parent* under PARENT.

natural mother. **1.** See *birth mother.* **2.** See *biological mother.*

psychological mother. See *psychological parent* under PARENT.

stepmother. The wife of one's father by a later marriage.

surrogate mother. **1.** A woman who carries out the gestational function and gives birth to a child for another; esp., a woman who agrees to provide her uterus to carry an embryo throughout pregnancy, typically on behalf of an infertile couple, and who relinquishes any parental rights she may have upon the birth of the child. • A surrogate mother may or may not be the genetic mother of a child. — Often shortened to *surrogate.* — Also termed *surrogate parent*; *gestational surrogate*; *gestational carrier*; *surrogate carrier.* **2.** A person who performs the role of a mother.

mother-in-law. The mother of a person's spouse.

motion. A written or oral application requesting a court to make a specified ruling or order.

ex parte motion (eks **pahr**-tee). A motion made to the court without notice to the adverse party; a motion that a court considers and rules on after hearing from fewer than all sides. • The court will typically grant an ex parte motion when there is immediate potential for family violence.

motion for reduction. A motion to lessen the amount of child-support payments. • This is a type of motion to modify.

motion to modify. A post-final-decree motion asking the court to change one of its earlier orders; esp., a request to change child support or visitation. — Also termed *complaint for modification*.

movable estate. See *personal property* under PROP-ERTY.

Multiethnic Placement Act of 1994. A model statute intended to (1) decrease the length of time that a child awaits adoption, (2) identify and recruit adoptive and foster parents who can meet the needs of available children, and (3) eliminate adoption discrimination based on race, color, or national origin of the child or the adoptive parents. — Abbr. MEPA.

multiple access. In a paternity suit, the defense that the mother had lovers other than the defendant around the time of conception. • The basis for the defense is that because the mother bears the burden of proof, she must be able to prove that only the defendant could be the child's father. In some jurisdictions, this is still known by its common-law name, the *exceptio plurium concubentium* defense, or as simply the *plurium* defense. Juries or judges who wished to dismiss the case because of the mother's promiscuity, rather than because of the improbability of the defendant's paternity, often accepted this defense. Most states have now abrogated the defense. In fact, in recent years the issue of multiple access has declined in importance with the rise of highly accurate paternity testing. Cf. NON-ACCESS.

multiple hearsay. See *double hearsay* under HEAR-SAY.

multiple-party account. See ACCOUNT.

Munchausen syndrome by proxy (mən-chow-zən). A condition in which a caregiver, usu. a parent, fabricates or induces a child's medical condition and seeks medical treatment for the child on the basis of the fabrications or induced symptoms. ● This syndrome is a kind of child abuse, especially when the victim is subjected to repeated medical examinations and treatment, often of an invasive nature, and sometimes even to physical injuries that induce symptoms consistent with the falsified medical condition. The parent is usually emotionally deprived and fabricates or causes the child's illness or medical condition as an attention-getting device.

municipal judge. See JUDGE.

mutual testament. See *mutual will* under WILL.

mutual will. See WILL.

N

naked expectancy. See *naked possibility* under POSSIBILITY.

naked owner. See OWNER.

naked possibility. See POSSIBILITY.

naked power. See POWER.

naked trust. See *passive trust* under TRUST.

nanny tax. See TAX.

National Council of Juvenile and Family Court Judges. An organization of judges and hearing officers who exercise jurisdiction over abuse, neglect, divorce, custody and visitation, support, domestic-violence, and other family-law cases. ● Founded in 1937, the Council has an educational and support facility located near Reno, Nevada. It provides training, technical support, and professional assistance in improving courtroom operations.

National Organ Transplant Act. A 1984 federal law banning the sale of human organs. 42 USCA §§ 273–274. — Abbr. NOTA.

natural-born citizen. See CITIZEN.

natural child. See CHILD.

natural cognation. See COGNATION (2).

natural death. See DEATH.

natural-death act. A statute that allows a person to prepare a living will instructing a physician to withhold life-sustaining procedures if the person should become terminally ill. See ADVANCE DIRECTIVE; LIVING WILL.

natural domicile. See *domicile of origin* under DOMICILE.

natural father. See *biological father* under FATHER.

natural guardian. See GUARDIAN.

natural heir. See HEIR.

natural infancy. See INFANCY.

naturalized citizen. See CITIZEN.

natural mother. See *birth mother* under MOTHER.

natural object. A person likely to receive a portion of another person's estate based on the nature and circumstances of their relationship. — Also termed *natural object of bounty*; *natural object of one's bounty*; *natural object of testator's bounty*.

natural succession. See SUCCESSION (2).

necessaries. 1. Things that are indispensable to living <an infant's necessaries include food, shelter, and clothing>. — Also termed *necessities*; *necessities of life*. **2.** Things that are essential to maintaining the lifestyle to which one is accustomed <a multimillionaire's necessaries may include a chauffeured limousine and a private chef>. ● The term includes whatever is reasonably needed for subsistence, health, comfort, and education, considering the person's age, station in life, and medical condition, but it excludes (1) anything purely ornamental, (2) anything solely for pleasure, (3) what the person is already supplied with, (4) anything that concerns someone's estate or business as opposed to personal needs, and (5) borrowed money. Under the common law, a husband was required to pay debts incurred by his wife or children for necessaries. Beginning in the late 1960s, most states began to change their statutes regarding the obligation to provide necessaries to include both husband and wife. See DOCTRINE OF NECESSARIES; FAMILY-EXPENSE STATUTE.

necessary domicile. See DOMICILE.

necessities. 1. Indispensable things of any kind. **2.** NECESSARIES (1).

necessities of life. See NECESSARIES (1).

ne exeat. [Latin "that he not depart"]. An equity writ restraining a person from leaving, or removing property from, the jurisdiction. ● A *ne exeat* is often issued to prohibit a person from removing a child or property from the jurisdiction — and sometimes from leaving the jurisdiction.

neglect, *n.* **1.** The omission of proper attention to a person or thing, whether inadvertent, negligent, or willful; the act or condition of disregarding. **2.** The failure to give proper attention, supervision, or necessities, esp. to a child, to such an extent that harm results or is likely to result. — **neglect,** *vb.* — **neglectful,** *adj.* Cf. ABUSE.

child neglect. The failure of a person responsible for a minor to care for the minor's emotional or physical needs. ● Child neglect is a form of child abuse. Local child-welfare departments investigate reports of child neglect. In a severe case, criminal charges may be filed against a person suspected of child neglect.

developmental neglect. Failure to provide necessary emotional nurturing and physical or cognitive stimulation, as a result of which a child could suffer from serious developmental delays.

educational neglect. Failure to ensure that a child attends school in accordance with state law.

medical neglect. Failure to provide medical, dental, or psychiatric care that is necessary to prevent or to treat serious physical or emotional injury or illness. ● In determining whether a parent's refusal to consent to medical treatment is neglectful, courts use any of three approaches: (1) an ad hoc test, (2) a best-interests-of-the-child test, or (3) a balancing test that weighs the interests of the parents, the child, and the state. Cf. FAITH-HEALING EXEMPTION.

physical neglect. Failure to provide necessaries, the lack of which has caused or could cause serious injury or illness.

willful neglect. Intentional or reckless failure to carry out a legal duty, esp. in caring for a child.

neglected child. See CHILD.

neglect hearing. See HEARING.

negotiated agreement. A settlement that disputing parties reach between themselves, usu. with the help of their attorneys, but without benefit of formal mediation. — Also termed *negotiated settlement.*

neonatal (nee-oh-**nayt**-əl), *adj.* Of or relating to the first four weeks of life. — **neonate** (**nee**-oh-nayt *or* **nee**-ə-nayt), *n.* Cf. PERINATAL.

neonaticide. See INFANTICIDE.

neonatology (nee-oh-nay-**tol**-ə-jee *or* nee-ə-nə-**tol**-ə-jee), *n.* The branch of medicine dealing with the development of newborn children, as well as various disorders of early infancy. — **neonatological** (nee-oh-nay-tə-**loj**-i-kəl *or* nee-ə-), *adj.* — **neonatologist** (nee-oh-nay-**tol**-ə-jist *or* nee-ə-nə-**tol**-ə-jist), *n.*

nephew. 1. The son of a person's brother or sister; sometimes understood to include the son of a person's brother-in-law or sister-in-law. ● This term is extended in some wills to include a grandnephew.

   half nephew. The son of one's half brother or half sister.

2. *Hist.* A grandchild. **3.** *Hist.* A descendant. Cf. NIECE.

nepotism (**nep**-ə-tiz-əm), *n.* Bestowal of official favors on one's relatives, esp. in hiring. — **nepotistic** (nep-ə-**tis**-tik), *adj.*

net estate. See *net probate estate* under PROBATE ESTATE.

net probate estate. See PROBATE ESTATE.

new asset. See ASSET.

next devisee. See DEVISEE.

next friend. A person who appears in a lawsuit to act for the benefit of an incompetent or minor plaintiff, but who is not a party to the lawsuit and is not appointed as a guardian. — Also termed *prochein ami.* Cf. *guardian ad litem* under GUARDIAN.

next of kin. 1. The person or persons most closely related to a decedent by blood or affinity. **2.** An intestate's heirs — that is, the person or persons entitled to inherit personal property from a decedent who has not left a will. See HEIR.

niece. The daughter of a person's brother or sister; sometimes understood to include the daughter of a person's brother-in-law or sister-in-law. • This term is extended in some wills to include a grandniece. Cf. NEPHEW.

> *half niece.* The daughter of one's half brother or half sister.

no-contact order. See STAY-AWAY ORDER.

no-contest clause. A provision designed to threaten one into action or inaction; esp., a testamentary provision that threatens to dispossess any beneficiary who challenges the terms of the will. — Also termed *in terrorem clause*; *noncontest clause*; *terrorem clause*; *anticontest clause*; *forfeiture clause*.

no-fault divorce. See DIVORCE.

nominal trust. See *passive trust* under TRUST.

nominee trust. See TRUST.

nonaccess. Absence of opportunity for sexual intercourse. • Nonaccess is often used as a defense by the alleged father in paternity cases. Cf. MULTIPLE AC-CESS.

nonage. See MINORITY.

nonancestral estate. See ESTATE.

noncode state. *Hist.* A state that, at a given time, had not procedurally merged law and equity, so that equity was still administered as a separate system. ● The term was current primarily in the early to mid-20th century. — Also termed *common-law state.* Cf. CODE STATE.

noncontestability clause. See INCONTESTABILITY CLAUSE.

noncontest clause. See NO-CONTEST CLAUSE.

noncontributory pension plan. See PENSION PLAN.

noncustodial parent. See PARENT.

nondiscretionary trust. See *fixed trust* under TRUST.

nonexempt property. A debtor's holdings and possessions that a creditor can attach to satisfy a debt. Cf. EXEMPT PROPERTY (1).

nonintercourse. The lack of access, communication, or sexual relations between husband and wife. Cf. NONACCESS.

nonintervention executor. See *independent executor* under EXECUTOR.

nonintervention will. See WILL.

nonlapse statute. See ANTILAPSE STATUTE.

nonmarital child. See *illegitimate child* under CHILD.

nonprobate, *adj*. **1.** Of or relating to some method of transmitting property at death other than by a gift by will <nonprobate distribution>. **2.** Of or relating to the property so disposed <nonprobate assets>. See *nonprobate asset* under ASSET.

nonprobate asset. See ASSET.

nonprosecution, affidavit of. See *affidavit of nonprosecution* under AFFIDAVIT.

nonqualified deferred-compensation plan. See EMPLOYEE BENEFIT PLAN.

nonqualified pension plan. See PENSION PLAN.

nonresident decedent. See DECEDENT.

nonresidential parent. See *noncustodial parent* under PARENT.

nonskip person. *Tax.* A person who is not a skip person for purposes of the generation-skipping transfer tax. IRC (26 USCA) § 2613(b). See SKIP PERSON.

nonsupport. The failure to support a person for whom one is legally obliged to provide, such as a child, spouse, or other dependent. • Nonsupport is a crime in most states. — Also termed *criminal nonsupport*; *criminal neglect of family*; *abandonment of minor children*; *abandonment of children*. Cf. SUPPORT.

nonvoluntary euthanasia. See EUTHANASIA.

NOTA. *abbr.* NATIONAL ORGAN TRANSPLANT ACT.

notarial will. See WILL.

notice of lis pendens. See LIS PENDENS.

notice of pendency. See LIS PENDENS.

notorious cohabitation. See COHABITATION.

nullity of marriage. **1.** The invalidity of a presumed or supposed marriage because it is void on its face or has been voided by court order. • A void marriage, such as an incestuous marriage, is invalid on its face and requires no formality to end. See *void marriage* under MARRIAGE. **2.** A suit brought to nullify a marriage. See ANNULMENT.

nuncupative will. See WILL.

nuptial (nəp-shəl), *adj.* Of or relating to marriage.

nurturing-parent doctrine. The principle that, although a court deciding on child support generally disregards a parent's motive in failing to maximize earning capacity, the court will not impute income to a custodial parent who remains at home or works less than full-time in order to provide a better environment for a child. ● The doctrine is fact-specific; courts apply it case by case.

O

OASDHI. *abbr.* Old Age, Survivors, Disability, and Health Insurance. See OLD-AGE AND SURVIVORS' INSURANCE.

OASDI. *abbr.* Old Age, Survivors, and Disability Insurance. See OLD-AGE AND SURVIVORS' INSURANCE.

OASI. *abbr.* OLD-AGE AND SURVIVORS' INSURANCE.

obediential obligation (ə-bee-dee-**en**-shəl). An obligation imposed on a person because of a situation or relationship, such as an obligation of parents to care for their children.

object (**ob**-jekt), *n.* A person or thing to which thought, feeling, or action is directed <the natural object of one's bounty>. See NATURAL OBJECT.

objectant. See CONTESTANT.

obligation, *n.* **1.** A legal or moral duty to do or not do something. **2.** A formal, binding agreement or acknowledgment of a liability to pay a certain amount or to do a certain thing for a particular person or set of persons. See DUTY; LIABILITY. **3.** *Civil law.* A legal relationship in which one person, the obligor, is bound to render a performance in favor of another, the obligee. La. Civ. Code art. 1756 (West 2000).

inheritable obligation. An obligation that may be enforced by a successor of the creditor or against a successor of the debtor. — Also termed *heritable obligation.*

obligee (ob-lə-**jee**). **1.** One to whom an obligation is owed; a promisee or creditor. **2.** Under the Uniform Interstate Family Support Act, any person to whom a duty of support is owed.

obligor (ob-lə-**gor** *or* **ob**-lə-gor). **1.** One who has undertaken an obligation; a promisor or debtor. **2.** Under the Uniform Interstate Family Support Act, any person who owes a duty of support.

obscenity, *n.* **1.** The characteristic or state of being morally abhorrent or socially taboo, esp. as a result of referring to or depicting sexual or excretory functions. **2.** Something (such as an expression or act) that has this characteristic. See CONTEMPORARY COMMUNITY STANDARD. Cf. INDECENCY.

commercialized obscenity. Obscenity produced and marketed for sale to the public.

obstinate desertion. See DESERTION.

occult marriage. See *confidential marriage* under MARRIAGE.

office of child-support enforcement. A state or federal agency established under Title IV(D) of the Social Security Act to help custodial parents collect child support. 42 USCA § 651 et seq. ● State offices of child-support enforcement generally come under the aegis of the Department of Human Resources. The federal Office of Child Support Enforcement has established the Parent-Locator Service.

officious testament. See TESTAMENT.

officious will. See *officious testament* under TESTAMENT.

offshore trust. See *foreign-situs trust* under TRUST.

old-age and survivors' insurance. (*often cap.*) A system of insurance, subsidized by the federal government, that provides retirement benefits for persons who turn 65 and payments to survivors upon the death of the insured. ● This was the original name for the retirement and death benefits established by the Social Security Act of 1935. As the scope of these benefits expanded, the name changed to Old Age, Survivors, and Disability Insurance (OASDI), and then to Old Age, Survivors, Disability, and Health Insurance (OASDHI). Today, the system is most often referred to as *social security*. — Abbr. OASI. See SOCIAL SECURITY ACT.

olograph. See HOLOGRAPH.

olographic will. See *holographic will* under WILL.

one-party consent rule. The principle that one party to a telephone or other conversation may secretly record the conversation. • This principle applies in most but not all states.

onerous gift. See GIFT.

onerous trust. See TRUST.

onomastic (on-ə-**mas**-tik), *adj.* **1.** Of or relating to names or nomenclature. **2.** (Of a signature on an instrument) in a handwriting different from that of the body of the document; esp., designating an autograph signature alone, as distinguished from the main text in a different hand or in typewriting. Cf. HOLOGRAPH; SYMBOLIC.

open adoption. See ADOPTION.

open and notorious. (Of adultery) known and recognized by the public and flouting the accepted standards of morality in the community.

open and notorious adultery. See ADULTERY.

oppressive child labor. See CHILD LABOR.

oral trust. See TRUST.

oral will. See WILL.

order. A written direction or command delivered by a court or judge. — Also termed *court order*; *judicial order*.

foreign support order. See SUPPORT ORDER.

health-insurance order. See HEALTH-INSURANCE ORDER.

income-withholding order. See INCOME-WITH-HOLDING ORDER.

modification order. See MODIFICATION ORDER.

protective order. See PROTECTIVE ORDER.

qualified domestic-relations order. See QUALI-FIED DOMESTIC-RELATIONS ORDER.

restraining order. See RESTRAINING ORDER.

separation order. See SEPARATION AGREEMENT.

support order. See SUPPORT ORDER.

temporary order. See TEMPORARY ORDER.

temporary restraining order. See TEMPORARY RESTRAINING ORDER.

visitation order. See VISITATION ORDER.

ordinary life insurance. See *whole life insurance* under LIFE INSURANCE.

orphan, *n.* **1.** A child whose parents are dead. **2.** A child with one dead parent and one living parent. — More properly termed *half orphan.* **3.** A child who has been deprived of parental care and has not been legally adopted; a child without a parent or guardian.

orphan's court. See *probate court* under COURT.

out-of-home placement. The placing of a child in a living arrangement outside the child's home (as in foster care or institutional care), usu. as the result of abuse or neglect; specif., in a child-abuse or child-neglect case, state action that removes a child from a parent's or custodian's home and places the child in foster care or with a relative, either temporarily or for an extended period. Cf. FOSTER-CARE PLACEMENT.

overlapping jurisdiction. See *concurrent jurisdiction* under JURISDICTION.

owner. One who has the right to possess, use, and convey something; a proprietor. See OWNERSHIP.

adjoining owner. A person who owns land abutting another's; abutter.

beneficial owner. **1.** One recognized in equity as the owner of something because use and title belong to that person, even though legal title may belong to someone else; esp., one for whom property is held in trust. — Also termed *equitable owner.* **2.** A corporate shareholder who has the power to buy or sell the shares, but who is not registered on the corporation's books as the owner.

equitable owner. See *beneficial owner* (1).

general owner. One who has the primary or residuary title to property; one who has the ultimate ownership of property. Cf. *special owner.*

legal owner. One recognized by law as the owner of something; esp., one who holds legal title to property for the benefit of another. See TRUSTEE.

limited owner. A tenant for life; the owner of a life estate. See *life estate* under ESTATE.

naked owner. *Civil law.* A person whose property is burdened by a usufruct. See USUFRUCT.

record owner. A property owner in whose name the title appears in the public records.

sole and unconditional owner. *Insurance.* The owner who has full equitable title to, and exclusive interest in, the insured property.

ownership. The collection of rights allowing one to use, manage, and enjoy property, including the right to convey it to others. • Ownership implies the right to possess a thing, regardless of any actual or constructive control. Ownership rights are general, permanent, and inheritable.

bare ownership. See *trust ownership.*

beneficial ownership. **1.** A beneficiary's interest in trust property. — Also termed *equitable ownership.* **2.** A corporate shareholder's power to buy or sell the shares, though the shareholder is not registered on the corporation's books as the owner.

contingent ownership. Ownership in which title is imperfect but is capable of becoming perfect on the fulfillment of some condition; conditional ownership.

corporeal ownership. The actual ownership of land or chattels.

incorporeal ownership. The ownership of rights in land or chattels.

joint ownership. Undivided ownership shared by two or more persons. • Typically, their interests, at death, pass to the surviving owner or owners by virtue of the right of survivorship.

ownership in common. Ownership shared by two or more persons whose interests are divisible. • Typically their interests, at death, pass to the dead owner's heirs or successors.

qualified ownership. Ownership that is shared, restricted to a particular use, or limited in the extent of its enjoyment.

trust ownership. A trustee's interest in trust property. — Also termed *bare ownership*.

vested ownership. Ownership in which title is perfect; absolute ownership.

P

palimony (**pal**-ə-moh-nee). [Portmanteau word from *pal* + *alimony*] A court-ordered allowance paid by one member to the other of a couple that, though unmarried, formerly cohabited. • Though not recognized under most state statutes, caselaw in some jurisdictions authorizes palimony claims. The term originated in the press coverage of *Marvin v. Marvin*, 557 P.2d 106 (Cal. 1976). Cf. ALIMONY.

parallel parenting. See PARENTING.

paraphernal property. See *extradotal property* under PROPERTY.

parcenary. See COPARCENARY.

parent. The lawful father or mother of someone. • In ordinary usage, the term denotes more than responsibility for conception and birth. The term commonly includes (1) either the natural father or the natural mother of a child, (2) the adoptive father or adoptive mother of a child, (3) a child's putative blood parent who has expressly acknowledged paternity, and (4) an individual or agency whose status as guardian has been established by judicial decree. In law, parental status based on any criterion may be terminated by judicial decree. In other words, a person ceases to be a legal parent if that person's status as a parent has been terminated in a legal proceeding. — Also termed *legal parent*.

absent parent. See *noncustodial parent.*

adoptive parent. A parent by virtue of legal adoption. See ADOPTION.

biological parent. The woman who provides the egg or the man who provides the sperm to form the zygote that grows into an embryo. — Also termed *genetic parent.*

birth parent. Either the biological father or the mother who gives birth to a child. — Sometimes written *birthparent.*

constructive parent. See *equitable parent.*

custodial parent. The parent awarded physical custody of a child in a divorce. See *physical custody* under CUSTODY. Cf. *noncustodial parent.*

de facto parent. An adult who (1) is not the child's legal parent, (2) has, with consent of the child's legal parent, resided with the child for a significant period, and (3) has routinely performed a share of the caretaking functions at least as great as that of the parent who has been the child's primary caregiver without any expectation of compensation for this care. • Because the status of de facto parent is subordinate to that of legal parent, a person who expects to be afforded the status of parent should, if possible, adopt the child. The primary function of the status of de facto parent is to provide courts with a means for maintaining a relationship between a child and an adult who has functioned as a parent when that adult is prohibited from legally adopting the child. The status of de facto parent is usually limited to a person who has assumed the role of parent with the knowledge and consent, either express or implied, of the legal parent. But it may also arise when there is a total failure or inability of the legal parent to perform parental duties. See *Principles of the Law of Family Dissolution: Analysis and Recommendations* § 2.03 (ALI, Tentative Draft No. 3, pt. I, 1998). Cf. *equitable parent*; *psychological parent*.

Disneyland parent. A noncustodial parent who indulges his or her children with gifts and good times during visitation and leaves most or all disciplinary responsibilities to the other parent; esp., a noncustodial parent who provides luxuries that the custodial parent cannot afford but performs no disciplinary duties, in an effort to gain or retain affection. See LOLLIPOP SYNDROME.

domiciliary parent. A parent with whom a child lives.

dual-residential parent. A parent who shares primary residential responsibility for a child with the other parent when each provides a residence that is substantially a primary residence. • In many jurisdictions, dual residence is referred to as joint physical custody. See RESIDENTIAL RESPONSIBILITY; CUSTODY. Cf. *residential parent*.

equitable parent. 1. A husband who, though not the biological father, is treated by the court as the

420

father in an action for custody or visitation, usu. when the husband (1) has treated the child as his own during the marriage to the child's mother, (2) is the only father the child has ever known, and (3) is seeking the rights of fatherhood. Restatement (Third) of Property: Wills and Other Donative Transfers § 2.5 (Tentative Draft No. 2, 1998). **2.** A mother or father, not by blood or adoption, but by virtue of the close parent-like relationship that exists between that person and a child. ● The status of equitable parent is a legal fiction that is used as an equitable remedy. Most commonly, the status of equitable parent arises when a person, living with the child and one of his or her legal or natural parents, forms a close bond with the child and assumes the duties and responsibilities of a parent. — Also termed *constructive parent*. See *adoption by estoppel* under ADOPTION. Cf. *psychological parent*; *de facto parent*.

foster parent. An adult who, though without blood ties or legal ties, cares for and rears a child, esp. an orphaned or neglected child who might otherwise be deprived of nurture, usu. under the auspices and direction of an agency and for some compensation or benefit. ● Foster parents sometimes give care and support temporarily until a child is legally adopted by others. See FOSTER CARE. Cf. *foster child* under CHILD.

genetic parent. See *biological parent*.

godparent. See GODPARENT.

intended parent. See *intentional parent*.

intentional parent. The person whose idea it is to have and raise a child and who (1) enters into a surrogacy contract with a surrogate mother, and (2) is the legal parent of the child regardless of any genetic link to the child. — Also termed *intended parent*. See *intended child* under CHILD.

noncustodial parent. In the child-custody laws of some states, a parent without the primary custody rights of a child; esp., the parent not awarded physical custody of a child in a divorce. ● The noncustodial parent is typically awarded visitation with the child. — Also termed *nonresidential parent*; *possessory conservator*; *absent parent*. See *physical custody* under CUSTODY. Cf. *custodial parent*.

nonresidential parent. See *noncustodial parent*.

parent by estoppel. A man who, though not a child's legal father, is liable for child support or who (1) has lived with the child for at least two years, (2) has had a good-faith belief that he was the child's father, (3) has fully accepted parental responsibilities for the child, and (4) has continued to make reasonable good-faith efforts to accept parental responsibilities although no longer believing that he was the child's father — or who has lived with the child since the child's birth and held out and accepted full and permanent parental responsibilities as part of a coparenting agreement with the child's mother when the court finds that recognition of the status of parent is in the best interests of the child. See *Principles of the Law of Family Dissolution: Analysis and Recommendations* § 2.03 (ALI, Tentative Draft No. 4, 2000). See ESTOPPEL.

primary domiciliary parent. In a joint-custody arrangement, the parent who exercises primary physical custody. See *joint custody* under CUSTODY.

psychological parent. A person who, on a continuing and regular basis, provides for a child's emotional and physical needs. ● The psychological parent may be the biological parent, a foster parent, a guardian, a common-law parent, or some other person unrelated to the child.

residential parent. A parent who has primary residential responsibility for a child and who is not a dual-residential parent. See RESIDENTIAL RESPONSIBILITY. Cf. *dual-residential parent.*

stepparent. The spouse of one's mother or father by a later marriage.

surrogate parent. **1.** A person who carries out the role of a parent by court appointment or the voluntary assumption of parental responsibilities. **2.** See *surrogate mother* (1) under MOTHER.

parentage (**pair**-ən-tij *or* **par**-). The state or condition of being a parent; kindred in the direct ascending line.

parentage action. See PATERNITY SUIT.

parental access. See VISITATION.

parental-alienation syndrome. See PARENT-ALIEN-ATION SYNDROME.

parental-autonomy doctrine. The principle that a parent has a fundamental right to raise his or her child and to make all decisions regarding that child free from governmental intervention, unless (1) the child's health and welfare are jeopardized by the parent's decisions, or (2) public health, welfare, safety, and order are threatened by the parent's decisions. ● The Supreme Court first recognized the doctrine of parental autonomy over the family in *Meyer v. Nebraska*, 262 U.S. 390, 43 S.Ct. 625 (1923). — Also termed *family-autonomy doctrine*. Cf. PARENTAL-PRIVILEGE DOCTRINE.

parental-consent statute. A statute that requires a minor to obtain his or her parent's consent before having medical treatment, such as an abortion. ● Without parental consent, a physician or other medical professional commits a battery upon a child when giving nonemergency medical treatment. To pass constitutional muster, a parental-consent statute must include a judicial-bypass provision. *Planned Parenthood of Southeastern Pa. v. Casey*, 505 U.S. 833, 112 S. Ct. 2791 (1992). — Also termed *parental-consent treatment statute*. See JUDICIAL-

BYPASS PROVISION. Cf. PARENTAL-NOTIFICATION STATUTE; MATURE-MINOR DOCTRINE.

parental-consent treatment statute. See PARENTAL-CONSENT STATUTE.

parental consortium. See CONSORTIUM.

parental-discipline privilege. A parent's right to use reasonable force or to impose reasonable punishment on a child in a way that is necessary to control, train, and educate. • Several factors are used to determine the reasonableness of the action, including whether the actor is the parent; the child's age, sex, and physical and mental state; the severity and foreseeable consequences of the punishment; and the nature of the misconduct. Cf. PARENTAL-PRIVILEGE DOCTRINE.

parental functions. See PARENTING FUNCTIONS.

parent-alienation syndrome. A situation in which one parent has manipulated a child to fear or hate the other parent; a condition resulting from a parent's actions designed to poison a child's relationship with the other parent. • Some mental-health specialists deny that this phenomenon amounts to a "psychological syndrome." — Also termed *parental-alienation syndrome.*

parental immunity. 1. The principle that children cannot sue their parents, and that parents cannot sue their children, for tort claims. • This tort immunity did not exist at English common law; it was created by American courts, first appearing in *Hewellette v. George*, 9 So. 885 (Miss. 1891). Many courts have abolished the doctrine for some purposes, such as actions by unemancipated minors against parents to recover for injuries sustained in motor-vehicle accidents. See, e.g., *Merrick v. Sutterlin*, 610 P.2d 891 (Wash. 1980) (en banc). Nor does the immunity apply when an injury is inflicted by the parent or child through willful, wanton, or criminal conduct. See, e.g., *Schenk v. Schenk*, 241 N.E.2d 12 (Ill. App. Ct. 1968). — Also termed *parent–child immunity*; *parental-immunity doctrine*. **2.** The principle that parents are not liable for damages caused by the ordinary negligence of their minor children. Cf. PARENTAL-LIABILITY STATUTE.

parental kidnapping. See KIDNAPPING.

Parental Kidnapping Prevention Act. A federal law, enacted in 1980, providing a penalty for child-kidnapping by a noncustodial parent and requiring a state to recognize and enforce a child-custody order rendered by a court of another state. 28 USCA § 1738A; 42 USCA §§ 654, 655, 663. — Abbr. PKPA. Cf. UNIFORM CHILD CUSTODY JURISDICTION ACT; FEDERAL KIDNAPPING ACT.

parental-liability statute. A law obliging parents to pay damages for torts (esp. intentional ones) committed by their minor children. • All states have these laws, but most limit the parents' monetary liability to about $3,000 per tort. Parents can also be held criminally liable for the acts of their children. One group of laws is aimed at contributing to the delinquency and endangering the welfare of a minor. More recently, the laws have been directed at improper supervision and failure to supervise. The first law aimed at punishing parents for the acts of their children was enacted in Colorado in 1903. By 1961 all but two states had enacted similar laws. At least five states make it a felony for a parent to intentionally, knowingly, and recklessly provide a firearm to a child, or permit the child to handle a firearm, when the parent is aware of a substantial risk that the child will use the weapon to commit a crime. — Also termed *parental-responsibility statute*; *failure-to-supervise statute*. Cf. PARENTAL-RESPONSIBILITY STATUTE.

parental-notification statute. A law that requires a physician to notify a minor's parent of her intention to have an abortion. Cf. PARENTAL-CONSENT STATUTE.

parental-preference doctrine. The principle that a fit parent of a minor child enjoys an advantage and should usu. be granted custody instead of someone who is not the child's parent. ● The preference can be rebutted by proof that the child's needs and best interests are to the contrary or that the parent is endangering the child's physical health or emotional welfare. — Also termed *parental-rights doc-*

trine; *parental-superior-rights doctrine*; *parental-presumption rule*. Cf. BEST INTERESTS OF THE CHILD.

parental-presumption rule. See PARENTAL-PREFER-ENCE DOCTRINE.

parental-privilege doctrine. The parent's right to discipline his or her child reasonably, to use reasonable child-rearing practices free of governmental interference, and to exercise decision-making authority over the child. Cf. PARENTAL-AUTONOMY DOCTRINE; PARENTAL-DISCIPLINE PRIVILEGE.

parental-responsibility statute. 1. A law imposing criminal sanctions (such as fines) on parents whose minor children commit crimes as a result of the parents' failure to exercise sufficient control over them. — Also termed *control-your-kid law*. **2.** PARENTAL-LIABILITY STATUTE.

parental rights. A parent's rights to make all decisions concerning his or her child, including the right to determine the child's care and custody, the right to educate and discipline the child, and the right to control the child's earnings and property. See TERMINATION OF PARENTAL RIGHTS.

parental-rights doctrine. See PARENTAL-PREFER-ENCE DOCTRINE.

parental-superior-rights doctrine. See PARENTAL-PREFERENCE DOCTRINE.

parent by estoppel. See PARENT.

parent–child immunity. See PARENTAL IMMUNITY (1).

parentela (par-ən-**tee**-lə), *n. pl.* [Law Latin] Persons who can trace descent from a common ancestor.

parentelic method (par-ən-**tee**-lik *or* -**tel**-ik). A scheme of computation used to determine the paternal or maternal collaterals entitled to inherit when a childless intestate decedent is not survived by parents or their issue. ● Under this method, the estate passes to grandparents and their issue; if there are none, to great-grandparents and their issue; and so on down each line until an heir is found. The Uniform Probate Code uses a limited parentelic system: it looks first to the grandparents and their issue, but if no heir is found in that line, the search ends and the estate escheats to the state. See DEGREE. Cf. GRADUAL METHOD.

parenting, *n.* **1.** Performance of the functions of a parent. **2.** One or more methods of child-rearing.

parallel parenting. A situation in which divorced parents, although disagreeing on some aspects of child-rearing, allow each other to handle discipline and daily regimens in their own individual ways when with the child.

shared parenting. Cooperation between divorced parents in child-rearing.

parenting agreement. See PARENTING PLAN.

parenting functions. Tasks that serve the direct or day-to-day needs of a child or of a child's family. ● Parenting functions include providing economic support, making decisions about the child's welfare, maintaining the family residence and the family vehicle, and buying food and clothes. See *Principles of the Law of Family Dissolution: Analysis and Recommendations* § 2.03 (ALI, Tentative Draft No. 3, pt. I, 1998). Cf. CARETAKING FUNCTIONS.

parenting plan. A plan for (1) allocating custodial responsibility and decision-making authority on behalf of a child, and (2) resolving subsequent disputes between parents. See *Principles of the Law of Family Dissolution: Analysis and Recommendations* § 2.03 (ALI, Tentative Draft No. 3, pt. I, 1998). — Also termed *parenting agreement*. See CUSTODY; CUSTODIAL RESPONSIBILITY; DECISION-MAKING RESPONSIBILITY.

parenting time. See VISITATION.

parliamentary divorce. See DIVORCE.

parol trust. See *oral trust* (1) under TRUST.

partial disability. See DISABILITY (1).

partial guardian. See GUARDIAN.

partial interdiction. See INTERDICTION.

partial intestate. See INTESTATE.

particular successor. See SUCCESSOR.

passive adoption-registry statute. See ADOPTION-REGISTRY STATUTE.

passive euthanasia. See EUTHANASIA.

passive trust. See TRUST.

paternal line. See LINE.

paternal-line descent. See DESCENT.

paternal property. See PROPERTY.

paternity (pə-**tər**-ni-tee). The state or condition of being a father, esp. a biological one; fatherhood. Cf. FILIATION.

paternity action. See PATERNITY SUIT.

paternity presumption. See PRESUMPTION OF PATERNITY.

paternity suit. A court proceeding to determine whether a person is the father of a child (esp. one born out of wedlock), usu. initiated by the mother in an effort to obtain child support. — Also termed *paternity action*; *parentage action*; *bastardy proceeding*.

paternity test. A test, usu. involving DNA identification or tissue-typing, for determining whether a given man is the biological father of a particular child. See DNA IDENTIFICATION; HUMAN-LEUKOCYTE ANTIGEN TEST; BLOOD TEST.

patient–physician privilege. See *doctor–patient privilege* under PRIVILEGE.

pauper. A very poor person, esp. one who receives aid from charity or public funds; INDIGENT. See IN FORMA PAUPERIS.

PDA. See PREGNANCY-DISCRIMINATION ACT.

pecuniary bequest. See BEQUEST.

pecuniary devise. See DEVISE.

pecuniary legacy. See LEGACY.

pendente lite (pen-**den**-tee **lı**-tee), *adv.* [Latin "while the action is pending"] During the proceeding or litigation; in a manner contingent on the outcome of litigation. — Also termed *lite pendente*. Cf. LIS PENDENS.

pendente lite administration. See *administration pendente lite* under ADMINISTRATION.

pension plan. An employer's plan established to pay long-term retirement benefits to employees or their beneficiaries; a plan providing systematically for the payment of definitely determinable benefits to employees over a period of years, usu. for life, after retirement. • Retirement benefits are typically determined by such factors as years of the employee's service and compensation received. ERISA governs the administration of many pension plans. See EMPLOYEE RETIREMENT INCOME SECURITY ACT. Cf. EMPLOYEE BENEFIT PLAN.

contributory pension plan. A pension plan in which both the employer and the employee contribute.

defined-contribution pension plan. See EMPLOYEE BENEFIT PLAN.

defined-pension plan. A pension plan in which the employer promises specific benefits to each employee. — Also termed *fixed-benefit plan.*

noncontributory pension plan. A pension plan contributed to only by the employer.

nonqualified pension plan. A deferred-compensation plan in which an executive increases retirement benefits by annual additional contributions to the company's basic plan.

qualified pension plan. A pension plan that complies with federal law (ERISA) and thus allows the employee to receive tax benefits for contributions and tax-deferred investment growth.

top-hat pension plan. An unfunded pension plan that is maintained by an employer primarily for the purpose of providing deferred compensation for a select group of managers or highly paid employees. ● Top-hat plans are generally not subject to the broad remedial provisions of ERISA because Congress recognized that certain individuals, by virtue of position or compensation level, can substantially influence the design or operation of their deferred-compensation plans. — Often shortened to *top-hat plan*.

pension trust. See TRUST.

per capita (pər **kap**-i-tə), *adj.* [Latin "by the head"] Divided equally among all individuals, usu. in the same class <the court will distribute the property to the descendants on a per capita basis>. Cf. PER STIRPES.

per capita with representation. Divided equally among all members of a class of takers, including those who have predeceased the testator, so that no family stocks are cut off by the prior death of a taker. ● For example, if T (the testator) has three children — A, B, and C — and C has two children but predeceases T, C's children will still take C's share when T's estate is distributed.

perfect usufruct. See USUFRUCT.

perinatal (per-i-**nayt**-əl), *adj*. Of or relating to the period from about the 12th week of gestation through the 28th day of life. Cf. NEONATAL.

periodic alimony. See *permanent alimony* under ALIMONY.

permanency hearing. See HEARING.

permanency plan. A proposed written strategy for the eventual permanent placement of a child who has been removed from his or her parents. • A permanency plan, ideally, provides either for the child's safe return to one or both parents or for the child's adoption. If neither of these alternatives is possible, then the plan will provide for long-term foster care, relative care, or guardianship. Under the Adoption and Safe Families Act, long-term foster care is the choice of last resort. — Also termed *permanent plan*.

permanency-planning hearing. See *permanency hearing* under HEARING.

permanent abode. See DOMICILE (1).

permanent alimony. See ALIMONY.

permanent disability. See DISABILITY (1).

permanent injunction. See INJUNCTION.

permanent plan. See PERMANENCY PLAN.

permanent ward. See WARD.

perpetual injunction. See *permanent injunction* under INJUNCTION.

perpetual trust. See TRUST.

perpetuities, rule against. See RULE AGAINST PERPE-TUITIES.

perpetuity (pər-pə-t[y]oo-ə-tee). **1.** The state of continuing forever. **2.** An interest that does not take effect or vest within the period prescribed by law. See RULE AGAINST PERPETUITIES.

persecution, *n.* Violent, cruel, and oppressive treatment directed toward a person or group of persons because of their race, religion, sexual orientation, politics, or other beliefs. — **persecute,** *vb.* See HATE CRIME.

person. 1. A human being. **2.** An entity (such as a corporation) that is recognized by law as having the rights and duties of a human being. **3.** The living body of a human being <contraband found on the smuggler's person>.

> ***adult disabled person.*** A child over the age of 18 for whom a parent continues to have a duty of support.

disabled person. A person who has a mental or physical impairment. See DISABILITY.

interested person. A person having a property right in or claim against a thing, such as a trust or decedent's estate.

natural person. A human being, as distinguished from an artificial person created by law.

person in loco parentis (in **loh**-koh pə-**ren**-tis). A person who acts in place of a parent, either temporarily (as a schoolteacher does) or indefinitely (as a stepparent does); a person who has assumed the obligations of a parent without formally adopting the child. See IN LOCO PARENTIS.

person of incidence. The person against whom a right is enforceable; a person who owes a legal duty.

person of inherence (in-**heer**-ənts). The person in whom a legal right is vested; the owner of a right.

private person. A person who does not hold public office or serve in the military.

protected person. A person for whom a conservator has been appointed or other protective order has been made.

personal estate. See *personal property* (1) under PROPERTY.

personal indignity. See INDIGNITY.

personal property. See PROPERTY.

personal representative. See REPRESENTATIVE.

personal-residence trust. See TRUST.

Personal Responsibility and Work Opportunity Reconciliation Act. A 1996 federal law that overhauled the welfare system, as well as requiring states to provide a means for collecting child support by (1) imposing liens on a child-support obligor's assets, and (2) facilitating income-withholding. ● The Act did away with Aid to Families with Dependent Children in favor of Temporary Assistance to Needy Families. It also limited the length of time that persons could receive welfare and tied states' receipt of federal child-support funds to their implementing enhanced paternity-establishment services. — Also termed *Welfare Reform Act*. See AID TO FAMILIES WITH DEPENDENT CHILDREN; TEMPORARY ASSISTANCE TO NEEDY FAMILIES. — Abbr. PRWORA.

personal service. See SERVICE.

personal trust. See *private trust* under TRUST.

personalty. See *personal property* (1) under PROPERTY.

person *in loco parentis*. See PERSON.

person in need of supervision. See *child in need of supervision* under CHILD. — Abbr. PINS.

person of incidence. See PERSON.

person of inherence. See PERSON.

per stirpes (pər **stər**-peez), *adv.* & *adj.* [Latin "by roots or stocks"] Proportionately divided between beneficiaries according to their deceased ancestor's share. — Also termed *in stirpes*. Cf. PER CAPITA.

petition, *n.* **1.** A formal written request presented to a court or other official body.

> *juvenile petition.* A juvenile-court petition alleging delinquent conduct by the accused. ● The accusations made in a juvenile petition are tried in an adjudication hearing. See *adjudication hearing* under HEARING.

2. In some states, a lawsuit's first pleading; COMPLAINT. — **petition,** *vb.*

petitioner. A party who presents a petition to a court or other official body. Cf. RESPONDENT (2).

physical child endangerment. See CHILD ENDANGERMENT.

physical cruelty. See CRUELTY.

physical custody. See CUSTODY.

physical disability. See DISABILITY (1).

physical endangerment. See *physical child endangerment* under CHILD ENDANGERMENT.

physical incapacity. See IMPOTENCE.

physical neglect. See NEGLECT.

physician–patient privilege. See *doctor–patient privilege* under PRIVILEGE.

physician's directive. See ADVANCE DIRECTIVE.

pickup tax. See TAX.

PINS. *abbr.* PERSON IN NEED OF SUPERVISION.

PKPA. *abbr.* PARENTAL KIDNAPPING PREVENTION ACT.

plaintiff. The party who brings a civil suit in a court of law. — Abbr. pltf. Cf. DEFENDANT.

plan. See EMPLOYEE BENEFIT PLAN.

pleading the baby act. See BABY ACT, PLEADING THE.

plenary guardianship. See GUARDIANSHIP.

pltf. *abbr.* PLAINTIFF.

plural marriage. See MARRIAGE (1); POLYGAMY.

plurium **defense.** See MULTIPLE ACCESS.

policy of insurance. See INSURANCE POLICY.

polyandry (**pol**-ee-an-dree). The condition or practice of having more than one husband. Cf. POLYGYNY.

polygamy (pə-**lig**-ə-mee), *n.* **1.** The state or practice of having more than one spouse simultaneously. — Also termed *simultaneous polygamy*; *plural marriage.* **2.** The fact or practice of having more than one spouse during one's lifetime, though never simultaneously. — Also termed *successive polygamy*; *serial polygamy*; *sequential marriage.* — **polygamous,** *adj.* — **polygamist,** *n.* Cf. BIGAMY; MONOGAMY.

polygyny (pə-**lij**-ə-nee). The condition or practice of having more than one wife. Cf. POLYANDRY.

pooled trust. See TRUST.

pornography, *n.* Material (such as writings, photographs, or movies) depicting sexual activity or erotic behavior in a way that is designed to arouse sexual excitement. • Pornography is protected speech under the First Amendment unless it is determined to be legally obscene. — **pornographic,** *adj.* See OBSCENITY.

  child pornography. Material depicting a person under the age of 18 engaged in sexual activity. • Child pornography is not protected by the First

Amendment — even if it falls short of the legal standard for obscenity — and those directly involved in its distribution can be criminally punished.

virtual child pornography. Material that includes a computer-generated image that appears to be a minor engaged in sexual activity but that in reality does not involve a person under the age of 18.

portion. A share or allotted part (as of an estate).

positive act. See ACT (2).

possessory conservator. See *noncustodial parent* under PARENT.

possibility. **1.** An event that may or may not happen. **2.** A contingent interest in real or personal property.

bare possibility. See *naked possibility.*

naked possibility. A mere chance or expectation that a person will acquire future property. ● A conveyance of a naked possibility is usually void for lack of subject matter, as in a deed conveying all rights to a future estate not yet in existence. — Also termed *bare possibility*; *naked expectancy.*

possibility coupled with an interest. An expectation recognized in law as an estate or interest, as occurs in an executory devise or in a shifting or springing use. ● This type of possibility may be sold or assigned.

possibility on a possibility. See *remote possibility*.

remote possibility. A limitation dependent on two or more facts or events that are contingent and uncertain; a double possibility. — Also termed *possibility on a possibility*.

possibility of reverter. A future interest retained by a grantor after conveying a fee simple determinable, so that the grantee's estate terminates automatically and reverts to the grantor if the terminating event ever occurs. ● In this type of interest, the grantor transfers an estate whose maximum potential duration equals that of the grantor's own estate and attaches a special limitation that operates in the grantor's favor. — Often shortened to *reverter*. Cf. REMAINDER (1); REVERSION.

possibility on a possibility. See *remote possibility* under POSSIBILITY.

POSSLQ (**pahs**-əl-kyoo). *abbr.* A person of opposite sex sharing living quarters. ● Although this term (which is used by the Census Bureau) is intended to include only a person's roommate of the opposite sex to whom the person is not married, the phrase literally includes those who are married. This overbreadth has occasionally been criticized. See CUPOS.

posthumous child. See CHILD.

postmarital, *adj.* **1.** Of, relating to, or occurring after marriage. Cf. PREMARITAL. **2.** Of, relating to, or occurring after divorce.

postnup, *n. Slang.* See POSTNUPTIAL AGREEMENT.

postnuptial (pohst-**nəp**-shəl), *adj.* Made or occurring during marriage <a postnuptial contract>. Cf. PRENUPTIAL.

postnuptial agreement (pohst-**nəp**-shəl). An agreement entered into during marriage to define each spouse's property rights in the event of death or divorce. ● The term commonly refers to an agreement between spouses during the marriage at a time when separation or divorce is not imminent. When dissolution is intended as the result, it is more properly called a *property settlement* or *marital agreement.* — Often shortened to *postnup.* — Also termed *postnuptial settlement.* Cf. PRENUPTIAL AGREEMENT.

postnuptial settlement. See POSTNUPTIAL AGREEMENT.

postnuptial will. See WILL.

pourover trust. See TRUST.

pourover will. See WILL.

power. **1.** The ability to act or not act. **2.** Dominance, control, or influence over another. **3.** The legal right or authorization to act or not act; the ability conferred on a person by the law to alter, by an act of will, the rights, duties, liabilities, or other legal relations either of that person or of another. **4.** A document granting legal authorization. **5.** An authority to affect an estate in land by (1) creating some estate independently of any estate that the holder of the authority possesses, (2) imposing a charge on the estate, or (3) revoking an existing estate. See POWER OF APPOINTMENT.

appendant power (ə-**pen**-dənt). **1.** A power that gives the donee a right to appoint estates that attach to the donee's own interest. **2.** A power held by a donee who owns the property interest in the assets subject to the power, and whose interest can be divested by the exercise of the power. ● The appendant power is generally viewed as adding nothing to the ownership and thus is not now generally recognized as a true power. — Also termed *power appendant*.

beneficial power. A power that is executed for the benefit of the power's donee, as distinguished from a *trust power*, which is executed for the benefit of someone other than the power's donee (i.e., a trust beneficiary).

general power. Power that can be exercised in anyone's favor, including the agent, to affect an-

other's interest in property; a power that authorizes the alienation of a fee to any alienee.

naked power. The power to exercise rights over
something (such as a trust) without having a
corresponding interest in that thing. Cf. *power
coupled with an interest.*

power appendant. See *appendant power.*

power coupled with an interest. A power to do
some act, conveyed along with an interest in the
subject matter of the power. ● A power coupled
with an interest is not held for the benefit of the
principal, and it is irrevocable due to the agent's
interest in the subject property. For this reason,
some authorities assert that it is not a true agency power. — Also termed *power given as security*;
proprietary power. See *irrevocable power of attorney* under POWER OF ATTORNEY. Cf. *naked power.*

power given as security. See *power coupled
with an interest.*

power of revocation (rev-ə-**kay**-shən). A power
that a person reserves in an instrument (such as
a trust) to revoke the legal relationship that the
person has created.

proprietary power. See *power coupled with an
interest.*

trust power. See *beneficial power.*

power appendant. See *appendant power* under POWER.

power coupled with an interest. See POWER.

power given as security. See *power coupled with an interest* under POWER.

power of appointment. A power conferred on a donee by will or deed to select and determine one or more recipients of the donor's estate or income. — Also termed *enabling power*.

> **general power of appointment.** A power of appointment by which the donee can appoint — that is, dispose of the donor's property — in favor of anyone at all, including oneself or one's own estate.

> **limited power of appointment.** A power of appointment by which the donee can appoint to only the person or class specified in the instrument creating the power, but cannot appoint to oneself or one's own estate. — Also termed *special power of appointment*.

> **special power of appointment.** See *limited power of appointment*.

> **testamentary power of appointment** (tes-tə-men-tə-ree *or* -tree). A power of appointment created by a will.

power-of-appointment trust. See TRUST.

power of attorney. 1. An instrument granting someone authority to act as agent or attorney-in-fact for the grantor. ● An ordinary power of attorney is revocable and automatically terminates upon the death or incapacity of the principal. — Also termed *letter of attorney*. **2.** The authority so granted. Pl. **powers of attorney.** See ATTORNEY (1).

durable power of attorney. A power of attorney that remains in effect during the grantor's incompetency. ● Such instruments commonly allow an agent to make healthcare decisions for a patient who has become incompetent.

general power of attorney. A power of attorney that authorizes an agent to transact business for the principal. Cf. *special power of attorney.*

irrevocable power of attorney (i-**rev**-ə-kə-bəl). A power of attorney that the principal cannot revoke. — Also termed *power of attorney coupled with an interest.* See *power coupled with an interest* under POWER.

power of attorney coupled with an interest. See *irrevocable power of attorney.*

power of attorney for healthcare. See ADVANCE DIRECTIVE.

special power of attorney. A power of attorney that limits the agent's authority to only a specified matter. Cf. *general power of attorney.*

springing power of attorney. A power of attorney that becomes effective only when needed, at some future date or upon some future occurrence, usu. upon the principal's incapacity. — Also termed *springing durable power of attorney*. See *durable power of attorney*; ADVANCE DIRECTIVE.

power of attorney coupled with an interest. See *irrevocable power of attorney* under POWER OF ATTORNEY.

power of attorney for healthcare. See ADVANCE DIRECTIVE.

power of revocation. See POWER.

precatory trust. See TRUST.

predator. See SEXUAL PREDATOR.

Pregnancy-Discrimination Act. A federal statute that prohibits workplace discrimination against a pregnant woman or against a woman affected by childbirth or a related medical condition. 42 USCA § 2000. • The Pregnancy-Discrimination Act is part of Title VII of the Civil Rights Act of 1964. — Abbr. PDA.

preliminary injunction. See INJUNCTION.

preliminary protective hearing. See *shelter hearing* under HEARING.

premarital, *adj.* Of, relating to, or occurring before marriage. Cf. POSTMARITAL.

premarital agreement. See PRENUPTIAL AGREEMENT.

premarital asset. See ASSET.

prenatal injury. Harm to a fetus or an embryo. Cf. BIRTH INJURY.

prenatal tort. See TORT.

prenup, *n. Slang.* See PRENUPTIAL AGREEMENT.

prenuptial (pree-**nəp**-shəl), *adj.* Made or occurring before marriage; premarital. — Also termed *antenuptial* (an-tee-**nəp**-shəl). Cf. POSTNUPTIAL.

prenuptial agreement. An agreement made before marriage usu. to resolve issues of support and property division if the marriage ends in divorce or by the death of a spouse. — Also termed *antenuptial agreement*; *antenuptial contract*; *premarital agreement*; *premarital contract*; *marriage settlement.* — Sometimes shortened to *prenup.* Cf. POSTNUPTIAL AGREEMENT.

prenuptial gift. See GIFT.

prenuptial will. See WILL.

presence-of-the-testator rule. The principle that a testator must be aware (through sight or other sense) that the witnesses are signing the will. • Many jurisdictions interpret this requirement liberally, and the Uniform Probate Code has dispensed with it.

present estate. See PRESENT INTEREST.

present interest. A property interest in which the privilege of possession or enjoyment is present and not merely future; an interest entitling the holder to immediate possession. — Also termed *present estate*. Cf. FUTURE INTEREST.

presumed father. See FATHER.

presumption-of-fertility rule. See FERTILE-OCTOGE-NARIAN RULE.

presumption of legitimacy. See PRESUMPTION OF PATERNITY.

presumption of maternity. The presumption that the woman who has given birth to a child is both the genetic mother and the legal mother of the child. — Also termed *maternity presumption*. Cf. *presumed father* under FATHER.

presumption of paternity. The presumption that the father of a child is the man who (1) is married to the child's mother when the child was conceived or born (even though the marriage may have been invalid), (2) married the mother after the child's birth and agreed either to have his name on the birth certificate or to support the child, or (3) welcomed the child into his home and later held out the child as his own. — Also termed *paternity presumption*; *presumption of legitimacy*; *legitimacy presumption*. See *presumed father* under FATHER.

presumptive death. See DEATH.

presumptive heir. See *heir presumptive* under HEIR.

presumptive trust. See *resulting trust* under TRUST.

pretermission (pree-tər-**mish**-ən). **1.** The condition of one who is pretermitted, as an heir of a testator. **2.** The act of omitting an heir from a will.

pretermission statute. See PRETERMITTED-HEIR STATUTE.

pretermit (pree-tər-**mit**), *vb.* **1.** To ignore or disregard purposely <the court pretermitted the constitutional question by deciding the case on procedural grounds>. **2.** To neglect, overlook, or omit accidentally <the third child was pretermitted in the will>. ● Although in ordinary usage sense 1 prevails, in legal contexts (esp. involving heirs) sense 2 is usual.

pretermitted child. See *pretermitted heir* under HEIR.

pretermitted heir. See HEIR.

pretermitted-heir statute. A state law that, under certain circumstances, grants an omitted heir the right to inherit a share of the testator's estate, usu. by treating the heir as though the testator had died intestate. ● Most states have a pretermitted-heir statute, under which an omitted child or spouse receives the same share of the estate as if the testator had died intestate, unless the omission was intentional. The majority rule, and that found in the Uniform Probate Code, is that only afterborn children — that is, children born after the execution of a will — receive protection as pretermitted heirs. Under that circumstance, an inference arises that their omission was inadvertent rather than purposeful. — Also termed *pretermission statute*.

pretermitted spouse. See *pretermitted heir* under HEIR.

pretrial detention. In a juvenile-delinquency case, the court's authority to hold in custody, from the initial hearing until the probable-cause hearing, any juvenile charged with an act that, if committed by an adult, would be a crime. ● If the court finds that releasing the juvenile would create a serious risk that before the return date the juvenile might commit a criminal act, it may order the juvenile detained pending a probable-cause hearing. Juveniles do not have a constitutional right to bail. The Supreme Court upheld the constitutionality of such statutes in *Schall v. Martin*, 467 U.S. 253, 104 S.Ct. 2403 (1984).

preventive injunction. See INJUNCTION.

preventive law. A practice of law that seeks to minimize a client's risk of litigation or secure more certainty with regard to the client's legal rights and duties. ● Emphasizing planning, counseling, and the nonadversarial resolution of disputes, preventive law focuses on the lawyer's role as adviser and negotiator.

priest–penitent privilege. See PRIVILEGE.

primary beneficiary. See BENEFICIARY.

primary caregiver. 1. The parent who has had the greatest responsibility for the daily care and rearing of a child. See TENDER-YEARS DOCTRINE; PRIMARY-CAREGIVER DOCTRINE. **2.** The person (including a nonparent) who has had the greatest responsibility for the daily care and rearing of a child. — Also termed *primary caretaker*.

primary-caregiver doctrine. The presumption that, in a custody dispute, the parent who is a child's main caregiver will be the child's custodian, assuming that he or she is a fit parent. ● This doctrine includes the quality and the quantity of care that a parent gives a child — but excludes supervisory care by others while the child is in the parent's custody. Under this doctrine, courts sometimes divide children into three age groups: those under the age of 6, those 6 to 14, and those 14 and older. For children under the age of 6, an absolute presumption exists in favor of the primary caretaker as custodian. For those 6 to 14, the trial court may hear the child's preference on the record but without the parents being present. For those 14 and older, the child may be allowed to choose which parent will be the custodian, assuming that both parents are fit. — Also termed *primary-caretaker doctrine*; *primary-caregiver presumption*; *primary-caretaker presumption*; *primary-caregiver preference*. Cf. MATERNAL-PREFERENCE PRESUMPTION; TENDER-YEARS DOCTRINE.

primary caretaker. See PRIMARY CAREGIVER.

primary devise. See DEVISE.

primary domiciliary parent. See PARENT.

primary residential responsibility. See RESIDENTIAL RESPONSIBILITY.

primogeniture (prɪ-mə-**jen**-ə-chər). **1.** The state of being the firstborn child among siblings. **2.** The common-law right of the firstborn son to inherit his ancestor's estate, usu. to the exclusion of younger siblings. — Also termed (in sense 2) *primogeniture-ship*.

primogenitureship. See PRIMOGENITURE (2).

principal, *n.* **1.** One who authorizes another to act on his or her behalf as an agent. **2.** One who has primary responsibility on an obligation, as opposed to a surety or indorser. **3.** The body of an estate, trust, investment, or other fund, not including interest, earnings, or profits.

prior-relationship rape. See *relationship rape* under RAPE.

privacy, invasion of. See INVASION OF PRIVACY.

privacy, right of. See RIGHT OF PRIVACY.

privacy act. See PRIVACY LAW (1).

Privacy Act of 1974. An act that regulates the government's creation, collection, use, and dissemination of records that can identify an individual by name, as well as other personal information. ● The Act was amended in 1990 and in 1994. 18 USCA § 552a.

privacy law. 1. A federal or state statute that protects a person's right to be left alone or restricts public access to personal information such as tax returns and medical records. — Also termed *privacy* *act.* **2.** The area of legal studies dealing with a person's right to be left alone and with restricting public access to personal information such as tax returns and medical records.

private adoption. See ADOPTION.

private agent. See AGENT.

private attorney. See ATTORNEY (1).

private placement. The placement of a child for adoption by a parent, lawyer, doctor, or private agency, rather than by a government agency. ● At least eight states have prohibited private-placement adoptions. — Also termed *direct placement.*

private-placement adoption. See *private adoption* under ADOPTION.

private trust. See TRUST.

privilege. An evidentiary rule that gives a witness the option to not disclose the fact asked for, even though it might be relevant; the right to prevent disclosure of certain information in court, esp. when the information was originally communicated in a professional or confidential relationship. ● Assertion of a privilege can be overcome by proof that an otherwise privileged communication was made in the presence of a third party to whom the privilege would not apply.

accountant–client privilege. The protection afforded to a client from an accountant's unauthorized disclosure of materials submitted to or prepared by the accountant.

antimarital-facts privilege. See *marital privilege* (2).

attorney–client privilege. The client's right to refuse to disclose and to prevent any other person from disclosing confidential communications between the client and the attorney. — Also termed *lawyer–client privilege*; *client's privilege*.

clergyman–penitent privilege. See *priest–penitent privilege*.

client's privilege. See *attorney–client privilege*.

doctor–patient privilege. The right to exclude from evidence in a legal proceeding any confidential communication that a patient makes to a physician for the purpose of diagnosis or treatment, unless the patient consents to the disclosure. — Also termed *physician–patient privilege*; *patient–physician privilege*.

husband–wife privilege. See *marital privilege*.

lawyer–client privilege. See *attorney–client privilege*.

marital privilege. **1.** The privilege allowing a spouse not to testify, and to prevent another from testifying, about confidential communications with the other spouse during the marriage. — Also termed *marital-communications privilege*. **2.** The privilege allowing a spouse not to testify in a criminal case as an adverse witness against the other spouse, regardless of the subject matter of the testimony. — Also termed (in sense 2) *privilege against adverse spousal testimony*; *antimarital-facts privilege*. **3.** The privilege immunizing from a defamation lawsuit any statement made between husband and wife. — Also termed (in all senses) *spousal privilege*; *husband–wife privilege*.

patient–physician privilege. See *doctor–patient privilege*.

physician–client privilege. See *doctor–patient privilege*.

priest–penitent privilege. The privilege barring a clergy member from testifying about a confessor's communications. — Also termed *clergyman–penitent privilege*.

privilege against adverse spousal testimony. See *marital privilege* (2).

psychotherapist–patient privilege. A privilege that a person can invoke to prevent the disclosure of a confidential communication made in the course of diagnosis or treatment of a mental or emotional condition by or at the direction of a psychotherapist. ● The privilege can be overcome under certain conditions, as when the examination is ordered by a court. — Also termed *psycho-therapist–client privilege*.

spousal privilege. See *marital privilege*.

privilege against adverse spousal testimony. See *marital privilege* (2) under PRIVILEGE.

probable-cause hearing. See *shelter hearing* under HEARING.

probate (**proh**-bayt), *n*. **1.** The judicial procedure by which a testamentary document is established to be a valid will; the proving of a will to the satisfaction of the court. ● Unless set aside, the probate of a will is conclusive upon the parties to the proceedings (and others who had notice of them) on all questions of testamentary capacity, the absence of fraud or undue influence, and due execution of the will. But probate does not preclude inquiry into the validity of the will's provisions or on their proper construction or legal effect. — Also termed *proof of will*.

independent probate. See *informal probate*.

informal probate. Probate designed to operate with minimal involvement and supervision of the probate court. ● Most modern probate codes encourage this type of administration, with an independent personal representative. — Also termed *independent probate*. Cf. *independent executor* under EXECUTOR.

probate in common form. Probate granted in the registry, without any formal procedure in court, on the executor's ex parte application. ● The judgment is subject to being reopened by a party who has not been given notice.

probate in solemn form. Probate granted in open court, as a final decree, when all interested parties have been given notice. ● The judgment is final for all parties who have had notice of the proceeding, unless a later will is discovered.

small-estate probate. An informal procedure for administering small estates, less structured than the normal process and usu. not requiring the assistance of an attorney.

2. Loosely, a personal representative's actions in handling a decedent's estate. **3.** Loosely, all the subjects over which probate courts have jurisdiction.

probate, *vb.* **1.** To admit (a will) to proof. **2.** To administer (a decedent's estate). **3.** To grant probation to (a criminal); to reduce (a sentence) by means of probation.

probate asset. See *legal asset* under ASSET.

probate bond. See BOND.

probate code. A collection of statutes setting forth the law (substantive and procedural) of decedents' estates and trusts.

probate court. See COURT.

probate distribution. See DISTRIBUTION.

probate duty. See DUTY (2).

probate estate. A decedent's property subject to administration by a personal representative. ● The probate estate comprises property owned by the decedent at the time of death and property acquired by the decedent's estate at or after the time of death. — Also termed *probate property*. See *decedent's estate* under ESTATE.

> **net probate estate.** The probate estate after the following deductions: (1) family allowances, (2) exempt property, (3) homestead allowances, (4) claims against the estate, and (5) taxes for which the estate is liable. See Restatement (Third) of Property: Wills and Other Donative Transfers § 1.1 (Tentative Draft No. 2, 1998). — Also termed *net estate*. Cf. *adjusted gross estate* (1) under ESTATE.

probate homestead. See HOMESTEAD.

probate in common form. See PROBATE (1).

probate in solemn form. See PROBATE (1).

probate judge. See JUDGE.

probate jurisdiction. See JURISDICTION.

probate property. See PROBATE ESTATE.

probate register. See REGISTER.

procedural due process. See DUE PROCESS.

prochein ami. [Law French] See NEXT FRIEND.

pro–con divorce. See DIVORCE.

proctor. See DIVORCE PROCTOR.

prohibited degree. See DEGREE.

prohibitory injunction. See INJUNCTION.

prolicide (**proh**-lə-sɪd). **1.** The killing of offspring; esp., the crime of killing a child shortly before or after birth. **2.** One who kills a child shortly before or after birth. — **prolicidal,** *adj.* Cf. INFANTICIDE.

promise in consideration of marriage. A promise for which the actual performance of the marriage is the consideration, as when a man agrees to transfer property to a woman if she will marry him. • A promise to marry, however, is not considered a promise in consideration of marriage.

promise to marry. See MARRIAGE PROMISE.

proof of will. See PROBATE (1).

pro per., *n*. See PRO SE.

pro persona (proh pər-**soh**-nə), *adv*. & *adj*. See PRO SE.

property. 1. The right to possess, use, and enjoy a determinate thing (either a tract of land or a chattel); the right of ownership <the institution of private property is protected from undue governmental interference>. **2.** Any external thing over which the rights of possession, use, and enjoyment are exercised <the airport is city property>.

   common property. Real property that is held by two or more persons with no right of survivorship. Cf. *joint property.*

   community property. See COMMUNITY PROPERTY.

   domestic-partnership property. Property that would have been marital property if the domestic partners had been married to each other. See *Principles of the Law of Family Dissolution: Analysis and Recommendations* § 6.04 (ALI, Tentative Draft No. 4, 2000). See DOMESTIC PARTNERS; DOMESTIC-PARTNERSHIP PERIOD.

   dotal property. *Civil law.* Separate property that the wife brings to the marriage to assist the husband with the marriage expenses. Cf. *extradotal property.*

   exempt property. See EXEMPT PROPERTY.

extradotal property. *Civil law.* **1.** That portion of a wife's property over which she has complete control. **2.** All of a wife's effects that have not been settled on her as dowry; any property that a wife owns apart from her dowry. • In Louisiana, after January 1, 1980, all property acquired by the wife that is not community is neither dotal nor extradotal; it is simply her separate property, as has always been true of the husband. — Also termed *paraphernal property.* Cf. *dotal property.*

intangible property. Property that lacks a physical existence. • Examples include stock options and business goodwill. Cf. *tangible property.*

joint property. Real or personal property held by two or more persons with a right of survivorship. Cf. *common property.*

marital property. Property that is acquired during marriage and that is subject to distribution or division at the time of marital dissolution. • Generally, it is property acquired after the date of the marriage and before a spouse files for divorce. The phrase *marital property* is used in equitable-distribution states and is roughly equivalent to *community property.* — Also termed *marital estate.* See COMMUNITY PROPERTY; EQUITABLE DISTRIBUTION.

maternal property. Property that comes from the mother of a party and other ascendants of the maternal stock.

mixed property. Property with characteristics of both real property and personal property — such as heirlooms and fixtures.

paraphernal property. See *extradotal property*.

paternal property. Property that comes from the father of a party and other ascendants of the paternal stock.

personal property. **1.** Any movable or intangible thing that is subject to ownership and not classified as real property. — Also termed *personalty*; *personal estate*; *movable estate*; (in plural) *things personal*. Cf. *real property*. **2.** Property not used in a taxpayer's trade or business or held for income production or collection.

qualified-terminable-interest property. Property that passes by a QTIP trust from a deceased spouse to the surviving spouse and that (if the executor so elects) qualifies for the marital deduction provided that the spouse is entitled to receive all income in payments made at least annually for life and that no one has the power to appoint the property to anyone other than the surviving spouse. ● The purpose of the marital deduction is to permit deferral of estate taxes until the death of the surviving spouse. But this property is included in the surviving spouse's estate at death, where it is subject to the federal estate tax. — Abbr. QTIP. See *QTIP trust* under TRUST.

quasi-community property. See COMMUNITY PROPERTY.

real property. Land and anything growing on, attached to, or erected on it, excluding anything that may be severed without injury to the land. ● Real property can be either corporeal (soil and buildings) or incorporeal (easements). — Also termed *realty; real estate.* Cf. *personal property* (1).

separate property. See SEPARATE PROPERTY.

tangible personal property. Corporeal personal property of any kind; personal property that can be seen, weighed, measured, felt, or touched, or is in any other way perceptible to the senses, such as furniture, cooking utensils, and books.

tangible property. Property that has physical form and characteristics. Cf. *intangible property.*

property division. See PROPERTY SETTLEMENT (1).

property settlement. 1. A judgment in a divorce case determining the distribution of the marital property between the divorcing parties. ● A property settlement includes a division of the marital debts as well as assets. — Also termed *property division; division of property.* **2.** A contract that divides up the assets of divorcing spouses and is incorporated into a divorce decree. — Also termed *integrated property settlement; property settlement agreement.* Cf. DIVORCE AGREEMENT. **3.** MARITAL AGREEMENT.

property settlement agreement. See PROPERTY SETTLEMENT (2).

proprietary power. See *power coupled with an interest* under POWER.

pro se (proh **say** *or* **see**), *adv.* & *adj.* [Latin] For oneself; on one's own behalf; without a lawyer <the defendant proceeded pro se> <a pro se defendant>. — Also termed *pro persona*; *in propria persona; pro per*.

pro se, *n.* One who represents oneself in a court proceeding without the assistance of a lawyer <the third case on the court's docket involving a pro se>. — Also termed *pro per*.

prospective heir. See HEIR.

protection order. See RESTRAINING ORDER (1).

protective order. 1. A court order prohibiting or restricting a party from engaging in conduct (esp. a legal procedure such as discovery) that unduly annoys or burdens the opposing party or a third-party witness. **2.** RESTRAINING ORDER (1).

protective trust. See TRUST.

protector. An unrelated, disinterested overseer of a trust who possesses broader authority than a trustee. ● Protectors are usually appointed to manage offshore trusts, but the concept is slowly being applied to domestic trusts. Protectors often possess broad powers to act for the benefit of the trust, as by removing trustees and clarifying or modifying trust terms to promote the settlor's objectives. For these reasons, a protector is generally not a trustee or beneficiary of the trust. Cf. TRUSTEE.

provisional alimony. See *temporary alimony* under ALIMONY.

provisional injunction. See *preliminary injunction* under INJUNCTION.

proxy directive. A document that appoints a surrogate decision-maker for the declarant's healthcare decisions. Cf. ADVANCE DIRECTIVE; INSTRUCTION DIRECTIVE; LIVING WILL.

proxy marriage. See MARRIAGE (2).

prudent-investor rule. *Trusts*. The principle that a fiduciary must invest in only those securities or portfolios of securities that a reasonable person would buy. • The origin of the prudent-investor rule is *Harvard College v. Amory*, 26 Mass. 446 (1830). This case stressed two points for a trustee to consider when making investments: probable income and probable safety. The trustee must consider both when making investments. Originally termed the *prudent-man rule*, the Restatement (Third) of

Trusts changed the term to *prudent-investor rule*. — Also termed *prudent-person rule*.

prudent-person rule. See PRUDENT-INVESTOR RULE.

PRWORA. *abbr.* PERSONAL RESPONSIBILITY AND WORK OPPORTUNITY RECONCILIATION ACT.

pseudo-stepparent adoption. See *second-parent adoption* under ADOPTION.

psychological father. See *psychological parent* under PARENT.

psychological mother. See *psychological parent* under PARENT.

psychological parent. See PARENT.

psychotherapist–patient privilege. See PRIVILEGE.

public administration. See ADMINISTRATION.

public administrator. See ADMINISTRATOR.

publication, *n.* The formal declaration made by a testator when signing the will that it is the testator's will. ● There is no requirement that the provisions of the will or the identities of the donees be revealed to the witnesses.

public attorney. See ATTORNEY (2).

public trust. See *charitable trust* under TRUST.

puisne judge (**pyoo**-nee). See *associate judge* under JUDGE.

punishment, *n.* **1.** A sanction — such as a fine, penalty, confinement, or loss of property, right, or privilege — assessed against a person who has violated the law. **2.** A negative disciplinary action administered to a minor child by a parent. — **punish,** *vb.*

   corporal punishment. Physical punishment; punishment inflicted on the body.

purchase, *n.* **1.** The act or an instance of buying. **2.** The acquisition of real property by one's own or another's act (as by will or gift) rather than by descent or inheritance. — **purchase,** *vb.* Cf. DESCENT (1).

purchase, words of. See WORDS OF PURCHASE.

purchase accounting method. See ACCOUNTING METHOD.

purchase-money resulting trust. See TRUST.

putative father. See FATHER.

putative-father registry. An official roster in which an unwed father may claim possible paternity of a child for purposes of receiving notice of a prospective adoption of the child.

Putative Fathers Act. See UNIFORM PUTATIVE AND UNKNOWN FATHERS ACT.

putative marriage. See MARRIAGE (1).

putative spouse. A spouse who believes in good faith that his or her invalid marriage is legally valid. See *putative marriage* under MARRIAGE (1).

putative-spouse doctrine. See *putative marriage* under MARRIAGE.

Q

QDOT. *abbr.* QUALIFIED DOMESTIC TRUST.

QDRO (**kwah**-droh). *abbr.* QUALIFIED DOMESTIC-RELA-TIONS ORDER.

QMCSO. *abbr.* QUALIFIED MEDICAL CHILD SUPPORT OR-DER.

QPRT. *abbr.* QUALIFIED PERSONAL-RESIDENCE TRUST.

QTIP (**kyoo**-tip). *abbr.* QUALIFIED-TERMINABLE-INTER-EST PROPERTY.

QTIP trust. See TRUST.

qualified domestic-relations order. A state-court order or judgment that relates to alimony, child support, or some other state domestic-relations matter and that (1) recognizes or provides for an alternate payee's right to receive all or part of any benefits due a participant under a pension, profit-sharing, or other retirement benefit plan, (2) otherwise satisfies § 414 of the Internal Revenue Code, and (3) is exempt from the ERISA rule prohibiting the assignment of plan benefits. ● Among other things, the QDRO must set out certain facts, including the name and last-known mailing address of the plan participant and alternate payee, the amount or percentage of benefits going to the alternate payee, and the number of payments to which the plan applies. The benefits provided under a

QDRO are treated as income to the actual recipient. IRC (26 USCA) § 414(p)(1)(A); 29 USCA § 1056(d)(3)(D)(i). — Abbr. QDRO.

qualified domestic trust. See TRUST.

qualified income trust. See *Miller trust* under TRUST.

qualified medical child-support order. A family-court order that enables a nonemployee custodial parent — without the employee parent's consent — to enroll the child, make claims, and receive payments as needed under the employee parent's group health plan, all at the employee parent's expense. ● The group-health-plan administrator must find that the order meets the requirements of a QMCSO, which are established by § 609(a) of the Employee Retirement Income Security Act, 29 USCA § 1169(a). — Abbr. QMCSO.

qualified ownership. See OWNERSHIP.

qualified pension plan. See PENSION PLAN.

qualified personal-residence trust. See TRUST.

qualified-terminable-interest property. See PROPERTY.

quality-of-products legislation. See LEMON LAW (2).

quasi-affinity. See AFFINITY.

quasi-community property. See COMMUNITY PROPERTY.

quasi-guardian. See GUARDIAN.

quasi-posthumous child. See CHILD.

quasi-rent. (*often pl.*) *Law and economics.* Value over and above one's opportunity cost or next best alternative; the excess of an asset's value over its salvage value. • In the economic theory of marriage, a quasi-rent is a spouse's excess value of the marriage over the value of the next best option of not being in that specific marriage. The next best option may be separation, divorce, or divorce and remarriage, depending on the spouse's preferences and opportunities.

quasi-trustee. See TRUSTEE.

quickie divorce. See DIVORCE.

R

rabbinical divorce. See DIVORCE.

racial discrimination. See DISCRIMINATION (2).

rape, *n.* **1.** At common law, unlawful sexual intercourse committed by a man with a woman not his wife through force and against her will. ● The common-law crime of rape required at least a slight penetration of the penis into the vagina. Also at common law, a husband could not be convicted of raping his wife. **2.** Unlawful sexual activity (esp. intercourse) with a person (usu. a female) without consent and usu. by force or threat of injury. ● Most modern state statutes have broadened the definition along these lines. Rape includes unlawful sexual intercourse without consent after the perpetrator has substantially impaired his victim by administering, without the victim's knowledge or consent, drugs or intoxicants for the purpose of preventing resistance. It also includes unlawful sexual intercourse with a person who is unconscious. Marital status is now usually irrelevant, and sometimes so is the victim's gender. — Also termed (in some statutes) *unlawful sexual intercourse*; *sexual assault*; *sexual battery*; *sexual abuse*. Cf. *sexual assault* under ASSAULT; *sexual battery* under BATTERY.

> **acquaintance rape.** Rape committed by someone known to the victim, esp. by the victim's social companion. Cf. *date rape*; *relationship rape*.

date rape. Rape committed by a person who is escorting the victim on a social occasion. ● Loosely, *date rape* also sometimes refers to what is more accurately called *acquaintance rape* or *relationship rape*.

marital rape. A husband's sexual intercourse with his wife by force or without her consent. ● Marital rape was not a crime at common law, but under modern statutes the marital exemption no longer applies, and in most jurisdictions a husband can be convicted of raping his wife. — Also termed *spousal rape*.

prior-relationship rape. See *relationship rape*.

rape by means of fraud. An instance of sexual intercourse that has been induced by fraud. ● Authorities are divided on the question whether rape can occur when a woman is induced by fraudulent statements to have sexual intercourse. But the term *rape by means of fraud* is not uncommon in legal literature.

rape under age. See *statutory rape*.

relationship rape. Rape committed by someone with whom the victim has had a significant association, often (though not always) of a romantic nature. ● This term encompasses all types of relationships, including family, friends, dates, cohabitants, and spouses, in which the victim has had more than brief or perfunctory interaction with the other person. Thus it does not extend to those with whom the victim has had only brief encounters or a nodding acquaintance. — Also termed *prior-relationship rape*. Cf. *date rape*; *acquaintance rape*.

spousal rape. See *marital rape*.

statutory rape. Unlawful sexual intercourse with a person under the age of consent (as defined by statute), regardless of whether it is against that person's will. • Generally, only an adult may be convicted of this crime. A person under the age of consent cannot be convicted. — Also termed *rape under age*. See AGE OF CONSENT.

rational-basis test. *Constitutional law.* A principle whereby a court will uphold a law as valid under the Equal Protection Clause or Due Process Clause if it bears a reasonable relationship to the attainment of some legitimate governmental objective. — Also termed *rational-purpose test*; *rational-relationship test*; *minimal scrutiny*; *minimum scrutiny*. Cf. STRICT SCRUTINY; INTERMEDIATE SCRUTINY.

rational-purpose test. See RATIONAL-BASIS TEST.

rational-relationship test. See RATIONAL-BASIS TEST.

real estate. See *real property* under PROPERTY.

real property. See PROPERTY.

realty. See *real property* under PROPERTY.

realty trust. See *nominee trust* (2) under TRUST.

reciprocal trust. See TRUST.

reciprocal will. See *mutual will* under WILL.

reconciliation (rek-ən-sil-ee-**ay**-shən), *n.* **1.** Restoration of harmony between persons or things that had been in conflict <a reconciliation between the plaintiff and the defendant is unlikely even if the lawsuit settles before trial>. **2.** Voluntary resumption, after a separation, of full marital relations between spouses <the court dismissed the divorce petition after the parties' reconciliation>. Cf. CONDONATION.

reconciliation agreement. A contract between spouses who have had marital difficulties but who now wish to save the marital relationship, usu. by specifying certain economic actions that might ameliorate pressures on the marriage. ● This type of agreement serves a limited purpose. In fact, many states have statutes prohibiting enforcement of contracts for domestic services, so if the agreement governs anything other than economic behavior, it may be unenforceable.

record owner. See OWNER.

recovered-memory syndrome. See REPRESSED-MEMORY SYNDROME.

recrimination (ri-krim-i-**nay**-shən), *n*. In a divorce suit, a countercharge that the complainant has been guilty of an offense constituting a ground for divorce. • When both parties to the marriage have committed marital misconduct that would be grounds for divorce, neither may obtain a fault divorce. Recriminations are now virtually obsolete because of the prevalence of no-fault divorce. — **recriminatory,** *adj*. Cf. COLLUSION; CONNIVANCE; CONDONATION.

reformation condition. See *conditional bequest* under BEQUEST.

register, *n*. **1.** A governmental officer who keeps official records <each county employs a register of deeds and wills>. Cf. REGISTRAR.

> *probate register.* One who serves as the clerk of a probate court and, in some jurisdictions, as a quasi-judicial officer in probating estates.

2. See *probate judge* under JUDGE. **3.** A book in which all docket entries are kept for the various cases pending in a court. — Also termed (in sense 3) *register of actions*.

registrar. A person who keeps official records; esp., a school official who maintains academic and enrollment records. Cf. REGISTER (1).

registration and community-notification law. See MEGAN'S LAW.

rehabilitative alimony. See ALIMONY.

reimbursement, *n*. **1.** Repayment. **2.** Indemnification. — **reimburse,** *vb*.

reimbursement alimony. See ALIMONY.

rejecting, *n*. A parent's or caregiver's pattern of refusing to acknowledge a child's worth or legitimate needs. Cf. ISOLATING; IGNORING.

relation. See RELATIVE.

relationship rape. See RAPE.

relative, *n*. A person connected with another by blood or affinity; a person who is kin with another. — Also termed *relation*; *kinsman*.

> **blood relative.** One who shares an ancestor with another.

> **collateral relative.** A relative who is not in the direct line of inheritance, such as a cousin.

> **relative by affinity.** Blood or adopted relatives of one's spouse. See AFFINITY.

> **relative of the half blood.** A collateral relative who shares one common ancestor. ● A half brother, for example, is a relative of the half blood. See *half blood* under BLOOD.

relative-responsibility statute. A law requiring adult children to support or provide basic necessities for their indigent elderly parents.

release, *n.* **1.** Liberation from an obligation, duty, or demand; the act of giving up a right or claim to the person against whom it could have been enforced. **2.** The relinquishment or concession of a right, title, or claim. **3.** A written discharge, acquittance, or receipt. ● Beneficiaries of an estate are routinely required to sign a release discharging the estate from further liability before the executor or administrator distributes the property.

religious-exemption statute. See FAITH-HEALING EXEMPTION.

remainder. 1. The property in a decedent's estate that is not otherwise specifically devised or bequeathed in a will. **2.** A future interest arising in a third person — that is, someone other than the creator of the estate or the creator's heirs — who is intended to take after the natural termination of the preceding estate. ● For example, if a grant is "to A for life, and then to B," B's future interest is a remainder. Cf. EXECUTORY INTEREST; REVERSION; POSSIBILITY OF REVERTER.

> ***accelerated remainder.*** A remainder that has passed to the remainderman, as when the gift to the preceding beneficiary fails.

alternative remainder. A remainder in which the disposition of property is to take effect only if another disposition does not take effect.

charitable remainder. A remainder, usu. from a life estate, that is given to a charity; for example, "to Jane for life, and then to the American Red Cross."

contingent remainder. A remainder that is either given to an unascertained person or made subject to a condition precedent. ● An example is "to A for life, and then, if B has married before A dies, to B." — Also termed *executory remainder*; *remainder subject to a condition precedent.*

cross-remainder. A future interest that results when particular estates are given to two or more persons in different parcels of land, or in the same land in undivided shares, and the remainders of all the estates are made to vest in the survivor or survivors. ● Two examples of devises giving rise to cross-remainders are (1) "to A and B for life, with the remainder to the survivor and her heirs," and (2) "Blackacre to A and Whiteacre to B, with the remainder of A's estate to B on A's failure of issue, and the remainder of B's estate to A on B's failure of issue." ● If no tenants or issue survive, the remainder vests in a third party (sometimes known as the *ulterior remainderman*). Each tenant in common has a reciprocal, or *cross*, remainder in the share of the others. This type of remainder could not be created by deed unless expressly stated. It could, however, be implied in a will.

defeasible remainder. A vested remainder that will be eliminated if a condition subsequent occurs. ● An example is "to A for life, and then to B, but if B ever sells liquor on the land, then to C." — Also termed *remainder subject to divestment*.

executed remainder. See *vested remainder*.

executory remainder. See *contingent remainder*.

indefeasible remainder. A vested remainder that is not subject to a condition subsequent. — Also termed *indefeasibly vested remainder*.

remainder subject to a condition precedent. See *contingent remainder*.

remainder subject to divestment. See *defeasible remainder*.

remainder subject to open. A vested remainder that is given to one person but that may later have to be shared with others. ● An example is "to A for life, and then equally to all of B's children." — Also termed *remainder subject to partial divestment*.

vested remainder. A remainder that is given to an ascertained person and that is not subject to a condition precedent. ● An example is "to A for life, and then to B." — Also termed *executed remainder*.

remainder bequest. See *residuary bequest* under BEQUEST.

remainderman. A person who holds or is entitled to receive a remainder. — Also termed *remainderer*; *remainderperson*; *remainor*.

> **ulterior remainderman.** A third party whose future interest in a property vests only if all the preceding reciprocal interests expire. See *cross-remainder* under REMAINDER.

remainder subject to a condition precedent. See *contingent remainder* under REMAINDER.

remainder subject to divestment. See *defeasible remainder* under REMAINDER.

remainder subject to open. See REMAINDER.

remainder subject to partial divestment. See *remainder subject to open* under REMAINDER.

remainor, *n.* See REMAINDERMAN.

remedial trust. See *constructive trust* under TRUST.

remote possibility. See POSSIBILITY.

renunciation (ri-nən-see-**ay**-shən), *n*. **1.** The express or tacit abandonment of a right without transferring it to another. **2.** The act of waiving a right under a will and claiming instead a statutory share. ● At one time, one *renounced* an inheritance by intestacy and *disclaimed* a gift by will. Today *disclaim* is common in both situations. — Also termed (in sense 2) *disclaimer*. See RIGHT OF ELECTION. Cf. DISCLAIMER. — **renounce**, *vb*. — **renunciative, renunciatory**, *adj*.

reparative injunction. See INJUNCTION.

representation, *n*. The assumption by an heir of the rights and obligations of his or her predecessor <each child takes a share by representation>. See PER STIRPES.

representative, *n*. One who stands for or acts on behalf of another. See AGENT.

independent personal representative. See *personal representative*.

lawful representative. **1.** A legal heir. **2.** An executor, administrator, or other legal representative. — Also termed *legal representative*. See *personal representative*.

legal-personal representative. **1.** When used by a testator referring to personal property, an executor or administrator. **2.** When used by a testator referring to real property, one to whom the real estate passes immediately upon the testator's death. **3.** When used concerning the death of a mariner at sea, the public administrator, executor, or appointed administrator in the seaman's state of residence.

legal representative. See *lawful representative.*

personal representative. A person who manages the legal affairs of another because of incapacity or death, such as the executor of an estate. ● Technically, while an executor is a personal representative named in a will, an administrator is a personal representative not named in a will. — Also termed *independent personal representative*; *legal representative.*

repressed-memory syndrome. A memory disorder characterized by an intermittent and extensive inability to recall important personal information, usu. following or concerning a traumatic or highly stressful occurrence, when the memory lapses cannot be dismissed as normal forgetfulness. ● The theoretical basis for this syndrome was proposed by Sigmund Freud in 1895. The American Psychiatric Association has recognized the syndrome officially by the medical term *dissociative amnesia.* Although the APA has affirmed that some people suffering partial or total dissociative amnesia may later recover some or all of the memory of the traumatic or stressful event, the existence of the syndrome is controversial. Some studies indicate that "repressed" memories, at least in some patients, may be a product of suggestions made by mental-health therapists rather than of any actual experience. — Abbr. RMS. — Also termed *recovered-memory syndrome; dissociative amnesia*. Cf. FALSE-MEMORY SYNDROME.

reproductive rights. A person's constitutionally protected rights relating to the control of his or her procreative activities; specif., the cluster of civil liberties relating to pregnancy, abortion, and sterilization, esp. the personal bodily rights of a woman in her decision whether to become pregnant or bear a child. ● The phrase includes the idea of being able to make reproductive decisions free from discrimination, coercion, or violence. Human-rights scholars increasingly consider reproductive rights to be protected by international human-rights law.

republication, *n.* Reestablishment of the validity of a previously revoked will by repeating the formalities of execution or by using a codicil. ● The result is to update the old will effective from the date of republication. — Also termed *revalidation*. — **republish,** *vb.* Cf. REVIVAL.

required-request law. A law mandating that hospital personnel discuss with a deceased patient's relatives the possibility of an anatomical gift. ● The Uniform Anatomical Gift Act (not in effect in all states) mandates a required-request law.

res. See CORPUS (1).

rescue syndrome. A situation in which a child in a custody battle expresses a preference for the parent perceived by the child to be the "weaker" of the two, in the belief that the parent needs the child. • This is a form of parent-alienation syndrome. One parent may overtly or subtly act increasingly dependent on the child, leading the child to believe that he or she is responsible for the parent's comfort, happiness, and protection. The child may also believe that one parent is actively harming the other and attempt to protect the "weaker" parent by choosing to stay with that parent, even if the child would actually prefer to live with the "stronger" parent. Cf. LOLLIPOP SYNDROME; PARENT-ALIENATION SYNDROME.

residence. 1. The place where one actually lives, as distinguished from a domicile <she made her residence in Oregon>. • *Residence* usually just means bodily presence as an inhabitant in a given place; *domicile* usually requires bodily presence plus an intention to make the place one's home. A person thus may have more than one residence at a time but only one domicile. Sometimes, though, the two terms are used synonymously. Cf. DOMICILE. **2.** A house or other fixed abode; a dwelling <a three-story residence>.

> **habitual residence.** A person's customary place of residence; esp., a child's customary place of residence before being removed to some other place. • The term, which appears as an undefined term in the Hague Convention, is used in deter-

mining the country having a presumed paramount interest in the child.

residency. The fact or condition of living in a given place <one year's residency to be eligible for in-state tuition>.

resident, *n.* **1.** A person who lives in a particular place. **2.** A person who has a home in a particular place. ● In sense 2, a resident is not necessarily either a citizen or a domiciliary. Cf. CITIZEN; DOMICILIARY.

residential care. Foster-care placement involving residence in a group home or institution. ● This type of foster care is most commonly used for adolescents who have been adjudged to be delinquents or status offenders.

residential custody. See *physical custody* (1) under CUSTODY.

residential parent. See PARENT.

residential responsibility. Overnight responsibility for a child. See *Principles of the Law of Family Dissolution: Analysis and Recommendations* § 3.02 (ALI, Tentative Draft No. 4, 2000). See CUSTODY; *dual-residential parent*, *residential parent* under PARENT.

> **primary residential responsibility.** Predominant overnight responsibility for a child.

residential time. See VISITATION.

residual estate. See *residuary estate* under ESTATE.

residuary (ri-**zij**-oo-er-ee), *adj.* Of, relating to, or constituting a residue; residual <a residuary gift>.

residuary, *n.* **1.** See *residuary estate* under ESTATE. **2.** See *residuary legatee* under LEGATEE.

residuary bequest. See BEQUEST.

residuary clause. A testamentary clause that disposes of any estate property remaining after the satisfaction of all other gifts.

residuary devise. See DEVISE.

residuary devisee. See DEVISEE.

residuary estate. See ESTATE.

residuary legacy. See LEGACY.

residuary legatee. See LEGATEE.

residue. **1.** Something that is left over after a part is removed or disposed of; a remainder. **2.** See *residuary estate* under ESTATE.

residuum. See *residuary estate* under ESTATE.

respondent. 1. The party against whom an appeal is taken; APPELLEE. **2.** The party against whom a motion or petition is filed. Cf. PETITIONER.

restorative justice. An alternative delinquency sanction that focuses on repairing the harm done, meeting the victim's needs, and holding the offender responsible for his or her actions. ● Restorative-justice sanctions use a balanced approach, producing the least restrictive disposition while stressing the offender's accountability and providing relief to the victim. The offender may be ordered to make restitution, to perform community service, or to make amends in some other way that the court orders.

restraining order. 1. A court order prohibiting family violence; esp., an order restricting a person from harassing, threatening, and sometimes merely contacting or approaching another specified person. ● This type of order is issued most commonly in cases of domestic violence. A court may grant an ex parte restraining order in a family-violence case if it is necessary to (1) achieve the government's interest in protecting victims of family violence from further abuse, (2) ensure prompt action where there is an immediate threat of danger, and (3) provide governmental control by ensuring that judges grant such orders only where there is an immediate danger of such abuse. *Fuentes v. Shevin,* 407 U.S. 67, 92 S.Ct. 1983 (1972). — Also termed *protection order*; *protective order*; *stay-away order*. See *ex parte* *motion* under MOTION. **2.** TEMPORARY RESTRAINING OR-DER. **3.** A court order entered to prevent the dissipation or loss of property.

restraint of marriage. A condition (esp. in a gift or bequest) that nullifies the grant to which it applies if the grantee marries or remarries. ● Restraints of marriage are usually void if they are general or unlimited in scope.

restricted visitation. See *supervised visitation* under VISITATION.

resulting trust. See TRUST.

retained income trust. See *grantor-retained income trust* under TRUST.

Retirement Equity Act of 1984. A federal law that requires private pension plans to comply with the court-ordered division of a pension and permits the plan administrator to pay all or part of a worker's pensions and survivor benefits directly to a former spouse if the plan has been served with a court order that meets the federal requirements for a qualified domestic-relations order. 29 USCA § 1056(d)(3). See QUALIFIED DOMESTIC-RELATIONS ORDER.

retirement plan. See EMPLOYEE BENEFIT PLAN.

reunification. The return of a child who has been removed from his or her parents because of abuse or neglect by one or both of them. ● When a child has been removed from the home because of abuse or neglect, the state's primary goal is family reunification as long as this is in the best interests of the child. The state is required, in most instances, to provide the parent or parents with services that will enable them to provide adequately for their child upon his or her return. After the enactment of the Adoption and Safe Families Act in 1997, states became more concerned with limiting the time that children are in foster care and less concerned with lengthy reunification plans. — Also termed *family reunification*. — **reunify,** *vb.* See ADOPTION AND SAFE FAMILIES ACT; PERMANENCY PLAN; ADOPTION ASSISTANCE AND CHILD WELFARE ACT.

revalidation. See REPUBLICATION.

reverse discrimination. See DISCRIMINATION (2).

reverse transfer statute. See TRANSFER STATUTE.

reversion, *n.* A future interest in land arising by operation of law whenever an estate owner grants to another a particular estate, such as a life estate or a term of years, but does not dispose of the entire interest. ● A reversion occurs automatically upon termination of the prior estate, as when a life tenant dies. — Also termed *reversionary estate*. — **revert,** *vb.* — **reversionary,** *adj.* Cf. POSSIBILITY OF REVERTER; REMAINDER (1).

reversionary estate. See REVERSION.

reverter. See POSSIBILITY OF REVERTER.

review hearing. See HEARING.

revival, *n.* The reestablishment of the validity of a revoked will by revoking the will that invalidated the original will or in some other way manifesting the testator's intent to be bound by the earlier will. — **revive,** *vb.* Cf. REPUBLICATION.

revocable trust. See TRUST.

revocation (rev-ə-**kay**-shən), *n.* Invalidation of a will by the testator, either by destroying the will or by executing a new one. ● A will, or parts of a will, may be revoked by operation of law. For example, most states have a statute providing for the revocation, upon divorce, of all provisions relating to the testator's former spouse. — **revoke,** *vb.*

right of assembly. The constitutional right — guaranteed by the First Amendment — of the people to gather peacefully for public expression of religion, politics, or grievances. — Also termed *freedom of assembly*; *right to assemble.* Cf. FREEDOM OF ASSOCIATION; UNLAWFUL ASSEMBLY.

right of election. A surviving spouse's statutory right to choose, upon the other spouse's death, either the gifts given by the deceased spouse in the will or a forced share or a share of the estate as defined in the probate statute. — Also termed *widow's election*. See ELECTION; *augmented estate* under ESTATE.

right of family integrity. A fundamental and substantive due-process right for a family unit to be free of unjustified state interference. ● While not specifically mentioned in the U.S. Constitution, this right is said to emanate from it. The contours of the right are nebulous and incompletely defined, but it at least includes the right to bear children, to rear them, and to guide them according to the parents' beliefs, as well as the right of children to be raised by their parents free of unwarranted interference by state officials. The right restricts state action under the Fourteenth Amendment. Interference is not permitted in the absence of a compelling state interest and is reviewed under a strict-scrutiny standard. Most courts require a state to establish by clear and convincing evidence that interference in a familial relationship is justified. — Also termed *right to family integrity*. See PARENTAL-AUTONOMY DOCTRINE; PARENTAL-PRIVILEGE DOCTRINE. Cf. *freedom of intimate association* under FREEDOM OF ASSOCIATION.

right of privacy. 1. The right to personal autonomy. ● The U.S. Constitution does not explicitly provide for a right of privacy, but the Supreme Court has repeatedly ruled that this right is implied in the "zones of privacy" created by specific constitutional guarantees. **2.** The right of a person and the person's property to be free from unwarranted public scrutiny or exposure. — Also termed *right to privacy*. See INVASION OF PRIVACY.

right of survivorship. A joint tenant's right to succeed to the whole estate upon the death of the other joint tenant. — Also termed *jus accrescendi*. See SURVIVORSHIP; *joint tenancy* under TENANCY.

right of visitation. See VISITATION RIGHT.

right to assemble. RIGHT OF ASSEMBLY.

right to choose. See FREEDOM OF CHOICE.

right to counsel. 1. A criminal defendant's constitutional right, guaranteed by the Sixth Amendment, to representation by a court-appointed lawyer if the defendant cannot afford to hire one. • The Supreme Court has recognized a juvenile delinquent defendant's right to counsel. *In re Gault*, 387 U.S. 1, 87 S.Ct. 1428 (1967). **2.** The right of a defendant in a suit for termination of parental rights to representation by a court-appointed lawyer if the defendant cannot afford to hire one. • Although some states appoint counsel for indigent defendants in a suit for termination of parental rights, the Supreme Court has held that the Constitution does not require that counsel be appointed for indigent defendants in all termination suits, but if a criminal charge may be made, the right to counsel may attach. *Lassiter v.*

Department of Soc. Servs., 452 U.S. 18, 101 S.Ct. 2153 (1981).

right to die. The right of a terminally ill person to refuse life-sustaining treatment. — Also termed *right to refuse treatment*. See ADVANCE DIRECTIVE.

right to family integrity. See RIGHT OF FAMILY INTEGRITY.

right to privacy. See RIGHT OF PRIVACY.

right to refuse treatment. See RIGHT TO DIE.

risk assessment. A process for ascertaining the likelihood that a person, usu. a parent, will harm a child. ● Before a child can be removed from his or her family by a governmental entity, a risk assessment should be performed to determine the likelihood of the child's being harmed in the future.

RMS. *abbr.* REPRESSED-MEMORY SYNDROME.

Roth IRA. See INDIVIDUAL RETIREMENT ACCOUNT.

rule against perpetuities. (*sometimes cap.*) The common-law rule prohibiting a grant of an estate unless the interest must vest, if at all, no later than 21 years after the death of some person alive when the interest was created. ● The purpose of the rule was to limit the time that title to property could be suspended out of commerce because there was no owner who had title to the property and who could sell it or exercise other aspects of ownership. If the terms of the contract or gift exceeded the time limits of the rule, the gift or transaction was void. See MEASURING LIFE.

rule of universal inheritance. See UNIVERSAL INHERITANCE RULE.

runaway, *n.* An unemancipated minor who has left home, often indefinitely. — **run away,** *vb.* Cf. THROWAWAY.

S

safe-storage statute. A law that prohibits persons from leaving firearms unattended in places where children may gain access to them. — Also termed *child-access prevention statute*.

salic marriage. See *morganatic marriage* under MARRIAGE (1).

same-sex marriage. See MARRIAGE (1).

sanity. The state or condition of having a relatively sound and healthy mind. Cf. INSANITY.

satisfaction, *n*. **1.** The payment by a testator, during the testator's lifetime, of a legacy provided for in a will; ADVANCEMENT. **2.** A testamentary gift intended to satisfy a debt owed by the testator to a creditor. See *ademption by satisfaction* under ADEMPTION. — **satisfy,** *vb*.

savings-account trust. See *Totten trust* under TRUST.

savings-bank trust. See *Totten trust* under TRUST.

Scotch marriage. See MARRIAGE (1).

sealed-record statute. See CONFIDENTIALITY STATUTE.

seaman's will. See *soldier's will* under WILL.

secondary abuse. See ABUSE.

secondary affinity. See AFFINITY.

secondary beneficiary. See *contingent beneficiary* (1) under BENEFICIARY.

secondary devise. See *alternative devise* under DEVISE.

second cousin. See COUSIN.

secondhand evidence. See HEARSAY.

second-parent adoption. See ADOPTION.

secretion of assets. The hiding of property, usu. for the purpose of defrauding an adversary in litigation or a creditor.

secret trust. See TRUST.

seduction. The offense that occurs when a man entices a woman of previously chaste character to have unlawful intercourse with him by means of persuasion, solicitation, promises, or bribes, or other means not involving force. ● Many states have abolished this offense for persons over the age of legal consent. Traditionally, the parent of a young woman had an action to recover damages for the loss of her services. But in measuring damages, the jury could consider not just the loss of services but also the distress and anxiety that the parent had suffered in being deprived of her comfort and companionship. Though seduction was not a crime at common law, many American states made it a statutory crime until the late 20th century.

self-authentication. See AUTHENTICATION.

self-destruct clause. A provision in a trust for a condition that will automatically terminate the trust. ● Discretionary trusts, especially supplemental-needs trusts, often include a self-destruct provision. For example, a trust to provide for the needs of a disabled person may terminate if the beneficiary becomes ineligible for a government-benefits program such as Medicaid.

self-destruction. See SUICIDE.

self-employed retirement plan. See KEOGH PLAN.

self-killing. See SUICIDE.

self-murder. See SUICIDE.

self-proved will. See WILL.

self-proving affidavit. See AFFIDAVIT.

self-settled trust. See TRUST.

self-slaughter. See SUICIDE.

semi-secret trust. See TRUST.

SEP. *abbr.* See *simplified employee pension plan* under EMPLOYEE BENEFIT PLAN.

separate and apart. See LIVING SEPARATE AND APART.

separate estate. See ESTATE.

separate maintenance. See MAINTENANCE.

separate property. 1. Property that a spouse owned before marriage or acquired during marriage by inheritance or by gift from a third party, and in some states property acquired during marriage but after the spouses have entered into a separation agreement and have begun living apart or after one spouse has commenced a divorce action. — Also termed *individual property*. Cf. COMMUNITY PROPERTY; *marital property* under PROPERTY. **2.** In some common-law states, property titled to one spouse or acquired by one spouse individually during marriage. **3.** Property acquired during the marriage in exchange for separate property (in sense 1 or sense 2).

separate-property state. See COMMON-LAW STATE.

separate-spheres doctrine. *Obsolete.* The common-law doctrine that wives were limited to control of the home — the personal or domestic sphere — and that husbands had control of the public sphere.

● Under this early-19th-century doctrine, the wife was to tend to the home and family and the husband was to be the breadwinner. — Also termed *doctrine of separate spheres*.

separate support. See *separate maintenance* under MAINTENANCE.

separation. 1. An arrangement whereby a husband and wife live apart from each other while remaining married, either by mutual consent (often in a written agreement) or by judicial decree; the act of carrying out such an arrangement. — Also termed *separation from bed and board*. See *divorce a mensa et thoro* under DIVORCE. **2.** The status of a husband and wife having begun such an arrangement, or the judgment or contract that brought about the arrangement. — Also termed (in both senses) *legal separation*; *judicial separation*.

separation agreement. 1. An agreement between spouses in the process of a divorce or legal separation concerning alimony, maintenance, property division, child custody and support, and the like. — Also termed *separation order* (if approved or sanctioned judicially). See TEMPORARY ORDER. **2.** DIVORCE AGREEMENT.

separation a mensa et thoro. See *divorce a mensa et thoro* under DIVORCE.

separation from bed and board. 1. SEPARATION (1). **2.** See *divorce a mensa et thoro* under DIVORCE.

separation order. See SEPARATION AGREEMENT.

sequential marriage. See BIGAMY (2).

serial polygamy. See POLYGAMY (2).

serious health condition. Under the Family and Medical Leave Act, an illness, injury, or physical or mental state that involves in-patient care or continuing treatment by a healthcare provider for several days. ● Excluded from the definition are cosmetic treatments and minor illnesses that are not accompanied by medical complications.

seriously harmful behavior. See HARMFUL BEHAVIOR.

serological test (seer-ə-**loj**-ə-kəl). A blood examination to detect the presence of antibodies and antigens, as well as other characteristics, esp. as indicators of disease. ● Many states require serological tests to determine the presence of venereal disease in a couple applying for a marriage license. See BLOOD TEST.

service, *n*. **1.** The formal delivery of a writ, summons, or other legal process <after three attempts, service still had not been accomplished>. — Also termed *service of process*. **2.** The formal delivery of some other legal notice, such as a pleading <be sure that a certificate of service is attached to the motion>.

actual service. See *personal service.*

constructive service. 1. See *substituted service.* 2. Service accomplished by a method or circumstance that does not give actual notice.

personal service. Actual delivery of process or of a notice to the person to whom it is directed. — Also termed *actual service.*

service by publication. The service of process on an absent or nonresident defendant by publishing a notice in a newspaper or other public medium.

sewer service. The fraudulent service of process on a debtor by a creditor seeking to obtain a default judgment.

substituted service. Any method of service allowed by law in place of personal service, such as service by mail. — Also termed *constructive service.*

service of process. See SERVICE (1).

settled estate. See ESTATE.

settlement, *n.* 1. An agreement ending a dispute or lawsuit <the parties reached a settlement the day before trial>. 2. The complete execution of an estate by the executor <the settlement of the estate was long and complex>. — **settle,** *vb.*

final settlement. A court order discharging an executor's duties after an estate's execution.

settlor (**set**-lər). A person who makes a settlement of property; esp., one who sets up a trust. — Also spelled *settler*. — Also termed *creator*; *donor*; *trustor*; *grantor*; *founder*.

seven-years'-absence rule. The principle that a person who has been missing without explanation for at least seven years is legally presumed dead. Cf. ENOCH ARDEN LAW.

several inheritance. See INHERITANCE.

sex. 1. The sum of the peculiarities of structure and function that distinguish a male from a female organism. **2.** Sexual intercourse. **3.** SEXUAL RELATIONS (2).

sex change. See SEX REASSIGNMENT.

sex discrimination. See DISCRIMINATION (2).

sex reassignment. Medical treatment intended to effect a sex change; surgery and hormonal treatments designed to alter a person's gender. — Also termed *sex change*.

sexual abuse. 1. See ABUSE. **2.** See RAPE.

sexual activity. See SEXUAL RELATIONS.

sexual assault. 1. See ASSAULT. **2.** See RAPE.

sexual battery. 1. See BATTERY. **2.** See RAPE.

sexual exploitation. The use of a person, esp. a child, in prostitution, pornography, or other sexually manipulative activity that has caused or could cause serious emotional injury. — Sometimes shortened to *exploitation*.

sexually dangerous person. See SEXUAL PREDATOR.

sexually transmitted disease. A disease transmitted only or chiefly by engaging in sexual acts with an infected person. • Common examples are syphilis and gonorrhea. — Abbr. STD. — Also termed *venereal disease*.

sexually violent predator. See SEXUAL PREDATOR.

sexual orientation. A person's predisposition or inclination toward a particular type of sexual activity or behavior; heterosexuality, homosexuality, or bisexuality. • There has been a trend in recent years to make sexual orientation a protected class, especially in employment and hate-crime statutes.

sexual predator. A person who has committed many violent sexual acts or who has a propensity for committing violent sexual acts. — Also termed *predator*; *sexually dangerous person*; *sexually violent predator*.

sexual relations. 1. Sexual intercourse. **2.** Physical sexual activity that does not necessarily culminate in intercourse. ● Sexual relations usually involve the touching of another's breast, vagina, penis, or anus. Both persons (the toucher and the person touched) engage in sexual relations. — Also termed *sexual activity*.

shaken-baby syndrome. The medical condition of a child who has suffered forceful shaking, with resulting brain injury. ● Common injuries in shaken-baby syndrome include retinal hemorrhage and subdural and subarachnoid hemorrhage, with minimal or no signs of external cranial trauma. Many victims of shaken-baby syndrome are permanently blind or die. Shaken-baby syndrome is one of the leading causes of infant death. It was first identified in the early 1970s.

sham marriage. See MARRIAGE (1).

shared custody. See *joint custody* under CUSTODY.

shared parenting. See PARENTING.

shared residency. See *joint physical custody* under CUSTODY (2).

shelter. A place of refuge providing safety from danger, attack, or observation.

   homeless shelter. A privately or publicly operated residential facility providing overnight accom-

modation free of charge to homeless people. •
Most homeless shelters accept occupants on a
first-come-first-served basis and are open only
from early evening to early morning. Those that
serve homeless families may remain open
throughout the day to women and children. Some
shelters offer occupants help such as advice on
finding and applying for public assistance, employment, and medical care.

women's shelter. A privately or publicly operated residential facility providing women (and their
children) who are victims of domestic violence
with temporary lodging, food, and other services
such as employment assistance, counseling, and
medical care. — Also termed *family shelter*.

youth shelter. **1.** A privately or publicly operated
residential facility offering young runaway or
throwaway children and homeless young people a
safe place to stay, usu. for a short time. • The
residents enter the shelter voluntarily and can
leave anytime they wish. Some shelters offer
long-term transitional training so that young people can leave street life and eventually lead independent, productive lives. **2.** An alternative type
of juvenile-detention center that is less physically
restrictive than a jail or boot camp. • Delinquent
juveniles are usually brought to these shelters by
police or ordered to reside there by a court. Residents attend school or work in the daytime and
may be permitted weekend visits at their family
homes.

shelter-care hearing. See *shelter hearing* under HEARING.

shelter hearing. See HEARING.

shifting trust. See TRUST.

short-term alimony. See *rehabilitative alimony* under ALIMONY.

sibling. A brother or sister.

sickness and accident insurance. See HEALTH INSURANCE.

significant connection/substantial evidence jurisdiction. See JURISDICTION.

simple assault. See ASSAULT (1), (2).

simple kidnapping. See KIDNAPPING.

simple trust. See *mandatory trust* under TRUST; *passive trust* under TRUST.

simplified employee pension plan. See EMPLOYEE BENEFIT PLAN.

simultaneous-death act. See UNIFORM SIMULTANEOUS DEATH ACT.

simultaneous-death clause. A testamentary provision mandating that if the testator and beneficiary die in a common disaster, or the order of their deaths is otherwise unascertainable, the testator is presumed to have survived the beneficiary. ● If the beneficiary is the testator's spouse, an express exception is often made so that the spouse with the smaller estate is presumed to have survived. Cf. SURVIVAL CLAUSE.

simultaneous polygamy. See POLYGAMY (1).

single-act statute. See LONG-ARM STATUTE.

single adultery. See ADULTERY.

singles' penalty. See MARRIAGE BONUS.

singular successor. See SUCCESSOR.

sister. A female with the same parents as another person.

> *half sister.* A female sibling with whom one shares the same father or the same mother, but not both; a sister by one parent only.

> *sister-german.* A full sister; a female child of both of one's own parents. See GERMAN.

> *stepsister.* The daughter of one's stepparent.

sister-in-law. The sister of one's spouse, the wife of one's brother, or the wife of one's spouse's brother.

skip person. *Tax.* A beneficiary who is more than one generation removed from the transferor and to whom assets are conveyed in a generation-skipping transfer. IRC (26 USCA) § 2613(a). See GENERATION-SKIPPING TRANSFER.

slayer rule. The doctrine that neither a person who kills another nor the killer's heirs can share in the decedent's estate. — Also termed *slayer's rule.*

slayer statute. *Slang.* A statute that prohibits a person's killer from taking any part of the decedent's estate through will or intestacy. • The Uniform Probate Code and nearly all jurisdictions have a slayer-statute provision.

small-estate probate. See PROBATE (1).

social-host act. See DRAM-SHOP ACT.

Social Security Act. A federal law, originally established in 1935 in response to the Great Depression, creating a system of benefits, including old-age and survivors' benefits, and establishing the Social Security Administration. 42 USCA §§ 401–433.

Social Security Administration. A federal agency created by the Social Security Act to institute a national program of social insurance. — Abbr. SSA.

Social Security Disability Insurance. A benefit for adults with disabilities, paid by the Social Security Administration to wage-earners who have accumulated enough quarters of coverage and then become disabled. ● Benefits are also available to disabled adult children and to disabled widows and widowers. — Abbr. SSDI.

social study. See HOME-STUDY REPORT.

sodomy (sod-ə-mee), *n*. **1.** Oral or anal copulation between humans, esp. those of the same sex. **2.** Oral or anal copulation between a human and an animal; bestiality. — Also termed *buggery*; *crime against nature*; *abominable and detestable crime against nature*; *unnatural offense*; *unspeakable crime*; (archaically) *sodomitry*. — **sodomize,** *vb*. — **sodomitic,** *adj*. — **sodomist, sodomite,** *n*.

soldier's and sailor's will. See *soldier's will* under WILL.

soldier's will. See WILL.

sole and unconditional owner. See OWNER.

sole custody. See CUSTODY.

solemnization. The performance of a formal ceremony (such as a marriage ceremony) before witnesses, as distinguished from a clandestine ceremony.

son. 1. A person's male child, whether natural or adopted; a male of whom one is the parent. **2.** An immediate male descendant.

son-in-law. The husband of one's daughter.

special administration. See ADMINISTRATION.

special administrator. See ADMINISTRATOR.

special appearance. See APPEARANCE.

special executor. See EXECUTOR.

special guardian. See GUARDIAN.

special legacy. See *specific legacy* under LEGACY.

special master. See MASTER (2).

special-needs trust. See *supplemental-needs trust* under TRUST.

special power of appointment. See *limited power of appointment* under POWER OF APPOINTMENT.

special power of attorney. See POWER OF ATTORNEY.

special relationship. A nonfiduciary relationship having an element of trust, arising esp. when one person trusts another to exercise a reasonable degree of care and the other knows or ought to know about the reliance. Cf. FIDUCIARY RELATIONSHIP.

special trust. See *active trust* under TRUST.

specific bequest. See BEQUEST.

specific devise. See DEVISE.

specific legacy. See LEGACY.

specific legatee. See LEGATEE.

speech. The expression or communication of thoughts or opinions in spoken words; something spoken or uttered. See FREEDOM OF SPEECH.

> *hate speech.* Speech that carries no meaning other than the expression of hatred for some group, such as a particular race, esp. in circumstances in which the communication is likely to provoke violence. Cf. HATE CRIME.

> *speech-plus.* See *symbolic speech*.

> *symbolic speech.* Conduct that expresses opinions or thoughts, such as a hunger strike or the wearing of a black armband. ● Symbolic speech does not enjoy the same constitutional protection that pure speech does. — Also termed *speech-plus*.

speech-plus. See *symbolic speech* under SPEECH.

spendthrift trust. See TRUST.

spiritual-treatment exemption. See FAITH-HEAL-ING EXEMPTION.

split custody. See CUSTODY.

split-funded plan. See EMPLOYEE BENEFIT PLAN.

split gift. See GIFT.

split income. See INCOME.

split-interest trust. See *charitable remainder trust* under TRUST.

sponge tax. See *pickup tax* under TAX.

sponsalia per verba de praesenti (spon-**say**-lee-ə pər **vər**-bə dee pri-**zen**-ti *or* pree-). *Eccles. law.* A type of informal marriage that occurred when the parties made an informal agreement to have each other as husband and wife. ● This type of informal marriage was based on nothing more than the present consent to be married but was entirely valid and would take precedence over a later formal ceremonial marriage that either of the parties attempted to contract with someone else. See *common-law marriage* under MARRIAGE (1).

sponsor. See GODPARENT.

spontaneous abortion. See MISCARRIAGE.

spousal abuse. See ABUSE.

spousal allowance. See ALLOWANCE (1).

spousal consortium. See CONSORTIUM.

spousal labor. Work by either spouse during the marriage. ● This term is typically used in community-property states.

spousal privilege. See *marital privilege* under PRIVILEGE.

spousal rape. See *marital rape* under RAPE.

spousal support. See ALIMONY.

spousal-unity doctrine. *Obsolete.* **1.** The common-law rule that a husband and wife were a legal unity. ● Under the spousal-unity doctrine, the husband had all rights to the possession, management, control, and alienation of property. The wife had no interests in property. — Also termed *doctrine of spousal unity*. Cf. LEGAL-UNITIES DOCTRINE. See MARRIED WOMEN'S PROPERTY ACTS. **2.** *Tax.* The rule that a person and that person's spouse are treated as one. ● This rule has been repealed. — Also termed *spousal-unity rule*.

spouse. One's husband or wife by lawful marriage; a married person.

> *surviving spouse.* A spouse who outlives the other spouse.

spouse-breach. See ADULTERY.

spray trust. See *sprinkle trust* under TRUST.

springing durable power of attorney. See *springing power of attorney* under POWER OF ATTORNEY.

springing power of attorney. See POWER OF ATTORNEY.

sprinkle power. In a sprinkle trust, the trustee's discretion about when and how much of the trust principal and income are to be distributed to the beneficiaries. See *sprinkle trust* under TRUST.

sprinkle trust. See TRUST.

SSA. *abbr.* SOCIAL SECURITY ADMINISTRATION.

SSDI. *abbr.* SOCIAL SECURITY DISABILITY INSURANCE.

SSI. *abbr.* SUPPLEMENTAL SECURITY INCOME.

stalking. 1. The act or an instance of following another by stealth. 2. The offense of following or loitering near another, often surreptitiously, with the purpose of annoying or harassing that person or committing a further crime such as assault or battery. • Some statutory definitions include an element that the person being stalked must reasonably feel harassed, alarmed, or distressed about personal safety or the safety of one or more persons for whom that person is responsible. And some definitions state that acts such as telephoning another and remaining silent during the call amount to stalking.

standby guardian. See GUARDIAN.

standby guardianship. See GUARDIANSHIP.

standby trust. See TRUST.

standing, *n.* A party's right to make a legal claim or seek judicial enforcement of a duty or right. — Also termed *standing to sue.*

> **third-party standing.** Standing held by someone claiming to protect the rights of others. • In most jurisdictions, only a parent has standing to bring a suit for custody or visitation; in some, however, a third party — for instance, a grandparent or a person with whom the child has substantial contacts — may have standing to bring an action for custody or visitation. See GRANDPARENT RIGHTS.

standing to sue. See STANDING.

state action. Anything done by a government; esp., in constitutional law, an intrusion on a person's rights (esp. civil rights) either by a governmental entity or by a private requirement that can be enforced only by governmental action (such as a racially restrictive covenant, which requires judicial action for enforcement).

status. **1.** A person's legal condition, whether personal or proprietary; the sum total of a person's legal rights, duties, liabilities, and other legal relations, or any particular group of them separately considered <the status of a landowner>. **2.** A person's legal condition regarding personal rights but excluding proprietary relations <the status of a father> <the status of a wife>. **3.** A person's capacities and incapacities, as opposed to other elements of personal status <the status of minors>. **4.** A person's legal condition insofar as it is imposed by the law without the person's consent, as opposed to a condition that the person has acquired by agreement <the status of a slave>.

status offense. Sanctionable conduct that can be committed only by a minor. ● Some examples of status offenses are being ungovernable or truant, violating a curfew, and running away. See *child in need of supervision* under CHILD.

status-offense jurisdiction. See JURISDICTION.

status quo (**stay**-təs *or* **stat**-əs **kwoh**). [Latin] The situation that currently exists.

statute of descent and distribution. See STATUTE OF DISTRIBUTION.

statute of distribution. A state law regulating the distribution of an estate among an intestate's heirs and relatives. ● Historically, the statute specified separate, and often different, patterns for distributing an intestate's real property and personal property. Generally, land descended to the heirs and personalty descended to the next of kin. — Also termed *statute of descent and distribution*.

statute of mortmain. See MORTMAIN STATUTE.

statute of wills. 1. (*cap.*) An English statute (enacted in 1540) that established the right of a person to devise real property by will. — Also termed *Wills Act*. **2.** A state statute, usu. derived from the English statute, providing for testamentary disposition and requiring an elaborate set of requirements for valid execution in that jurisdiction.

statutory exclusion. The removal, by law, of certain crimes from juvenile-court jurisdiction. ● More than half the states now remove certain particularly serious crimes committed by older juveniles from the jurisdiction of the juvenile courts. In this kind of case, the juvenile court never has jurisdiction, so a transfer hearing is not required or necessary. Cf. MANDATORY WAIVER.

statutory forced share. See ELECTIVE SHARE.

statutory guardian. See GUARDIAN.

statutory rape. See RAPE.

statutory share. See ELECTIVE SHARE.

stay-away order. 1. In a domestic-violence case, an order forbidding the defendant to contact the victim. ● A stay-away order usually prohibits the defendant from coming within a certain number of feet of the victim's home, school, work, or other specific place. Stay-away orders are most often issued in criminal cases. **2.** RESTRAINING ORDER (1). **3.** In a juvenile-delinquency case, an order prohibiting a youthful offender from frequenting the scene of the offense or from being in the company of certain persons. — Also termed *no-contact order*; *stay-away order of protection*.

stepbrother. See BROTHER.

stepchild. See CHILD.

stepfather. See FATHER.

stepmother. See MOTHER.

stepparent. See PARENT.

stepparent adoption. See ADOPTION.

stepsister. See SISTER.

step-up visitation. See VISITATION.

stillborn, *adj.* (Of an infant) born dead. — Also termed *deadborn*.

stipital. See STIRPITAL.

stipulated judgment. See *agreed judgment* under JUDGMENT.

stirpal (**stər**-pəl), *adj.* See STIRPITAL.

stirpes (**stər**-peez). (*pl.*) STIRPS.

stirpital (**stər**-pə-təl), *adj.* Of or relating to per stirpes distribution. — Also termed *stipital*; *stirpal*. See PER STIRPES.

stirps (stərps), *n.* [Latin "stock"] A branch of a family; a line of descent. Pl. **stirpes** (**stər**-peez). See PER STIRPES.

stock, *n.* The original progenitor of a family; a person from whom a family is descended <George Harper Sr. was the stock of the Harper line>.

stopgap tax. See TAX.

straight life insurance. See *whole life insurance* under LIFE INSURANCE.

stranger in blood. 1. One not related by blood, such as a relative by affinity. **2.** Any person not within the consideration of natural love and affection arising from a relationship.

street gang. See GANG.

strict scrutiny. *Constitutional law.* The standard applied to suspect classifications (such as race) in equal-protection analysis and to fundamental rights (such as voting rights) in due-process analysis. ● Under strict scrutiny, the state must establish that it has a compelling interest that justifies and necessitates the law in question. See COMPELLING-STATE-INTEREST TEST; SUSPECT CLASSIFICATION; FUNDAMENTAL RIGHT. Cf. INTERMEDIATE SCRUTINY; RATIONAL-BASIS TEST.

student-benefit theory. A principle that allows state funds to be provided to private-school pupils if the allotment can be justified as benefiting the child. ● The Supreme Court upheld a Louisiana law that allowed the purchase of textbooks for all children throughout the state — even those in private schools — under this theory. *Cochran v. Louisiana State Bd. of Educ.*, 281 U.S. 370, 50 S.Ct. 335 (1930). — Also termed *child-benefit theory.*

subpoena (sə-**pee**-nə), *n.* [Latin "under penalty"] A writ commanding a person to appear before a court or other tribunal, subject to a penalty for failing to comply. Pl. **subpoenas.**

sub potestate parentis (səb poh-tes-**tay**-tee pə-**ren**-tis). [Latin] *Archaic.* Under the protection of a parent.

subscribing witness. See WITNESS.

substantial change in circumstances. See CHANGE IN CIRCUMSTANCES.

substantial-compliance rule. See SUBSTANTIAL-PERFORMANCE DOCTRINE.

substantial-performance doctrine. The equitable rule that, if a good-faith attempt to perform does not precisely meet the terms of an agreement or statutory requirements, the performance will still be considered complete if the essential purpose is accomplished. ● Under the Uniform Probate Code, a will that is otherwise void because some formality has not been followed may still be valid under the substantial-performance doctrine. But this rule is not widely followed. — Also termed *substantial-compliance rule.*

substantive due process. See DUE PROCESS.

substituted executor. See EXECUTOR.

substituted-judgment doctrine. A principle that allows a surrogate decision-maker to attempt to establish, with as much accuracy as possible, what decision an incompetent patient would make if he or she were competent to do so. ● The standard of proof is by clear and convincing evidence. Generally, the doctrine is used for a person who was once competent but no longer is. — Also termed *doctrine of substituted judgment*. Cf. SPIRITUAL-TREATMENT EXEMPTION; *medical neglect* under NEGLECT.

substitute gift. See GIFT.

substitutional gift. See *substitute gift* under GIFT.

substitutional legacy. See LEGACY.

succession, *n.* **1.** The act or right of legally or officially taking over a predecessor's office, rank, or duties. **2.** The acquisition of rights or property by inheritance under the laws of descent and distribution; DESCENT (1). — **succeed,** *vb.*

hereditary succession. See *intestate succession.*

intestate succession. **1.** The method used to distribute property owned by a person who dies without a valid will. **2.** Succession by the common law of descent. — Also termed *hereditary succession; descent and distribution.* See DESCENT. Cf. *testate succession.*

irregular succession. Succession by special laws favoring certain persons or the state, rather than heirs (such as testamentary heirs) under the ordinary laws of descent.

legal succession. The succession established by law, usu. in favor of the nearest relation of a deceased person.

natural succession. Succession between natural persons, as in descent on the death of an ancestor.

testamentary succession. *Civil law.* Succession resulting from the institution of an heir in a testament executed in the legally required form.

testate succession. The passing of rights or property by will. Cf. *intestate succession.*

universal succession. Succession to an entire estate of another, living or dead (though usu. the latter). ● This type of succession carries with it the predecessor's liabilities as well as assets. Originally developed by Roman law and later continued by civil law, this concept has now been widely adopted as an option endorsed and authorized by the Uniform Probate Code.

vacant succession. *Civil law.* **1.** A succession that fails either because there are no known heirs or because the heirs have renounced the estate. **2.** An estate that has suffered such a failure. See ESCHEAT.

successional, *adj.* Of or relating to acquiring rights or property by inheritance under the laws of descent and distribution.

succession tax. See *inheritance tax* (1) under TAX.

successive, *adj. Archaic.* (Of an estate) hereditary.

successive polygamy. See POLYGAMY (2).

successor. A person who succeeds to the office, rights, responsibilities, or place of another; one who replaces or follows another.

> ***particular successor.*** *Civil law.* One who succeeds to rights and obligations that pertain only to the property conveyed.

> ***singular successor.*** One who succeeds to a former owner's rights in a single piece of property.

> ***universal successor.*** One who succeeds to all the rights and powers of a former owner, as with an intestate estate or an estate in bankruptcy.

successor fiduciary. See FIDUCIARY.

successor guardian. See GUARDIAN.

successor trustee. See TRUSTEE.

sudden-death jurisdiction. A jurisdiction in which a will once revoked cannot be revived, and instead must be reexecuted. See REVIVAL.

suicide, *n.* **1.** The act of taking one's own life. — Also termed *self-killing; self-destruction; self-slaughter; self-murder; felony de se.*

assisted suicide. The intentional act of providing a person with the medical means or the medical knowledge to commit suicide. — Also termed *assisted self-determination*. Cf. EUTHANASIA.

attempted suicide. An unsuccessful suicidal act.

2. A person who has taken his or her own life. — **suicidal,** *adj*.

suicide clause. *Insurance*. A life-insurance-policy provision either excluding suicide as a risk or limiting the liability of the insurer in the event of a suicide to the total premiums paid.

summons, *n*. **1.** A writ or process commencing the plaintiff's action and requiring the defendant to appear and answer. **2.** A notice requiring a person to appear in court as a juror or witness. Pl. **summonses.**

sunna. See FEMALE GENITAL MUTILATION.

supernumerary witness. See WITNESS.

supervised visitation. See VISITATION.

supplemental-needs trust. See TRUST.

Supplemental Security Income. A welfare or needs-based program providing monthly income to the aged, blind, or disabled. ● It is authorized by the Social Security Act. — Abbr. SSI.

support, *n*. **1.** Sustenance or maintenance; esp., articles such as food and clothing that allow one to live in the degree of comfort to which one is accustomed. See MAINTENANCE; NECESSARIES. **2.** One or more monetary payments to a current or former family member for the purpose of helping the recipient maintain an acceptable standard of living. See ALIMONY. Cf. NONSUPPORT.

child support. See CHILD SUPPORT.

family support. See FAMILY SUPPORT.

spousal support. See ALIMONY.

support order. A court decree requiring a party (esp. one in a divorce or paternity proceeding) to make payments to maintain a child or spouse, including medical, dental, and educational expenses.

foreign support order. An out-of-state support order.

support trust. See TRUST.

surname. A person's family name, derived from the common name of his or her parent. ● Although a person's surname is usually the father's surname, there is nothing to prevent someone from taking the mother's surname. Cf. MAIDEN NAME; GIVEN NAME.

531

surrogacy. 1. The act of performing some function in the place of someone else. **2.** The process of carrying and delivering a child for another person.

> ***gestational surrogacy.*** A pregnancy in which one woman (the genetic mother) provides the egg, which is fertilized, and another woman (the surrogate mother) carries the fetus and gives birth to the child.

> ***traditional surrogacy.*** A pregnancy in which a woman provides her own egg, which is fertilized by artificial insemination, and carries the fetus and gives birth to a child for another person.

surrogacy contract. See SURROGATE-PARENTING AGREEMENT.

surrogate (sər-ə-git), *n.* **1.** A judge on a probate court <the surrogate held that the will was valid>. See *probate judge* under JUDGE. **2.** One who acts in place of another. See *surrogate mother* under MOTHER. — **surrogate,** *adj.* — **surrogacy** (sər-ə-gə-see), **surrogateship,** *n.*

surrogate carrier. See *surrogate mother* (1) under MOTHER.

surrogate court. See *probate court* under COURT.

surrogate mother. See MOTHER.

surrogate parent. See PARENT; *surrogate mother* under MOTHER.

surrogate-parenting agreement. A contract between a woman and typically an infertile couple under which the woman provides her uterus to carry an embryo throughout pregnancy; esp., an agreement between a person (the intentional parent) and a woman (the surrogate mother) providing that the surrogate mother will (1) bear a child for the intentional parent, and (2) relinquish any and all rights to the child. • If the surrogate mother is married, her husband must also consent to the terms of the surrogacy contract. The agreement usually provides that the woman will relinquish to the couple any parental rights she may have upon the birth of the child. Complex issues arise concerning who is the parent of the resulting child: the genetic donor of egg or sperm, a spouse of either donor, the surrogate, or the person intending to care for the resulting child? American jurisdictions are split on the interpretation and enforceability of these contracts. — Also termed *surrogacy contract.* See *surrogate mother* under MOTHER; *intended child* under CHILD; *intentional parent* under PARENT.

surrogate's court. See *probate court* under COURT.

survival action. A lawsuit brought on behalf of a decedent's estate for injuries or damages incurred by the decedent immediately before dying. • A survival action derives from the claim that a decedent would have had — such as for pain and suffering — if he or she had survived. In contrast is a claim that the beneficiaries may have in a wrongful-death action, such as for loss of consortium or loss of support from the decedent. Cf. WRONGFUL-DEATH ACTION.

survival clause. A testamentary provision conditioning a bequest on a beneficiary's living for a certain period, often 60 days, after the testator's death. ● If the beneficiary dies within the stated period, the testamentary gift usually accrues to the residuary estate. — Also termed *survivorship clause*. Cf. SIMULTANEOUS-DEATH CLAUSE.

survival statute. A law that modifies the common law by allowing certain actions to continue in favor of a personal representative after the death of the party who could have originally brought the action; esp., a law that provides for the estate's recovery of damages incurred by the decedent immediately before death. Cf. DEATH STATUTE.

surviving spouse. See SPOUSE.

survivor. 1. One who outlives another. **2.** A trustee who administers a trust after the cotrustee has been removed, has refused to act, or has died.

survivorship. 1. The state or condition of being the one person out of two or more who remains alive after the others die. **2.** The right of a surviving party having a joint interest with others in an estate to take the whole. See RIGHT OF SURVIVORSHIP.

survivorship clause. See SURVIVAL CLAUSE.

suspect class. A group identified or defined in a suspect classification.

suspect classification. *Constitutional law.* A statutory classification based on race, national origin, or alienage, and thereby subject to strict scrutiny under equal-protection analysis. ● Examples of suspect classifications are a law permitting only U.S. citizens to receive welfare benefits and a law setting quotas for the government's hiring of minority contractors. See STRICT SCRUTINY. Cf. FUNDAMENTAL RIGHT.

symbolic, *adj.* (Of a signature) consisting of a symbol or mark. Cf. ONOMASTIC (2); HOLOGRAPH.

symbolic speech. See SPEECH.

T

tableau of distribution. *Civil law.* A list of creditors of an estate, stating what each is entitled to. See *judgment homologating the tableau* under JUDGMENT.

TANF. *abbr.* TEMPORARY ASSISTANCE TO NEEDY FAMILIES.

tangible personal property. See PROPERTY.

tangible-personal-property memorandum. A handwritten or signed document that lists items of tangible personal property (such as jewelry, artwork, or furniture) and the persons who should receive the property upon the owner's death. ● This memorandum is a separate document from the property owner's will, and if referred to by the will, it is a valid testamentary disposition. Unif. Probate Code § 2–513. — Abbr. TPPM.

tangible property. See PROPERTY.

target benefit plan. See EMPLOYEE BENEFIT PLAN.

tax, *n.* A monetary charge imposed by the government on persons, entities, or property to yield public revenue. ● Most broadly, the term embraces all governmental impositions on the person, property, privileges, occupations, and enjoyment of the people, and includes duties, imposts, and excises. Although a tax is often thought of as being pecuniary in nature, it is not necessarily payable in money. — **tax,** *vb*.

additional tax. See *stopgap tax*.

collateral-inheritance tax. A tax levied on the transfer of property by will or intestate succession to a person other than the spouse, a parent, or a descendant of the decedent. Cf. *legacy tax*.

death tax. See *estate tax*.

estate tax. A tax imposed on property transferred by will or by intestate succession. — Also termed *death tax*. Cf. *inheritance tax*.

generation-skipping tax. A tax on a property transfer that skips a generation. ● The tax limits the use of generation-skipping techniques as a means of avoiding estate taxes.

generation-skipping transfer tax. A gift or estate tax imposed on a generation-skipping transfer or a generation-skipping trust. — Sometimes shortened to *generation-skipping tax*; *transfer tax*. IRC (26 USCA) §§ 2601–2663. See DIRECT SKIP; GENERATION-SKIPPING TRANSFER; *generation-skipping trust* under TRUST; TAXABLE DISTRIBUTION.

gift tax. A tax imposed when property is voluntarily and gratuitously transferred. ● Under federal law, the gift tax is imposed on the donor, but some states tax the donee.

inheritance tax. **1.** A tax imposed on a person who inherits property from another (unlike an estate tax, which is imposed on the decedent's estate). • There is no federal inheritance tax, but some states provide for one (though it is deductible under the federal estate tax). — Also termed *succession tax.* Cf. *estate tax.* **2.** Loosely, an estate tax.

kiddie tax. *Slang.* A federal tax imposed on a child's unearned income at the parents' tax rate if the parents' rate is higher and if the child is under 14 years of age.

legacy tax. A tax on a legacy, often with the provision that the rate increases as the relationship of the legatee becomes more remote from the testator. — Also termed *legacy duty.* Cf. *collateral-inheritance tax.*

nanny tax. *Slang.* A federal social-security tax imposed on the employer of a domestic employee if the employer pays that employee more than a specified amount in total wages in a year. • The term, which is not a technical legal phrase, was popularized in the mid-1990s, when several of President Clinton's nominees were found not to have paid the social-security tax for their nannies.

pickup tax. *Slang.* A state death tax levied in an amount equal to the federal death-tax credit. — Also termed *sponge tax.*

sponge tax. See *pickup tax.*

stopgap tax. A generation-skipping transfer tax that prohibits property from passing over one generation to another without the imposition of an estate-transfer tax. — Also termed *additional tax*.

succession tax. See *inheritance tax*.

transfer tax. **1.** A tax imposed on the transfer of property, esp. by will, inheritance, or gift. **2.** See *stock-transfer tax*. **3.** See *generation-skipping transfer tax*.

unified transfer tax. The federal transfer tax imposed equally on property transferred during life or at death. ● Until 1977, gift-tax rates were lower than estate taxes. — Also termed *unified estate and gift tax*.

taxable distribution. A generation-skipping transfer from a trust to the beneficiary (i.e., the *skip person*) that is neither a direct skip nor a taxable termination. See GENERATION-SKIPPING TRANSFER; *generation-skipping transfer tax* under TAX; *generation-skipping trust* under TRUST; SKIP PERSON.

taxable estate. See ESTATE.

taxable gift. See GIFT.

tax-apportionment clause. A testamentary provision that inheritance and estate taxes be paid out solely from the residue of the estate.

tax credit. An amount subtracted directly from one's total tax liability, dollar for dollar, as opposed to a deduction from gross income. — Often shortened to *credit*. Cf. DEDUCTION.

> **child- and dependent-care tax credit.** A tax credit available to a person who is employed full-time and who maintains a household for a dependent child or a disabled spouse or dependent.

> **unified estate-and-gift tax credit.** A tax credit applied against the federal unified transfer tax. ● The 1999 credit is $211,300, meaning that an estate worth up to $650,000 passes to the heirs free of any federal estate tax. The credit will gradually increase so that, after 2005, it will be $345,800, meaning that no federal estate tax will be due on an estate worth up to $1 million. — Often shortened to *unified credit*. — Also termed *applicable exclusion amount*.

tax deduction. See DEDUCTION.

tax-deferred annuity. See *403(b) plan* under EMPLOYEE BENEFIT PLAN.

tax-sheltered annuity. See *403(b) plan* under EMPLOYEE BENEFIT PLAN.

teen court. See COURT.

temporary administration. See ADMINISTRATION.

temporary alimony. See ALIMONY.

Temporary Assistance to Needy Families. A combined state and federal program that provides limited financial assistance to families in need. 42 USCA §§ 601–603a. ● This program replaced Aid to Families with Dependent Children. TANF differs from AFDC because families are limited to no more than five years of assistance, and states have more control over eligibility requirements. — Abbr. TANF.

temporary disability. See DISABILITY (1).

temporary executor. See *acting executor* under EXECUTOR.

temporary fiduciary. See FIDUCIARY.

temporary injunction. See *preliminary injunction* under INJUNCTION.

temporary judge. See *visiting judge* under JUDGE.

temporary order. A court order issued during the pendency of a suit, before the final order or judgment has been entered.

temporary restraining order. 1. A court order preserving the status quo until a litigant's application for a preliminary or permanent injunction can be heard. ● A temporary restraining order may sometimes be granted without notifying the opposing party in advance. **2.** See *ex parte injunction* under INJUNCTION. — Abbr. TRO. — Often shortened to *restraining order*.

temporary total disability. See DISABILITY (1).

temporary ward. See WARD.

tenancy. 1. The possession or occupancy of land by right or title, esp. under a lease; a leasehold interest in real estate. **2.** The period of such possession or occupancy. See ESTATE.

> ***common tenancy.*** See *tenancy in common.*

> ***cotenancy.*** A tenancy with two or more coowners who have unity of possession. ● Examples are a joint tenancy and tenancy in common.

> ***joint tenancy.*** A tenancy with two or more coowners who take identical interests simultaneously by the same instrument and with the same right of possession. ● A joint tenancy differs from a tenancy in common because each joint tenant has a right of survivorship to the other's share (in some states, this right must be clearly expressed in the conveyance — otherwise, the tenancy will be presumed to be a tenancy in common). See RIGHT OF SURVIVORSHIP. Cf. *tenancy in common.*

> ***tenancy by the entirety*** (en-tı-ər-tee). See *estate by entirety* under ESTATE.

tenancy in common. A tenancy by two or more persons, in equal or unequal undivided shares, each person having an equal right to possess the whole property but no right of survivorship. — Also termed *common tenancy*; *estate in common.*

tenancy in coparcenary. See COPARCENARY.

tenancy in tail. See FEE TAIL.

tenant, *n.* One who holds or possesses lands or tenements by any kind of right or title. See TENANCY.

joint tenant. See *joint tenancy* under TENANCY.

life tenant. See LIFE TENANT.

tenant in common. See *tenancy in common* under TENANCY.

tender-years doctrine. The doctrine holding that custody of very young children (usu. five years of age and younger) should generally be awarded to the mother in a divorce unless she is found to be unfit. ● This doctrine has been rejected in most states and replaced by a presumption of joint custody. See MATERNAL-PREFERENCE DOCTRINE; PRIMARY-CARE-GIVER DOCTRINE.

tender-years hearsay exception. See HEARSAY EXCEPTION.

tentative trust. See *Totten trust* under TRUST.

teratogen (tə-**rat**-ə-jən), *n*. An agent, usu. a chemical, that causes injury to a fetus or any of various birth defects <alcohol is a teratogen to the developing brain of a fetus>. — **teratogenic** (tə-rat-ə-**jen**-ik), *adj*.

termination hearing. See *termination-of-parental-rights hearing* under HEARING.

termination of parental rights. The legal severing of a parent's rights, privileges, and responsibilities regarding his or her child. ● Termination of a parent's rights frees the child to be adopted by someone else. — Abbr. TPR. See *termination-of-parental-rights hearing* under HEARING; PARENTAL RIGHTS.

term life insurance. See LIFE INSURANCE.

terrorem clause. See NO-CONTEST CLAUSE.

terrorizing, *n*. A parent's or caregiver's act of orally assaulting, bullying, or frightening a child, or causing the child to believe that the world is a hostile place.

testacy (**tes**-tə-see), *n*. The fact or condition of leaving a valid will at one's death. Cf. INTESTACY.

testament (**tes**-tə-mənt). **1.** Traditionally, a will disposing of personal property. Cf. DEVISE (4). **2.** WILL.

inofficious testament. *Civil law.* A will that does not dispose of property to the testator's natural heirs; esp., a will that deprives the heirs of a portion of the estate to which they are entitled by law. — Also termed *inofficious will*; *unofficious will.* See *forced heir* under HEIR.

officious testament. *Civil law.* A will that disposes of property to the testator's family; a will that reserves the legitime for the testator's children and other natural heirs. — Also termed *officious will.* See LEGITIME.

testamentary (tes-tə-**men**-tə-ree *or* -tree), *adj.* **1.** Of or relating to a will or testament <testamentary intent>. **2.** Provided for or appointed by a will <testamentary guardian>. **3.** Created by a will <testamentary gift>.

testamentary capacity. See CAPACITY.

testamentary class. See CLASS.

testamentary gift. See GIFT.

testamentary guardian. See GUARDIAN.

testamentary heir. See HEIR.

testamentary intent. See INTENT.

testamentary power of appointment. See POWER OF APPOINTMENT.

testamentary succession. See SUCCESSION.

testamentary trust. See TRUST.

testamentary trustee. See TRUSTEE.

testate (**tes**-tayt), *adj*. Having left a will at death <she died testate>. Cf. INTESTATE.

testate, *n*. See TESTATOR.

testate succession. See SUCCESSION.

testation (te-**stay**-shən). **1.** The disposal of property by will; the power to dispose of property by will. **2.** *Archaic*. Attestation; a witnessing.

testator (**tes**-tay-tər *also* te-**stay**-tər). A person who has made a will; esp., a person who dies leaving a will. ● Because this term is usually interpreted as applying to both sexes, *testatrix* has become archaic. — Also termed *testate*. Cf. INTESTATE.

testatrix (te-**stay**-triks *or* **tes**-tə-triks). *Archaic*. A female testator. ● In modern usage, a person who leaves a will is called a testator, regardless of sex. Pl. **testatrixes, testatrices.**

testimonial incapacity. See INCAPACITY.

testimonium clause. A provision at the end of an instrument (esp. a will) reciting the date when the instrument was signed, by whom it was signed, and in what capacity. ● This clause traditionally begins with the phrase "In witness whereof." Cf. ATTESTATION CLAUSE.

therapeutic abortion. See ABORTION.

things personal. See *personal property* (1) under PROPERTY.

third cousin. See COUSIN.

third-party standing. See STANDING.

throwaway, *n. Slang.* **1.** An unemancipated minor whose parent or caregiver has forced him or her to leave home. **2.** A runaway whose parent or caregiver refuses to allow him or her to return home. Cf. RUNAWAY.

TILA. *abbr.* Truth in Lending Act. See CONSUMER CREDIT PROTECTION ACT.

title by descent. A title that one acquires by law as an heir of the deceased owner.

title by devise. A title created by will.

title division. *Archaic.* A common-law system for dividing property acquired during marriage upon the dissolution of the marriage, the divisions being based on who holds legal title to the property. ●

Under title division, when a marriage ends in divorce, property purchased during the marriage is awarded to the person who holds title to the property. Cf. COMMUNITY PROPERTY; EQUITABLE DISTRIBUTION.

top-hat pension plan. See PENSION PLAN.

torpedo doctrine. See ATTRACTIVE-NUISANCE DOCTRINE.

tort (tort). A civil wrong for which a remedy may be obtained, usu. in the form of damages; a breach of a duty that the law imposes on everyone in the same relation to one another as those involved in a given transaction.

> ***marital tort.*** A tort by one spouse against the other. ● Since most jurisdictions have abolished interspousal tort immunity, courts have had to decide which tort claims to recognize between married persons. Among those that some, but not all, courts have chosen to recognize are assault and battery, including claims for infliction of sexually transmitted disease, and intentional and negligent infliction of emotional distress. — Also termed *domestic tort.* Cf. HUSBAND–WIFE IMMUNITY.

> ***prenatal tort.*** **1.** A tort committed against a fetus. ● If born alive, a child can sue for injuries resulting from tortious conduct predating the child's birth. **2.** Loosely, any of several torts relating to reproduction, such as those giving rise to

wrongful-birth actions, wrongful-life actions, and wrongful-pregnancy actions.

tortious battery. See BATTERY (2).

total disability. See DISABILITY (1).

Totten trust. See TRUST.

TPPM. *abbr.* TANGIBLE-PERSONAL-PROPERTY MEMORANDUM.

TPR. *abbr.* TERMINATION OF PARENTAL RIGHTS.

tracing, *n.* The process of tracking property's ownership or characteristics from the time of its origin to the present. ● Parties in a divorce will be expected to trace the origins of property in existence at the time of marital dissolution in order to characterize each asset as separate or marital property (or as community property in some states). — Also termed *tracing of funds*; *tracing of property*. Cf. COMMINGLE.

traditional surrogacy. See SURROGACY.

transfer, *n.* **1.** Any mode of disposing of or parting with an asset or an interest in an asset, including a gift, the payment of money, release, lease, or creation of a lien or other encumbrance. ● The term embraces every method — direct or indirect, absolute or conditional, voluntary or involuntary — of disposing of or parting with property or with an

549

interest in property, including retention of title as a security interest and foreclosure of the debtor's equity of redemption. **2.** Negotiation of an instrument according to the forms of law. ● The four methods of transfer are by indorsement, by delivery, by assignment, and by operation of law. **3.** A conveyance of property or title from one person to another.

> *colorable transfer.* A sham transfer having the appearance of authenticity; a pretended transfer. See ILLUSORY-TRANSFER DOCTRINE.

> *incomplete transfer.* A decedent's inter vivos transfer that is not completed for federal estate-tax purposes because the decedent retains significant powers over the property's possession or enjoyment. ● Because the transfer is incomplete, some or all of the property's value will be included in the transferor's gross estate. IRC (26 USCA) §§ 2036–2038.

> *inter vivos transfer* (**in**-tər **vi**-vohs *or* **vee**-vohs). A transfer of property made during the transferor's lifetime.

> *transfer in contemplation of death.* See *gift causa mortis* under GIFT.

transfer hearing. See HEARING.

transfer statute. A provision that allows or mandates the trial of a juvenile as an adult in a criminal court for a criminal act. ● Every state has some form of transfer statute. The Supreme Court has held that a juvenile cannot be transferred to criminal court under a discretionary statute "without ceremony — without hearing, without effective assistance of counsel, without a statement of reasons." *Kent v. United States*, 383 U.S. 541, 554, 86 S.Ct. 1045, 1053–54 (1966).

> ***automatic-transfer statute.*** A law requiring the transfer from delinquency court to criminal court for certain statutorily enumerated offenses if certain statutory requirements are met.

> ***discretionary-transfer statute.*** A law that allows, but does not mandate, the transfer from delinquency court to criminal court for certain statutorily enumerated offenses if certain statutory requirements are met. ● The prosecutor has discretion to request the transfer, and the judge has discretion to order the transfer.

> ***reverse transfer statute.*** A provision that allows a criminal court to return certain cases to juvenile court.

Transfers to Minors Act. See UNIFORM TRANSFERS TO MINORS ACT.

transfer tax. See *generation-skipping transfer tax* under TAX.

transgressive trust. See TRUST.

transitional alimony. See *rehabilitative alimony* under ALIMONY.

transmutation. A change in the nature of something; esp., in family law, the transformation of separate property into marital property, or of marital property into separate property.

transnational adoption. See *international adoption* under ADOPTION.

transracial adoption. See ADOPTION.

transsexual. A person born with the physical characteristics of one sex but who has undergone, or is preparing to undergo, sex-change surgery. See SEX REASSIGNMENT.

trial calendar. See DOCKET (2).

trial court. See COURT.

Tribal Court. Under the Indian Child Welfare Act, a court with child-custody jurisdiction that is (1) a Court of Indian Offenses, (2) a court established and operated under the code or custom of a tribe, or (3) any other tribal administrative body that is vested with authority over child-custody proceedings. • The Tribal Court is composed of tribal members, is usually situated on the reservation, and varies in its characteristics from tribe to tribe. It is not part of any state's judicial system, instead operating more or less as a judicial system of a foreign nation. See INDIAN CHILD WELFARE ACT.

trigamy (**trig**-ə-mee), *n*. The act of marrying a person while legally married to someone else and bigamously married to yet another.

TRO. *abbr*. TEMPORARY RESTRAINING ORDER.

truancy (**troo**-ən-see), *n*. The act or state of shirking responsibility; esp., willful and unjustified failure to attend school by one who is required to attend. — **truant,** *adj*. & *n*.

truancy officer. An official responsible for enforcing laws mandating school attendance for minors of specified ages (usu. 16 and under). — Also termed *truant officer*; *attendance officer*.

trust, *n*. **1.** The right, enforceable solely in equity, to the beneficial enjoyment of property to which another person holds the legal title; a property interest held by one person (the *trustee*) at the request of another (the *settlor*) for the benefit of a third party (the *beneficiary*). ● For a trust to be valid, it must involve specific property, reflect the settlor's intent, and be created for a lawful purpose. The two primary types of trusts are *private trusts* and *charitable trusts* (see below). **2.** A fiduciary relationship regarding property and charging the person with title to the property with equitable duties to deal with it for another's benefit; the confidence placed in a trustee, together with the trustee's obligations toward the property and the beneficiary. ● A trust arises as a result of a manifestation of an intention to create it. See FIDUCIARY RELATIONSHIP. **3.** The property so held; TRUST ESTATE.

A-B trust. See *bypass trust*.

accumulation trust. A trust in which the trustee must accumulate income and gains from sales of trust assets for ultimate disposition with the principal when the trust terminates. ● Many states restrict the time over which accumulations may be made or the amount that may be accumulated.

active trust. A trust in which the trustee has some affirmative duty of management or administration besides the obligation to transfer the property to the beneficiary. — Also termed *special trust*. Cf. *passive trust*.

alimony trust. A trust in which the payor spouse transfers to the trustee property from which the payee spouse, as beneficiary, will be supported after a divorce or separation.

annuity trust. A trust from which the trustee must pay a sum certain annually to one or more beneficiaries for their respective lives or for a term of years, and must then either transfer the remainder to or for the use of a qualified charity or retain the remainder for such a use. ● The sum certain must not be less than 5% of the initial fair market value of the property transferred to the trust by the donor. A qualified annuity trust must comply with the requirements of IRC (26 USCA) § 664.

asset-protection trust. See *self-settled trust*.

bank-account trust. See *Totten trust*.

blended trust. A trust in which the beneficiaries are a group, with no member of the group having a separable individual interest. • Courts rarely recognize these trusts.

blind trust. A trust in which the settlor places investments under the control of an independent trustee, usu. to avoid a conflict of interest.

bond trust. A trust whose principal consists of bonds that yield interest income.

bypass trust. A trust into which a decedent's estate passes, so that the surviving heirs get a life estate in the trust rather than the property itself, in order to avoid estate taxes on an estate larger than the tax-credit-sheltered amount ($700,000 in 2000, increasing to $1 million after 2005). — Also termed *credit-shelter trust*; *A-B trust*; *marital life-estate trust*. See *unified estate-and-gift tax credit* under TAX CREDIT.

charitable lead trust. An irrevocable trust that is made in favor of a charity and that allows the charity to receive income from the trust property for a specified period, after which the property reverts to the settlor's estate.

charitable-remainder annuity trust. A charitable-remainder trust in which the beneficiaries receive for a specified period a fixed payment of 5% or more of the fair market value of the original principal, after which the remaining principal passes to charity. — Abbr. CRAT. — Also termed *charitable-remainder-trust retirement fund.*

charitable-remainder trust. A trust that consists of assets that are designated for a charitable purpose and that are paid over to the trust after the expiration of a life estate or intermediate estate. — Also termed *split-interest trust.*

charitable-remainder-trust retirement fund. See *charitable-remainder annuity trust.*

charitable trust. A trust created to benefit a specific charity, specific charities, or the general public rather than a private individual or entity. • Charitable trusts are often eligible for favorable tax treatment. — Also termed *public trust*; *charitable use*. See CHARITABLE DEDUCTION; CY PRES. Cf. *private trust.*

Claflin trust. See *indestructible trust.*

community trust. See COMMUNITY TRUST.

complete voluntary trust. See *executed trust.*

constructive trust. A trust imposed by a court on equitable grounds against one who has obtained property by wrongdoing, thereby preventing the wrongful holder from being unjustly enriched. ● Such a trust creates no fiduciary relationship. The phrase *constructive trust* is, strictly speaking, a misnomer, since it denotes a court-imposed remedy as opposed to a real trust. — Also termed *implied trust*; *involuntary trust*; *trust de son tort*; *trust ex delicto*; *trust ex maleficio*; *remedial trust*; *trust in invitum*. See *trustee de son tort* under TRUSTEE. Cf. *resulting trust*.

contingent trust. An express trust depending for its operation on a future event.

credit-shelter trust. See *bypass trust*.

Crummey trust. A trust in which the trustee has the power to distribute or accumulate income and to give the beneficiary the right to withdraw the amount of the annual exclusion (or a smaller sum) within a reasonable time after the transfer. ● This type of trust can have multiple beneficiaries and is often used when the beneficiaries are minors. Gifts to a *Crummey* trust qualify for the annual exclusion regardless of the age of the beneficiaries. The trust assets are not required to be distributed to the beneficiaries at age 21. The validity of this type of trust was established in *Crummey v. Commissioner*, 397 F.2d 82 (9th Cir. 1968). — Also termed *discretionary trust*. See

CRUMMEY POWER; *annual exclusion* under EXCLUSION. Cf. *2503(c) trust.*

custodial trust. A revocable trust for which a custodial trustee is named to manage the assets for an incapacitated or disabled beneficiary. • The beneficiary does not have to be disabled or incapacitated at the time the trust is created. An adult beneficiary who is not disabled or incapacitated may terminate the trust at any time before his or her disability, incapacity, or death.

defective trust. A trust that is treated, for income-tax purposes, as if it were the same entity as the grantor, but for estate-tax purposes is treated as an entity separate from the grantor. • Typically a trust is an independent entity that is taxed separately from the settlor. Because trust income is taxed at higher rates than individual income, the settlor may intentionally create a defect in the trust terms so that the trust's income will be taxable to the grantor. This is achieved by violating the grantor-trust rules of IRC §§ 671–677 in a way that does not affect the completeness of the gift under IRC §§ 2035–2042. A violation renders the trust "defective" because the settlor must recognize the income even if the settlor does not actually receive it. The attribution of tax liability and payment of taxes on trust income do not give the grantor an ownership in the trust, which remains separate from the settlor's estate and is not subject to estate taxes.

destructible trust. A trust that can be destroyed by the happening of an event or by operation of law.

directory trust. **1.** A trust that is not completely and finally settled by the instrument creating it, but only defined in its general purpose and to be carried into detail according to later specific directions. **2.** See *fixed trust*.

direct trust. See *express trust*.

discretionary trust. **1.** A trust in which the settlor has delegated nearly complete or limited discretion to the trustee to decide when and how much income or property is distributed to a beneficiary. ● For example, a support trust operates to provide a standard for or limit on the exercise of discretion. This is perhaps the most common type of trust used in estate planning. **2.** See *Crummey trust*. Cf. *mandatory trust*; CRUMMEY POWER.

donative trust. A trust that establishes a gift of a beneficial interest in property for a beneficiary. ● Most trusts are donative trusts. — Also termed *gratuitous trust*.

dry trust. **1.** A trust that merely vests legal title in a trustee and does not require that trustee to do anything. **2.** See *passive trust*.

dynasty trust. A generation-skipping trust funded with the amount that is permanently exempt from generation-skipping tax and designed to last more than two generations. ● In 2000, a settlor could contribute $1 million to a dynasty trust. Almost half the states allow dynasty trusts, despite their potential for lasting more than 100 years. — Also termed *GST supertrust*.

educational trust. **1.** A trust to found, endow, or support a school. **2.** A trust to support someone's education.

estate trust. A trust of which all or part of the income generated is to be accumulated during the surviving spouse's life and added to the trust property, with the accumulated income and trust property being paid to the estate of the surviving spouse at death. ● This type of trust is commonly used to qualify property for the marital deduction. See *marital deduction* under DEDUCTION (1).

ex delicto trust (də-**lik**-toh). A trust that is created for an illegal purpose, esp. to prevent the settlor's creditors from collecting their claims out of the trust property.

executed trust. A trust in which the estates and interests in the subject matter of the trust are completely limited and defined by the instrument creating the trust and require no further instruments to complete them. — Also termed *complete voluntary trust*.

executory trust (eg-**zek**-yə-tor-ee). A trust in which the instrument creating the trust is intended to be provisional only, and further conveyances are contemplated by the trust instrument before the terms of the trust can be carried out. — Also termed *imperfect trust*.

express active trust. A testamentary trust that confers upon the executor authority to generally manage the estate property and pay over the net income to the devisees or legatees.

express private passive trust. A trust in which land is conveyed to or held by one person in trust for another, without any power being expressly or impliedly given to the trustee to take actual possession of the land or exercise any ownership rights over it, except at the beneficiary's direction.

express trust. A trust created with the settlor's express intent, usu. declared in writing; an ordinary trust as opposed to a resulting trust or a constructive trust. — Also termed *direct trust*.

family-pot trust. A trust in which all the assets are kept in a single fund for the trustee to use for multiple beneficiaries (usu. children). ● Family-pot trusts are typically testamentary and used to administer a donor's property until the donor's minor children have completed their education.

family trust. A trust created to benefit persons who are related to one another by blood, affinity, or law.

fixed trust. A trust in which the trustee may not exercise any discretion over the trust's management or distributions. — Also termed *directory trust*; *nondiscretionary trust*.

foreign-situs trust (sɪ-təs). A trust created under foreign law. ● This type of trust usually has no significant income-tax benefits and is subject to greater reporting requirements than a domestic trust. Because creditors cannot easily reach the foreign trust's assets, it is frequently used as a means of asset-protection. — Also termed *foreign trust*; *offshore trust*.

generation-skipping trust. A trust that is established to transfer (usu. principal) assets to a skip person (a beneficiary more than one generation removed from the settlor). ● The transfer is often accomplished by giving some control or benefits (such as trust income) of the assets to a nonskip person, often a member of the generation between the settlor and skip person. This type of trust is subject to a generation-skipping transfer tax. IRC (26 USCA) §§ 2601 et seq. See DEEMED TRANSFEROR; GENERATION-SKIPPING TRANSFER; *generation-skipping transfer tax* under TAX; SKIP PERSON. Cf. *dynasty trust*.

governmental trust. **1.** A type of charitable trust established to provide a community with facilities ordinarily supplied by the government, esp. by a municipality, and to promote purposes that are sufficiently beneficial to the community to justify permitting the property to be perpetually devoted to those purposes. ● Examples of such

562

facilities include public buildings, bridges, streets, parks, schools, and hospitals. **2.** A type of charitable trust established for general governmental or municipal purposes, such as defraying the expenses of a governmental entity or paying the public debt. Restatement (Second) of Trusts §§ 373, 374 (1959).

grantor-retained annuity trust. An irrevocable trust into which the grantor transfers property in exchange for the right to receive fixed payments at least annually, based on original fair market value of the property transferred. — Abbr. GRAT.

grantor-retained income trust. A trust in which a gift's value can be reduced by the grantor's retaining an income interest, for a specified time, in the gifted property. — Sometimes shortened to *retained income trust.* — Abbr. GRIT.

grantor-retained unitrust. An irrevocable trust into which the grantor transfers property in exchange for the right to receive annual payments, the amount of which fluctuates based on the increase or decrease in the value of the property transferred. — Abbr. GRUT. Cf. *grantor-retained annuity trust.*

grantor trust. A trust in which the settlor retains control over the trust property or its income to such an extent that the settlor is taxed on the trust's income. • The types of controls that result in such tax treatment are set out in IRC (26

USCA) §§ 671–677. An example is the revocable trust.

gratuitous trust. See *donative trust.*

GST supertrust. See *dynasty trust.*

honorary trust. A trust that is legally invalid and unenforceable because it lacks a proper beneficiary. • Examples include trusts that honor dead persons, maintain cemetery plots, or benefit animals. But the modern trend is to recognize the validity of such a trust for the care of pets, if the trustee is willing to accept the responsibility.

illusory trust. An arrangement that looks like a trust but, because of powers retained in the settlor, has no real substance and is not a completed trust.

imperfect trust. See *executory trust.*

implied trust. See *constructive trust*; *resulting trust.*

indestructible trust. A trust that, because of the settlor's wishes, cannot be prematurely terminated by the beneficiary. — Also termed *Claflin trust.*

insurance trust. A trust whose principal consists of insurance policies or their proceeds.

inter vivos trust (**in**-tər **vi**-vohs *or* **vee**-vohs). A trust that is created and takes effect during the settlor's lifetime. — Also termed *living trust*. Cf. *testamentary trust*.

involuntary trust. See *constructive trust*.

irrevocable trust (i-**rev**-ə-kə-bəl). A trust that cannot be terminated by the settlor once it is created. ● In most states, a trust will be deemed irrevocable unless the settlor specifies otherwise.

life-insurance trust. A trust consisting of one or more life-insurance policies payable to the trust when the insured dies.

limited trust. A trust created for a limited period. Cf. *perpetual trust*.

liquidating trust. A trust designed to be liquidated as soon as possible. ● An example is a trust into which a decedent's business is placed to safeguard the business until it can be sold.

living trust. See *inter vivos trust*.

mandatory trust. A trust in which the trustee must distribute all the income generated by the trust property to one or more designated beneficiaries. — Also termed *simple trust*. Cf. *discretionary trust*.

marital-deduction trust. A testamentary trust created to take full advantage of the marital deduction; esp., a trust entitling a spouse to lifetime income from the trust and sufficient control over the trust to include the trust property in the spouse's estate at death. See *marital deduction* under DEDUCTION (1).

marital life-estate trust. See *bypass trust.*

Medicaid-qualifying trust. A trust that is deemed to have been created in an effort to reduce someone's assets so that the person may qualify for Medicaid, and that will be included as an asset for purposes of determining the person's eligibility. • Someone who wants to apply and qualify for Medicaid, but who has too many assets to qualify, will sometimes set up a trust — or have a spouse or custodian set up a trust — using the applicant's own assets, under which the applicant may be the beneficiary of all or part of the payments from the trust, which are distributed by a trustee with discretion to make trust payments to the applicant. Such a trust may be presumed to have been established for the purpose of attempting to qualify for Medicaid, and may be counted as an asset of the applicant, resulting in a denial of benefits and the imposition of a penalty period during which the applicant cannot reapply. Nonetheless, Medicaid rules allow three types of trusts that do not impair Medicaid eligibility, since the trust assets are not considered the beneficiary's property: *Miller trust, pooled trust,* and *under-65 trust.*

Miller trust. An irrevocable trust funded with the income of an incompetent beneficiary who seeks to qualify for Medicaid in a state with an income cap. ● Funding is strictly limited to the beneficiary's income (from any source). The assets in the trust are not included in the beneficiary's estate for Medicaid purposes if the trust assets will be used to reimburse the state after the beneficiary's death. Trust distributions are kept below the income cap in order to preserve the beneficiary's Medicaid eligibility. This type of trust was first judicially sanctioned in *Miller v. Ibarra*, 746 F.Supp. 19 (D. Colo. 1990). — Also termed *Miller's trust*; *qualified income trust*.

ministerial trust. See *passive trust*.

minor's trust. See *2503(c) trust*.

mixed trust. A trust established to benefit both private individuals and charities.

naked trust. See *passive trust*.

nominal trust. See *passive trust*.

nominee trust. 1. A trust in which the beneficiaries have the power to direct the trustee's actions regarding the trust property. **2.** An arrangement for holding title to real property under which one or more persons or corporations, under a written declaration of trust, declare that they will hold any property that they acquire as trustees for the benefit of one or more undisclosed beneficiaries. — Also termed (in sense 2) *realty trust*.

nondiscretionary trust. See *fixed trust*.

offshore trust. See *foreign-situs trust.*

onerous trust. A trust that places exceptionally heavy and time-consuming duties of responsibility and care on the trustee, often without providing for compensation. ● Because of the burden and inequity of requiring the trust to be administered voluntarily, courts often grant a trustee a reasonable sum for the tasks performed.

oral trust. **1.** A trust created by the settlor's spoken statements as opposed to a written agreement. ● Trusts of real property must usually be in writing (because of the statute of frauds), but trusts of personal property can usually be created orally. — Also termed *parol trust.* **2.** A trust created by operation of law, such as a resulting trust or a constructive trust.

parol trust. See *oral trust* (1).

passive trust. A trust in which the trustee has no duty other than to transfer the property to the beneficiary. — Also termed *dry trust*; *nominal trust*; *simple trust*; *naked trust*; *ministerial trust.* See *bare trustee* under TRUSTEE. Cf. *active trust.*

pension trust. An employer-funded pension plan; esp., a pension plan in which the employer transfers to trustees amounts sufficient to cover the benefits payable to the employees.

perpetual trust. A trust that is to continue as long as the need for it continues, such as for the lifetime of a beneficiary or the term of a particular charity. Cf. *limited trust.*

personal-residence trust. An irrevocable trust to which the settlor transfers ownership of his or her personal residence while retaining the right to live there for a specified term of years. • The trust cannot hold any assets other than the residence and proceeds resulting from damage to or destruction of the residence. Cf. *qualified personal-residence trust.*

personal trust. See *private trust.*

pooled trust. An irrevocable, discretionary trust that (1) is established and managed by a nonprofit association, (2) is funded with the assets of disabled persons, and (3) maintains a separate trust account for each beneficiary, but (4) pools the trust assets for investment purposes. • If the trust provides for distribution of a deceased beneficiary's interest to the state in reimbursement of Medicaid expenditures, a pooled-trust beneficiary may be eligible for Medicaid benefits. The assets contributed to the trust for the individual's benefit are not treated as the beneficiary's property. — Also termed *pooled-assets trust.*

pourover trust. An inter vivos trust that receives property (usu. the residual estate) from a will upon the testator's death. Cf. *pourover will* under WILL.

power-of-appointment trust. A trust in which property is left in trust for the surviving spouse. ● The trustee must distribute income to the spouse for life, and the power of appointment is given to the spouse or to his or her estate. A power-of-appointment trust is commonly used to qualify property for the marital deduction. See *marital deduction* under DEDUCTION (1).

precatory trust (**prek**-ə-tor-ee). A trust that the law will recognize to carry out the wishes of the testator or grantor even though the statement in question is in the nature of an entreaty or recommendation rather than a positive command.

presumptive trust. See *resulting trust.*

private trust. A trust created for the financial benefit of one or more designated beneficiaries rather than for the public benefit; an ordinary trust as opposed to a charitable trust. ● Three elements must be present for a private trust: (1) sufficient words to create it, (2) a definite subject matter, and (3) a certain or ascertained object. — Also termed *personal trust.* Cf. *charitable trust.*

protective trust. A trust that is designed to protect the trust property to ensure the continued support of the beneficiary.

public trust. See *charitable trust.*

purchase-money resulting trust. A resulting trust that arises when one person buys property but directs the seller to transfer the property and its title to another. ● Although a purchase-money resulting trust is properly understood as a court-imposed equitable remedy rather than as a true trust, the buyer is occasionally referred to as the "beneficiary" and the titleholder as the "trustee." — Abbr. PMRT.

QTIP trust (**kyoo**-tip). A trust that is established to qualify for the marital deduction. ● Under this trust, the assets are referred to as qualified-terminable-interest property, or QTIP. See *qualified-terminable-interest property* under PROPERTY. Cf. *qualified domestic trust.*

qualified domestic trust. A trust for noncitizens that defers estate taxes in a citizen's estate until the death of the noncitizen surviving spouse. ● When the second spouse dies, the assets in the QDOT are taxed in the estate of the first spouse to die. — Abbr. QDOT. Cf. *QTIP trust.*

qualified personal-residence trust. An irrevocable trust that is funded with cash and the personal residence of the grantor, who retains the right to dwell in the residence for a specified term of years. ● The trust can receive and hold additional cash to pay for trust expenses, mortgage installments, and improvements to the residence. — Abbr. QPRT. Cf. *personal-residence trust.*

reciprocal trust. A trust arrangement between two parties in which one party is beneficiary of a trust established by the other party, and vice versa. • Such trusts are common between husband and wife.

remedial trust. See *constructive trust*.

resulting trust. A remedy imposed by equity when property is transferred under circumstances suggesting that the transferor did not intend for the transferee to have the beneficial interest in the property. — Also termed *implied trust*; *presumptive trust*. Cf. *constructive trust*.

retained income trust. See *grantor-retained income trust*.

revocable trust (**rev**-ə-kə-bəl). A trust in which the settlor reserves the right to terminate the trust and recover the trust property and any undistributed income.

savings-account trust. See *Totten trust*.

savings-bank trust. See *Totten trust*.

secret trust. An instrument, usu. a will, that appears to give an absolute gift to another although the donee has orally agreed with the grantor that he or she is to use the property for the benefit of some third party. • Courts admit evidence of the promise to prevent unjust enrichment and enforce it by imposing the remedy of a constructive trust upon the reneging "trustee." Cf. *semi-secret trust*.

self-settled trust. A trust in which the settlor is also the person who is to receive the benefits from the trust, usu. set up in an attempt to protect the trust assets from creditors. ● In most states, such a trust will not protect trust assets from the settlor's creditors. Restatement (Second) of Trusts § 156 (1959). — Also termed *asset-protection trust*.

semi-secret trust. An instrument that indicates who is to serve as a trustee but fails to identify the beneficiary. ● Traditionally, this trust was deemed to fail for want of an ascertainable beneficiary. But the modern view is to provide the same relief as that given for a secret trust: to receive evidence of the donor's intent, including the intended beneficiary, and impose a constructive trust in his or her favor. Cf. *secret trust*.

shifting trust. An express trust providing that, upon a specified contingency, it may operate in favor of an additional or substituted beneficiary.

simple trust. **1.** See *mandatory trust*. **2.** See *passive trust*.

special-needs trust. See *supplemental-needs trust*.

special trust. See *active trust*.

spendthrift trust. A trust that prohibits the beneficiary's interest from being assigned and also prevents a creditor from attaching that interest.

split-interest trust. See *charitable-remainder trust*.

spray trust. See *sprinkle trust*.

sprinkle trust. A trust in which the trustee has discretion to decide how much will be given to each beneficiary. — Also termed *spray trust*. See SPRINKLE POWER.

standby trust. A trust created to manage a person's assets while he or she is out of the country or disabled.

supplemental-needs trust. A trust established to provide supplemental income for a disabled beneficiary who is receiving or may be eligible to receive government benefits. ● This type of irrevocable trust is often used by parents of disabled children to ensure the beneficiary's eligibility for government benefits by expressly prohibiting distributions that may be used for the beneficiary's food, shelter, or clothing.

support trust. A discretionary trust in which the settlor authorizes the trustee to pay to the beneficiary as much income or principal as the trustee believes is needed for support, esp. for "comfortable support" or "support in accordance with the beneficiary's standard of living." ● The beneficiary's interest can be reached by creditors for necessaries, but usually not by general creditors.

tentative trust. See *Totten trust.*

testamentary trust (tes-tə-**men**-tə-ree *or* -tree). A trust that is created by a will and takes effect when the settlor (testator) dies. — Also termed *trust under will.* Cf. *inter vivos trust.*

Totten trust. A revocable trust created by one's deposit of money, typically in a savings account, in the depositor's name as trustee for another. • A Totten trust is an early form of "pay on death" account, since it creates no interest in the beneficiary unless the account remained at the depositor's death. Its name derives from the earliest decision in which the court approved the concept, even though the formalities of will execution were not satisfied: *In re Totten,* 71 N.E. 748 (N.Y. 1904). A Totten trust is commonly used to indicate a successor to the account without having to create a will, and thus it is a will substitute. — Also termed *tentative trust; bank-account trust; savings-account trust; savings-bank trust; trustee bank account.*

transgressive trust. A trust that violates the rule against perpetuities. See RULE AGAINST PERPETUITIES.

trust de son tort (də sawn [*or* son] **tor**[t]). See *constructive trust.*

trust ex delicto. See *constructive trust.*

575

trust ex maleficio. See *constructive trust.*

trust in invitum. See *constructive trust.*

trust under will. See *testamentary trust.*

2503(c) trust. A trust with only one beneficiary, who must be a minor and must have the power to withdraw all assets from the trust upon attaining the age of 21. ● This type of trust derives its name from the requirements set forth in IRC (26 USCA) § 2503(c). Although the trust may continue after the beneficiary turns 21, gifts to the trust will no longer qualify for the annual exclusion if the beneficiary has no immediate right to withdraw the gift.

under-65 trust. A discretionary trust established for the sole benefit of a Medicaid recipient who is under the age of 65. ● This type of trust may be established by anyone except the beneficiary, who must be less than 65 years old at the time of creation. The assets in trust will not be included in the beneficiary's estate for purposes of determining Medicaid eligibility. The beneficiary may receive distributions from the trust during life, but any balance remaining in the trust must be used to reimburse the state for the beneficiary's Medicaid expenditures.

unitrust. A trust from which a fixed percentage of the fair market value of the trust's assets, valued annually, is paid each year to the beneficiary.

voluntary trust. **1.** A trust that is not founded on consideration. ● One having legal title to property may create a voluntary trust by (1) declaring that the property is to be held in trust for another, and (2) transferring the legal title to a third person who acts as trustee. **2.** An obligation arising out of a personal confidence reposed in, and voluntarily accepted by, one for the benefit of another.

voting trust. A trust used to hold shares of voting stock in a closely held corporation, usu. transferred from a parent to a child, and empowering the trustee to exercise the right to vote. ● The trust acts as custodian of the shares but is not a stockholder.

wasting trust. A trust in which the trust property is gradually depleted by periodic payments to the beneficiary.

trust agreement. See *declaration of trust* (2) under DECLARATION.

trust deed. See *declaration of trust* (2) under DECLARATION.

trust de son tort. See *constructive trust* under TRUST.

trust distribution. See DISTRIBUTION.

trustee (trəs-**tee**), *n.* One who, having legal title to property, holds it in trust for the benefit of another

and owes a fiduciary duty to that beneficiary. ●
Generally, a trustee's duties are to convert to cash
all debts and securities that are not qualified legal
investments, to reinvest the cash in proper securities, to protect and preserve the trust property, and
to ensure that it is employed solely for the beneficiary, in accordance with the directions contained in
the trust instrument.

bare trustee. A trustee of a passive trust. ● A
bare trustee has no duty other than to transfer
the property to the beneficiary. See *passive trust*
under TRUST.

corporate trustee. A corporation that is empowered by its charter to act as a trustee, such as a
bank or trust company.

indenture trustee. A trustee named in a trust
indenture and charged with holding legal title to
the trust property; a trustee under an indenture.

joint trustee. See COTRUSTEE.

judicial trustee. A trustee appointed by a court
to execute a trust.

quasi-trustee. One who benefits from a breach
of a trust to a great enough degree to become
liable as a trustee.

successor trustee. A trustee who succeeds an
earlier trustee, usu. as provided in the trust
agreement.

testamentary trustee (tes-tə-**men**-tə-ree *or* -tree). A trustee appointed by or acting under a will; one appointed to carry out a trust created by a will.

trustee ad litem (ad **lı**-tem *or* -təm). A trustee appointed by the court.

trustee de son tort (də sawn [*or* son] **tor**[t]). A person who, without legal authority, administers a living person's property to the detriment of the property owner. See *constructive trust* under TRUST.

trustee ex maleficio (eks mal-ə-**fish**-ee-oh). A person who is guilty of wrongful or fraudulent conduct and is held by equity to the duty of a trustee, in relation to the subject matter, to prevent him or her from profiting from the wrongdoing.

trustee bank account. See *Totten trust* under TRUST.

trust estate. See CORPUS (1). — Also termed *trust*.

trust ex delicto. See *constructive trust* under TRUST.

trust ex maleficio. See *constructive trust* under TRUST.

trust fund. The property held in a trust by a trustee; CORPUS (1).

common trust fund. A trust fund set up within a trust department to combine the assets of numerous small trusts to achieve greater investment diversification. ● Common trust funds are regulated by state law.

trust indenture. A document containing the terms and conditions governing a trustee's conduct and the trust beneficiaries' rights. — Also termed *indenture of trust*.

trust in invitum (in in-**vi**-təm). See *constructive trust* under TRUST.

trust instrument. See *declaration of trust* (2) under DECLARATION.

trust legacy. See LEGACY.

trust officer. A trust-company official responsible for administering funds held by the company as a trustee.

trustor. One who creates a trust; SETTLOR.

trust ownership. See OWNERSHIP.

trust power. See *beneficial power* under POWER.

trust property. See CORPUS (1).

trust res (reez *or* rays). See CORPUS (1).

trust under will. See *testamentary trust* under TRUST.

Truth in Lending Act. See CONSUMER CREDIT PROTECTION ACT. — Abbr. TILA.

turntable doctrine. See ATTRACTIVE-NUISANCE DOCTRINE.

2503(c) trust. See TRUST.

U

UAA. *abbr*. UNIFORM ADOPTION ACT.

UAGA. *abbr*. UNIFORM ANATOMICAL GIFT ACT.

UCCJA. *abbr*. UNIFORM CHILD CUSTODY JURISDICTION ACT.

UCCJEA. *abbr*. UNIFORM CHILD CUSTODY JURISDICTION AND ENFORCEMENT ACT.

UDRA. *abbr*. UNIFORM DIVORCE RECOGNITION ACT.

UGMA. *abbr*. Uniform Gifts to Minors Act. See UNIFORM TRANSFERS TO MINORS ACT.

UHCDA. *abbr*. UNIFORM HEALTH-CARE DECISION ACT.

UIFSA. *abbr*. UNIFORM INTERSTATE FAMILY SUPPORT ACT.

UIJC. *abbr*. UNIFORM INTERSTATE JUVENILE COMPACT.

UJCA. *abbr*. UNIFORM JUVENILE COURT ACT.

ulterior remainderman. See REMAINDERMAN.

UMDA. *abbr*. UNIFORM MARRIAGE AND DIVORCE ACT.

unborn beneficiary. See BENEFICIARY.

unborn child. See CHILD.

unborn-widow rule. The legal fiction, assumed under the rule against perpetuities, that a beneficiary's widow is not alive at the testator's death, and thus a succeeding life estate to her voids any remainders because the interest would not vest within the perpetuities period. See RULE AGAINST PERPETUITIES.

unclean-hands doctrine. See CLEAN-HANDS DOCTRINE.

unconditional delivery. See DELIVERY.

unconditional heir. See HEIR.

uncontestable clause. See INCONTESTABILITY CLAUSE.

uncontested divorce. See DIVORCE.

uncontested hearing. See HEARING.

UNCRC. *abbr.* UNITED NATIONS CONVENTION ON THE RIGHTS OF THE CHILD.

under-65 trust. See TRUST.

undue influence. 1. The improper use of power or trust in a way that deprives a person of free will and substitutes another's objective. ● Consent to a contract, transaction, or relationship or to conduct is voidable if the consent is obtained through undue influence. **2.** Coercion that destroys a testator's free will and substitutes another's objectives in its place. • When a beneficiary actively procures the execution of a will, a presumption of undue influence may be raised, based on the confidential relationship between the influencer and the person influenced. — Also termed *improper influence*. See COERCION; DURESS.

unfit, *adj.* Morally unqualified; incompetent <the judge found the mother unfit and so found that awarding custody of the child to the father was in the child's best interests>.

unfitness of a parent. A parent's failure to exhibit a reasonable concern for, interest in, or responsibility for a child's welfare. • Regardless of the specific ground for an allegation of unfitness, a court considers the parent's actions and the circumstances surrounding the conduct in deciding whether unfitness has been demonstrated.

unified credit. See *unified estate-and-gift tax credit* under TAX CREDIT.

unified estate-and-gift tax. See *transfer tax* under TAX.

unified estate-and-gift tax credit. See TAX CREDIT.

unified family court. See COURT.

unified transfer tax. See *transfer tax* under TAX.

Uniform Adoption Act. A 1994 model statute aimed at achieving uniformity in adoption laws. • The current version of the UAA was promulgated in 1994 by the National Conference of Commissioners on Uniform State Laws. State adoption of the Uniform Adoption Act has been largely unsuccessful. Earlier versions, in 1953 and 1971, were amended many times but were enacted in only a few states. — Abbr. UAA.

Uniform Anatomical Gift Act. A 1968 model statute that created protocols that govern the giving and receiving of anatomical gifts. • Under the Act, persons may donate their body or parts of their body for purposes of transplantation, therapy, research, or education. The original Act has been adopted in some form in all 50 states. It was revised in 1987, and the revised version has been adopted in some form in at least 22 states. — Abbr. UAGA.

Uniform Child Custody Jurisdiction Act. A 1968 model statute that sets out a standard (based on the child's residence in and connections with the state) by which a state court determines whether it has jurisdiction over a particular child-custody matter or whether it must recognize a custody decree issued by another state's court. • The Uniform Child Custody Jurisdiction Act was replaced in 1997 by the Uniform Child Custody Jurisdiction and Enforcement Act. — Abbr. UCCJA. See HOME STATE. Cf.

PARENTAL KIDNAPPING PREVENTION ACT; UNIFORM CHILD CUSTODY JURISDICTION AND ENFORCEMENT ACT.

Uniform Child Custody Jurisdiction and Enforcement Act. A 1997 model statute that provides uniform methods of expedited interstate custody and visitation orders. ● This Act was promulgated as a successor to the Uniform Child Custody Jurisdiction Act. The UCCJEA brings the Uniform Child Custody Jurisdiction Act into conformity with the Parental Kidnapping Prevention Act and the Violence Against Women Act. The Act revises child-custody jurisdiction, giving clearer standards for original jurisdiction and a standard for continuing jurisdiction. The Act also provides a remedial process for enforcing interstate child custody and visitation. — Abbr. UCCJEA. Cf. UNIFORM CHILD CUSTODY JURISDICTION ACT.

Uniform Determination of Death Act. A 1978 model statute that provides a comprehensive basis for determining death. ● This is a technical act that merely defines death clinically and does not deal with suicide, assisted suicide, or the right to die. The Act was revised in 1980. It has been adopted in almost all states.

Uniform Disposition of Community Property at Death Act. A 1971 model statute designed for non-community-property states to preserve the rights of each spouse in property that was community property before the spouses moved to non-community-property states, unless they have severed or altered their community-property rights.

Uniform Divorce Recognition Act. A 1947 model code adopted by some states regarding full-faith-and-credit issues that arise in divorces. — Abbr. UDRA.

Uniform Durable Power of Attorney Act. A 1979 model statute that provides a simple way for a person to deal with his or her property by providing a power of attorney that will survive after the incompetence of the principal. ● The Act was revised in 1987 and has been adopted in almost every state.

Uniformed Services Former Spouses' Protection Act. A federal statute that governs the disposition of military pension benefits to former spouses of persons in the armed services. 10 USCA §§ 1401 et seq. ● The Act permits state courts to treat military-retirement pay as marital property and to order payment of up to 50% of the retirement pay directly to the former spouse if the spouses were married for at least ten years while the employee served in the military. — Abbr. USFSPA.

Uniform Gifts to Minors Act. — Abbr. UGMA. See UNIFORM TRANSFERS TO MINORS ACT.

Uniform Health–Care Decision Act. A 1993 model statute that facilitates and encourages the making of advance directives. — Abbr. UHCDA. See ADVANCE DIRECTIVE; LIVING WILL.

Uniform Interstate Family Support Act. A 1992 model statute establishing a one-order system by which an alimony or child-support decree issued by one state can be enforced against a former spouse who resides in another state. ● This statute has been adopted in every state and is the basis of jurisdiction in child-support suits. The purpose of the Act is to make the pursuit of interstate child support and paternity more effective, consistent, and efficient by requiring all states to recognize and enforce consistently support orders issued in other states. Before its enactment, there was considerable disparity among the states in the way they handled interstate child-support proceedings, since each state had differing versions of the earlier uniform law, the Uniform Reciprocal Enforcement of Support Act. The Act was revised in 1996. — Abbr. UIFSA.

Uniform Interstate Juvenile Compact. An agreement that regulates the treatment of juveniles who are not under proper supervision or control, or who have run away or escaped, and who are likely to endanger their own or others' health, morals, or welfare. ● The Compact is relied on by the state to transport juvenile runaways back to their home states. It has now been universally adopted in the United States, but not always in its entirety. — Abbr. UIJC.

Uniform Juvenile Court Act. A 1968 model statute designed to (1) provide for the care, protection, and moral, mental, and physical development of the children who come under its provisions, (2) provide juvenile delinquents with treatment, training, and rehabilitation rather than criminal punishment, (3) attempt to keep families together unless separation of parents and children is necessary for the children's welfare or is in the public interest, (4) provide a judicial procedure for a fair hearing and protection of juvenile delinquents' constitutional and other legal rights, and (5) provide simple interstate procedures to carry out cooperative measures among the juvenile courts of different states. — Abbr. UJCA.

Uniform Marriage and Divorce Act. A 1970 model statute that defines marriage and divorce. • Extensively amended in 1973, the Act was an attempt by the National Conference of Commissioners on Uniform State Laws to make marriage and divorce laws more uniform. The Act's greatest significance is that it introduced, as the sole ground for divorce, irreconcilable differences. Although the UMDA has been enacted in part in only a handful of states, it has had an enormous impact on marriage and divorce laws in all states. — Abbr. UMDA. — Also termed *Model Marriage and Divorce Act*. See IRRECONCILABLE DIFFERENCES.

Uniform Parentage Act. A 1973 model statute that provides a means for determining parenthood for the general welfare of the child and for assigning child support. ● The Act abolishes distinctions between legitimate and illegitimate status for children. Instead, it directs courts to determine rights and responsibilities based on the existence of a parent–child relationship. The Act has been adopted in all states.

Uniform Premarital Agreements Act. A 1983 model statute that governs the drafting of prenuptial contracts and provides a more certain framework for drafting complete and enforceable agreements. ● Under the UPAA, a premarital agreement must be in writing and signed by the parties. It becomes effective only upon marriage. The agreement may govern the parties' assets, support, and obligations during the marriage, at death, and upon divorce. The UPAA has been adopted in some form in about one-third of the states. — Abbr. UPAA.

Uniform Probate Code. A 1969 model statute that modernizes the rules and doctrines governing intestate succession, probate, and the administration of estates. ● It has been extensively amended many times since 1969 and has been enacted in a majority of states. — Abbr. UPC.

Uniform Prudent Investor Act. A 1994 model statute that sets a standard for the acts of a trustee, adopts a prudent-investor standard, and prefers a modern portfolio approach to investing. ● Under the Uniform Prudent Investor Act, the trustee is given significant power to delegate the selection of investments. The prudent-investor standard replaces the prudent-person standard of investing. The portfolio approach provides that no investment will be viewed in isolation; rather, it will be viewed as part of the entire portfolio. Under this theory, even though an investor loses trust assets on an investment, if there is an overall positive return, the investor will not be liable to the beneficiaries. — Abbr. UPIA. See PRUDENT-INVESTOR RULE.

Uniform Putative and Unknown Fathers Act. A 1988 model statute aimed at codifying Supreme Court decisions on the rights of an unwed father in relation to his child. ● The Act deals primarily with an unwed father's right to notice of a termination and adoption proceeding, to adjudication of paternity, to visitation, and to custody. — Abbr. UPUFA. — Also termed *Model Putative Fathers Act*; *Putative Fathers Act*.

Uniform Reciprocal Enforcement of Support Act. A 1950 model statute (now superseded) that sought to unify the way in which interstate support matters were processed and the way in which one jurisdiction's orders were given full faith and credit in another jurisdiction. ● This Act, which was amended in 1958 and 1960, was replaced in 1997 with the Uniform Interstate Family Support Act. — Abbr. URESA. See UNIFORM INTERSTATE FAMILY SUPPORT ACT.

Uniform Simultaneous Death Act. A 1940 model statute creating a rule that a person must survive a decedent by at least 120 hours in order to avoid disputes caused by simultaneous deaths (as in a common disaster) or by quickly successive deaths of persons between whom property or death benefits pass on the death of one survived by the other. ● In the absence of the 120-hour period of survival, each person is presumed to have survived the other for purposes of distributing their respective estates. The Act was revised in 1993 and has been adopted in some form by almost all states. See COMMORIENTES.

Uniform Status of Children of Assisted Conception Act. A 1988 model statute aimed at ensuring certainty of legal parentage when assisted conception has been used. ● The adopting state has the option of regulating or prohibiting contracts with surrogate mothers.

Uniform Transfers to Minors Act. A 1983 model statute providing for the transfer of property to a minor and permitting a custodian who acts in a fiduciary capacity to manage investments and apply the income from the property to the minor's support. ● The Act has been adopted in most states. It was revised in 1986. — Abbr. UTMA. — Also termed *Transfers to Minors Act*. — Formerly also termed *Uniform Gifts to Minors Act*; *Gifts to Minors Act*.

unincorporated association. See ASSOCIATION.

United Nations Convention on the Rights of the Child. An international instrument covering children's civil, political, economic, social, and cultural rights. ● The Convention was adopted by the United Nations General Assembly on November 20, 1989. Sixty-one nations signed the Convention on the first day it was open for signature. Having now been ratified by almost every nation, it is the most widely ratified human-rights treaty in history. The United States did not sign the Convention until February 23, 1995, and the U.S. Senate had not, as of 2000, considered it for ratification. — Abbr. UNCRC.

unities doctrine of marriage. See LEGAL-UNITIES DOCTRINE.

unitrust. See TRUST.

universal agent. See AGENT.

universal inheritance. See INHERITANCE.

universal-inheritance rule. A doctrine holding that an intestate estate escheats to the state only if the decedent leaves no surviving relatives, no matter how distant. ● Through the first half of the 20th century, this rule was broadly followed in American jurisdictions. The Uniform Probate Code abandons the universal-inheritance rule and provides that if no member of the third or a nearer parentela survives the decedent, the intestate estate escheats to the state. — Also termed *rule of universal inheri-*

tance. See PARENTELA. Cf. *laughing heir* under HEIR; GRADUAL METHOD.

universal legatee. See LEGATEE.

universal succession. See SUCCESSION.

universal successor. See SUCCESSOR.

unlawful assembly. A meeting of three or more persons who intend either to commit a violent crime or to carry out some act, lawful or unlawful, that will constitute a breach of the peace.

unlawful sexual intercourse. See RAPE.

unnatural offense. See SODOMY.

unnatural will. See WILL.

unofficious will. See *inofficious testament* under TESTAMENT.

unsolemn will. See WILL.

unspeakable crime. See SODOMY.

unwritten will. See *nuncupative will* under WILL.

UPAA. *abbr.* UNIFORM PREMARITAL AGREEMENTS ACT.

UPC. *abbr.* UNIFORM PROBATE CODE.

UPIA. *abbr.* UNIFORM PRUDENT INVESTOR ACT.

UPUFA. *abbr.* UNIFORM PUTATIVE AND UNKNOWN FATHERS ACT.

URESA. *abbr.* UNIFORM RECIPROCAL ENFORCEMENT OF SUPPORT ACT.

USFSPA. *abbr.* UNIFORMED SERVICES FORMER SPOUSE PROTECTION ACT.

usufruct (**yoo**-zə-frəkt), *n. Roman & civil law.* A right to use another's property for a time without damaging or diminishing it, although the property might naturally deteriorate over time. ● In Roman law, the usufruct was considered an encumbrance. In modern civil law, the owner of the usufruct is similar to a life tenant, and the owner of the thing burdened is the *naked owner.* — Also termed *usufructus*; *perfect usufruct*; (in Scots law) *life-rent.*

usufructus. See USUFRUCT.

uterine (**yoo**-tər-in), *adj.* Born of the same mother but having different fathers.

uterine brother. See BROTHER.

UTMA. *abbr.* UNIFORM TRANSFERS TO MINORS ACT.

uxor (ək-sor), *n.* [Latin] Wife. — Abbr. *ux.* See ET UXOR. Cf. VIR.

uxoricide (ək-**sor**-ə-sɪd *or* əg-**zor**-), *n.* **1.** The murder of one's wife. **2.** A man who murders his wife. — **uxoricidal,** *adj.* Cf. MARITICIDE.

V

vacant succession. See SUCCESSION.

VAWA. *abbr.* VIOLENCE AGAINST WOMEN ACT.

venereal disease. See SEXUALLY TRANSMITTED DISEASE.

verbal will. See *nuncupative will* under WILL.

verification, *n.* **1.** A formal declaration made in the presence of an authorized officer, such as a notary public, or (in some jurisdictions) under oath but not in the presence of such an officer, whereby one swears to the truth of the statements in the document. ● Traditionally, a verification is used as a conclusion for all pleadings that are required to be sworn. Cf. ACKNOWLEDGMENT (2). **2.** An oath or affirmation that an authorized officer administers to an affiant or deponent. — **verify,** *vb.* — **verifier,** *n.*

verified copy. See *certified copy* under COPY.

vertical equality. In per capita distribution of an estate, a system that results in equal distribution among children's families. See Restatement (Third) of Property: Wills and Other Donative Transfers § 2.3 (Tentative Draft No. 2, 1998). See PER CAPITA. Cf. HORIZONTAL EQUALITY.

vested estate. See ESTATE.

vested gift. See GIFT.

vested legacy. See LEGACY.

vested ownership. See OWNERSHIP.

vested remainder. See REMAINDER.

Victims of Child Abuse Laws. An organization of persons who claim to have been wrongly accused of sexually abusing children. — Abbr. VOCAL. Cf. FALSE MEMORY SYNDROME FOUNDATION.

Video Privacy Protection Act. A federal statute that bars video stores from disclosing to third parties the names of customers' rentals. 18 USCA § 2710.

viewpoint discrimination. See DISCRIMINATION (2).

violence. The use of physical force, usu. accompanied by fury, vehemence, or outrage; esp., physical force unlawfully exercised with the intent to harm.

domestic violence. **1.** Violence between members of a household, usu. spouses; an assault or other violent act committed by one member of a household against another. See BATTERED-CHILD SYNDROME; BATTERED-WOMAN SYNDROME. **2.** The infliction of physical injury, or the creation of a reasonable fear that physical injury or harm will be inflicted, by a parent or a member or former member of a child's household, against a child or against another member of the household. — Also termed *domestic abuse*; *family violence*.

Violence Against Women Act. A federal statute that established a federal civil-rights action for victims of gender-motivated violence. 42 USCA § 13981. ● In 2000, the Supreme Court invalidated the statute, holding that neither the Commerce Clause nor the Enforcement Clause of the 14th Amendment authorized Congress to enact the civil-remedy provision of this Act. *United States v. Morrison*, 120 S.Ct. 1740 (2000). — Abbr. VAWA.

vir (veer), *n.* [Latin] **1.** An adult male; a man. **2.** A husband. ● In the Latin phrases and maxims that once pervaded English law, *vir* generally means "husband," as in the expression *vir et uxor* (husband and wife). See ET VIR. Cf. UXOR.

virtual adoption. See *adoption by estoppel* under ADOPTION.

virtual child pornography. See PORNOGRAPHY.

visitation. A relative's, esp. a noncustodial parent's, period of access to a child. — Also termed *parental access*; *access*; *parenting time*; *residential time*.

> ***grandparent visitation.*** A grandparent's court-approved access to a grandchild. ● The Supreme Court recently limited a grandparent's right to have visitation with his or her grandchild if the

parent objects, citing a parent's fundamental right to raise his or her child and to make all decisions concerning the child free from state intervention absent a threat to the child's health and safety. *Troxel v. Granville*, 120 S.Ct. 2054 (2000).

restricted visitation. See *supervised visitation*.

stepped-up visitation. Visitation, usu. for a parent who has been absent from the child's life, that begins on a very limited basis and increases as the child comes to know the parent. — Also termed *step-up visitation*.

supervised visitation. Visitation, usu. court-ordered, in which a parent may visit with the child or children only in the presence of some other individual. ● A court may order supervised visitation when the visiting parent is known to be prone to physical abuse, sexual abuse, or violence. — Also termed *restricted visitation*.

visitation credit. A child-support reduction that reflects the amount of time the child lives with the noncustodial parent.

visitation order. 1. An order establishing the visiting times for a noncustodial parent with his or her child. **2.** An order establishing the visiting times for a child and a person with a significant relationship to the child. ● Such an order may allow for visitation between (1) a grandparent and a grandchild, (2) a child and another relative, (3) a child and a stepparent, or (4) occasionally, a child and the child's psychological parent. — Also termed *access order*.

visitation right. A noncustodial parent's or grandparent's court-ordered privilege of spending time with a child or grandchild who is living with another person, usu. the custodial parent. • The noncustodial parent with visitation rights may sometimes be a parent from whom custody has been removed because of abuse or neglect. — Also termed *right of visitation*.

visiting judge. See JUDGE.

vital statistics. Public records — usu. relating to matters such as births, marriages, deaths, diseases, and the like — that are statutorily mandated to be kept by a city, state, or other governmental division or subdivision. • On the admissibility of vital statistics, see Fed. R. Evid. 803(9).

VOCAL. *abbr.* VICTIMS OF CHILD ABUSE LAWS.

voidable marriage. See MARRIAGE (1).

void legacy. See LEGACY.

void marriage. See MARRIAGE (1).

voluntary abandonment. See ABANDONMENT.

voluntary arbitration. See ARBITRATION.

voluntary association. See ASSOCIATION.

voluntary commitment. See COMMITMENT.

voluntary consent. See CONSENT.

voluntary euthanasia. See EUTHANASIA.

voluntary-registry law. See ADOPTION-REGISTRY STATUTE.

voluntary trust. See TRUST.

voting trust. See TRUST.

W

wage assignment. 1. ATTACHMENT OF WAGES. **2.** IN-COME-WITHHOLDING ORDER.

wage-assignment order. See INCOME-WITHHOLDING ORDER.

wage-withholding. See ATTACHMENT OF WAGES.

wage-withholding order. See INCOME-WITHHOLDING ORDER.

waiver of service. A defendant's voluntary submission to the jurisdiction made by signing an acknowledgment of receipt of the petition and stating that he or she waives all further service.

ward. A person, usu. a minor, who is under a guardian's charge or protection. See GUARDIAN.

permanent ward. A ward who has been assigned a permanent guardian, the rights of the natural parents having been terminated by a juvenile court.

temporary ward. A minor who is under the supervision of a juvenile court but whose parents' parental rights have not been terminated.

ward of the state. A person who is housed by, and receives protection and necessities from, the government.

wasting trust. See TRUST.

wedding. See MARRIAGE CEREMONY.

whole blood. See *full blood* under BLOOD.

whole life insurance. See LIFE INSURANCE.

widow, *n.* A woman whose husband has died and who has not remarried.

widower. A man whose wife has died and who has not remarried.

widower's allowance. See *spousal allowance* under ALLOWANCE (1).

widow's allowance. See *spousal allowance* under ALLOWANCE (1).

widow's election. See RIGHT OF ELECTION.

wife. A married woman; a woman who has a lawful husband living.

> *common-law wife.* **1.** The wife in a common-law marriage; a woman who contracts an informal marriage with a man and then holds herself out to the community as being married to him. See *common-law marriage* under MARRIAGE (1). **2.** *Archaic.* Loosely, a concubine.

wife's equity. See EQUITY TO A SETTLEMENT.

wife's settlement. See EQUITY TO A SETTLEMENT.

will, *n.* A document by which a person directs his or her estate to be distributed upon death <there was no mention of his estranged brother in the will>. — Also termed *testament*; *will and testament.* — **will,** *vb.*

antenuptial will. See *prenuptial will.*

attested will. A will that has been signed by a witness.

bogus will. An unauthentic will, esp. one involving fraud or unauthorized changes.

conditional will. A will that depends on the occurrence of an uncertain event for the will to take effect. ● Most jurisdictions hold a conditional will valid even though the testator's death does not result from or on the occasion of the condition mentioned in the will. The courts generally hold that the condition is the inducement for making the will rather than a condition precedent to its operation. See *Eaton v. Brown,* 193 U.S. 411, 24 S.Ct. 487 (1904); *In re Will of Cohen,* 491 A.2d 1292 (N.J. Super. Ct. App. Div. 1985). Cf. *contingent will.*

conjoint will. See *joint will.*

contingent will. A will that takes effect only if a specified event occurs. Cf. *conditional will.*

counter will. See *mutual will.*

double will. See *mutual will.*

duplicate will. A will executed in duplicate originals by a testator who retains one copy and gives the second copy to another person. ● The rules applicable to wills apply to both wills, and upon application for probate, both copies must be tendered into the registry of the probate court.

holographic will (hol-ə-**graf**-ik). A will that is handwritten by the testator. ● Such a will is typically unattested. Holographic wills are rooted in the civil-law tradition, having originated in Roman law and having been authorized under the Napoleonic Code. French and Spanish settlers introduced holographic wills in America, primarily in the South and West. Today they are recognized in about half the states. — Also termed *olographic will.* See HOLOGRAPH.

inofficious will. See *inofficious testament* under TESTAMENT.

international will. A will that is executed according to formalities provided in an international treaty or convention, and that will be valid although it may be written in a foreign language by a testator domiciled in another country.

invalid will. A will that fails to make an effective disposition of property.

joint and mutual will. A will executed by two or more people — to dispose of property they own separately, in common, or jointly — requiring the surviving testator to dispose of the property in accordance with the terms of the will, and showing that the devises are made in consideration of one another. • The word "joint" indicates the form of the will. The word "mutual" describes the substantive provisions. — Also termed *joint and reciprocal will*.

joint and reciprocal will. See *joint and mutual will*.

joint will. A single will executed by two or more testators, usu. disposing of their common property by transferring their separate titles to one devisee. — Also termed *conjoint will*.

last will. The most recent will of a deceased; the instrument ultimately fixing the disposition of real and personal property at the testator's death. — Also termed *last will and testament*.

last will and testament. See *last will*.

living will. See LIVING WILL.

lost will. An executed will that cannot be found at the testator's death. • Its contents can be proved by parol evidence in many jurisdictions. The common-law presumption — still the view of the overwhelming majority of American jurisdictions — is that there is a presumption of revocation if a lost will is proved to be in the possession of the testator and has been lost.

mariner's will. See *soldier's will.*

mutual will. (*usu. pl.*) One of two separate wills in which two persons, usu. a husband and wife, establish identical or similar testamentary provisions disposing of their estates in favor of each other. ● It is also possible (though rare) for the testators to execute a single mutual will, as opposed to separate ones. And it is possible (though, again, rare) for more than two parties to execute mutual wills. — Also termed *reciprocal will*; *counter will*; *double will*; *mutual testament.*

nonintervention will. A will that authorizes an independent executor. See *independent executor* under EXECUTOR.

notarial will. A will executed by a testator in the presence of two witnesses and a notary public.

nuncupative will (**nəng**-kyə-pay-tiv *or* nəng-**kyoo**-pə-tiv). An oral will made in contemplation of imminent death from an injury recently incurred. ● Nuncupative wills are invalid in most states, but in those states allowing them, the amount that may be conveyed is usually limited by statute, and they traditionally apply only to personal property. — Also termed *oral will*; *unwritten will*; *verbal will.*

olographic will. See *holographic will.*

oral will. A will made by the spoken declaration of the testator and usu. dependent on oral testimony for proof. Cf. *nuncupative will.*

postnuptial will (pohst-**nəp**-shəl). A will executed after marriage.

pourover will (**por**-oh-vər). A will giving money
or property to an existing trust. Cf. *pourover trust*
under TRUST.

prenuptial will (pree-**nəp**-shəl). A will executed
before marriage. • At common law, marriage automatically revoked a spouse's will, but modern
statutes usu. provide that marriage does not revoke a will (although divorce does). But if this
marriage was not contemplated by the will and
there is nothing otherwise on its face to indicate
that the testator intentionally left nothing to any
future spouse, the pretermitted spouse may be
entitled to a special forced share of the estate.
Unif. Probate Code § 2–508. — Also termed *antenuptial will*.

reciprocal will. See *mutual will*.

seaman's will. See *soldier's will*.

self-proved will. A will proved by a self-proving
affidavit. See *self-proving affidavit* under AFFIDA-
VIT.

soldier's will. A soldier's informal oral or written will that is usu. valid despite its noncompli-
ance with normal statutory formalities, as long as
the soldier was in actual service at the time the
will was made. — Also termed *seaman's will*;

mariner's will; *military testament*; *soldier's and sailor's will*.

unnatural will. A will that distributes the testator's estate to strangers rather than to the testator's relatives, without apparent reason.

unofficious will. See *inofficious testament* under TESTAMENT.

unsolemn will. *Civil law.* A will in which an executor is not named.

unwritten will. See *nuncupative will*.

verbal will. See *nuncupative will*.

will and testament. See WILL.

will contest. The litigation of a will's validity, usu. based on allegations that the testator lacked capacity or was under undue influence.

willful, continued, and obstinate desertion. See *obstinate desertion* under DESERTION.

willful neglect. See NEGLECT.

Wills Act. 1. STATUTE OF WILLS (1). **2.** An 1837 English statute that allowed people to dispose of every type of property interest by will and that had an elaborate set of requirements for valid execution. • Some states today continue to adhere to these stringent requirements. Cf. Unif. Probate Code

§ 2–502. — Also termed (in sense 2) *Lord Lang-dale's Act*.

will substitute. A document or instrument that allows a person, upon death, to dispose of an estate in the same or similar manner as a will but without the formalities and expense of a probate proceeding. • The most common will substitutes are trusts, life-insurance plans, and retirement-benefits contracts. The creation of will substitutes has been one of the most important developments in the area of dece-dents' estates in the past 50 years. Cf. *nonprobate asset* under ASSET.

witness, *n.* **1.** One who sees, knows, or vouches for something <a witness to a testator's signature>. **2.** One who gives testimony under oath or affirmation (1) in person, (2) by oral or written deposition, or (3) by affidavit <the witness to the signature signed the affidavit.>. — **witness,** *vb.*

attesting witness. One who vouches for the au-thenticity of another's signature by signing an instrument that the other has signed <proof of the will requires two attesting witnesses>.

interested witness. A witness who has a direct and private interest in the matter at issue. • Most jurisdictions provide that a person witnessing a will may not be a devisee under the will. The Uniform Probate Code, however, has abrogated this rule.

subscribing witness. One who witnesses the signatures on an instrument and signs at the end of the instrument to that effect.

supernumerary witness. An unrequired witness, such as a third witness to a will where only two are required.

women's shelter. See SHELTER.

words of purchase. Language in a deed or will designating the persons who are to receive the grant. ● For example, the phrasing "to A for life with a remainder to her heirs" creates a life estate in A and a remainder in A's heirs. See PURCHASE (2).

worldwide military-locator service. A search service that locates the current duty station of a member of any branch of the United States military services, esp. for enforcing the service member's child-support obligations. ● Each branch of the armed forces maintains a worldwide locator service that is available to military and nonmilitary persons, their counsel, and Title IV-D agencies. Use of the locator service requires the member's full name and social-security number.

worthier-title doctrine. 1. *Hist.* The common-law doctrine that if a beneficiary of a will would receive an identical interest as an heir under the laws of intestacy, the person takes the interest as an heir rather than as a beneficiary. ● The doctrine has been abolished in most states. **2.** *Property.* The

doctrine that favors a grantor's intent by construing a grant as a reversion in the grantor instead of
as a remainder in the grantor's heirs. — Also
termed *doctrine of worthier title*.

writ of capias. See CAPIAS.

writ of injunction. See INJUNCTION.

written directive. See ADVANCE DIRECTIVE.

wrongful adoption. 1. An adoption in which the
adoption agency fails to provide adoptive parents
with full or accurate information regarding the
child's physical or psychological background. ● The
adoptive parents usually do not seek to nullify the
adoption. Rather, they seek damages, usually for
medical care and for emotional distress. **2.** An adoptive parent's legal claim against an adoption agency
for not fully or accurately disclosing the child's
physical or psychological background.

wrongful-birth action. A lawsuit brought by parents against a doctor for failing to advise them
prospectively about the risks of their having a child
with birth defects.

wrongful-conception action. See WRONGFUL-PREG-
NANCY ACTION.

wrongful-death action. A lawsuit brought on behalf of a decedent's survivors for their damages

resulting from a tortious injury that caused the decedent's death. — Also termed *death action*; *death case*. Cf. SURVIVAL ACTION.

wrongful-life action. A lawsuit brought by or on behalf of a child with birth defects, alleging that but for the doctor-defendant's negligent advice, the parents would not have conceived the child or, if they had, would have aborted the fetus to avoid the pain and suffering resulting from the child's congenital defects. • Most jurisdictions reject these claims.

wrongful-pregnancy action. A lawsuit brought by a parent for damages resulting from a pregnancy following a failed sterilization. — Also termed *wrongful-conception action*.

XYZ

younger-generation devise. See DEVISE.

youth court. See *teen court* under COURT.

youthful offender. See JUVENILE DELINQUENT.

youth shelter. See SHELTER.

zero-tolerance policy. An established plan or method of action stating that certain acts will not be permitted or condoned. • School districts often have a zero-tolerance policy regarding the use of drugs and alcohol on school premises or at school-sponsored functions. In 1995 Congress enacted a nationwide zero-tolerance statute to combat underage drinking.

ZIFT. *abbr.* ZYGOTE INTRAFALLOPIAN TRANSFER.

zygote. A two-celled organism formed by the joining of egg and sperm. Cf. EMBRYO; FETUS.

zygote intrafallopian transfer. A procedure in which mature eggs are fertilized in a test tube or petri dish and then injected into a woman's fallopian tubes. — Abbr. ZIFT. — Also termed *zygote intrafallopian-tube transfer*. Cf. ARTIFICIAL INSEMINATION; GAMETE INTRAFALLOPIAN TRANSFER; IN VITRO FERTILIZATION.

Table of Cases